TURKEY'S RELIGIOUS SITES

Anna G. Edmonds

DAMKO
Publications

Turkey's Religious Sites

First published in Turkey 1997 by Damko A.Ş.
CC 177, Mecidiyeköy 80303, İstanbul
Fax. 90 (212) 273 1792 - 90 (212) 669 4731

Writer: Anna G. Edmonds
The photographs by Haluk Özözlü other than the following:
Photograhps on pages 33, 57, 116, 120, 128,130, 132, 137, 146, 161 below, 164, 169 below, 170, 171, 203, 218, 221, 224 below, 226, 228, 231, 232, 235, 239, 240, 242, 246, 247, 248 by Anna G. & William Edmonds; photographs on pages 21, 22 above and below left, 23, 24, 25, 26, 29, 30, 32, 42, 43, 46, 54, 60, 64, 73, 75, 84, 86, 87, 94, 101 above, 103, 105, 109, 111 above, 134, 144, 149 above, 163, 166, 167, 168 above, 177, 186, 190, 193, 194, 195, 206, 207 below, 208, 214, 217, 219, 245 from the DAMKO A.Ş. archives; photographs on pages 71,107, 113 from the Turkish Touring and Automobile Association archives; photograph on page 152 by Oğuz Hamza; photographs on pages 182 and 198 by Halis Yenipınar; photographs on pages 216, 230 by Arnold C. Hanson; photograph of the rubbing on page 31 by Dorothe Gould Pratt

Design and page composition: Gülseren Ramazanoğlu
Cover design and illustrations: Aydın Erkmen; Illustration on page 134: Nazan Erkmen
Artwork: Meridyen
Color separation and printing: MAS Matbaacılık, İstanbul, Turkey

Distributed by: Be-Ra Promosyon
Mail order: Zeytinoğlu Cad., Bahar Sitesi, Mimoza 1, Daire 1, Akatlar, İstanbul, Turkey
Tel: (90-212) 269 44 26 - 278 76 86, Fax. (90-212) 278 68 96

The responsibility for the contents of the book lies solely with the writer.

FIRST EDITION - 1997

ISBN-975-8227-00-9

Printed in Turkey

TURKEY'S RELIGIOUS SITES

CONTENTS

4 Contents

When the Muslim Turks from Central Asia settled in Anatolia, they built stately mosques with their elegant interior decorations, their imposing domes and minarets that proclaim their Islamic beliefs that God is One. Each and every one is a magnificent work of art. At the same time, the Turks have cared for the places of worship that belonged to the people who were resident in Anatolia before them. They have continued to respect the religious beliefs and practices of people of differing faiths.

Religious feeling is a natural human impulse. People express their beliefs and their religious feelings by way of their worship. The places of worship are the places where beliefs and worship are performed freely and without stress. Protecting the temples is as important as building them. In this regard the Holy Koran says, "The monasteries, churches, synagogues and mosques where the name of God is often invoked and recited must be protected and not destroyed." (Hac 22:40). Therefore in observance of this, the places of worship for people of differing faiths in Anatolia are open, often next to each other.

Respect for human rights involves respect for the faith, religious practices and the holy places of all people.

Mehmet Nuri Yılmaz
Head of Religious Affairs
Administration

1 September 1997

ՊԱՏՐԻԱՐՔԱՐԱՆ ՀԱՅՈՑ
ԳՈՒՄԳԱՓԸ - ՍՏԱՆՊՈԼ

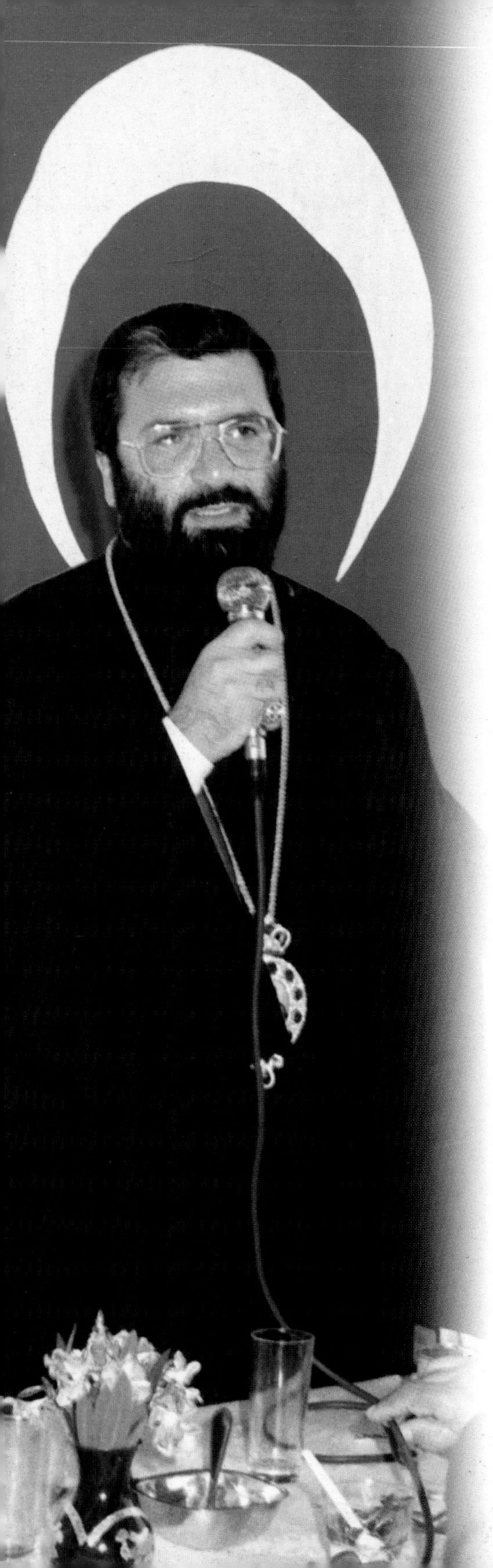

ERMENİ PATRİKLİĞİ

The roots of the Christian Church are in Palestine and Anatolia. Three of the most ancient branches of the worldwide Church of Christ, namely the Armenian, Syrian and Greek Orthodox churches, are essentially Anatolian in character. Although the Imperial Church of Byzantium has been well studied, most of the manuscripts of the Eastern and Southern Anatolian churches remain unpublished in local or foreign languages.

We welcome the publication of *Turkey's Religious Sites* and recommend it to all who would like to survey the pagan, Jewish, Christian and Moslem religious sites in our country at the threshold of the Second Millenium. A book of this scope would naturally avoid details, however, we are sure that the reader will be led by Ms. Anna G. Edmonds' skilled treatment of the subject to a deeper inquiry of the Anatolian civilizations.

As the three major monotheistic religions get ready to celebrate the traditional birthyear of Jesus Christ, the Messiah, in the year 2000, the Armenian Church of Turkey prepares to mark in the year 2001 the 1700th anniversary of the official acceptance of Apostolic Christianity by the Armenians in Anatolia, as a consequence of the tireless efforts of Saint Gregory the Illuminator of Caesarea Cappadocia (301 AD). This publication is an invaluable tool for all who prepare for those major festivities.

We know that the reader will greatly profit from this book also in order to gain an understanding of the dialogue of life which exists in our country between the adherents of different religions.

We count it our blessing and privilege to live in this beautiful land of culture and religion, prayer and feasts, music and art... And it will be our joy to share it with all visitors of good will. Welcome to Turkey!

Mesrob Mutafyan

✠ Mesrob Mutafyan
Archbishop of the Princes' Islands
& Head of the Religious Council
Armenian Patriarchate of Istanbul

TÜRKİYE ERMENİ PATRİKLİĞİ İSTANBUL 1461

16 September 1997

RUM PATRİKHANESİ

İstanbul

History has never been so generous to any land as it has to the lands on which we are living. People who lived here long before history began developed material and spiritual values that they offered to humanity. Of these, one of the most important is Christianity.

These lands are where many Christian religious leaders, prime among them St. Andrew, the founder of our Patriarchate, have lived. Here also the Ecumenical Councils took place and Christianity was formally accepted by an Empire -- an important turning point in the history of Christianity.

Our Patriarchate, the founder and pillar of our faith in Jesus Christ throughout this period, is completing its 1600 years of existence as we near the third millennium. One of the difficulties we face with this prestigious responsibility is the fact that the knowledge of history has been distorted and pushed aside because of certain anxieties. Prejudices originating from ignorance have impeded the rightful feelings of pride in the rich history of Christianity in Anatolia for those living in these lands.

A very important step towards peaceful coexistence will be realized when it is understood that differences are a richness. Therefore we congratulate your success, and pray God that this work, *Turkey's Religious Sites*, will forward our eternal aims of peace and tolerance.

Vekili

Metropolit Filippos

Filippos, Metropolitan of Tyana
The acting Grand Chancellor

Photo: His All Holiness Bartholomew,
Ecumenical Patriarch

18 September 1997

Türkiye
Hahambaşılığı
הרבנות הראשית
בתורקיה

Paul Dumond, a French researcher, began his 227-page annual report in 1893 with this sentence:

"Among the most civilized and enlightened countries of the world, in few do Jews enjoy a more complete equality than they do in Turkey."

About 400 years before this report was published, Rabbi İzak Sarfati of Edirne sent the following letter to his religious brethren in Germany:

"Brothers and teachers, friends and acquaintances! I, İzak Sarfati, declare that Turkey is a country where nothing is lacking and where everything will be good for you... If you listen to me, the road to Turkey is the road of life. Do not dally, but come to this place of comfort. Here everyone lives happily and peacefully in the shade of his own vine and fig tree..."

Today, five hundred years after that letter was written, who can claim that the tolerance shown to all religions in Turkey is any less?

Throughout the years that I have served as Chief Rabbi in the Turkish Republic, I can state without hesitation that all religions have been practiced in our country freely and unhindered.

Rav David Asseo
Chief Rabbi of Turkey

3 September 1997

PUBLISHER'S LETTER

The idea of this book was conceived two years ago when I published an issue of the *Hilton Turkey Magazine* containing general information about the religious sites - Christian, Jewish and Islamic - of Turkey. The magazines, placed in the guest rooms of all the Hilton hotels in Turkey, normally are taken away by the guests within three months. The disappearance from the guest rooms of this issue in no time and the encouraging comments of the readers emphasized the need for such a book.

We made a decision immediately. We would produce a book to meet the growing demand for information on Turkey's religious sites. People were starting to discover one of the richest and oldest aspects of Turkey. The book needed a writer worthy of its concept, knowledgeable on the subject, unprejudiced, cooperative, and pleasant to work with. Anna G. Edmonds was the answer. As she had been one of the contributing writers to the *Hilton Turkey Magazine* for years, I knew her well. She has spent 40 years in Turkey, constantly trying to discover new things, and she is very knowledgeable about religious subjects. I enjoyed every minute of the work with her, and I hope our readers will also share my feelings. I owe gratitude to John Robbins, a Harvard graduate and once the President of Mobil Companies in Turkey, who is well-versed on Christianity and ancient Anatolian history, for his encouraging remarks and constructive criticism just before we went to press.

The book has three themes. We thought general information on religions that have flourished in Turkey was essential; not only the three religions which continue to be important in the western world, but also a variety of worship practiced before they arose in Anatolia, a crossroads for religions and cultures. On this basis the book concentrates on religious sites. For the convenience of the readers we divided Turkey in five sections depending on geography. We have added a general introduction section on history, culture and the nature of the religions that have affected life in Anatolia and Anatolian Thrace. As Turkey is very rich in historical ruins we could not overlook them. The information provided in this respect is just to whet the appetite of the readers for their future visits. For more detailed and specific information we give at the end of the book a long list of suggested readings about Turkey.

At the end of the book you will find a map of the Religious Heritage of Turkey indicating selected as well as recommended sites for you to choose to read about in this book or plan to visit in addition to the map on page 79 indicating the locations of all the religious sites mentioned in this book. The very last page of the book, like a dictionary, gives a summary of the religious sites of Turkey.

Turkey is exciting and entertaining. With her very ancient history, every inch of the country offers something interesting. With the pleasant climate and the vitality of the people (most of the population is young), the country offers a great variety of interests to a great variety of tastes. In short, Turkey and Turkish people may get in your blood if you understand them and you keep on coming back.

Turks are known for their hospitality, their friendliness, their tolerance and their sensitivity. These traits put the Turks always on the side of oppressed people; thus it is one of the rare countries in the world where you do not observe discrimination. Immediately after the conquest of İstanbul in 1453, Sultan Mehmet the Conqueror accepted the Byzantine people as Ottoman citizens and permitted them freedom of worship. He also insisted on giving a decent funeral to the emperor, killed on the last day, as he respected the leader who had valiantly defended his country. Being a lover of art, he refrained from destroying the great religious treasures and mosaics of Christ, his family, and the apostles, and ordered them to be covered with a thin layer of whitewash in conformity with the Muslim interdiction against depicting human forms. When Aya Sophia (originally, the Church of the Holy Wisdom) was converted into a museum in 1936, the whitewash over the mosaics was cleaned; thanks to Fatih Sultan Mehmet, people are now able to admire the splendor of Byzantine artwork.

Since the early days of the Ottoman Empire Turks have opened their doors and their arms to those who have been oppressed or persecuted. In 1492, the same year in which she sent Christopher Colombus on his way across the Atlantic, Queen Isabella exiled all the Jewish residents of Spain (to say nothing of the Muslim Moors, whom she had defeated them). This happened, remember, more than 500 years ago, in an era of religious intolerance and persecution. The Ottoman Sultan Bayezit II sent ships to Spain to welcome the exiled Jews of Spain to Anatolia. In 1856 the Ottoman citizens, Muslim and non-Muslim alike, became equal under the law; most of the important government positions were held by non-Muslims.

In İstanbul the presence of the Greek Orthodox Patriarchate, the Armenian Orthodox Patriarchate, the Rabbinate, and many active churches and synagogues points to the Turks' respect for the beliefs of other people.

In their time, Paganism, Christianity and Judaism flourished in Anatolia where ninety-nine percent of the population is now Muslim. St. Paul started on his travels from Anatolia to spread Christianity. Soon after that, St. John addressed letters to the seven churches located in western Anatolia: his warnings are found in the Book of Revelation. Seven Ecumenical Councils took place here. Cappadocia was the place where early Christians escaped from persecution by hiding in caves or in the underground dwellings. There they painted beautiful frescoes. Southwestern Anatolia was the home of St. Nicholas, better known in the west as Santa Claus.

Located on the crossroads of civilizations between Europe and Asia for thousands of years, Anatolia has been home to people of different races, nationalities, and beliefs who have intermarried and coexisted in peace. They share the same legacy, beauties, advantages, and disadvantages of this country, so rich in fables and legends.

We like to share the splendors of our country with visitors, whoever they are and wherever they come from. In the words of our 13th-century mystic poet Mevlana:

> *Come, come again, whoever, whatever you may be, come:*
> *Heathen, fire worshiper, sinful of idolatry, come.*
> *Come even if you have broken your penitence a hundred times,*
> *Ours is not the portal of despair and misery; come.*
>
> (Translated from *Mesnevi* by Talat Sait Halman)

Gülseren Ramazanoğlu
İstanbul, 1997

TIME CHART

(Major periods and events are in bold face type.)

10,000 BC	**New Stone Age,** Neolithic Period	1150	Nebuchadnezzar I (1124-1103)
8000	Karain, Beldibi caves	1050	**Neo-Hittite Kingdom**
6000	Çatal Höyük; Mother Goddess	1000	Phoenicians a sea power Latin tribes began to settle in Anatolia
5000	**Chalcolithic Period**		
3200	**Early Bronze Age** King Gilgamesh of Erech 2650; Abraham?	850	**Homeric Greece**
		750	**Urartu** King Sardur II King Tiglath-Pileser III (745-727) King Sennacherib (704-681) built palace at Nineveh King Asitawanda in Karatepe (c. 720) Rusa I of Urartu fought Merodach- baladan of Babylon Sargon II (c. 740-705) King Midas (c. 725-696)
2500	Kanesh: **Hatti rule** in Anatolia		
2000	Abraham? Mycenaeans (2000-1700)		
1900	**Middle Bronze Age** Assyrian traders in Anatolia; cuneiform writing; Indo-European invasion (Hittites, Hivites)	700	King Gyges of **Lydia** Byzantium founded by Megarans Height of Assyrian power Sack of Tarsus by Sennacherib (695)
1850	Beginning of **Hittite power** (to c. 1100)	650	Battle of Carchemish (605) Nebuchadnezzar II (605-562)
1800	**Hurrians** (later organized as Mitanni Empire)	600	Sack of Smyrna by Lydians (595); **Persian influence** in Asia Minor Urartu overthrown Solar eclipse 28 May 585
1700	Minoan culture (to 1500)		
1600	Babylonian Empire destroyed by Hittites **Mitanni Empire** (to 1330)	550	Cyrus the Great defeated Croesus (547)
1550	Harran a major city Hittite Lawgiver King Telipinu (c. 1525-1500)		Temple to Diana in Ephesus Xerxes I (519-463)
1500	Mitannis used chariots in warfare	500	**Classical Greek Civilization** Persian War (499-449) Herodotus (c.490-425)
1400	Hittite King Suppiluliama I (c. 1380-1346)	450	Xenophon (430-355)
1350	Mitanni Kingdom overthrown **Ugarit Kingdom**	400	King Mausolus' tomb in Halicarnassus (352) Alexander the Great born 356, ruled 336-323
1300	Hurri Kingdom overthrown; Battle of Kadesh (c. 1290); Hattusilis (1289-1265), Puduhepa (c. 1288-1250)	350	**Hellenistic Period** (323-31)
		300	Rome became major power
1200	**Trojan Wars** Aegean **Sea Peoples invasion** **Phrygians** (c. 1200-600)	250	Attalus I of Pergamum (241-197)

200	Syrian War (192-189); Rome conquered Asia Minor	1200	Fourth Crusade (1204); Latin Kingdom of Constantinople (1204-1261)
150	Attalus III gave Pergamum to Rome (133) Formation of Roman Province of Asia (133)		Hacı Bektaş Veli **Mongol invasions** (1240-1402) Celaleddin Rumi (1207-1273) Marco Polo (1254-1324) Osman I (c. 1290-1326): **Ottoman Empire** (1290-1923)
100	First Triumvirate of Julius Caesar, Pompey, Crassus (60-53) Strabo (?63 BC-AD 24) Antiochus I of Commagene (64-38)	1300	Yunus Emre (d. c. 1320) Tamerlane (?1336-1405)
50	**Roman Empire** established (27); *Pax Romana* (14 BC-AD 191) **Jesus** (c. 4 BC-AD 30)	1400	Battle of Ankara (1402) **Ottoman conquest of Constantinople** (1453) Conquest of Trebizond (1461) Welcome to Jews of Europe (1492)
AD 1	**Paul's missionary journeys** (c. 47-57)		
50	Paul and Peter martyred in Rome (? 62)	1500	Süleyman I (the Magnificent) (1520-1566) Mosque of Selim II in Edirne by architect Sinan (1575)
150	Polycarp martyred (?155) Tatian	1600	Blue Mosque (1617) Sabbatai Zebi (1626-1676)
200	Diocletian (284-286)		
300	**Eastern Roman (Byzantine) Empire** (325-1453) Constantine the Great (306-337) Edict of Milan 313; First Ecumenical Council: Niceae (325); Second: Constantinople (381); Third: Ephesus (431); Fourth: Chalcedon (451) Gregory the Illuminator (c. 257-335)	1700 1800	Tulip Period (1703-1736) Suppression of the janissaries (1826) *Tanzimat* (Reform Period, (1839-1876) Crimean War (1853-1856)
500	Jacob Baradi (c. 500-578) Fifth Ecumenical Council: Constantinople (553); Sixth: Constantinople (680-81); Seventh: Nicaea (787) Justinian (527-565); St. Sophia completed (537) **Muhammad** (c. 570- 632); **Hegira** (622) Jerusalem captured by Omar (637) Arab attack on Constantinople (c. 677) Iconoclastic controversy (726-843)	1900	**Turkish Republic** (1923-) Treaty of Lausanne (1923) Dervish orders abolished (1925) **Mustafa Kemal Atatürk** (1881-1938) Roman Catholic, Greek Orthodox excommunications annulled (1965)
1000	**Selçuk Empire** (c. 1000-1300); Battle of Manzikert (1071); Battle of Nicaea (1080) Mutual anathemas between Orthodox and Catholic prelates (1054) **First Crusade** (1095); capture of Antioch (1098)		
1100	Second Crusade (1146) Saladin (1138-1193)		

RULERS REFERRED TO IN TEXT

(Dates for a number of rulers are approximate)

Hittites
1525 - 1500 BC	Telipinu
1380 - 1346	Suppiluliama I
1315 - 1296	Muwatallis
1296 - 1289	Urhi Teshub
1289 - 1265	Hattusilis - Puduhepa
1265 - 1235	Tuthaliya IV

Neo-Hittite
c. 720	Asitawanda

Assyrians, Akkadians, Chaldeans
? 3800 BC	Sargon I
1792 - 1750	Hammurabi
1124 - 1103	Nebuchadnezzar I
858 - 824	Shalmaneser III
745 - 727	Tiglath-Pileser III
721 - 705	Sargon II
704 - 681	Sennacherib
681 - 669	Esarhaddon
669 - 627	Assurpanipal
605 - 562	Nebuchadnezzar II

Urartu
840 - 830	Sardur I
810 - 786	Menua
780 - 756	Argishti I
764 - 735	Sardur II
735 - 714	Rusa I

Persians
553 - 528	Cyrus I
528 - 521	Cambyses
521 - 485	Darius I
485 - 465	Xerxes I
424 - 404	Darius II
404 - 359	Artaxerxes II

Lydians
725 - 696	Midas
c. 710	Candaules
c. 700	Gyges
560 - 546	Croesus

Greeks, Hellenes
490 - 429	Pericles
359 - 336	Philip of Macedon
336 - 323	Alexander the Great
323 - 280	Seleucis
323 - 281	Lysimachus
323 - 301	Antigonus

Pergamenes
282 - 263	Phileterus
263 - 241	Eumenes I
241 - 197	Attalus I
197 - 160	Eumenes II
160 - 138	Attalus II
138 - 133	Attalus III

Bithynia
c. 279 - 255	Nicomedes I
228 - 185	Prusias I

Pontus
120 - 63	Mithradates VI Eupator

Commagene
69 - 34	Antiochus I Theos
63 - 47	Pharnaces

Armenia
94 - c. 56 BC	Tigranes I
AD 238 - 314	Tiridates
989 - 1020	Gagil (Gagik I) Artsruni

Roman Kings
82 - 60 BC	Sulla
60 - 46	First Triumvirate: Julius Caesar, Pompey, Crassus
46 - 43	Julius Caesar
43 - 27	Second Triumvirate: Octavian, Mark Anthony, Lepidus

Roman Emperors
27 BC - AD 14	Octavian (Augustus)
14 - 37	Tiberius I
37 - 41	Caligula
41 - 54	Claudius I
54 - 68	Nero
69 - 79	Vespasian
79 - 81	Titus
81 - 96	Domitian
98 - 117	Hadrian
117 - 138	Antoninus Pius
161 - 180	Marcus Aurelius
161 - 169	Lucius Verus
193 - 211	Septimium Severus
284 - 305	Diocletian
286 - 305	Maximian
308 - 324	Licinius

Byzantine Emperors
(306) 324 - 337	Constantine the Great
337 - 361	Constantius
361 - 363	Julian the Apostate
364 - 378	Valens
379 - 395	Theodosius the Great
408 - 450	Theodosius II

457 - 474	Leo I the Great
518 - 527	Justin I
527 - 565	Justinian the Great,
	Theodora
741 - 775	Constantine V
	Copronymus
775 - 780	Leo IV the Khazar
780 - 797	Constantine VI
797 - 802	Irene
813 - 820	Leo V the Armenian
820 - 829	Michael II the Stammerer
867 - 886	Basil I
886 - 912	Leo VI the Philosopher
913 - 959	Constantine VII
	Porphyrogenitus
1025 - 1028	Constantine VIII
1028 - 1034	Romanus III Argyrus
1034 - 1041	Michael IV
1041 - 1042	Michael V Calaphates
1042	Theodora and Zoe
1042 - 1055	Constantine IX
	Monomachus
1055 - 1056	Theodora
1056 - 1057	Michael VI
1057 - 1059	Isaac I Comnenus
1059 - 1067	Constantine X Ducas
1067 - 1071	Romanus IV Diogenes
1071 - 1078	Michael VII Ducas
1078 - 1081	Nicephorus III Boaniates
1081 - 1118	Alexius I Comnenus
1204	Alexius V Ducas

Latin Occupation

1204 - 1205	Baudouin I
1205 -1216	Henri
1261 - 1282	Michael VIII Paleologus
1341 - 1354	John VI Cantacuzene
1448 - 1453	Constantine XI Dragases

Selçuk Sultans

c. 1040	Tuğrul Bey
	Çakır Bey
1063 - 1072	Alp Arslan
c. 1075	Kutulmuş
1072 - 1092	Malik Shah
1084 - 1086	Süleyman
1092 - 1107	Kılıç Arslan
1107 - 1116	Malik Shah (son of Kılıç Arslan)
- 1155	Masut
1155 - 1192, 1204	Kılıç Arslan II
1193 - 1199	Keykusrev
1199 - 1204	Rukneddin Süleyman
1207 - 1211	Keykusrev (again)
	Kılıç Arslan III
1211 - 1219	Kaykavus
1219 - 1237	Alaettin Kaykubat I
1237 - 1245	Giyasettin Keykusrev II
1245	İzzettin Kaykavus
1245 - 1265	Ruknettin Kılıç Arslan IV
1267 - 1284	Giyasettin Keykusrev III
1284 - 1295	Masut
1295 - ? 1300	Feramerz

Mongols

1162 - 1227	Genghis Khan
1256 - 1265	Hulagu
1259 - 1294	Kublai Khan
1294 - 1311	Timur Khan (Oldjeitu)
1360 - 1404	Tamerlane

Ottoman Sultans

1288 - 1324	Osman Gazi
1324 - 1360	Orhan Gazi
1360 - 1389	Murat I
1389 - 1402	Bayezit I
interregnum	
1413 - 1421	Mehmet I
1421-44, 1446-51	Murat II
1444-6, 1451-81	Mehmet II Fatih
1481 - 1512	Bayezit II
1512 - 1520	Selim I
1520 - 1566	Süleyman I
1566 - 1574	Selim II
1574 - 1595	Murat III
1595 - 1603	Mehmet III
1603 - 1617	Ahmet I
1617-18, 1622-3	Mustafa I
1618 - 1622	Osman II
1623 - 1640	Murat IV
1640 - 1648	İbrahim
1648 - 1687	Mehmet IV
1687 - 1691	Süleyman II
1691 - 1695	Ahmet II
1695 - 1703	Mustafa II
1703 - 1730	Ahmet III
1730 - 1754	Mahmut I
1754 - 1757	Osman III
1757 - 1774	Mustafa III
1774 - 1789	Abdülhamit I
1789 - 1807	Selim III
1807 - 1808	Mustafa IV
1808 - 1839	Mahmut II
1839 - 1861	Abdülmecit I
1861 - 1876	Abdülaziz
1876	Murat V
1876 - 1909	Abdülhamit II
1909 - 1918	Mehmet V
1918 - 1922	Mehmet VI
1922 - 1924	Abdülmecit II (caliph only)

Turkish Presidents

1923 - 1938	Mustafa Kemal Atatürk
1938 - 1950	İsmet İnönü
1950 - 1960	Celal Bayar
1961 - 1966	Cemal Gürsel
1966 - 1973	Cevdet Sunay
1973 - 1980	Fahri Korutürk
1982 - 1989	Kenan Evren
1989 - 1993	Turgut Özal
1993 -	Süleyman Demirel

FOREWORD

The purpose of this book is to describe places of continuing and diverse religious interest in Turkey. It presents a brief survey of the events and some of the people who are memorable in the religious life of Asia Minor. It does not attempt to give full information about other places that may be as important and interesting as religious sites *per se*. For that the reader needs to turn to more general references such as those listed under Suggested Readings in the Appendix.

The word "God" with a capital letter has been used throughout for the Jewish, Christian and Muslim deity. This is not to deny or to minimize the differences in the concept that each faith holds dear. While the beliefs are important to each, the discussion of them is outside the purview of this book. A short Vocabulary can serve as reference for Turkish terms used throughout the book.

The book is organized first to introduce Turkey with an overview of the long and complicated history of Asia Minor and then of Turkey's current situation. There is a geographic description, a brief survey of Turkish arts, then a general discussion of the peoples whose names are associated with certain regions. That is followed by a discussion of paganism as it was practiced in Asia Minor. The main religious groups are described as they and their histories relate to Turkey. For the pagan religions, the chief references are to Homer's *Iliad* and *Odyssey*; for Judaism and Christianity to the Bible; and for Islam, to an English interpretation of the Koran and to the *Shorter Encyclopaedia of Islam*.

Since this is intended as a guide to specific sites, the arrangement of places that are discussed is geographic. The various sites are organized according to broad geographic areas: Marmara and Thrace, Aegean Turkey, Mediterranean Turkey, Central Turkey, and Eastern Turkey. Within the areas the listing is generally as one might visit the sites, going from one to the next.

Place names are given both with their Turkish spelling as they are found on Turkish road maps and with their older names. There has also been an attempt to use them as they were common at the time of the reference. That is, in describing the monastery of St. John of Studion, the city is referred to as Constantinople, while the Topkapı Palace is in Istanbul. In the Index, Constantinople is listed with a reference to the main entry of "Istanbul, Byzantium, Constantinople," and the pages are given at that place. Thus the Index provides a cross reference between the historical and the current names. There are stylistic inconsistencies between English and Turkish: For instance, the description of the mosque in Eminönü in Istanbul is of Yeni Cami, not the New Mosque. Other inconsistencies crop up because at times the Turkish name for a place is most commonly used in English (i.e., Kayseri, not Caesarea Mazaka) and at others few people know the old name (Divriği, not Tephrice).

Distances are in the metric system because that is the common measure in Turkey. Regional maps will help locate the places. The Time Chart shows a chronological order of events. See also p. 79 for a comprehensive map.

This book has grown out of the author's experiences and study gained from living and working in Turkey during the four decades from 1949 to 1991. She visited almost all the places described, many of them several times and she has returned to them more recently. While her perspective on the religious sites has remained that of a Western Christian, the experiences have given her more questions now than she had answers fifty years ago. Among her responsibilities as a writer for Redhouse Press, she co-authored with Everett C. Blake the book, *Biblical Sites in Turkey*. In this present book she continues to look at those and other sites both with a sense of the unknowables and the absurdities of religion and with what she hopes is a nonjudgmental respect for the beliefs of people of all religions. If there are mistakes — undoubtedly there are — she would welcome being corrected. As the wise Turkish Nasreddin Hoca points out, when you are listening to those who know a subject, you need to pay attention; when someone else is listening to you, you need to listen even more carefully to yourself.

Warm and hearty thanks are due first to those who shared their understanding of the country. More specifically, thanks go to her husband Bill and son James for their unfailing support and careful criticisms, to Paul and Gladys Minear, and to Gülseren Ramazanoğlu without whose help and encouragement this book would not have been published.

Anna G. Edmonds
İstanbul, 1997

INTRODUCTION

GEOGRAPHY

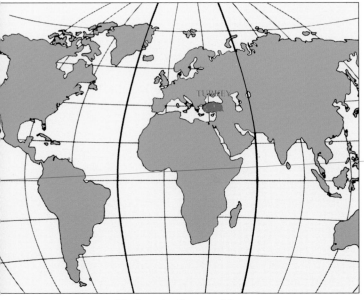

Turkey in the world

Turkey, exotic, colorful, many-faceted, romantic, ever-old and ever-new, is the gateway and the key to the fabled East. It is in the context of its unique geographic location and its age-long history that its religious sites continue to be significant.

Speaking in more concrete terms, Turkey includes the large peninsula of Western Asia, called both Asia Minor and Anatolia, and a part of Thrace in Europe. It covers an area of just over 783,500 square kilometers (300,000 square miles), comparable to slightly less than California, Oregon and Washington combined, or to the countries of Spain and Italy together. It is roughly a rectangle stretching from about 26° N to 42° N, and from 26° E to 45° E. The capital of Turkey is Ankara.

To the south and west are the Mediterranean and Aegean Seas respectively; to the north is the Black Sea. In clockwise order, Turkey shares borders with Greece,

Turkey and her neighbors

Bulgaria, Georgia, Armenia, Iran, Iraq and Syria. The inland waters of the Dardanelles, the Sea of Marmara and the Bosphorus divide Europe from Asia.

Fertile plains fringe the coast; mountain ranges separate them from the high central plateau. Nineteen mountains are over 4,100 meters (13,800 feet) high; of them Mt. Ararat (Ağrı Dağı) is the highest at 5,073 meters (16,910 feet). Both the Tigris and the Euphrates Rivers (Dicle and Firat) rise in Anatolia. Van is a large natural lake in eastern Turkey; Beyşehir, Salt (Tuz), and Eğridir are lakes in central Turkey. Winters in eastern Turkey are severe and summers in the south central region are hot. The contrasts of climate and geography enable the country to produce a great variety of foodstuffs.

The economy of the country is based on agriculture, industry, tourism and natural resources. Two-fifths of the land is arable; of that, half is used for growing cereals. Among the other crops are olives, fruits, nuts, tea, cotton, tobacco, sugar beets, potatoes and other vegetables. Animal husbandry focuses on sheep, goats and cattle. The once prosperous fishing industry is currently suffering a decline. Important mineral deposits include iron, coal, bauxite, boron, chrome and copper; the petroleum resources are insufficient for the nation's requirements. A network of dams on the major rivers creates power and irrigation for Turkey.

The current population of Turkey is over 65 million people, of whom sixty percent live in the cities. The ten most populous cities in order are İstanbul, Ankara, İzmir, Adana, Bursa, Gaziantep, Konya, Eskişehir, Kayseri and Diyarbakır. More than half the population is under the age of 20. Ninety-eight percent are Muslims; there are small Christian and Jewish communities, mostly located in İstanbul and İzmir. Over eighty percent of the people are literate. Turkish is the official language, but many speak at least one other language.

Politically, Turkey is divided into eighty provinces. Five regions give a more general geographic division: Marmara and Thrace, Aegean, Mediterranean, Central, and Eastern (including the Black Sea). Turkey is a constitutional republic. Its legislature is called the Grand National Assembly (GNA); it is composed of 550 members who are elected every five years. All citizens over the age of 18 are required to vote. The head of state is the president, elected by the GNA for one seven-year term; the head of the government, the prime minister, is the head of the majority party elected by popular vote.

THE ARTS OF TURKEY

Turkish arts derive from the early cultural milieus of Central Asia, from whence the Turkish tribes migrated beginning in the 8th century AD, and the Middle East, particularly Anatolia, where those tribes settled. Since the 9th century the esthetic has also been strongly informed by Islam. While each of these artistic elements deserves an in-depth study, the following paragraphs give a brief survey of the subject.

Central Asia, the Far East. The common heritage of Turkish and Far Eastern Arts can be recognized for instance in motifs used in all media. Objects dating from the Bronze Age (c. 3000 BC) that were found near the Yenisey River area near Lake Baikal in Siberia have stylized animal figures that carry through into the Ottoman *rumi* designs. (*Rumi* is the design that evolved from drawings of animals and developed into intertwining curves and scrolls that look like sweet peas; it was often worked into arabesques.) Other Eastern symbolic patterns commonly found in Turkish art include the Chinese dragons (*çintamani* in Turkish) which are two parallel wavy lines (duality) and three beads, the tree of life and the vine loaded with grapes (symbols of longevity and fertility, also found in Greek art), stylized flowers *(hatayi),* and yin-yang (the Chinese female-male duality). The Turkish adaptation of yin-yang at times appears as swaying cypress trees. *Çintamani* appears as a talisman; the *hatayi* blossom is a lotus in profile.

A second art form that probably entered Turkey from the Far East is the shadow theater. While it seems to have originated in Java, China and India, it came to Turkey via Egypt in the early 16th century. The Turkish shadow theater takes its name from the main character, Karagöz (see p. 85).

Middle East, Anatolia. A mixture of Hittite, Hellenistic, and oriental motifs (eagles, deer, griffins, crescent moons) were used in the arabesques of Selçuk artists in Iran in the 11th to 13th centuries. Although by then they were Muslim artists, the Selçuks were not loath to use reliefs of animals and birds in their stonework, nor did they hesitate to represent the human figure, often in hunting scenes. This continued in the ceramic and textile arts of the 11th to 14th century Selçuk capital, Konya. While the Hittites had used embroidery in their costumes in the 2nd millennium BC, the art of appliqué which was developed in Central Asia was apparently carried on the Turkmen tents into Anatolia and the West in the 14th century AD.

Cultural exchanges between the resident Anatolians and the newcomers occurred in other media also. In the 10th century the Selçuks brought with them the knowledge of knotted pile rugs. They and their relatives the Ottomans found and developed in Turkey the knowledge of how to cover a large rectangular room with a domed ceiling. The Turks took over the local folk heroes and gave them a Turkish character in their legends and songs (see St. George, p.47 and 197).

Tiles and wood inlay, Topkapı Palace Museum

Islamic Expression. Even beyond these cultural influences, a quality that must be recognized in understanding Turkish art is that it is almost always an Islamic expression, of which the controlling characteristic is the concept that God is One. There is no philosophical distinction between the sacred and the secular worlds. Islamic art, therefore, is more unified than Western art because Islam itself is a totality. The spiritual world, according to Islamic thought, can best be expressed in pure mathematics. The Jewish and Christian iconoclastic aversion to representational art

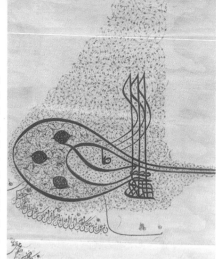

Tuğra of Sultan Süleyman the Lawmaker

also probably had an important influence on what Islamic artists produced. Thus the criteria applied in a discussion of Western art do not necessarily pertain in the discussion of Islamic or Turkish art. Rather than in the representational art of the temporal world, Turkish artists created their masterpieces in geometric and rhythmic intricacy.

The Fine Arts. The arts of Turkey fall into several groupings, depending on the media used by the artists. Among them are architecture, calligraphy, textiles, rugs, ceramics, glass, stonecarving, woodwork, metalwork (and the related field of intarsia), illumination, poetry, music, and culinary arts.

Architecture. The architecture of the mosques is a prime example of the interdependence of art and religion. The mosques were built with the intent to express the power and awe and grace of the Islamic comprehension of God. The basic design of a mosque is intended to maximize the number of worshippers who can be close to the front of the building. The centrality of God is symbolized in the soaring central dome, while the equality among all worshippers is evidenced in the absence of any special separation in the central prayer area. Notice also that the lower windows of mosques are clear glass: the outside world should be the same as the inner. The other fine arts have been used to enhance the experience of worship in the mosque.

Calligraphy. Calligraphy, particularly the Arabic script, was developed with a spiritual purpose in mind. Although it existed before the 7th century, its use was greatly encouraged by the need to transcribe in a permanent form God's word as revealed to people through the Prophet Muhammad.

The first style of Arabic writing was the angular Kufic, later the more flowing *nesih* and bold *sülüs* styles were invented. Turkish masters of calligraphy have contributed to the

Calligraphy (left); the silhouette of the Süleymaniye Mosque designed by Sinan (right)

A kaftan made of a 16th century textile,
Topkapı Palace Museum

development of the art. In the 11th century the Turkish Yakut Müstesami, working in Baghdad, refined both those styles and *hakkik, reyhani, tevkii* and *rik'al* by cutting the point of his pen on a slant. From the Ottoman Sultan Orhan (1324) on, stylized script was used by each of the rulers for his monogram, called a *tuğra*. The tuğra included the sultan's name on the first line and that of his father above it. The early sultans wrote their own tuğras; Sultan Ahmet III (d. 1730) was considered a skilled calligrapher.

By the 15th century the city of Amasya northeast of Ankara had become the center of calligraphic art. One of the greatest Turkish calligraphers, Sheyh Hamdullah (1436-1520) lived there and taught his art to the son of Sultan Mehmet II. When that son became Sultan Bayezit II, he brought Sheyh Hamdullah and his family to İstanbul to add to the artistic treasures of his capital. The sheyh's work is distinguished by its classic elegance; it can be seen in the Bayezit mosques both in İstanbul and in Amasya. The ceiling medallion of the Mosque of Süleyman the Magnificent in İstanbul is the work of the 16th century master, Ahmet Karahisari. The value of calligraphy was so great that in the 17th century a single copy of the Koran cost almost as much as the erection of a public fountain. Ahmet Kemal Akdik was the last chief Ottoman calligrapher for the sultan. When the Latin alphabet was introduced by Atatürk in 1928 the art of Arabic calligraphy disappeared in Turkey.

Textiles, rugs. After the value of knotted rugs was recognized in the West, by the 15th century Turkish rugs and carpets were so prized that they were gifts for the rich and powerful of Europe, as can be seen in paintings by Holbein (1497) and Lotto (1480-1556).

The floors of mosques are usually covered with prayer rugs. Often these were woven by hand as a gift to the mosque. The patterns in these rugs both show the direction that the person praying will face and also have some kind of geometric or floral decoration, often suggesting a mosque. Rather than being replaced when they began to wear, a new rug might be placed on top of the old one. Thus some remarkable old pieces have been recovered from under the newer layers.

The Selçuks also stimulated the arts of textile weaving, particularly using silk thread combined with other materials. One of the gold brocade robes of honor from the 13th century is in the museum in Lyons, France. Its decorations are of lions and an inscription giving the name of the ruling Sultan Keykubat of Konya. Silk brocades and velvets woven between the 16th and 19th centuries often have elaborate designs of multicolored sprays of

The oldest Turkish rug, discovered in the glaciers of the Altai mountains

Selçuk stonework, Konya *Woodcarved minber of the Blue Mosque*

flowers. They may be further decorated with gold or silver threads. Embroideries were often added to kerchiefs and towels used for ceremonial purposes such as wrapping or cleaning religious items.

Ceramics, Glass. The development of ceramic art can be traced in the mural tiles of the Turkish mosques. At first the colored pieces of ceramic -- usually black or turquoise -- were cut in geometric shapes, sometimes to form Arabic characters (such as in the Arslanhane Camii in Ankara and the Karatay Medresesi in Konya). They were fitted in place into the plaster on the wall. This technique was perfected by the Selçuk Turks. It was used also for exterior decoration, such as on the shafts of minarets (notice the Çifte Minareli Medrese in Sivas). Later, the technique of drawing many colors on a single tile was added, increasing the repertory of designs and colors available to the ceramists. The 16th century mural ceramics show in particular the exceptionally high degree of artistry in which craftsmen in the Ottoman Empire balanced color, line, and rhythm in geometric designs. Because of a slight boss created when it was fired, the unique tomato red Armenian bole from the İznik kilns between about 1556 and 1620 produced a gleam beyond the luster of the glass in the mural tiles. (An outstanding example of this period is found in the Rüstem Paşa Camii in İstanbul where the walls are totally covered with patterned tiles.)

Stained glass was also used in geometric shapes and embedded in plaster in the upper level windows. Such work can be seen in the Mosque of Süleyman the Magnificent in İstanbul.

Stonecarving, Woodwork, Metalwork, Inlay. Stonecarving, woodwork, and metalwork artists created similar geometric patterns in their media. At times the minber of the mosque is made of intricately carved wood, at times it is carved stone. Besides the magnificently carved stone doorways (the İnce Minareli Medresesi in Konya and the Yeşil Cami in Bursa), the careful carving on thousands of gravestones is evidence of the value given to this art. Among the examples of the carved wood are the window shutters in the Mosque of Süleyman in İstanbul and many of the imam's thrones. Iron grillwork protecting the windows of ablution fountains similarly demonstrates the esthetic in geometry.

At times the designs were intensified when a second material was inlaid on the original surface. One of the windows on the courtyard of the Mosque of Fatih Mehmet II in İstanbul has an inlaid marble inscription. Much of the furniture in the Palace of Beylerbeyi is heavily decorated with ivory and mother-of-pearl marquetry.

Poetry, Music, Dance. The outpouring of mystical inspiration in poetry, music, and dance is found in some religious services. The 15th century Birth-song of the Prophet *(Mevlut)* by Süleyman Çelebi is familiar to almost all Turks. This is recited frequently in services both in mosques and in private homes.

Works by the two 13th century poets, Yunus Emre and Celâleddin Rumi, are considered masterpieces of religious expression, as is the 16th century epic poem *Leyla ve Mecnun* by Fuzuli.

Music and dance are prominent in the dervish ceremonies. Particular instruments are reserved for this music -- the *ney* (bamboo flute), *rebab* (stringed instrument) and

An exquisite 16th century tile from Rüstem Paşa Camii in İstanbul

*Stained glass, the
Süleymaniye Mosque*

kudum (small, double drums). A number of hymns have been written expressing dervish thought. Religious dance is represented by the whirling of the Mevlevis.

Turkish music had a great influence on Western music in the 17th and 18th centuries when the janissary bands accompanied the sultans' armies on their European campaigns. Most commonly the janissaries were members of the Bektaşi dervish order. Their instruments and musical themes found their way into the music of Mozart, Beethoven, and Gluck, among many others.

Culinary Arts. Culinary arts belong in this discussion for several reasons. Turks pride themselves that their foods are recognized internationally to be among the world's great cuisines. They are connoiseurs of water, and can often identify the specific spring from which their drinking water comes. Speaking in more religious terms, the art of viticulture is reputed to have originated in Turkey; according to the Bible, after Noah landed on Mt. Ararat he planted the first vineyard. To a degreee uncommon today in the West except perhaps in the sacrament of communion, Turks are aware of the relationship between bread and worship, between food and culture, between the produce of the earth and their very being. Not only is there an almost ritualistic performance of insuring that there is fresh bread for every meal, one particular bread, *pide*, has been reserved for the meals during the Islamic month of fasting.

On many old fountains there is an inscription in Arabic which translated reads, "From water comes all life." The word for water, as it comes in the form of rain, is "blessing" *(rahmet)*; when it is offered to a thirsty person the polite form of thanks is "May you be as holy as water." *(Su gibi aziz olasın!)*

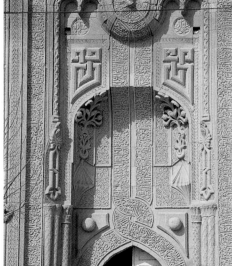

Calligraphy, woodwork, tiles, Selimiye Mosque, Edirne (left); Selçuk stonecarving (right)

OVERVIEW OF HISTORY

One of the earliest and the most persistent themes that still appears in the history of the many peoples of Anatolia is their balancing between feuding with and tolerating each other. As a great world crossroads, the land has seen the struggles and the accommodations to each other of the Hattis and the Assyrians, the Sea Peoples, the Trojans and the Greeks, the Byzantines, the Crusaders and the Ottomans, the Russians, the Kurds, the Armenians and the Turks, to name only the most well-known. More than once the personal loyalties have been weighted more on the side of a desire for feuding, or for land, or for tolerance than they have been on the side of ethnic or religious identity. It is also important

The silk road between Sardis and Susa

to remember when discussing the history in a generalized survey that throughout there have been enclaves of people — identified often not by themselves but by their enemies in terms of religion, language or family — who because of the very rugged topography have maintained their culture unresponsive to and ignored by whatever group claimed to rule the land.

Another major element in the long history is the importance of the trade routes that made a network linking Anatolia to the East, to Egypt and to Europe. The roads usually followed the paths of least resistance; they went over the mountain passes, along the river valleys and across the safest fords. As fully as their builders were able to engineer them, they were all-weather roads; they often were elevated, high ways. They were politically important in that they were part of the mechanism keeping a government in Rome or in Susa in touch with what was happening in Sardis, for example. They were important economically in enabling goods and services to move with dispatch (if not without adventure). They were important tools in facilitating the communication of ideas. The spread of Christianity and later of Islam followed the trade routes. Regularly at about the distance that could be traveled in a day there was some kind of shelter for people and their animals to spend the night. Many of the towns and cities described in this book evolved as part of this system of roads, shelters, caravansaries, and marketplaces.

Besides the routes on land, people also used a relay of fire towers to communicate quickly over long distances. Crusader castles were sited on hilltops so as to be places of defense and alarm, and so as to be able to signal to each other. A complicated system linked the castle in Sis (Kozan) with Anavarza, Mamistra (Yakapınar/Misis), and Til Hamdoun (Toprak Kalesi), among others. Probably Yılankale and Hierapolis Castabala (Bodrum) were included in this circuit, but their medieval names are uncertain. In Istanbul, well into the 19th century the rulers watched the fire signals on Mt. Bulgurlu (Çamlıca) for current news of their far-flung empire.

THE STONE AGE (c. 8,000 - 4,000 BC). Evidence of human habitation as early as about 400,000 years ago has been found in caves on the lake of **Küçük Çekmece** near İstanbul. However, the earliest true settlements appear to be in Anatolia from the Stone Age beginning about 8,000 BC. This was the time when people who used stone tools evolved from being hunters to becoming farmers. Up until then

A ceremonial Hittite standard

they had been food-gatherers; they had been at the mercy of the elements and the hunt. Afterwards they became food-producers, able with increasing skills to control more and more of their environment. This revolution is the critical division between primitive existence and culture; this marks the beginning of civilization. Before the Stone Age little evidence of human presence has been found by archaeologists beyond stone tools; before it came to an end the archaeological evidence is of a well developed artistic expression of formal religious thought and emotion. The Stone Age people accomplished the change in the remarkably short time of about 4,000 years. But why it happened at this time and in this place no one knows for sure. During the Neolithic Revolution people in the Middle East began to domesticate their food. They found — or maybe hybridized — a wheat that gave much more food than the wild emmer or einkorn but that depended on their reaping and sowing it to grow in abundance. They tamed animals, planted crops, and stored enough harvest to last through the bleak winters. The Revolution meant a new kind of social organization and discipline; it created an economic need to settle and manage the stock piles; politically it meant a possibility and a responsibility of supporting a large and complex community.

The first settlements that are known in Anatolia are in some caves (**Karain, Beldibi**) on the Mediterranean coast. There archaeologists discovered remains of barley, lentils, and primitive wheat along with the stone implements for cutting the sheaves. Those knives had been used so long they were covered with a patina. In the caves were also bits of pottery and a line drawing of graceful, running deer.

Some of the factors that we know contributed to the Revolution were the variety of resources available in the Middle East: There were native grains and animals, arable soil, materials for making tools, and a temperate climate with enough rain and seasonal variation to make things grow. The foothills of the Taurus Mountains and the drainage basins of the Tigris and Euphrates Rivers — long considered part of the Fertile Crescent — fulfilled the requirements for people to develop the available natural resources. Without question these possibilities existed in other places around the world. People were living with similar resources in other places and had done so for thousands of years. However, also at this time, in this place people gained some new, radically different understanding of what to do with their resources.

With the more certain continuing supply of food came the complexities and the security of relatively permanent communities in which not everyone was compelled to do everything all the time. There could be specialization. Surely some people's hands were skillful in chipping flint so that a straight knife edge

Cuneiform inscriptions on an Assyrian tablet, the Museum of Ancient Orient Arts, İstanbul

would be formed, while others were prized as swift-running hunters. Surely some were as quick to grasp the implications of inter-tribal relationships as our contemporary diplomats. Some certainly would have thrown pots, some could tend the fields, some were called on to govern. Some would have spent their time in the priestly rituals of placating the gods to bring the community good harvests and successful battles. Evidence of this developing society has been found in **Çatal Höyük** south of Konya.

THE BRONZE AGE (C. 3200 BC), THE HATTIS (C. 2500 BC). About 3200 BC the new knowledge and skills of metallurgy characterized the Bronze Age. A temple at **Midas Şehri** northeast of Afyon was where priests, using this new technology, probably cast and blessed the bronze weapons that gave their soldiers a strength superior to their enemies (see p. 203).

A group calling itself Hatti (resident in central Anatolia before the Bronze Age) established a capital at **Kanesh** between today's Kayseri and Sivas. By about 2500 BC they had become prosperous through trading with Assyria. The carved seals, the baked letters found there, and the gold found in **Alaca Höyük** (both a Hattic and a Hittite city) suggest the wealth and artistry of the Hatti. These Hatti seem to have understood something of the relationship between the sun and the planets as shown in their symbol of a sun disc. Their worship of the Mother Goddess and their many statuettes of bulls and stags betoken connections between them, the Mycenaeans, and the much later Greeks.

But rather than the Hatti, it was their Assyrian partners living on the outskirts of Kanesh who brought a major contribution, that of writing, to Anatolia. Because of cuneiform inscriptions about commercial dealings that these foreign traders preserved on mud tablets, a written history exists for these people dating back to 1900 BC. These were records cut into the soft clay with a triangular instrument, baked, enclosed in an incised clay envelope and baked again. Most of the tablets were business accounts between the Assyrians and their home markets, but also some human details appear in them — a son who felt his father cheated him, a man who attempted to smuggle forbidden goods.

THE HITTITES (C. 2000 - 600 BC). Some time during the 3rd millennium BC Indo-European tribes took possession of much of Anatolia. They centered at the crossroads of the trade routes that crisscrossed from the Aegean to the east, and from the Black Sea through the Cilician Gates to the Mediterranean. One name they used was the "Land of the Hattis," referring to the people who were there before them. Our word for these newcomers, "Hittites," comes from that and from their biblical identification (Gen. 15:20). The Hittites picked up several Hatti ideas, including some of their mythology and their awareness of relations between celestial objects as expressed in their "sun discs."

The Hittite civilization flourished in Anatolia from about 1900 to 1200 BC. From the objects that have been recovered — sculptures, paintings, documents — we can see a high level of cultural and artistic development. Many of the objects that they left behind them had some religious significance: the stone reliefs of gods and priests before an altar, the temple at Yazılıkaya, tablets that give details of religious ceremonies and lengthy questions put to the gods in search of a favorable answer.

THE PHRYGIANS (C. 1200 - 600 BC).

The origins of the Phrygians are among the enigmas of the past. They seem to have been a varied group that came originally from southeastern Europe or from Greece and the Balkans. What spurred their migration is not known, but as they moved south through the Middle East beginning about 1200 BC they spread

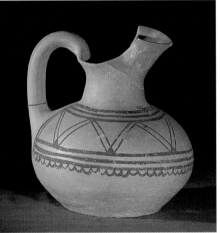

warfare and destruction. One theory is that the eruption of Thera (Santorini) created major disruptions of peoples in the eastern Mediterranean by forcing migration. Or, perhaps, it was the region's prosperity that attracted the invaders' cupidity and brought the disaster. Whoever they were, they apparently occasioned the downfall of the Hittite Empire, and possibly they were the ones who burned and sacked the Troy of Homer's epic. It took over two hundred years on the coast and four hundred in the interior for the residents to recover from the havoc they wreaked.

These invaders settled in Asia Minor and along the Mediterranean coast. The names we know them by are not what they used for themselves, but what they were called by the people they fought. In northwestern

Phrygian painted pitcher Anatolia they were usually called the Ionians and the Aeolians. The Egyptian Pharaoh Ramses III who defeated them about 1190 BC gave them the name "Sea Peoples." He pictured them as tall, skinny soldiers who wore short skirts and tufted helmets. They came into conflict with the Israelites on the Mediterranean coast, and were called Philistines by them (Gen. 10:14, Jer. 47:4). For the Assyrians they were the Muski; this name is thought to be related to the biblical Meshech who was the sixth son of Japheth (Gen. 10:2).

By the 8th century, a group in central Anatolia who were descendants of these warriors had become known as Phrygians. They were a settled power concentrated in the valley of the Sangarius River (Sakarya); at their height their power extended from Sinop on the Black Sea, into the Troad (the Çanakkale Peninsula) and including Mt. Sipylus (Manisa Dağı), through the Taurus Mountains to the Assyrian kingdom in the south. While their power was relatively short-lived, they acted as the intermediaries who transmitted the art and culture of central Anatolia to the West. Their capital, Gordium, was on the Persian "Royal Road" between Susa and Sardis — the main commercial highway of the time.

Later the Greeks believed that the Phrygians spoke the oldest language of the world, that their kings were half-divine, and that their name meant "free men." The early Greek writers (Homer, Hesiod, Herodotus, Thucydides, Strabo and Plutarch among them) are the best sources for our knowledge about this period. Phrygian contributions to music, including the invention of cymbals, have lasted into the present. Pythagoras, who discovered the relationship of music to mathematics and, with that discovery, the octave scale, also held the doctrine that morality meant a proper tuning of the soul to the harmony of the universe. Pythagoras influenced the later identifications of Dorian, Aeolian, Ionian and Phrygian modes. The Phrygian cadence is described as the ending of a piece of music (which up to then has been in a major key) on the dominant chord of that key's relative minor key. The effect (used often by J. S. Bach) might be compared to the ideas of a completed thought followed by, "However…"

Phrygians are known in art for their bronze artifacts, their kilims and gold embroidery, pottery and their stylized lions (companions of the goddess Cybele) resembling the Hittite lions, which appear to have been copied on the gateway at Mycenae in Greece. Their paintings of warriors and graceful animals also seem to be precursors of a Greek style. Phrygian cauldrons with bull head handles show a possible influence stemming back to the shrines in Stone Age Çatal Höyük.

Phrygian importance reached its climax under King Midas (c. 725-696 BC) who is still synonymous with "the golden touch." Legend says that King Midas was present during a contest between the gods Pan and Apollo. When Midas favored Pan, the judge Tmolus gave him a pair of donkey's ears as a comment on his bad judgment.

URARTIANS, LYDIANS, THRACIANS, GALATIANS (C. 750 - 230 BC). About the time that the Hittites were losing their power in the area, several other communities were gaining importance. East of the Euphrates River the Urartians ruled a land known in the Bible as Ararat (Gen. 8:4); they reached the height of their power in the middle of the 8th century BC. The Urartu stronghold was on Lake Van. Similarities in their art with that of the Minoans and the Etruscans raise questions about what contacts there were among these people and when they occurred.

A different group who some think were related to Lud, one of Noah's grandsons, were the Lydians. The Lydians, whose capital was Sardis, are best known for their wealthy King Croesus who ruled from 560 to 546 BC. The outstanding contribution the Lydians made to world trade was to guarantee the value of their gold and silver coinage. The guarantee is thought not only to have facilitated business arrangements, but also, by making life easier for everyone, to have freed some of the Lydians for time to develop a musical style and to tell stories. Aesop is said to have lived at Croesus' court; it may be because Aesop was such a good story-teller that Croesus is known so well. (Herodotus also helped tell his story.) In 547 BC Croesus was defeated by the Persian Cyrus the Great. This initiated about two hundred years of Persian dominance, during which time they

Urartu figures

engineered an excellent system of roads, including the Royal Road from Susa to Sardis. In addition to these peoples, several other early groups have left their names as geographic identities in Turkey. The Thracians, one of whose fabled sons was Orpheus, lived in what is now European Turkey. The Galatians, who settled around Ankara, were originally soldiers from southern France (Gaul) hired by the Bithynian

Hittite reliefs

King Nicomedes I in 279 BC and defeated by King Attalus I of Pergamum in 230 BC.

PERSIANS (546 - 190 BC). Between the time of the Greeks and the Romans, in the 6th century BC, Asia Minor was invaded from the east by the Persians. Under Cyrus the Great Sardis was captured from Croesus (546 BC); this completed the Persian control of Asia Minor. This Cyrus is the man who freed the Jews in Babylon (539 BC) and helped rebuild the temple to Yahweh in Jerusalem. Part of the Persian contribution to the people of Anatolia was the introduction of the cult of Mithraism.

GREEK AND ROMAN PERIOD (C.1200 BC - AD 300) Even though the Persians ruled the region and exacted financial returns from it, the daily life of the people remained much as it had been until Alexander the Great embarked on his world conquest in 334 BC, inaugurating the Hellenistic Period. Hellenism blended into the Roman Period as Rome took over governing one after another of the eastern provinces, starting in 190 BC. While most of the names of these provinces are no longer used except by historians or archaeologists, some are important in locating the path that Paul took on his missionary journeys or in distinguishing which place is being referred to when the same name occurs more than once.

The early Greek-speaking residents of western Anatolia developed a remarkable and complex culture that has affected the politics, economy, philosophy, astronomy, and mathematics of the world. Their contributions ranged from their social structure based on an organized government and their eagerness to question the why's and how's of their universe, to their tool of writing with which they recorded their thoughts.

While Homer lived long before Alexander, the poems he composed shaped the ethos of the Hellenistic Period — and still today are part of the Western cultural heritage. Homer may have been born in İzmir; he is supposed to have lived about 850 BC — around four hundred years after the events that he sang about took place and three hundred years before his poetry was written down. In his portrayal of the conflict between freedom and responsibility, the Western world has ever since recognized a standard of ethical behavior.

During the Hellenistic period there were flowerings of city states, of art and architecture, and of science. The Hellenistic influence was felt largely among the residents of the coastal areas of the Aegean and Mediterranean Seas. Ruins of theaters, temples, libraries, fountains, gymnasiums, city council chambers, and market places still attest to the wealth and the achievements of the residents.

Greek theaters regularly had temples to Dionysus near by. Dionysus was the actors' patron god and was associated with the beginnings and development of drama. Arion, a 7th century BC poet from Lesbos (Mytilene) is credited with giving artistic shape to the highly emotional hymn, the *dithyramb,* that was sung by a chorus around the altar of Dionysus to commemorate the story of his joys and sufferings. Thespis, who lived in the mid-6th century, is supposed to have introduced dialogue to the hymn, thus starting Greek tragedy on its way.

Theatrical performances were religious festivals. In the classical period serious plays were given only during special festivals. They were not events that ran for an extended season. Like the athletic events, the theatrical events were also a com-

Theater of Ephesus

petition. Each competing poet presented a tragic trilogy, usually centered on one subject, followed by a lighter satire. Later for the Romans a theatrical entertainment might include, besides the comedies and tragedies, rather coarse farces and dances, character sketches and pantomimes.

The tragedies were usually given in the morning and the comedies in the afternoon. Their timing was associated with the cultivation of grapes. The Great Dionysia was a spring festival when the vines were pruned. Another festival coincided with the harvest. The lesser festival of the wine-press came when the new wine was first sampled.

Dionysus is one of many examples of beliefs that were borrowed and modified among the residents of Anatolia. Dionysus was the god of fertility, and particularly the god of wine. As such, he is curiously, though logically, related to the Hittite god of agriculture, Telipinu, who dies in winter and comes back to life in spring. Dionysus as a child was supposed to be horned: is this the Neolithic-Hittite male symbol of the bull? Another story about Dionysus in which he shares a voyage on a new-moon boat with a large number of animals seems to echo both the *Gilgamesh Epic* and the story of Noah and the Deluge.

When Alexander the Great died in 323 BC his empire was divided by his three generals Antigonus, Lysimachus and Seleucis (he founded the Seleucid dynasty), with Lysimachus ruling the western region and Seleucis the southern. Antigonus was killed in battle in 301, and Lysimachus soon after. At that time much of Lysimachus's kingdom was taken over and enlarged by the kings of Pergamum. Two events were critical in the transfer of control in the change from the Hellenistic period to the Roman. The first came in 190 BC when the Seleucids were defeated by the Roman army at Magnesia-on-the-Meander. Then in 133 BC the Pergamene King Attalus III bequeathed his kingdom to Rome, to the astonishment and annoyance of his would-be heirs.

Pax Romana (14 BC - AD 191) defines a time of political stability, economic and commercial development (with the building and upkeep of roads a contributing factor), and of a unified language. Latin was used for official documents while Greek was the vernacular. Most of the inscriptions from this period are in Greek, largely to enable people to read them. It was also both a time of despotic rule and a time of the birth and spread of Christianity. Public buildings built during the Roman period were ostentatious. Theaters were replaced by amphitheaters (places of contest).

While the roads were relatively good, travel still had its problems. In general, the inns were poor. They were dirty, smoky and infested with vermin. Travelers either put up with the conditions or contrived to stay with their friends. A traveler often carried his own bedding and went by cart. On top of these complications, any stranger in the neighborhood was generally suspect. The usual assumption was that the person was an outlaw. As such he was potentially fair game for mistreatment of any kind, including robbery and murder, and the bully could claim that the stranger had deserved his fate. Perhaps it is no wonder that both Paul and Ignatius had military guards when they were being taken to Rome. If ordinary people were rich enough to be able to ride horseback, they usually rode only for a relatively short distance. A day's travel might average 60 km; a messenger going by foot was fortunate to cover 40 km. The deluxe way to travel was in a covered carriage that might be fitted with a bed on which the passenger could get some sleep. The emperor's messengers were expected to hurry: From Antioch-on-the-Orontes to Rome the trip averaged about 50 days, and duplicate letters were often sent because of the uncertainties of the mail. People rarely traveled in winter, particularly by sea.

The regional names used to identify provinces give an indication of the backgrounds of the groups: the Phrygians from Thrace who probably helped in the downfall of both Troy VII and Hattusas, the Aeolians from Thessaly and Boeotia (in Greece) who settled between Smyrna and Pergamum, and the Ionians from Attica who were concentrated south of Smyrna. The Lydians whose capital was Sardis, and the Lycians whose capital was Xanthus, are thought to have been descendants of Hittite, Etruscan, and pre-Hittite people who mingled with and were influenced by the invaders. The Carians thought that they were the first residents; other names were more political than ethnic, among them Asia, Cappadocia and Cilicia.

The regions populated by Ionians and Aeolians came under Roman control gradually. Chronologically, the order in which the eastern provinces were taken over by Rome were these: Achaea (southern Greece: 190 BC); Macedonia (northern Greece: 146 BC); Asia (133 BC); Pontus (85 BC); Bithynia (74 BC); Syria (c. 64 BC); Cilicia (64 BC); Galatia (which included parts of Phrygia, Pisidia, Lycaonia and Isauria: 25 BC); Paphlagonia (added to Galatia: 5 BC); Illyrium (on the Dalmatian coast: AD 9); Cappadocia (AD 17); Lesser Armenia (added to Cappadocia in AD 70 and then both merged with Galatia to form a double governorship); Lycia (AD 43); Thrace (AD 46); Commagene (added to Syria: AD 72); and Pamphylia (AD 74). The borders of the provinces were blurred; thus, for instance, it is next to impossible to determine where Paul was when he journeyed to Galatia.

Greek and Roman place names in Anatolia

The following short description is in geographical, not chronological order beginning with the Marmara and Thracian areas, continuing south through the Troad, along the Aegean and Mediterranean coast, then central, and finally eastern Anatolia.

Bithynia was a relatively small region bounded by the Sangarius River (Sakarya) on the east, the Rhyndachus (Koca Çay) on the south and west, and the Propontus (Sea of Marmara) and Black Sea on the north. Its cities were Nicomedia (İzmit) and Nicaea (İznik) whose citizens vied with each other for leadership, Chrysopolis (Üsküdar), and Prusa (Bursa) at the foot of Bithynian Mt. Olympus (Uludağ). Nicaea was named by Alexander's general Lysimachus for his wife Nikaia. Prusa was founded by King Prusias I towards the end of the 3rd century BC. This Prusias was the man who sheltered Hannibal from the Romans.

A persistent tradition credits the Apostle Andrew with founding the Christian church in Bithynia. It also says that Andrew continued farther north into Thrace and across the Black Sea. At the time of Trajan, Pliny the Younger was governor of Bithynia and Pontus (AD 110-113); following a destructive fire in Nicomedia, he petitioned Trajan for permission to form a volunteer fire brigade. Trajan turned him down, fearing that it might become a "political club," an action which some scholars have seen as a veiled reference to Trajan's attitude towards the early Christian church.

The Province of **Thrace** extended north from the Hellespont, the Propontus and the Bosphorus into today's Bulgaria and west to Macedonia. The kings' palace was at Bizye (Vize). The main river was the Hebrus (Meriç Nehri); among the cities were Philipopolus (Plovdiv), Hadrianople (Edirne), Perinthus/Heraclea (Marmara Ereğlisi) and Byzantium (İstanbul). According to the historian Herodotus, the indigenous Thracians observed several barbaric customs, including tattooing; somewhat later they became known as musicians and poets. The province came under Roman control during the reign of the emperor Vespasian (AD 69-79), but because it was on one of the outer edges of the Empire it suffered from repeated attacks by the Goths and the Huns. Constantine the Great was involved in driving the Goths back between 321 and 336. The Goths won the battle of Hadrianople in 378, but then made peace with Theodosius the Great in 381.

In Greek legend, the **Troad** (the northwest peninsula from Mt. Ida — Kazdağı — to the Hellespont — Çanakkale Boğazı) was settled by King Teucer and his band who escaped from a famine in Crete and who interpreted an oracle to mean that they should found a city where mice attacked them. Teucer built his Temple to Apollo Smintheus (Apollo, the killer of mice) where the town of Gülpınar is now located. Shortly thereafter Prince Dardanus landed on the same coast. Teucer gave Dardanus both his daughter and land enough for a city which he called Dardania. Dardanus' grandson was Tros who named his people Trojans. In turn, his grandson, Ilius, won a spotted cow from the king of Phrygia and was told to found his city Ilion (or Troy) where the cow lay down. Ilius's grandson was Priam who fathered Paris, Hector and Cassandra, characters in Homer's *Iliad*. The Troad was sometimes considered to be part of the district of Mysia.

The **Aeolians** (the people living between Smyrna and Pergamum) considered themselves to be two of the four nations who were sons of Hellen. Hellen was the father of all the Greeks.They spoke various dialects of Greek. Deucalion — Hellen's father — in one account, incidentally, was warned of an approaching world flood by his father Prometheus and therefore with his wife Pyrrha built an ark to save themselves from it. Once the waters subsided — they knew that this was happening because of a dove — Deucalion and Pyrrha repopulated the world by veiling their heads and throwing the "bones" (i.e.stones) of their Mother Earth behind them. This story must have come from the East with its many parallels with both the *Gilgamesh Epic* and the story of Noah (Gen. 6:9 - 9:29).

Ionia was the coastal region of Asia Minor from the Meander River (Menderes Nehri) north to Smyrna (İzmir). The Ionians who gave their name to the region are thought to have come from Greece in about the 10th century BC. In biblical accounts the name appears as Javan (Isa 66:19); Javan refers to a group of people living on the coast of Asia Minor and the adjacent islands. Javan was the fourth son of Japheth (Gen. 10:2). The derivative of Javan, Yunan, continues to be used in Turkish to mean Greek.

The Ionians in the 6th and 5th centuries BC fostered an amazingly rich community of philosophers who sought to find a rational explanation of their physical world in terms of matter, movement and energy. Thales of Miletus (?640-546 BC), called the father of Greek geometry, astronomy and philosophy, believed in a universal material cause — he said the primordial material was water. He gained his fame from having predicted the eclipse of the sun in 585 BC; the eclipse stopped a battle between the Medes and the Lydians and led to their agreeing on a lasting peace. Thales seems to have gotten a boost in astronomy from the Babylonians who knew that eclipses reoccurred regularly. Two other Miletians carried on his search for the ultimate substance, Anaximander (611-547 BC) and Anaximenes (?600-530 BC). Anaximander called it the "infinite," and believed that it was subject to laws, while Anaximenes was convinced that everything resulted from air. A little later Anaxagoras (?500-426 BC) of Clazomene thought that everything existed originally in tiny, infinite, disordered particles (seeds — atoms) which were given a rational order by *nous* or mind. His theories about the universe got him into trouble in Athens and he was forced to retire to Lampsacus (Lapseki) on the southeastern corner of the Hellespont (Çanakkale Boğazı). Xenophanes (570-?470 BC) of Colo-

Reconstruction of the Mausoleum, after Kristian Jeppessen

phon asserted that god — he defined god as true existence — was One, Undivided, Unmoving, Eternal, Identical with the universe, totally unlike man in either form or understanding.

The first of the Roman holdings was the **Province of Asia.** Asia at that time meant the area for which Ephesus was the capital. Later Asia was expanded to include Miletus to the south, Sardis to the east, and Smyrna and Pergamum to the north. It was the wealthiest of all the Roman provinces and the most attentive in worshipping the emperor. This cult of emperor worship was associated with the worship of Diana of the Ephesians. However, the association did not mean that the two were equated, but rather that the cult added a religious dimension to the figure of the emperor.

Because the term "Asia" came to be used for the whole continent by the 5th century AD, the name "Asia Minor" became the popular distinction for the peninsula. The first references to "Anatolia" were made in the 10th century AD.

Carians claimed that they were natives of the region; Homer located them around Miletus. Later under King Mausolus (377 - ?350 BC) their capital was Mylasa (Milas) until with his work of Hellenizing his land he concentrated his subjects in Halicarnassus (Bodrum). Halicarnassus not only was the place of the Mausoleum, one of the Seven Wonders of the World, its Crusader fortress ranks among the great castles of the 14th to 16th centuries. Evidences of the efforts of Alexander's general, Seleucis, to continue Alexander's desire to Hellenize Anatolia in the 3rd century BC, can be seen in the Carian city of Aphrodisias. Enough of the buildings that are left there show that the site rivals Ephesus. It affords tourists today a glimpse of a thriving, beautiful ancient city.

Galatia got its name from the mercenary Celtic soldiers from Gaul who were hired by Nicomedes I of Bithynia in 279 BC to help him fight his brother. This Nicomedes was the founder of the city of Nicomedia (İzmit). The Gauls originally were about 20,000 strong, about half being women or children. After almost fifty years of continual fighting with the older residents of Asia Minor, they were trounced by Attalus I of Pergamum. He forced them to settle around Ankara. The geographical boundaries of their Galatia are not known, but they may have reached as far south as Iconium (Konya). At the same time it is not impossible that Paul may have traveled to Tavium, Ancyra, and Pessinus in Galatia before he tried unsuccessfully to go into Bithynia (Acts 16:8).

Cappadocia was a political unit during the time of the Persian domination of Asia Minor beginning about 550 BC. It became a Roman province in AD 17 when its last king, who had supported first Mark Anthony and then Octavian, died in prison in Rome. Cappadocia included much of the old Hittite kingdom. The northwest region included some of Galatia. The capital was Caesarea Mazaca (Kayseri). Other cities of note were Archelais (Aksaray), Morimene (Hacıbektaş), Tyana (south of Niğde), Comana/Hierapolis (south of Pınarbaşı) and Melitine (Malatya). The area was the largely treeless plain, home to shepherds with their large flocks of sheep. Harassed in turn by Arabs, Crusaders, Mongols and Selçuks, it became part of the Ottoman Empire in the 14th century. Into the 19th century significant percentages of the population were of Greek or Armenian background.

Today Cappadocia refers only to the area south of Kayseri and east of Nevşehir distinguished by the "fairy chimneys" or fantastically eroded volcanic tuff into which caves were hollowed to make homes and churches. The largest collection of these troglodyte rooms lies between Kayseri and Aksaray; this region includes the caves of the Peristrima valley southeast of Aksaray (Belisirma and Ihlara), the underground cities of Derinkuyu and Kaymaklı, and the caves of Göreme, Zelve and Soğanlı. There are many more outside this area.

Lycia extended on the Mediterranean coast between Asia and Pamphylia. Its main city was Xanthus; the port was Patara at the mouth of the Xanthus River (Koca Çay). The Letoon, a temple sanctuary, was dedicated to Apollo and Leto. The province also included the cities of Telmessus (Fethiye), Didyma (Didim), Myra (Demre) and Phaselia. The Lycian federal system of government with proportional representation was used as a model by the men who wrote the United States constitution.

Pamphylia was at first a narrow coastal district between Lycia and Cilicia. Under the Romans it came to include all of Pisidia. Its only seaport in antiquity was Side; today the main port city is Antalya. Perge, Aspendus and Sillyum (Asar Köyü) remain interesting for the variety and quality of their existing ruins.

Rome divided **Cilicia** into two regions: "Rough Cilicia" was the mountainous region west from Silifke; "Level Cilicia" was the eastern fertile plain, called in Turkish Çukurova — the "sunken plain." The pass through the Taurus Mountains into the Cappadocian interior was the Cilician Gates (Gülek Boğazı). Alexander the Great's army widened the pass in 333 BC; the work of his engineers is marked by a small inscription in the rock at the narrowest point. Sea cities of Rough Cilicia include Alanya and Anamur; Mersin, Tarsus and Adana are busy cities of today's Çukurova. Many still-imposing Crusader castles can be found in Cilicia: Bakraş Kalesi, Toprakkale, Yılankale, Anavarza (Anazarbus), Namrun (Lampron) and Anamur, to name those that are the best preserved.

The Province of **Syria** was generally located along the basin of the Orontes River (Asi Nehri); its capital of Antioch (Antakya) was the most desired of the proconsular appointments from Rome. At one time or another it included the land from the Tigris to the Mediterranean and from Egypt to the Taurus Mountains. Syria became part of the Ottoman Empire in 1516; by 1938 the present borders between Syria and Turkey were established.

The kingdom of **Commagene** was absorbed into the Roman province of Syria. It lay between the eastern slopes of the Taurus Mountains and the Euphrates River. Samosata (Samsat, now lost under the Atatürk Dam) was its capital when it was ruled by Seleucid kings, of whom Antiochus I of Commagene immortalized himself with his temple on Nemrut Dağı. Lucian, one of the Roman satiric wits, was born in Samosata about 120 AD. His *True History* about "Moonites" is a lampoon on voyagers who are similar to Jules Verne's heroes. His barbs were aimed at what he considered false value judgments; his essay on Peregrine is a contemporary Roman's ridicule of gullible people. (The people happened to be Christians.) He burlesques Greek philosophers in a Peter Sellers-like banquet scene in which the solemn gentlemen's discussion degenerates into a quarrel and the men end up hitting each other with the chickens they have been served.

The southeastern shore of the Black Sea was known as **Pontus**. It included the fertile sea coast and some of the mountainous country that borders the Black Sea. Its main rivers are the Halys (Kızılırmak) which drains into the sea at Bafra and the Iris (Yeşilırmak) which empties out just east of Samsun. Pontus was the home of the Amazons, the mythical women warriors who, according to legend, lived on the Thermodon River near present-day Terme.

Comana of Pontus was famous for its Temple to Ma, a moon-goddess (Artemis). The temple was served by six thousand priests. Remains of that city are just north of Tokat. It was in Comana that the Patriarch John Chrysostom died in AD 407 as he was returning to Constantinople from exile. Zela, another religious center known now as Zile, was the site of the battle in 47 BC between Julius Caesar and Pharnaces, the son of Mithradates the Great, where Caesar "came, saw and conquered."

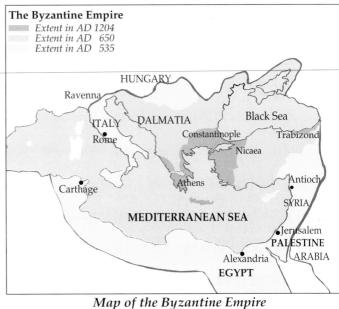

The Byzantine Empire
Extent in AD 1204
Extent in AD   650
Extent in AD   535

Map of the Byzantine Empire

THE BYZANTINE EMPIRE (AD 330 - 1453). The Eastern Roman Empire (often called the Byzantine Empire) is generally dated from AD 330. When the Emperor Constantine the Great moved his capital from Rome, Byzantium then became his city, Constantinople. Under Constantine's influence, the empire developed as a state in which religion and politics acted in concert. The empire saw its most glorious years under the reign of Justinian (527-556). Justinian is applauded for having codified the laws and for building one of the masterpieces of the world, the Church of St. Sophia. His wife Theodora, who as a popular circus performer had caught his attention, shared credit for the buildings. She saved his throne and probably his life by scorning flight at the time of the Nika riots in 532. The empire weakened as the government, often led by its emperors, succumbed to the corruptions of power. An irreparable disaster occurred in 1204 when the Fourth Crusaders, ostensibly intent upon regaining Jerusalem for Christianity, sacked and looted Constantinople and then set up their Latin kingdom there for 57 years. Confined to a smaller and smaller area, the Byzantine Empire faltered until its capital was conquered by the Ottoman Sultan Mehmet II on May 29, 1453.

THE TURKISH PEOPLE. The Turkish people trace their ethnic origins to a group of Ural-Altaic tribes who in the second millennium BC were located in what is today Outer Mongolia. Nomads, these people from the steppes of Central Asia migrated south, east and west. By the seventh century AD the groups came in contact with Arabs who were conquering Persia. Muslims themselves, the Arabs were zealous in making converts to Islam. The Turkish conversion was mostly accomplished in the ninth century.

In 1055 the ruler of the Selçuk Turks, Tuğrul Bey, conquered Baghdad and took over not only the Moslem caliphate but also control of the western Islamic world. The Selçuks were one of the first distinctive Turkish tribes moving into Anatolia. Others included the Oğuz, the Karakoyunlu, and the Akkoyunlu. In part they were following the centuries-old trade routes of caravans carrying silk and spices from China to the west.

The Turkish migration did not take place without disruption to the government already present in Anatolia. Two critical events that still reverberate occurred in the 11th century. The first was a battle in 1071 near the town of Malazgirt (Manzikert) northwest of Lake Van. Here the Selçuk Sultan Alp Arslan, nephew of Tuğrul Bey, defeated the Byzantine Emperor Romanus IV Diogenes. Historians note this as the break in the Byzantine defense against Turkish inroads.

From the eleventh century through the thirteenth century the Selçuk state, with its tributary Turkoman principalities, grew in power and territory in central Anatolia. In 1078 the Selçuks took possession of İznik in western Anatolia. Konya became its political capital and was also an intellectual and religious center. The great mystic philosopher and poet, Celaleddin Rumi started the Mevlevi Dervish order in Konya in the 13th century (see pp. 206 - 207).

The Selçuk conflict with Byzantium led to the second critical event. Overland routes for pilgrims from Europe going to Jerusalem crossed through Selçuk territory. Harassment of the Christians by the Muslims brought a call for help from the Byzantine Emperor Alexius I to the West. The response to him was the First Crusade which reconquered İznik for Alexius in 1097. The First Crusade continued south through Anatolia, stopping in Antioch before going on to capture Jerusalem in 1099. Battles between the Crusaders, the Byzantines, and the Turkic groups flared up throughout the next three hundred years, leaving among each a residue of the fear of and the hostility to each other's religion and culture that have yet to be transcended.

THE OTTOMAN EMPIRE (AD 1290 - 1923). The Ottomans, a Turkish tribe related to the Selçuks, date their history from the reign of Osman I in the 1290s. Osman's principality started in the region around Söğüt between Bursa and Kütahya. It abutted on the Byzantine Empire. Through the 13th and 14th centuries the Ottomans were often allies of the Byzantines. But increasingly, the weak Byzantine and Selçuk powers gave way to the vigorous, tolerant Ottomans who often were preferred by the general populace over their former rulers. Except for the interregnum (when there was a power struggle among the sultan's surviving sons) between 1402 and 1413, until the dissolution of the empire in 1923 the Ottoman power continued without interruption. Equally impressive, the last sultan, Mehmet VI (1918-1922), was a direct descendent of Osman I: the Ottoman family had reigned for over six hundred years.

One of the Ottoman practices instituted by the first sultans was the *millet* (religious community) system whereby the major non-Islamic religious groups were given a degree of autonomy in governing their own people. While this contributed to each community's sense of separateness, the official tolerance secured a religious freedom which lasted through the Empire. The end of the system and the Empire came when the weak central government was confronted by outside political interests coupled with 19th century ideas of nationhood.

The reign of Sultan Süleyman the Magnificent (1520-1566) is considered to be the climax of the Ottoman period. It was a time of great conquest: Süleyman's father Selim I had taken Tabriz, Damascus, Jerusalem, Medina, Mecca and Cairo.

The Selçuk and the Ottoman Empires from 1100 to 1689

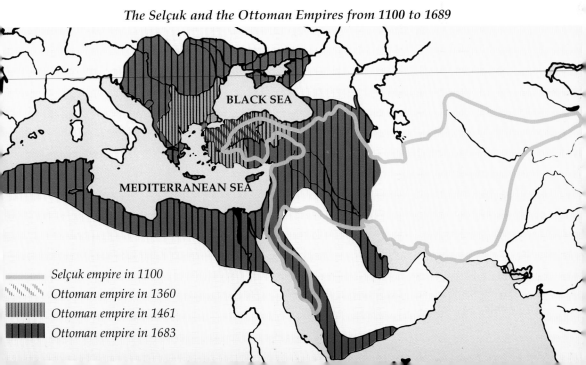

BLACK SEA

MEDITERRANEAN SEA

Selçuk empire in 1100
Ottoman empire in 1360
Ottoman empire in 1461
Ottoman empire in 1683

Süleyman added Baghdad, Rhodes, Belgrade and Buda, but failed before Vienna. While people in the West either prayed to be delivered from his military power or envied the splendor of his court, he and his countrymen held that his greatest accomplishment was that of lawgiver: The Ottoman sultans believed that their first responsibility was to ensure justice for their people.

Süleyman's reign was distinguished by the buildings of his Chief Architect Sinan. Sinan's works are found across the width and breadth of Turkey. Of them, his masterpiece is generally considered to be the Mosque of Selim II in Edirne. His genius is not so much in his amazing productivity as it is in his definition of classical Ottoman architecture. Sinan was a man who both understood and communicated the cultural ideals of his time in his medium, and one who created works of art that have transcended his age. He stated in architectural terms the spiritual vitality of Islam and the political power of the Ottoman Empire.

The command which the sultan had over his empire lessened after Süleyman's death, though the Empire continued to expand well into the 17th century. The early 17th century was the time of very young and/or weak sultans controlled by their mothers. Some of the sultans in the 18th century attempted reform, influenced in their ideas particularly by France. However, by the time that Sultan Mahmut II overthrew his janissaries in 1826, Europe was far advanced beyond the Ottoman Empire in military and economic power. Still, the westernizing movement did result in a forty-year period of reform (the *Tanzimat*) that began in 1839.

Called by Western observers the "Sick Man of Europe," the Empire struggled along, increasingly torn apart by many groups: those who were determined to conserve the past at the expense of reasoned change, those who saw their strength in nationhood, those who espoused Islam as the supranational unifying identity, and those who used anarchy to maneuver for their own increased power and territory. The sultan was forced into a constitutional government in 1876 and again in 1908. Turkish secret organizations worked to bring order out of the domestic and foreign chaos of the period (and to preserve the sultanate). One was the Committee of Union and Progress, the members of which were called the Young Turks. Ottoman interests took the side of the Axis Powers in World War I. When Germany was defeated, the Allies set about to dismember the Empire. French, Italian, Greek, Russian, and British foreign armies each occupied strategic regions.

Among those fostering the instability were ethnic groups who desired their own nation-states. At the end of the 19th century two Armenian revolutionary parties joined with Russia in an attempt to establish an Armenian republic. The resulting fighting left at least three million people dead, Turks, Armenians, Kurds and others. By 1922 in some of the eastern areas of Anatolia more than fifty percent of the population had died, and great areas — farmland and towns — had been destroy-

Atatürk introducing the Latin alphabet in a public park in İstanbul

ed. This disintegration mirrored the balkanization that had already led to the founding of Greece (1829) and Bulgaria (1908) and that so tragically continues today. As one historian of the period has said, even the attempt to describe the suffering is obscene.

MUSTAFA KEMAL ATATÜRK AND HIS REFORMS. The turning point in Turkey's fortunes came in 1919 when Turkish forces successfully defended the Gallipoli peninsula against attack by the British and French armies. Out of that emerged the figure of the Turkish colonel Mustafa Kemal as a dynamic, tireless, charismatic leader. Starting in eastern Turkey, Mustafa Kemal organized resistance to the foreign occupation and inspired the nationalist movement that established the political borders of the new Republic of Turkey. With the

Mustafa Kemal Atatürk, the founder of modern Turkey

signing of the Treaty of Lausanne in July 1923, Turkey was recognized as an independent equal among the world nations.

On October 29, 1923 Mustafa Kemal was elected by the Grand National Assembly to be the first president of the Turkish Republic in its new capital Ankara. Shortly thereafter he took the surname Atatürk, "father of the Turks." The government which he led accomplished a remarkable number of reforms. The sultanate was abolished, as was the caliphate. The Republic was proclaimed to be secular: Islamic canonical law (sheriat) was replaced by Turkish law which was a combination of European codes. The metric system was adopted. Schools were secularized, and education through fifth grade was both required and free. (Public education through university is still free if you do not consider the minimal fees.) The Islamic calendar was replaced with the Gregorian, and Sunday became the day of rest. The Ottoman alphabet, based on Arabic, was changed to a modified Latin alphabet, and the Turkish Language Association attempted — generally successfully — to purify and simplify the language as one of the many programs unifying the country. Dress was westernized, and men were required to wear hats with brims rather than fezzes. Surnames were required, and the old titles or professional distinctions forbidden. Voting for men and women alike was made obligatory. Western music and art were encouraged, and — a significant symbolic act — St. Sophia, the great church of Byzantium that the Ottomans had made a mosque, was turned into a public museum. Atatürk's foreign policy, the forerunner of peaceful co-existence and nonintervention, was expressed in his goal of "peace in the country, peace in the world." This continues to be the country's motto. The reforms are frequently weighed, both in specific instances (dress code, mandatory education age), and in their rationale, but in principle they still define the nation.

Recognizing Atatürk's international stature, UNESCO dedicated the year 1981 (his centennial) to him. Although he had been unsuccessful in instituting a two-party political system, that did come about in 1950; today there is a multiplicity of parties. Faced with an almost total loss of Turkey's resources during the War of Independence (1919-1923), Atatürk envisioned and then applied an economic and industrial development plan reflecting the extent of his genius. Under his presidency this gave the country its most steady economic development.

With his genius and determination in establishing his reforms, Mustafa Kemal Atatürk laid the foundation for modern Turkey.

TURKEY SINCE 1938. Atatürk died in 1938 before the upheaval of World War II. Through most of that war Turkey remained neutral, but joined the Allies in 1945 in time to become a charter member of the United Nations. Since then membership has included NATO, the Council of Europe, the Organization for Economic Cooperation and Development, the Regional Cooperation for Development, and the Islamic Community. Turkey joined the Customs Union of the European Community on January 1, 1996.

Turkey's population has grown from about 14 million people in 1927 to over 65 million in 1996. When the Republic was established, three-fourths of the people were engaged in agriculture and lived in the country; today only forty percent live in the rural areas. Technological changes in farming methods have encouraged this migration.

Since the 1980s Turkey's manufactured goods have accounted for more value in exports than its agricultural products. Although it buys natural gas from Russia and Bulgaria, it expects to be selling electricity to Syria, Iraq, Iran and the Turkic republics because of the power generated by the new dams on the Tigris and Euphrates Rivers. Bulgaria helps supply northern Turkey with electricity when needed. In spite of political unease, the country is moving ahead, thanks to the dynamism of the private sector and its many well-trained, dedicated people.

Relations remain strained between Turkey and Iraq following Desert Storm; they have been exacerbated by the Kurdish problems in the southeastern region. Also outstanding is the impasse between Turkey and Greece over the unilaterally-declared Turkish Republic of Northern Cyprus and over rights in the Aegean Sea.

There have been social changes in the years since Atatürk: the old, closely knit multi-generational family living in one house has split into separate units. In many cases both the father and the mother must work outside the house to support their family. The formal observance of old customs is giving way to international behavior codes. The change in the balance from an agrarian Turkey to an urban nation has strained the ability of the large cities to provide the needed infrastructure. The experiences of many Turkish workers in Europe in the last thirty years have influenced the economy of the country and some conceptions about Turkey's rightful place in the Middle East. Within the last few years Turkish foreign policy has moved from being strongly pro-United States to a position representing the country's desires to be included as a European nation, to be the cultural as well as the geographic bridge between Europe and Asia, and at the same time to be a leader among its Middle Eastern neighbors.

PAGANISM:
LEGENDS, MYTHS, FOLKLORE

THE CONTINUUM
STONE AGE BELIEFS
HITTITE BELIEFS
PHRYGIAN BELIEFS
GREEK AND ROMAN MYTHOLOGY
MITHRAISM
FOLKLORE

THE CONTINUUM. An extraordinary convergence of major religions — paganism, Judaism, Christianity and Islam — has occurred in the land now known as Turkey. Each one of them, with some of its roots here, has acted on the others. A description of them appears to be a continuum of places, events and ideas. The fact that so much has happened raises the question of what effect geography has had on this persistent religious history. Certainly the geography of a land bridge between Europe and Asia has made this a thoroughfare for many people. They have carried their skills, their commerce and their beliefs back and forth. Undoubtedly also the hospitable climate and the land's resources have been important: People have wanted to stay and use the riches that they found. In addition, this is a country with fertile valleys, rushing streams, fields of golden wheat, forests and orchards, combined with a raw, desolate wasteland, rugged coasts and snow-capped mountains. The land has called forth a sense of grandeur, a challenge to survival and an aesthetic appeal to the imagination.

Not only in beliefs, but also in the related fields of law, science, mathematics and art the ethical standards and disciplines that one group developed have been modified and used by others. For instance, in law, among many other interpersonal relations, the code of the Hittites in Hattusas covered homicide, ownership of slaves, contamination from sorcery and sexual offenses. The execution ordered by law of a man and his kin who defied the king's judgment seems to parallel the story in Joshua (7:10-26) in which a man named Achan who confessed to stealing religious items was stoned to death along with his family. The Chaldeans of Harran who studied the yearly course of the heavenly objects contributed to the refinement of both mathematics and science. Thales of Miletus probably learned his astronomy from his Eastern colleagues. Scholars in Edessa translated the Greek classics into Arabic, and these were reintroduced to Western students by the Crusaders who held Edessa in the 12th century.

Symbols have also had a permanence: The cross, the crescent and the star can be found with religious meaning in pagan temples near Antalya, on statues on Nemrut Dağı and as designs in the flags of the nations of the Middle East. Apollo's laurel tree is perhaps related to the pattern of the tree of life in contemporary Turkish rug patterns. The Stone Age **Mother Goddess**, the Greek egg-and-dart pattern and the present-day folk talismans made of wheat, seeds and blue beads are easily-recognizable symbols of fertility. Angels or heavenly messengers are found in all these belief systems. While the ethical values of some of these examples are lost to us, we can recognize in them the intensity of the religious thought that produced them originally.

STONE AGE BELIEFS. Eight thousand years ago daily life and ritual/religion were probably closely intertwined. The satisfactory hunt, the plenteous harvest were thought to be dependent on the favor of elements or beings that were greater than people and whose whimsies or angers might be appeased by ritual and right behavior. Mysteries such as weather, celestial events, birth, death and natural events were celebrated as religious events.

The main deity in the Stone Age seems to have been feminine. She was shown in figures usually made of baked clay or stone and in one of three forms: a young girl, a mother giving birth and an old woman. The Mother Goddess was the symbol of the divine force of fertility, and the purpose of worshipping her seems to have been to insure abundant life in this world and the next. If not all the religious attention was focused on appeasement, perhaps there was room for wonder at and respect for new life. The Mother Goddess was sometimes seated between leopards (to symbolize strength? control?) which she used as arm rests while she was in labor. Among the images were scenes of a woman giving birth to a bull's head or a ram's head. Symbols such as bulls' horns were perhaps intended to suggest strength or to ward off evil. These images seem to connect the beliefs and traditions of people in Anatolia with later symbols in Crete (the bull of Minos), in Antioch of Pisidia (bulls' heads on cornices) and İstanbul (gargoyles on secular buildings on İstiklâl Caddesi).

While groups of figures were infrequent, the male image as a son or lover and as an old man, or as a bull or ram sometimes was found with the goddess. There were also models apparently of Siamese twins. A few stone sculptures have been found of embracing couples. Another is a statue of a bearded man riding a bull. Bulls were symbols of strength and thus were probably also the symbols of masculinity. The animals had an additional importance: They could be used in plowing the fields, both pulling a plow and being made to root with their horns.

HITTITE BELIEFS. For the Hittites around four thousand years ago, head priest and political leader were the same person. The major yearly religious festivals involved an elaborate ritual led by a large number of trained priests and priestesses and performed in a large sanctuary.

The main god was the Weather-god, called **Teshub** (a name they borrowed from their neighbors the Hurrians). Teshub was represented driving a wagon that was pulled by bulls and that thundered across the mountain peaks. (Does this reecho in the image of Zeus's thunder coming when he rattled across the mountains in his chariot?) Teshub had another duty: he was the god responsible for international relations. Teshub's consort was **Hepat**,

Seated goddess a goddess perhaps equal in importance to Teshub; their roles
(6000 BC) sometimes overlapped. Her sacred animal was a lion and she was

represented as the dispenser of justice. When she was the Sun-goddess, she was the one to whom the king prayed for help in battle.

The Hittites had many, many other gods and goddesses. Among them, one of the sons of Teshub and Hepat was **Telipinu**; he was the god of agriculture. Telipinu represented the death of nature in the winter and its rebirth in spring. The goddess **Shauskha** was the same as the Assyrian **Ishtar**. She was a winged goddess who stood on a lion. **Kubaba** became the chief goddess for the Neo-Hittites in later years. She started as a deity known to them only in Carchemish, but their successors the Phrygians adopted her as **Cybele**. Her cult and her symbol were transported to Rome in 204 BC in the Romans' effort to save the city from the attack by the Carthaginian general Hannibal (see p. 202).

The homes of the deities were temples. The priests and priestesses were considered to be their domestic staff. They took care of the deity's daily needs which included food, a bath, flattery and entertainment. These were religiously exact ceremonies, with the deity's approval dependent upon their perfect performance. In contrast, the deity was not required to be reliable. He might be asleep when called on, or off someplace entertaining himself. He (or she) was quite capable of making the wrong decision. Evil spirits could be waiting to profit by his mistake. The king or priest could then do no more than remind him of his duty.

The religious year seems to have culminated in the service marking the beginning of spring (perhaps cued to the first sighting of the star Sirius in the east at sunrise). A recitation of the Myth of the Slaying of the Dragon **Illuyankas** was part of this service. Like other primitive winter-spring stories symbolizing the returning life, the evil dragon was portrayed as stupid and gluttonous. At first he overcame the good Weather-god. Then Illuyankas was defeated by a trick played on him by a human acting for the Weather-god, after which both the dragon and the human were killed. The story seems to be related not only to Hurrian and Sumerian myths; the dragon was also carried into Greek mythology in the form of the monster **Typhon**, the symbol of fire and smoke and the earth's interior rumblings. A curious parallel continues in the Christian story of St. George and the Dragon. This man who lived in the 3rd century and who became the patron saint of England came from the region of Anatolia that had been ruled by the Hittites; the 3rd century "dragon" he fought was the Emperor Diocletian.

Tablets have been found detailing the ritual of the Hittite religious ceremonies with instructions on what the king and queen should wear, how they should process to the temple with jesters playing music before and behind them, where the dignitaries and body guards would walk, when they would kneel inside the temple, when they would sit, when they would wash their hands, who would give them a towel to wipe their hands, through to the presentation of all the sacrifices and gifts: hours and hours of preparation, and more hours and hours of performance. If the spring happened to turn out to be disastrous — with floods destroying the crops, for instance — some flaw in the ritual would be pointed out as the cause for the Weather-god's anger, and appropriate sacrifices would have to be made to appease him.

Another of the Hittite/Hurrian myths was that of the Missing God of Fertility, Telipinu. Telipinu was believed at one time to have deserted his people in a huff, putting his left boot on his right foot, and his right boot on his left. His departure

caused devastation, famine and drought, with dust clouding the sky and sheep dying in the fold. The Sun-goddess tried to appease the other gods, while the Weather-god set out to look for him. At last the goddess **Hanna-hannas** (meaning "grandmother") came up with the solution: She told the Weather-god to send a bee to sting Telipinu. (Bee stings were thought to cure paralysis.) Although at first this made Telipinu even more vindictive, at last he was brought back on the wings of an eagle. When he reached home he restored abundance to the land.

Procession of Gods, Yazılıkaya

PHRYGIAN BELIEFS. The Phrygians, who came after the Hittites, have a share in the bigger-than-life characters of Greek mythology. One Phrygian was the unfortunate shepherd **Marsyas.** After Athena invented the flute out of the bones of a stag, she threw the instrument away cursing it because she thought that she looked ugly playing it. Marsyas picked it up and played it so well that he made Apollo jealous; in his anger Apollo flayed him alive. The river that issues out of the cave near today's Dinar where his skin was hung is called the Marsyas River (Çine Çayı).

In a different contest, this one between Apollo and the god **Pan**, the Phrygian king Midas was the judge. Midas decided that Pan was the better flutist and Apollo punished him with donkey's ears for that insult. Two elderly Phrygians who lived south of today's Niğde and who had no riches beyond their love for each other became immortals when they were hospitable to a couple of strangers. To their surprise, **Baucis** and **Philemon** found that they had entertained Zeus and Hermes. The gods rewarded them first with a beautiful temple and then on their death changed them into an oak and a linden. A third Phrygian reference in mythology is to Aphrodite who pretended to be a Phrygian princess in order to seduce King Anchises of Trojan fame was when he slept on Mt. Ida (Kaz Dağı). His son Aeneas was born from that union.

The main Phrygian deity was **Cybele.** Depending on the location and the language used she was also known as the Great Mother, as Rhea or as Kubaba. She was worshipped as the power of nature to create life. She was the symbol of the art of agriculture; for the Phrygians she was the one who cultivated the vine. Note that other traditions point to the origins of viticulture in eastern Anatolia. This ties in with the biblical account of Noah who was the one to begin vineyards (Gen.9:20). (The Greeks gave this attribute to Dionysus.) Because of the value of farming, she was thought to be the one responsible for social progress and civilization; thus she was the founder of cities. Cybele was Mother Earth, the fruitful parent of all living things, particularly wild nature. She herself was beautiful and chaste, but her worship culminated in frenzied, orgiastic excesses.

According to Greek mythology, Cybele was the mother of the gods of Olympus — Zeus, Hera, Poseidon, Demeter. In Anatolia she was accompanied by her grandson, **Attis**, a man who castrated himself because of unrequited love. Violets grew from the foot of the pine tree where his blood fell. In imitation of him all her priests were castrated; they wore female dresses and perfumed their long hair.

Another god who accompanied Cybele was **Sabazius**, the barley god who was cut down every year. He was identified with **Cronus**, the Crow-god, and with Dionysus whose worship spread as the cultivation of grapes spread. Sabazius's use of wine supplanted beer as an intoxicant. Sabazius's symbol was a snake.

The main festival to Cybele was held in the spring when she led a train of eunuch priests and followers who carried lighted torches and danced wildly to the music of flutes, horns, cymbals and tambourines. Their excitement led to their own self-castration in envy of Attis. According to Roman theology, Cybele's love for Attis was interpreted as the love of Mother Earth for its fruits; his emasculation was the harvesting of the fruit; his yearly death was the divine preservation of the harvest; and his resurrection was the new sowing of seed in the spring. This came to be celebrated in dramas playing out that story. Other festivals included the sacrifice of a bull and the purifying baptism for the celebrants in its blood.

The cult gained a great following and was popular into the Christian centuries. Along with the cults of Isis and of Mithra it was not only a strong rival to Christianity, but, more than that, its mystic communion with the divine and its promise of rebirth may have paved the way to an acceptance of the discipline of Christianity when the revulsion grew against the excesses of paganism.

THE GREEK AND THE ROMAN MYTHOLOGY. The Greek (and later the Roman) pantheon was ruled over by **Zeus** (**Jupiter** to the Romans), the father of the gods. His consort was the jealous **Hera** (**Juno**). Worship of them had been superseded by that of Cybele and of Mithra even before paganism faded out. The sea was controlled by **Poseidon** (**Neptune**) to whom black bulls were sacrificed, and the underworld by **Hades** (**Pluto**). Among the other gods and goddesses whose ruined temples can be seen in Turkey are **Apollo** the god of light and agriculture, **Artemis** (**Diana**) the goddess of chastity (whose temple in Ephesus may have been started by Amazons), **Aphrodite** (**Venus**) the goddess of love, and **Dionysus** (**Bacchus**) the god of wine and patron of the theater. Dionysus probably was first a Thracian god. Sometime near the shortest day of the year women celebrated his return with wild dances.

Many other gods and goddesses and semi-mythical figures appear in references to places in Turkey. A short list of them includes these:

Adonis was born from the bark of the myrtle tree. (His mother **Smyrna** had been turned into that tree.). Adonis was loved by **Aphrodite** who was inconsolable when he was gored to death by a boar. Therefore she created anemones from his blood. The Feast of Adonis, a women's celebration, took place in summer. He is sometimes identified with the Persian god **Tammuz.**

Amazons were women warriors who lived on the southern shore of the Black Sea near today's Terme. By some accounts they founded Smyrna, Ephesus and Sinop.

Ares (**Mars**), the god of war, was the lover of Aphrodite, by whom his son **Eros** (**Cupid**) was born. Ares favored the land of the wild Thracians.

Argonauts were the men who sailed with Jason in the Argo to Colchis at the far end of the Black Sea. Following the course of Greek traders, they sailed through the Hellespont, stayed at Cyzicus (Erdek) where by mistake they killed the king who had given them shelter, got past the Symplegades (two huge rocks that clashed together to prevent ships from sailing past them) at the entrance to the Black Sea, avoided the Amazons, and returned successfully from Colchis.

Asclepius, the god of healing, was thought to reveal himself as a snake because snakes could shed their skins. His temple at Pergamum was a major medical center. Those who were healed offered a cock as a sacrifice and hung up a tablet inscribed with their names and their diseases at the temple.

Astarte, a Semitic goddess, was womanhood personified. A nature goddess, her qualities and the stories about her were combined with those of **Aphrodite**, **Artemis**, **Diana**, **Hera**, and **Venus**. She appeared in the sky as the planet Venus. The Hebrew prophets railed against her worship because she was the consort of the god Baal. As the moon goddess she may have been identified with the Egyptian Isis. She was sometimes represented with sheep's horns.

Athene (Minerva) was the goddess of war, of wisdom, of art and of science.

Attis (sometimes confused with **Pan**, **Sabazius**, **Men** and **Adonis**) was driven insane by Cybele when he did not return her love. He died castrating himself. In honor of him the priests of Cybele were all emasculated.

Bellerophon, grandson of **Sisyphus** (the man who was condemned to roll a stone forever up a hill), was commissioned to destroy the Chimera. He managed this task riding on the winged horse **Pegasus.** In another engagement he fought and defeated the Amazons. Then, proud of his accomplishments he tried to ride Pegasus into the home of the gods. He fell off and was killed, but Pegasus went on to become the one to carry Zeus' thunder and lightning.

Hecate, the sister of Leto, was sometimes identified with **Artemis**, sometimes with **Persephone (Proserpina)** who spent half the year with her husband Pluto in the underworld and half with her mother **Demeter (Ceres)** helping crops to grow. Her worship may have originated in Thrace.

Helios (Sol) was the sun god, the brother of **Selene (Moon)** and **Eos (Dawn)**. He was all-seeing because his rays could penetrate everything.

Heracles (Hercules) was the consummate Greek hero, able to accomplish everything. Of his twelve labors, one took place on the Black Sea when he killed the Amazon Queen Hippolyte in order to get her girdle. On that same adventure he also killed a sea monster near Troy. For a year Heracles was the slave and consort of Queen Omphale of Lydia. When they were inspecting their vineyard on Mt. Tmolus (Boz Dağları), the god Pan tried to abduct Omphale. Heracles saved her and made a fool of Pan by disguising himself and taking the Queen's place.

Hermaphrodites, the son of **Hermes** and **Aphrodite**, was born on Mt. Ida. Too handsome by far, he rejected the love of a Nymph when he bathed in her fountain in Halicarnassus. In spite, the **Nymph** prayed to be so united with him that they could never be separated.

Hermes (Mercury) was the god of mining, of roads and of dreams. He was the messenger of the gods and the one who took souls to the underworld. He discovered music, mathematics and astronomy. He was mischievous, giving **Pandora** the ability to lie. The caduceus which he carried was a symbol of his influence over life and death; it became the herald's staff and the doctor's symbol.

The young girl **Io** was changed into a heifer by Hera who was jealous because Zeus was in love with her. A gad-fly drove her to ford the strait separating Europe from Asia; the strait thus was known as the "ox's ford" or the Bosphorus.

Jason was considered to be the patron of navigation. He was the leader of the

Argonauts. His adventures began when he presented himself at his uncle's court wearing only one shoe. His uncle had been warned about such a man, and therefore sent Jason away to Colchis (on the eastern end of the Black Sea) to get the Golden Fleece. He hoped the task would spell Jason's death. Instead, Jason got the Fleece and, with the help of his wife **Medea**, returned to take vengeance on his uncle.

Leto (Latona) preceded Hera as Zeus's wife. She was the mother of Apollo and Artemis and was a goddess of fertility.

Niobe met her misfortune when she gloated over Leto. Niobe had six sons and six daughters while Leto had only two. For her pride she lost all her children and was changed to a weeping stone.

The weeping stone in Manisa

Orpheus was the son of the king of Thrace and of **Calliope**, the muse of epic poetry. He was born in Thrace on the bank of the Hebrus (Meriç) River.

Serapis was the Egyptian god of the underworld. When his worship spread to Asia Minor he became identified as the god of healing. There were temples to him in Ephesus and Pergamum.

Tantalus was king of Sipylus and the father of Niobe. For insulting the gods he was thrown into Hades where he was tortured by being able neither to eat nor drink.

Like their predecessors, the early Greeks considered the gods to be external powers that were outside of human control. Some were personifications of nature, some others grew out of historical events. The gods and goddesses acted indiscriminately; they were not bound by human limitations. They had free rein to interfere in human affairs, while people were able to relate to them only by trying to stay on their good side. The gods had little connection with morality: they were licentious, deceitful, quarrelsome and fickle. They were to be worshipped at games and athletic events, at theatrical performances, before military undertakings and generally in daily life. The combination of theology and morality came slowly and unevenly; perhaps it showed up first in the requirement of the priests to be ceremonially pure at religious services.

During the time of Socrates and Plato, the gods were regarded as absolute and eternal. But as Greeks were more and more influenced by Eastern religions, the particular deities became to them trivial and boring. At the same time there was an attempt to ennoble them with richer and more spiritual truths. Thus the story of Niobe, whose "tears" still flow off her stone face on Manisa Dağı, was more a story about a parent who was guilty of pride than of a woman who lost a fight with a goddess. Mythology was reinterpreted in a more ethical concept of human relations to the powers that were beyond human comprehension.

Pagan temples served a number of purposes. They were first and foremost a place of worship. In addition, they usually were located in a beautiful place with a good view. The buildings themselves provided an aesthetic experience; they contained art works such as friezes and statues. They were often set in an enclosed park with fruit trees and flowering shrubs.

Many temples were also museums and zoos. The park was a bird preserve and a place for sacred animals. Each temple had its own collection of marvels: in Rome, for instance, there was a cut stone collection. Natural freaks (including an elephant tusk), barbarians' costumes, foreign weapons, relics from famous men and — most popular — remains from the Trojan war were also displayed for people to wondered at. Alexander's steps were as lovingly treasured as George Washington's beds in the United States.

Temples often included a library and places outside where suppliants could sit for their picnics while they waited for the prophetess's utterances to be reported to them.

Offering a sacrifice was a common daily act at home; it expressed a petition, a thanksgiving, or a desire for pardon. At the same time, many people journeyed on special occasions to the more famous temples such as that to Diana in Ephesus. A suppliant in the temple usually stood upright, holding his outstretched hands palms up. However, when he was praying to the gods of the underworld he might bend over and knock sharply on the ground to attract their attention. The priests and temple servants often acted as guides around their premises. Plutarch remarked that his visit to Delphi had been unpleasantly long because the guides insisted on reading all the inscriptions, and that they weren't able to answer any questions he put to them outside the common patter. Lucian added, "If the legends were banished from Greece, the guides would starve, for truth is unpalatable."

Of these Greek and Roman writers, the following are frequently used to give details and insights on the people who were in Anatolia. Lucian, a satirist, was born in Samosata (Samsat) about AD 120. Among other writers referred to for their knowledge of beliefs and early history are the following: Homer (? 950 BC) was a blind poet whose works, the *Iliad* and the *Odyssey*, were probably composed on the coast of Asia Minor. Hesiod (c. 776 BC), also an epic poet, wrote the *Theogony*, a discussion of the origin of the world and the birth of the gods. His father came from Cyme, a seaport northwest of Smyrna. Aesop, the ugly slave, was in Croesus's court about 560 BC; many Far Eastern tales have become associated with his *Fables*. Thucydides was born about 491 BC; he is known for his *History of the Peloponnesian War* (431-404 BC). Strabo, the geographer, was born in Amasya about 63 BC. A great traveler, he wrote a 17-book *Geography*. Xenophon, leader of the Ten Thousand from Babylon through central Anatolia in about 399 BC wrote the *Anabasis* describing his accomplishments. Herodotus (c. 484-420 BC), the Father of History, was born in Halicarnassus. The orator, senator and consul Cicero (106-43 BC) was proconsul of Cilicia in 51-50 BC. Vergil, author of the *Aeneid* lived from 70 to 19 BC. Josephus, author of the *History of the Jewish Wars* and *Jewish Antiquities*, lived from AD 37 to 93. Plutarch lived from about AD 50 to 120; his biographies (*Lives*) contrasting famous Greeks and Romans were written toward the end of his life. Tacitus (? AD 55-118) was a Roman historian known for his careful scholarship; his *Annals* cover the years from AD 14 to 96. Writer and friend of the Emperor Trajan, Pliny the Younger was governor of Bithynia from AD 112 - 114. Eusebius Pamphili, author of the *Eccelsiastical History*, lived from about AD 260 to 340. He was bishop of Caesarea of Palestine; as such he was present at the First Ecumenical Council in Nicaea.

For the Romans, "pagan" meant merely a person who lived in the country. The word, however, held something of the contemptuous attitude toward the pagan that "provincial," meaning someone from the provinces, has had in English. By the time of the early Christians, pagan was used as a term of criticism, probably because a large number of those who held to their traditional beliefs lived in the rural areas. Thus a pagan became one who worshipped false gods or who belonged to a nation that practiced idolatry and believed in polytheism. The term was not applied to the Jews; not only were they monotheists, but many of the new Christians, like Paul, were themselves Jews, to say nothing of Jesus and Mary. During the time of the Crusades, Christians considered Muslims to be pagans (although Muslims are uncompromising monotheists) and infidels; Muslims considered Christians to be giaours or infidels.

MITHRAISM. Standing someplace between paganism and monotheism, Mithraism originated in Persia at least 4,000 years ago. It was a secret cult; few records about its requirements or its rites were left by its members. Much of what we know comes either from statues such as the one of Apollo-Mithra-Helios-Hermes at Nemrut Dağı, from the frieze originally in Pergamum (now in Berlin) or from a number of remains in Rome where it had become popular among members of the Roman army and the Roman merchant class by the 2nd century. Some also comes from what contemporary outsiders said about it. To the Persians, Mithra was the god of light and air; he was loyalty and truth personified. He was the god of fertility; he blessed the good and destroyed the bad. He was a military god who gave victory to the army's heroes. He was a redeemer and protected souls as they went to paradise.

Mithra's miraculous birth from a stone was believed to have been seen only by shepherds who then brought gifts and worshipped him. At once Mithra ate the fruit of the fig tree and took its leaves to make clothes for himself. He created life on earth from the blood of a sacred bull. Men of all classes — and including young boys — could be admitted as members, but they first had to swear to secrecy and then to undergo an initiation ordeal that included various deprivations. As the members progressed through the seven levels (among them raven, soldier, lion and Persian), they celebrated their advancement with a communion banquet of bread and wine. Libations, chants, bells, music and candles were used in the rites. The Mithraic community was not only a group of worshippers, it became a legal body that owned property and elected officers. Its support was mostly in the form of voluntary contributions.

The importance of Mithraism came not only from the impressive, mystic ceremonies in which worshippers were purified from their sins, promised a better life in the hereafter and entrusted with ancient, secret wisdom, but also from the equality of all the members, slave and senator alike, and from the stern moral rectitude demanded of each one.

The similarities between Mithraism and Christianity suggest some borrowing back and forth. Both were Eastern in origin, and both became prominent in the West about the same time. Their early communities were democratic in behavior. Both had stories of adoring shepherds, of a flood and an ark, and of drawing water from a rock. Mithra — the Sun — was born on December 25th. Sunday was the holy day for both. Both demanded high moral standards and atoning sacrifice, and both believed in the immortality of the soul, the last judgment and the fiery end of the universe. However, Mithraism was polytheistic and therefore was not judged illegal by Rome. Its central figure was a mythical not an historic person, and it excluded half of humanity — women — from its membership and its privileges. Mithraism died out by the 5th century as Christianity became the ascendant religion.

FOLKLORE. In addition to the established religions practiced today — Islam, Christianity, Judaism — there are a number of religious customs that are common among many peoples and that cut across religious lines. Belonging to one of the main religious groups does not preclude belief patterns that cannot be labeled mainstream. Some people also accept elements of a number of other religious beliefs, some of which are superstitions, some of which center on folk heroes such as the Turkish wit Nasreddin Hoca, or local saints, some of which are mixed with convenient politics or economics.

The superstitions and traditions are many; some are trifling, some are held to be mere hocus-pocus. Some are observed out of respect for older family members. Many are primitive in origin and in location, including beliefs about mountain tops, ancient trees, and graves that have been considered holy. Some of the legends have been preserved in poetry and songs such as *Köroğlu*, the ballad of a boy seeking revenge for his father. Some are told in dance such as the Aegean *zeybek* about brave men who are as free as the eagles of the mountains.

People may tie a piece of cloth torn from their clothes to the shrubbery or fence in the hopes of reminding the local saint to grant their prayers. They may pick up a small stone from near the saint's grave and keep it, returning it to the grave when their prayer is answered. They may light candles at the shrine, or walk a certain number of times around it, or leave a token of their faith or of their problem. A number of holy sites are wells or springs (*ayazma*); they probably have been places of reverence for thousands of years.

Some of the religious practices are identifiably Christian or Muslim, but have been observed in one way or another by the other group. For instance, women have always visited certain holy sites to pray that they may have children. They have taken their children who were obstreperous to the tomb of Eyüp Sultan in İstanbul because they believed that this saint who loved children would have a good effect on them. In İstanbul, Muslims have waited until the Greek Orthodox patriarch blessed the sea before they set out on their first voyage in the spring. The idea of *Noel Baba* (Father Noel) is a popular one around January 1st in the stores of the major cities.

People may hang a talisman in their home made of beads and buttons arranged in a geometric pattern against a colored background. Or the talisman may be made of grain worked into a design. The patterns woven into the rugs, particularly the flatweaves, are chosen for their meaning to the weaver and her community: the "tree of life" for longevity, the "snake" for good luck, the "hands on hip" for fertility. Blue beads, the protection against the Evil Eye, can be pinned on a baby's shirt, hung above the windshield of a taxi or bus, or embedded in the masonry of a house. Bridges, including the Bosphorus Bridge in İstanbul, are protected with a blue bead. One way or another the talismans are a tie with the past.

The blue bead reputed to ward off the evil eye

JUDAISM, CHRISTIANITY AND ISLAM IN TURKEY

SIMILARITIES AND DIFFERENCES
JUDAISM: Noah's Sons, Jews in Anatolian History
CHRISTIANITY: Early Communities, Paul's Missionary Journeys, Eastern Roman
               (Byzantine) Empire, Eastern Christianity, Ecumenical Councils,
               Politics, The Crusades, Other Christian Traditions
ISLAM: The Koran, God's Attributes, Five Duties, Muslim Teaching vis-à-vis
               Other Religions, the Mosque, the Caliphate, Muslim Sects, Sufism,
               Tarikats, Mevlevis, Bektaşis, Shiite Alevis, Turks and Islam

Turkey is a unique setting for seeing the histories of the three monotheistic religions, Judaism, Christianity and Islam.[1] In few, if in any other places, does the chronicle of Western belief from pagan times to the present appear so concretely and so fully. It was here that Abraham was challenged by God; it was here that Paul heard the call to carry his message into Europe. In all parts of the country there are places celebrated for some pivotal event, for the work of some master artist, for the home of some religious leader. The unusual concentration is due in no small way to Turkey's geography as the juncture of two peninsulas that bridge Asia and Europe. Many different peoples have converged here upon each other. In this relatively confined space, what they did in one corner sooner or later was felt by the rest, often with redoubled effect. The peninsulas have focused the affairs of trade route, forum, battlefield and marketplace; the resulting struggle has produced both an abundance and a challenge of new ideas. Out of this also has come a confluence of religions.

Followers of each of these religions have had a special tie to the land. Judaism, the first of them to develop, has consistently been in the minority. In spite of that, resident Jews have frequently been accorded positions of distinction and authority. Grounded in Judaism, the early Christian church started in Anatolia. In an acknowledgment of the close relationship of Islam to the other religions, the leaders of the Ottoman Empire and the secular Turkish Republic have officially practiced religious tolerance through the *millet* (religious community) system and the Turkish constitution. However, it must be acknowledged that the peaceful coexistence of these three has never been without its problems or its price, and tolerance has not been simply a matter of charity. Pragmatism, foreign pressures, proximity and shared human necessities continue to add their frequent challenges.

This chapter is a brief survey of the monotheistic religions as a preface to the descriptions of the sites that occupy the rest of the book. That the three are treated unequally is in part related to their quite distinct features and in part to the place of this land in their histories. The sites of pagan worship (discussed in the previous chapter) represent a legacy of belief and art in which all people can trace some of their own backgrounds and developments. In contrast, the Jewish, Christian and Muslim sites, both past and present, are part of living traditions. Surveying them and tracing the importance of these sites may contribute towards understanding the values of all religions in their unique historical and geographical settings.

In important ways the three faiths are similar. Their adherents hold that God is One and Almighty. The same patriarchs and prophets have been reverenced by all three. Adam and Eve, Noah and Abraham are examples of the theme of God's continuing involvement in human life and of his promise — embodied in the rainbow — of mercy toward those who fear him. The faiths have shared locations for their places of worship, sometimes taking over earlier buildings, although the particular beliefs and rituals associated with those buildings have changed. Often pagan temples were adapted by a later faith. For churches that have become mosques, the buildings have been untouched, but the Christian symbolism has been removed and the prayer niche (*mihrap*) has been located so that in facing the niche worshippers turn towards Mecca.

The three faiths share their roots in eastern Anatolia. The people of these faiths, the "People of the Book," as they are identified in the Koran (ii: 103; xxix: 45, etc.), look back to the paradisiacal time of the Garden of Eden, to the time of cleansing of the earth's pollution in the Deluge, and to the time when Abraham was called to leave his father's home in Harran to go to a new country where he would found a great nation that worshipped One God.

Jewish mercantile communities have been influential on the trade routes and in city life in Asia Minor from very early times, but Judaism has never been the religious identity of a majority of the people. Christianity gained ascendance around the 4th century AD. It, too, at first followed the main highways. Many events in early Christian history took place here. The first Muslim inroads became apparent before the end of the 7th century, less than fifty years after the death of the Prophet Muhammad. Turks themselves became Muslims largely before they entered Asia Minor; many non-Turks were converted to Islam in the 12th and 13th centuries. Today ninety-eight percent of the population of Turkey is Muslim; no city, no town, no village is without at least one mosque.

There are other differences, for example the concepts of time.

For Jews, the new day starts with sunset. There are seven days to the week and twelve months to the year, except that in seven out of every nineteen years there is an additional "leap" year. The last day of the week, the Sabbath, is the day of rest and worship because that was the day that God rested after Creation. The year begins with the month Teshri that starts on or immediately after the new moon after the fall equinox. The years are numbered from Creation, considered to be 3760 years and three months before the beginning of the Christian calendar.

The Christian day begins at midnight. The first day of the week, Sunday, is the day of rest and worship because that was the day of Christ's resurrection. The year begins in January, following Roman practice; the numbering begins with the date thought to be when Christ was born. The Roman calendar was kept until the 16th century. By that time, Easter was ten days off in relation to the first new moon in spring. Pope Gregory XIII remedied the problem in 1582 by readjusting the dates; because of that, Westerners now call their calendar "Gregorian."

The Muslim day, like the Jewish, begins at sunset. Friday is the day for the faithful to gather at the mosque for noon prayers and the sermon. Muslim months begin with the new moon, irrespective of the season. Thus the Muslim year is ten or eleven days shorter than the Gregorian year, and the Muslim months complete a cycle around the seasons in about thirty-two and a half years. The Muslim era began with the emigration of Muhammad from Mecca to Medina in AD 622. In the Muslim calendar, the 1st of Muharrem 1417 corresponded to May 19, 1996; Muharrem 1, 1418 was May 9, 1997.

The holy book for Jews is the Bible. It is made up of the books of the law (the first five books), the books of the Prophets, and the books of Writings. It is a collection of inspired works written over a period of about 800 years from the 10th to the 2nd century BC. As such it is incidentally one of the major sources for information about the early history of the Hebrew people.

The holy book for Christians combines the Old Testament with the New. The New Testament concerns the life of Jesus and includes some of the works written about his teaching soon after he died. The Bible was not intended to be a geography textbook, but it has become one of the major references for archaeologists who are studying Anatolia.

For Muslims, the holy book is the Koran. It was revealed to Muhammad in the 7th century AD.[2]

In trying to communicate with others, each tradition has tried to express its understanding of the Ineffable, of that which is beyond expression. Judaism has done this by forbidding the use of the name of God; Christianity repeats the commandment that "You shall not take the name of the Lord your God in vain"; and Islam says that "God is greater (*Allahuekber*)," leaving to infinity the completion of that comparison.

JUDAISM

Of the Anatolian land, the northern plain of the Fertile Crescent between the Tigris and the Euphrates (Mesopotamia) was home to people who contributed to some of the earliest development of Western civilization and of Hebraic insight into the nature of God. In the account in Genesis, Noah's family spread from the mountains of Ararat across the land. It is presumed that some of these people settled the fertile plain of Anatolia.[3]

NOAH'S SONS. Noah's sons who survived the Flood were Shem (the Semites), Ham (the Hamites) and Japheth (the Japhethites). The following is a summary, as given in chapter 10 of Genesis, of their children who have connections with Anatolia. Four of Shem's sons (Asshur, Arphaxad, Lud and Aram), three of Ham's sons (Cush, Mizraim and Canaan) and all of Japheth's sons (Gomer, Magog, Madai, Javan, Tubal, Meshech and Tiras) may have lived, intermarried and fought with their relatives in Anatolia. (In some cases these names may have first

Harran temple/university

been people; in some the names may have been places from which people took their names.)

Asshur, Shem's son, was the ancestor of the Assyrians whose empire along the northern Tigris River was a major power in the second and first millennia BC. Among the Assyrian kings who figure in biblical accounts are Shalmaneser III (who fought King Ahab — I Kings 22), Sennacherib (who fought King Hezekiah — II Kings 18, 19), Tiglath-Pileser III (who demanded heavy taxes from King Ahaz — II Kings 16:17-18) and Sargon II (who conquered Carchemish — Isa. 10:9 — and who not long after was killed in a battle in southern Anatolia described by Isaiah as so great a disaster that the stars, the moon and the sun all refused to shine — Isa. 13:10).

Arphaxad was both the ancestor of Abraham and a geographic place somewhere in Mesopotamia. There is uncertainty over whether the place was located in Babylon or farther north. Nahor, one of Arphaxad's descendants, lived near the source of the Cullab Çayı, a tributary of the Euphrates that once flowed past Harran. Nahor's son Terah moved to Harran; other members of the family who were in Harran at one time or another were Lot, Laban, Rebecca, Leah and Rachel (Gen. 11:31, Gen. 24). (In another reference Laban is identified as an Aramean — Gen. 24:10.)

Apparently two groups of people may have been related to Lud. One was located in North Africa; the other may have been those later known as the Lydians who, if they were sons of Shem, had lost their Semitic identity by the 8th century BC.

The Arameans, presumably the descendants of Aram, were powerful in the 1st millennium BC. They were found throughout northern Mesopotamia, and Aramaic was the main language of the Middle East up to the 4th century BC; a dialect of it is still spoken among the Suriani Christians who come from the Mardin region. The Arameans contributed to the development of the Roman alphabet by adapting the Phoenician letters and using them in their diplomatic documents.[4]

The three sons of Ham who may have Anatolian connections are Cush, Mizraim and Canaan. Nimrod, the son of Cush and "a mighty hunter before the Lord," appears in the Muslim story of Abraham, and in the names of two mountains (both called Nemrut Dağı) in southeastern Turkey. Of Mizraim's family (generally thought to be the Egyptians), the Lydians, as mentioned above, seem to be connected or confused with Shem's son, Lud. The Lydian center was at Sardis; in the 6th century BC they ruled the Aegean coast until their King Croesus was defeated in 546 by the Persian King Cyrus the Great (Isa. 45:1). So far as is known, the Lydians of Sardis had little intercourse with other people in the Old Testament except for Sepharad exiles from Jerusalem who were mentioned by the prophet Obadiah (Obad. 20-21). The date of Obadiah is thought to be just after the destruction of the Temple in Jerusalem in the 6th century BC (II Kings 25:10). These exiles may have been slaves who were sold to the people of Sardis when the Babylonians took Jerusalem. Or, they may have been expatriate merchants who helped conduct the commerce between Lydia and Israel, and who were caught without a homeland during the 6th century Exile. Whatever the source of the community may be, two synagogues excavated at Sardis give clear evidence of a Semitic community there well into the Christian centuries.

Heth, the son of Canaan, is the presumed father of the Hittites who were important in central Anatolia from the second millennium into the 6th century BC. Although the Hittite Empire did not extend into Israel, several Hittite references

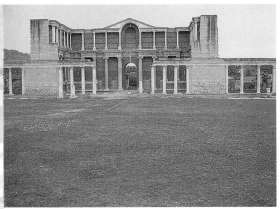

Gymnasium at Sardis

appear in the Bible. Isaac and Rebecca were disturbed that their son Esau married a Hittite woman Judith. The prophet Ezekiel scolded Jerusalem, calling her mother a Hittite. (This is thought to be a symbolic reference, perhaps to some pagan Hittite practices.) The soldier Uriah, whose wife King David lusted after, was a Hittite.

The descendants of another son of Canaan, the Hivites (or maybe the Horites), present a problem in identification. They may be related to the Hurrians who lived north of the Dead Sea; they may or may not be related to the Mitanni (also the Hurrians) who were in northern Mesopotamia. Or, these two Hurrian groups may themselves be related. Part of the trouble in determining who they were comes because in Hebrew writing the letters "r" and "v" can easily be confused.

All of Japheth's sons apparently have Anatolian connections: Gomer is the name associated with the Cimmarians, nomads who were in southern Russia and northeastern Anatolia. Magog (perhaps the word means the land of Gog) seems to have lived north of Israel; Gog may have been the 7th century BC King Gyges of Lydia. Madai is thought to refer to the Medes of northern Iran; they are linked with the Persians and the Kurds. Javan is the name for Ionia, the Greek-speaking northwest coast of Anatolia, the Aegean islands, Thrace and Macedonia. The name continues to be used in the Turkish word for the country of Greece, *Yunanistan*. Tubal may have been a family group living in central Anatolia around Kayseri. Meshech (also Muski) was both a region and a people living in central Anatolia. They were associated with Tubal as skilled workers in copper and iron. Their King Midas fought and was defeated by the Assyrian king Sargon II in 709 BC. Tantalizing clues of this culture are evident in the letters "MIDAI" (a name for Cybele) that appear in the geometric frieze over a site thought to be a temple and a forge at Midas Şehri, and in the letters "MITA" that are carved into the rock called Yazılıkaya south of Eskişehir, but neither inscription is fully understood. Tiras has been tentatively identified with the Sea Peoples, the Thracians, or the Etruscans. Most of these peoples would be identified now as Indo-Europeans. Their listing in the Bible has been the best source of information that scholars have had to piece together the history of the ancient Middle East.

JEWS IN ANATOLIAN HISTORY. The percentage of Jews in Anatolia in relation to the total population has never been great, but the community has long played an important role in the commercial and intellectual life. According to the records, King Sargon II (Isa. 20) resettled over 27,000 Israelites in northern Mesopotamia in the years around 720 BC, and during the time of Alexander the Great again a large number of people were encouraged to move northwestward from Palestine into the newly conquered Greek lands. Many of these were traders and merchants.

By the 2nd century AD there may have been a million Jews in Asia Minor; they

After Paul, John is the person who holds the greatest interest in the early history of Christianity in Anatolia. His Book of Revelation, written while he was in exile on the island of Patmos, is the last book in the New Testament. He is thought to have written it during the years that the emperor Domitian was repressing the Christians. This would date the book about AD 95 or 96. While John addressed it ostensibly to the congreations of the Seven Churches of Asia Minor, his message must have been intended for a broader readership. Even so, the locations of those seven churches have acquired a special meaning because of the intensity of John's message.

At the end of the 1st century Christianity under the Roman Empire in western Anatolia was an illegal sect. Its members acknowledged the sole sovereignty of God. This put them in conflict with the sovereign claims of the State and the cult of emperor worship. Christians were critical of the status quo and rejected the popular mores and customs. They were required by the state to conform to the laws, but they held that their religious standards superseded state law. Therefore the government considered them traitors and, when they persisted in their defiance, punished them with death.

Among the first Christian martyrs in Anatolia was Polycarp who died in Smyrna about AD 150 .[5] Christianity grew in spite of the persecutions, particularly under the Emperor Diocletian (284-305). Bringing an era of persecution to an end, the Roman Emperors Constantine and Licinius issued the Edict of Milan in 313 proclaiming the official toleration of Christianity.

PAUL'S MISSIONARY JOURNEYS. The missionary work of Paul in western Anatolia was accomplished between about AD 47 and 57. Some of the places that

St. Paul's trips and locations of the Seven Churches of Asia Minor

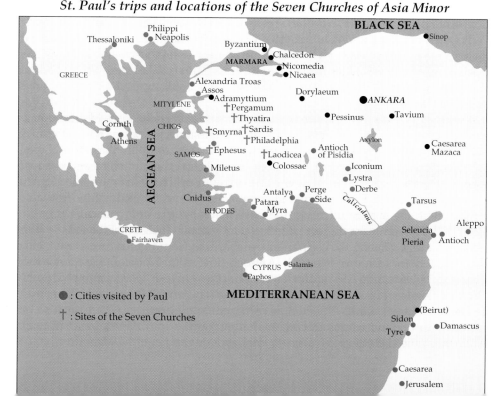

● : Cities visited by Paul

† : Sites of the Seven Churches

Paul visited and preached in Anatolia have always been identified as such. Buildings that he would have known — the theater in Ephesus, the City Council in Miletus, for instance — still exist. Some cities have not been located for sure, as is the case with Lystra and Derbe. For some, there is a difference of opinion on whether he actually got there — the meaning of "Galatia" may include Ankara and Pessinus; it may mean only the region around Antioch-of-Pisidia.

For people who find inspiration in tracing Paul's steps and his spiritual journey, something of his problems, his path and the dates can be suggested from what is recorded in Acts. Luke, thought to be the author of Acts, probably joined Paul in Alexandria Troas on his second journey, which may explain why the route up until that time is obscure. In any case, Luke certainly had no intention of writing a tour guide.

Neither Luke nor Paul dwelt on the difficulties of their journeys, although Paul noted that he met a number of dangers (II Cor. 11:25-27). He probably started on his first missionary journey some time in the spring between AD 47 and 49. He set out from Antioch-on-the-Orontes with two other Christians, Barnabas and Barnabas's cousin John Mark. From the port of Seleucia they sailed to Cyprus and then back to the mainland, landing probably at Attalia (Antalya), but possibly at Side. They stopped in Perge where John Mark left them, evidently after some disagreement which made Paul angry with him. From there they went to Antioch-of-Pisidia. Paul's sermon and the large crowd of outsiders who attended the service in the synagogue turned the leading Jewish women of the city against him, and the missionaries "shook the dust off their feet" as they traveled on to Iconium (Konya). The people of Iconium were even less friendly, so Paul and Barnabas moved to Lystra. There the irate Jewish citizens from Antioch-of-Pisidia and Iconium caught up with them and came close to stoning Paul to death. The missionaries escaped to Derbe, and then returned before the winter storms set in through Lystra and Iconium to Antioch-of-Pisidia where they had only recently been attacked. (The men were no cowards!) Having preached to the people they had converted, they started back, stopping in Perge and Attalia before sailing to Seleucia and Antioch-on-the Orontes.

The second missionary journey probably took place after Paul and Barnabas had been to Jerusalem to settle the questions concerning the matter of circumcision and the gift of the Holy Spirit as requirements for acceptance into the faith. Again this journey started from Antioch-on-the-Orontes. The dates are suggested to be about AD 50 to 53. This time Paul's companion was Silas. They apparently went overland through Syria (probably up and over the Amanus Mountains to İskenderun) and then through Cilicia (and through Paul's home of Tarsus) to Derbe. In Lystra the young man Timothy joined Paul. They traveled through Phrygia and Galatia, but the exact route they took is not known. Paul had wanted to go into Asia or into Bithynia, but instead he traveled through Mysia to Alexandria Troas. From there he sailed to Macedonia. His route in Greece took him from Neapolis eventually to Athens and Corinth before he sailed to Ephesus and finally back to Antioch-on-the-Orontes.

The beginnings of the third missionary journey are somewhat less clear, being mixed with the end of the second. Paul seems not to have spent much time in Antioch-on-the-Orontes before going from place to place in Galatia and Phrygia and then to Ephesus. There he stayed more than two years until the riot of the silversmiths made him move to Macedonia. The tradition is that he traveled by land through Smyrna and Pergamum before he reached Greece, but those cities are not named in the biblical account. (Could the winter season when people did not easily venture onto the seas have determined his route?) After several months in Greece (Corinth, Cenchraea, Philippi, Neapolis) Paul was back in Alexandria Troas for a week in the spring, following Passover. From Assos he took a ship to Mytilene and Chios; perhaps the ship touched at Erythrea before going to Samos and then Miletus. His visit in Miletus was an emotional farewell to the church elders. From Miletus his ship took him to Cos, Rhodes and Patara. In Patara he boarded a larger vessel that skirted Cyprus and landed at Tyre from whence he went on to Ptolemais (Acre), Caesarea in Palestine, and Jerusalem.

Interior of St. Irene, founded by Justinian and Theodora, AD 537

On Paul's journey to Rome under Roman guard, his ship touched at Myra (Demre). There he transshipped to a vessel sailing for Rome. The captain wanted to stop at Cnidus, but a storm kept them from landing. They anchored briefly at Fair Havens on Crete where Paul protested their continuing, saying it was too late in the year. The captain chose to go on, hoping that the weather would hold. Soon the ship was storm-tossed and they were driven out of control by it for days on end. At last they were shipwrecked and rescued by people on Malta. From there they continued on to Syracuse, Rhegium, Puteoli and at last to Rome. It is thought that Paul arrived in Rome about AD 60 (Acts 27, 28).

Paul's account is a dramatic example of the dangers of travel by sea in the winter and of the reason that Anatolia has been so important as a land bridge between Asia and Europe for migrants, traders, armies and ordinary travelers.

THE EASTERN ROMAN (BYZANTINE) EMPIRE.[6] Christians continued as members of a minority religion, either ignored or persecuted, until the time of the Emperor Constantine the Great who ruled from AD 324 to 337. Two decrees between 311 and 314 had put Christianity on a level with all other religions, including paganism. Constantine increased the privileges of the clergy and gave their communities legal standing. Historians judge that he was primarily committed to unifying his empire, and that he saw Christianity as the new political tool whereby he could do so. They point to the fact that he was not baptized until he was dying in order to shed doubt on his commitment to Christianity as a faith. It was not until the reign of the Emperor Theodosius I (AD 379-395) that Christianity became the religion of the state and that paganism was outlawed.

Whether Constantine only made a show of his religion or not, he determined two critical changes in Western history: He espoused Christianity and he moved the center of political power from Rome to Constantinople. Constantinople rapidly became the leading world capital, and Byzantine commerce and civilization the forces that changed the course of events for Europe. Rather than the government in Rome, it was the government in Constantinople that was the bulwark for Europe against aggression by the Eastern powers. In the 6th century the Emperor Justinian built on the greatness that Constantine had begun. With the support of his wife Theodora, he enlarged the Empire, codified its laws and built the cathedral of St. Sophia. In spite of many threats (religious controversies that led to nationalistic movements), weak emperors and rapacious Crusaders (particularly those of the Fourth Crusade), the Empire continued well over a thousand years until it was conquered by the Muslim Ottoman army.

EASTERN CHRISTIANITY

The spread of Christianity in eastern Anatolia and the conflicts its members struggled with are less well documented and equally less well-known among Western Christians. Lack of information, however, in this instance does not mean lack of activity. The belief did spread: converts were made; perhaps in some areas the practices still maintained are closer to the original forms than those accepted among the Western churches. Among the early churches in Eastern Turkey are those whose members spoke Armenian and those who spoke Syriac, a dialect of Aramaic. A long-standing tradition credits the Apostle Thaddeus with taking the Gospel to the Assyrians in the area of Harran and Edessa at the same time that Paul was journeying among the Pisidians and the Galatians.

One of the earliest Christian communities was the Armenian. The Armenians in the 9th century BC were perhaps a Semitic group. Under King Tiridates (AD 238-314) they were converted to Christianity by Gregory the Illuminator. They accepted Christianity as the state religion in the 4th century, some years before Constantine the Great had imposed it on the Roman Empire. Mesrop invented the Armenian alphabet, and the Bible was translated into the common Armenian language in 410. This had the effect of drawing the various Armenian communities together, while at the same time lessening the influence of Constantinople and the Greek Orthodox Church.

The Armenians were strongest in the east, led by a Bagratid dynasty that claimed descent from Herod the Great. A substantial group of Armenians migrated to Cappadocia and to Cilicia in part because of the Mongol invasion in the 13th century. A Bagratid principality, established in the 11th century in Cilicia, became known as Lesser Armenia; it cooperated with the Crusaders against the Byzantine monarchs.[7]

Another early group of Christians were those who spoke Aramaic. Aramaic is a Semitic language; it was the lingua franca of the Middle East from the 8th to the 4th centuries BC. It was spoken by the Arameans and the Assyrians among others, and probably was the language Jesus spoke. In the early Christian centuries the Aramaic dialect, Syriac, was the language of the Christian writers from Antioch-on-the-Orontes east; they were concentrated in the university centers of Edessa and Nisibin. Today's Surianis, members of the Syrian Orthodox Church, who live in the Tur Abdin region still speak this language and cling to their Syrian Orthodox tradition.

THE ECUMENICAL COUNCILS. The Ecumenical Councils continue to be important in church history because their members defined orthodox belief, because they initiated formal church-state interdependence, and because they can be used to point to reasons for separations between Eastern, Oriental and Western church practice. There have been attempts in the 20th century to hold an Eighth Ecumenical Council; the ideal remains unrealized.

In 325 Constantine called the first of the seven church councils that were attended by representatives from all the churches.[8] This one is said to have been attended by 318 bishops, some of whom carried the scars of persecutions that had been sanctioned by previous emperors.

First Ecumenical Council, AD 325, in Constantine's palace in Nicaea

The purpose of the First Ecumenical Council was first to spell out the correct, doctrinally sound faith of the Christian church. This was accomplished when the Council drew up a statement of belief, a creed. With a few later refinements, this is now known as the Nicene Creed (named for the site). The Council stated that Christ is "truly God, one in essence with the Father." Those churchmen who did not subscribe to this doctrine were exiled, including Arian of Alexandria and Eusebius of Nicomedia. (Arianism continued for years to be a thorn in the side of Church politics.) The second purpose (at least as far as Constantine was concerned) was to prevent a worsening of the political struggles among his subjects. In the long run this led to the interference of church and state in each other's affairs. Two people from this Council stand out: Constantine (who each time he appeared was wearing a wig of a different color), and the writer Eusebius Pamphili whose *Ecclesiastical History* is an unsurpassed reference for those seeking to understand the beginnings of Christianity.

Second Ecumenical Council, AD 381, in the Church of St. Irene in Constantinople

Inspired by the wisdom of several theologians, the Second Ecumenical Council expanded and refined the Nicene Creed. Those men were Athanasius of Alexandria, Gregory of Nazianzus (a.k.a. Gregory the Theologian), Basil the Great of Caesarea (who had died shortly before the Council convened) and his brother Gregory of Nyssa. They stressed the doctrine of the Trinity: that the Father, Son and Holy Spirit are three persons in one essence.

Popular interest in the theological debate was at such a height that everyone in town discussed it, from the bishops to the rag pickers. Gregory of Nyssa remarked irascibly, "If I complained that the cost of a loaf of bread was too great, the baker told me that the Father was greater than the Son. If I asked the maid if she had produced the bath water, she replied that the Son had been produced out of nothing." Gregory of Nazianzus, Patriarch of Constantinople when the Council convened, denounced the conduct of the actual debate, comparing the rancorous proceedings to the noise of wasps or magpies.

Third Ecumenical Council, AD 431, in the Double Church in Ephesus

Nestorius (originally from Antioch but at the time of the Third Council the Bishop of Constantinople) provoked the major controversy in this Council which centered on the understanding of the person of Christ. His view that distinguished between Christ's manhood and his divinity was condemned as heresy.

Fourth Ecumenical Council, AD 451 in the Church of St. Euphemia in Chalcedon

The bishops who gathered proclaimed that Christ was "truly God, truly man" in one person. From now on this would be the doctrine of both the Latin Catholic and the Eastern Orthodox Churches, but it would divide them from the Oriental Orthodox Churches (the Armenian Orthodox and the Syrian Orthodox) who held to the Monophysite position that Christ had one composite nature and who from this time on did not take part in the Councils. By the mid-fifth century Christianity had spread so that its members no longer came from the same cultural background or spoke the same language. These differences increasingly added to the misunderstandings and hard feelings among the members.

Fifth Ecumenical Council, AD 553 in the Church of St. Sophia in Constantinople

Called by the Emperor Justinian, the Fifth Council met in his new cathedral to refine the thinking on the nature of Christ. While not all the Christian traditions were represented, this and the later Councils are called "ecumenical."

Sixth Ecumenical Council, AD 680-681, in St. Sophia in Constantinople

Again much of the discussion was on the issue of the nature of Christ. In 622, between the Fifth and the Sixth Ecumenical Councils, Muhammad had led the Hegira. So rapid and so forceful was the expansion of Islam that less than fifty years later (in 668) a Muslim army attacked the walls of Constantinople. Both the military and the intellectual conflicts between Christianity and Islam have influenced the history of the Middle East since this time.

Seventh Ecumenical Council, AD 787, in the Church of St.Sophia in Nicaea

The last ecumenical council that has been recognized by both the Latin Catholic and the Eastern Orthodox Churches took place in the Church of St. Sophia in Nicaea. One of the major issues was about the place that icons should have in worship. The iconoclasts (icon breakers) considered that the use of icons anywhere represented a form of idolatry; the iconodules (icon worshippers) believed that icons could be venerated. The position of the iconodules won (although the controversy surfaced briefly later), thus incidentally allowing for the flowering of Christian art.

POLITICS. From the beginning of the Councils, politics influenced the outcome of the discussions. The several bishops, particularly those of Rome and Constantinople, frequently contended over who was supreme. In 1054 the Latin Catholic Pope Leo IX, wanting to restore the unity of the church under his authority, sent a representative to Constantinople. Following an angry exchange, his representative delivered a "Papal Bull of Excommunication" which was countered by a reciprocal excommunication from Patriarch Michael Cerularius. These two decrees remained in effect envenoming relations until Pope Paul VI and Patriarch Athenagoras annulled them in 1965 before Pope Paul's visit to Turkey.

Christianity had officially been made the state religion by the Emperor Theodosius I in 381 with the Second Ecumenical Council. By 438 Theodosius II could claim that there were no pagans in his empire. The reign of Justinian (527-565) is counted the height of the Eastern Roman Empire. During his time the empire circled the Mediterranean and extended into Persia. Not only did he contribute the great churches of St. Sophia and St. Irene, but he is also considered to have been a great legalist, having produced a code of laws to which reference is still made.

The Eastern Roman Empire continued through a succession of more or less incompetent rulers for almost another 900 years until it was ended with the conquest of Constantinople by the Turkish Sultan Mehmet II in 1453. Less than a hundred years later Muslim forces under Süleyman the Magnificent were challenging the European forces at the gates of Vienna. But much before that, one of the greatest challenges to Byzantium and to Christian-Muslim understanding came from Western Christianity in the form of the Crusades.

THE CRUSADES. From 1095 until the 16th century a series of wars were fought in the Middle East, ostensibly inspired by European Christians who wanted to control Jerusalem and the places where Jesus lived. More than eight Crusades were launched; the first four were fought in part in Asia Minor as the Crusaders made their way toward the Holy Land. The fortresses which these soldiers and their Armenian allies built, and which are so strikingly a part of the landscape today, stand as reminders of their vigor, their architectural genius, their religious fervor and their greed.

Several factors contributed to the beginnings of the Crusades. The Selçuk Turks had defeated the Byzantine army at the Battle of Manzikert (Malazgirt) in 1071, opening the whole of Anatolia to their occupation. Frequently the people of the areas that they moved into welcomed their generous control as an improvement over the misgovernment of the Byzantines. The Turks encroached farther and farther west, and as a consequence the Christians lost more and more territory. Thus the Byzantine government turned to the West and to its co-religionists to help against the "infidel." The West's response was to a large degree self-serving. For some time the Greek Orthodox Church had been in conflict with the Roman Catholic Church over the question of supremacy. The issues were both political and theological, and both Churches had declared anathema on each other in 1054. However, the threat of losing everything to the Selçuks drove the Byzantine emperors to seek help from Rome against the desires of their churchmen. Rome, for its part, was eager for a reconciliation between the communities. Another factor that contributed to igniting the Crusades was a growing restlessness among many people in Europe, a restlessness which the popes tried to channel. They used the challenge of a Holy War to focus this energy.

Lastly, during those same years the Muslim control of Syria and Palestine was in dispute, meaning that pilgrims had to travel through politically unstable regions to get to Jerusalem. Jerusalem had been captured by the Muslim general Omar in 637; but until the Selçuk Turks took it over in 1071 it had been administered with a clemency toward Western Christians, and the intercourse between Jerusalem and the West was undisturbed. The Selçuks were not intolerant, but they made travel and business difficult. This forced the Westerners to find new commercial routes to the Far East and to try a variety of measures to ease the difficulty of pilgrimage to Jerusalem.

Pope Urban II saw that if he sent an army to support the request of the Byzantine Emperor Alexius II Comnenus for aid against the Selçuks, he might be able to heal the rift between Eastern and Western Christianity and to establish the position of the pope above that of the patriarch. He also expected the army to continue south and to capture Jerusalem. In part for publicity, the garments of the soldiers who went on this venture carried a distinguishing identity: Their name, "Crusader," meant that they had been "marked with the cross." While men had long worn devices quickly recognizable in the heat of battle, heraldry for Western Europe really developed at the time of the Crusades.

Pope Urban's appeal came in 1095; it was answered with unexpected enthusiasm. By 1096 members of the First Crusade began arriving in Constantinople. Already they were a disputatious, unruly horde of soldiers, pilgrims, opportunists and camp followers which Emperor Alexius was hard put to use. Among them were the ruffian followers of Peter the Hermit and Walter the Penniless. Peter the Hermit's undisciplined mob was annihilated by the Selçuks almost as soon as they moved into Anatolia.

The leaders of the more organized armies included Godfrey of Bouillon, Raymond of Potiers, Bohemund and Robert Guiscard. Alexius tried to get the leaders to promise that they would turn over to him whatever they captured in Anatolia. The knights, on their part, expected titles and property in return, a pact which Alexius hesitated to accept. Crossing into Anatolia, the Crusaders attacked and defeated the Selçuk Turks at Nicaea in June of 1097. But, when Alexius used his own soldiers to protect Nicaea from being looted, the Crusaders resented his interference. Alexius accompanied the foreign army as far as Dorylaeum (Eskişehir) where the combined Christian forces defeated the Selçuks again. There he turned back, leaving the Crusaders to continue south with the feeling that he had deserted them.

By October the Crusaders had split into two groups. One followed Godfrey's brother Baldwin to Edessa where he set up his personal countship. The second went south to camp outside of Antioch-on-the-Orontes. That group had expected Alexius to join them again, but when he got only as far as Philomelia (Akşehir) he was scared off by the report that a strong Muslim force was approaching from Mosul. By returning to Constantinople Alexius lost out on three counts: on regaining Antioch for the Byzantine Empire, on saving his own credibility in the eyes of the Europeans and on improving relations in general between East and West.

The Crusaders took Antioch in June 1098. A year later they captured Jerusalem, massacring many Muslims and Jews when they entered the city. The First Crusade was successful in its objectives of limiting the extent of the Selçuk Empire and of returning Jerusalem to Christian control, but it intensified the differences between the Eastern and the Western Churches.

The Second Crusade (1145-1148) was sparked by the fall of Edessa in 1144 to İmadeddin Zengi, the Muslim ruler of Mosul and Aleppo. To avenge that disgrace King Louis VII of France and King Conrad III of Germany led their armies into Anatolia in 1147. King Conrad's army was soundly defeated near Dorylaeum (Eskişehir), and King Louis's at Laodicea (near Denizli). King Louis continued south with his much reduced forces to St. Simeon (Seleucia), the port of Antioch (where he quarreled with his queen). From there he went on to Jerusalem without challenging the Muslim forces in Aleppo or trying to recover Edessa.

The Third Crusade was fueled because the Muslim leader Saladin had retaken Jerusalem and many of the Crusaders' cities and castles by 1187. This Crusade was led by King Richard the Lionhearted of England, King Philip II Augustus of France

(King Louis VII's son) and King Frederick I Barbarossa of Germany (who was also Holy Roman Emperor). The first two men (who were already disputing Richard's possessions in France) were not important in Anatolian history. Barbarossa had been with his uncle, King Conrad, on the Second Crusade forty years earlier. He started by making his peace with the Byzantine Emperor Isaac II Angelus in Constantinople and then continued into Anatolia where he allied himself with the Armenian King Leo the Great. On June 10, 1190, when he was crossing the Calycadnus (Göksu) River just above Silifke he drowned, and his part of the Third Crusade came to an end. Richard's career was not much better: He was captured in Vienna on his way home and languished in prison until the English paid his ransom.

The Fourth Crusade, which originally was led by French nobles who intended to fight for the recovery of Jerusalem, was diverted from its course by the desires of the Venetians (to whom the French had become indebted) in order to interfere in the politics of Constantinople. The Crusaders attacked that city and conquered it on April 12, 1204. In the pillage that followed, they destroyed many of the buildings and most of the art. The Latin kingdom which the Crusaders set up in Constantinople lasted only 57 years until 1261 when the Byzantines retook the city.

Later Crusades were mounted against the Ottoman Turks in contest for parts of Asia Minor rather than for the possession of Jerusalem. In 1344 Crusaders from Venice, from Cyprus and the Knights Hospitallers captured Smyrna. They held it until Tamerlane took it from them in 1402. A few of the Hospitallers who escaped from Tamerlane moved down the coast and strengthened a fortress on the small peninsula at Halicarnassus. That fortress had been held by their group since 1309. Once strengthened, the fortress was given the name of the Castle of St. Peter; Petros to the Greeks became Petronium to the Latins and thus Bodrum to the Turks. As a fort it worked in cooperation with castles in Cos and in Rhodes to control the coastal shipping until it was captured in 1523 by Sultan Süleyman the Magnificent.

The southwestern region of Turkey is spotted with many, many Crusader-period castles, some along the sea as at Ayaş, Kızkalesi and Anamur, some slightly inland as at Silifke and others on strategic high points on the main routes, among them Bakraş, Kozan, Anavarza, Yılan Kalesi, Toprakkale and Namrun. They are imposing, romantic and deserted: The development of the use gunpowder some time before the 14th century contributed to the end of the usefulness of castles in defensive warfare. In addition, the strength and stability of the Middle East under the Ottoman Empire meant that while European rulers continued to talk about the profits that they had accrued from the Crusades, by 1500 they had no interest left in collecting an army and setting off on another large-scale operation.

OTHER CHRISTIAN TRADITIONS. Besides the Eastern (Greek) Orthodox Church and the Oriental (Armenian and Syrian) Orthodox Church, there are three other major Christian traditions represented in some numbers in Turkey. The Latin (Roman) Catholic Church membership traces its roots to the Crusaders, the early merchants and sailors, and some expatriate communities. The Eastern Rite Catholic Church represents members who have broken with the Orthodox Church and are joined with Rome. (Of this group, the Maronite Church claims never to have interrupted its communion with Rome.) The Evangelical (Protestant and Anglican) Churches stem largely from the evangelical revival in the West that took place in the early 19th century and that sent missionaries throughout the world. In order to protect the new Protestant community from persecution by members of the Orthodox Churches, Sultan Abdülmecit formally recognized it as a *millet* in 1847, making it a legal entity. This was part of the Ottoman westernizing reform movement known as the *Tanzimat* (1839-1876), and one of the many evidences of Ottoman fair dealings with the diverse communities they ruled.

Interior, the Blue Mosque

"Islam" means submission (to God/Allah); an adherent is called a "Muslim," one who submits (to God). God is One: totality, unity. In its unity and comprehensiveness Islam pervades the whole of life. *Allahuekber* (God is incomparable) are the words calling people to prayer. Nothing exists that is not God; even that which is beyond human imagination is God. God cannot be separated from anything. Out of this understanding of the nature of God comes the corollary that all aspects of human life are ordered by and must be performed in accordance with God. All human beings are God's slaves. All the categories into which human behavior is often divided (i.e., religion, politics, economics, social behavior) are one and related. Thus, for instance, Islam denies a separation of politics and religion.

In practice, Islam has no religious hierarchy and no complicated creed. The education offered in the İmam-Hatip (religious training) schools is valuable, but it does not necessarily confer a cachet on the students.

Anyone who has the respect of the community may be the religious leader in any mosque. At the same time, no priestly intercessor may come between God and God's slaves. Moral judgment is God's province alone. The requirements of Islam can be comprehended by everyone, and in its teachings there are both commonplace guides and inspiration for profound insights.

Islam is the most recent of the three great monotheistic religions, having developed from the revelations by God to the Prophet Muhammad. Muhammad was born as a member of the Kuraish tribe in Mecca and lived from about AD 570 to June 8, 632. His activity as a prophet encompassed the ten years before his death.

THE KORAN, THE SUNNA, THE ICMA. The holy book of Islam is the Koran; it is believed to be the revelation of God to Muhammad. It contains 114 *Suras* (chapters) and 6,666 *ayets* (verses). The first Sura is the *Fatiha*; it is a prayer and is the one most frequently recited by Muslims. Muhammad conveyed the revelations orally to those who learned them by heart. The one who had memorized the Koran (the *Hafız*) chanted them for the public to hear and learn. After the death of Muhammad, the Caliph Abu Bakr collected them in written form on individual pages. It was in Caliph Othman's time (AD 644-656) that caligraphers compiled them in a book. Because the Koran was revealed in Arabic, the language spoken by Muhammad, it was written in Arabic. Muslims maintain that it cannot be translated. There are, however, foreign language "interpretations" of it, including Turkish and English. Arabic is the language of Islam all over the world, hence the common custom of referring to God in Islam with the Arabic word, Allah.

The foundation of Islam is the Koran, the divine word; but so little of this is dogmatic or legislative that early Muslims found it an incomplete authority for determining the proper behavior for the good life. This was especially true when Islam first began to spread among many diverse peoples. Thus the body of the *Sunna* developed, supplementing the Koran. The Sunna is a collection of traditions, moral sayings and anecdotes (*Hadiths*) of Muhammad. "Sunna" means the accepted system of social and legal behavior based on Muhammad's deeds, utterances and unspoken approval. It is the theory and practice of the entire Islamic community. The Sunna is almost as important as the Koran because it embodies all the elaborations of Koranic teaching.

Over time there have been serious disagreements concerning the Hadiths, and interpretations of the Koran and the Sunna have varied so much as to be contradictory. This situation is generally resolved by reference to what has become perhaps the most important of all the sayings attributed to Muhammad, "My community will never agree in an error." The principle that this expresses is called *Icma*, the agreement of Islam; according to it, every Muslim knows that a belief entertained by the greater part of the community over the course of time is infallibly true, and that a practice (for instance, the cult of saints) that has been allowed by most over a long period must be legitimate and good. Another way of expressing this is to state that the people of the Sunna do not deviate from dogma and practice.

The Koran, the Sunna, and the Icma are thus the three supports of Islam. It is the Icma that has given Islam its constant unity with its past and its continuous flexibility. But while the Icma speaks with the voice of authority, Muslims have been saved from internal intolerance and extreme sectarianism by another Hadith of Muhammad which says, "The differences of opinion in my community are a divine mercy."

GOD'S ATTRIBUTES. For a Muslim, God is supreme and indivisible. Muslims submit to His will; they constantly praise and glorify Him; and in Him alone they hope. He is transcendent, majestic, almighty, eternal, just, loving, merciful and good.[9] Nothing may be compared to Him, and to Him alone they pray. All Muslims (perhaps with the exception of Shiites) jealously preserve the distinction between Creator and creature. They seldom ask God for favors, limiting their prayer to thanksgiving and adoration. According to the Islamic view of the Apocalypse, God's final judgment will come at the end of time when heaven will await the faithful and hell the infidels. The pious Muslim does not distinguish faith from works; both are indispensable and mutually supplementary.

FIVE DUTIES IN ISLAM. The five duties (sometimes called the Five Pillars of Islam) are 1) the statement of the creed, 2) prayer, 3) alms, 4) fasting, and 5) pilgrimage. The Creed (*Kelime-i Şehadet*) in Islam is the statement in the frame. Once in his life the believer must state this with full understanding and absolute acceptance.[10]

Kelime-i Şehadet

"There is no god but God and Muhammad is His prophet."

Prayer (*namaz*) is performed five times daily. At dawn, at noon, in mid-afternoon, at dusk, and after dark a muezzin announces the time of prayer by giving the Call to

Prayer (*ezan*) broadcast from the minaret of a mosque. (The hours vary according to the time of the year.) The prayers are preceded by ablutions; they are set and are accompanied by traditional postures. When a Muslim prays he covers his head, removes his shoes and places a carpet under him. He faces Mecca, kneeling, prostrating himself and standing with his hands open. During the noon prayer time on Friday set prayers are said, the Koran is read, and a sermon is given by the *imam* (preacher). The most frequently recited prayer is the Fatiha:

> ## Fatiha
> *In the name of God, the merciful, the compassionate: / Praise be to God, the Lord of the worlds, the merciful, the compassionate, / The ruler of the judgment day! / You we serve, and of You we ask for aid. / Guide us in the right path, / The path of those to whom You are gracious, / Not of those with whom You are angry nor of those who err.*

An illuminated page from the Holy Koran

Alms (*zekât*) are expected from every Muslim; he is expected to give gener-ously and beyond the minimum pres-cribed. The alms should be in the form of something he himself has produced.

The fast (*oruç*) is kept through the month of Ramazan; it is the ninth month of the Islamic year. The first revelation of the Koran is commemorated in this month. Muslims must fast during the daylight hours. All indulgence of any sort is forbidden during the fast, but the physically weak, the sick, the soldiers, travelers and a few others are exempted. Because the Muslim calendar is based on a lunar year the months rotate around the seasons. Each year, for instance, Ramazan begins ten or eleven days earlier than the previous year according to the Gregorian calendar.[11] There are two canonical festivals in the Muslim year. The major one is the Festival of Sacrifice (in Turkish, *Kurban Bayramı*) which commemorates Abraham's willingness to sacrifice his son İsmael. It begins on the tenth of Zilhicce. The Festival of Breaking the Fast (*Şeker Bayramı*, or Candy Festival) begins on the first of Şevval. A joyous holiday, it celebrates the end of Ramazan.

Pilgrimage (*hac*) to Mecca is expected of every Muslim once during his lifetime if he can afford it physically and financially. The pilgrimage -- probably the greatest in the world -- is timed so that the person can be in Mecca from the ninth to the twelfth of Zilhicce. In 1996 these dates were from the 28th of April to the 1st of May. [12]

MUSLIM TEACHING VIS-À-VIS OTHER RELIGIONS. According to Muslim teaching, God has given successive revelations through His prophets. Muhammad is the last, the "Seal of the Prophets." The end of the world will come when Islam is triumphant. Abraham and Jesus are two principal prophets. Abraham was the

Father of the Faithful and the first Muslim. Jesus was born of Mary and performed many miracles. Contrary to Christian teaching, Jesus was not crucified, but was instead taken away by God who left a shadow in his place. Jesus will return at the end of the world as the *Mahdi* (the divinely guided one) to restore the true Islam and fight the Antichrist.

The close relationship acknowledged between Judaism, Christianity and Islam has meant that Jews and Christians have been treated in principle with special tolerance in Muslim countries. It is thought that Muhammad derived his ideas about the other two religions not from reading but from his intercourse with contemporary Arabian Jews and Christians.

THE MOSQUE. The building in which Muslims worship is a mosque (*cami*). In Turkey, where the climate can be cold in winter, mosques are enclosed buildings. They are oriented so that when the congregation stands facing the front they pray towards Mecca. The niche in the center wall (*mihrap*) indicates the direction of Mecca. To the right of it is the pulpit (*minber*) from which the preacher (*imam*) gives the Friday sermon. Usually the names of God (Allah), Muhammad, and the first six caliphs (Abu Bakr, Ali, Omar, Othman, Hasan and Husain) are displayed on the walls around the central worship area. One or more minarets accompany a mosque; they may or may not be attached to the building. Representational art in any form is forbidden, so only geometric patterns, calligraphy or floral designs decorate a mosque. The magnificence of the mosques and their meticulous decoration led the way to the development of Islamic art in the field of architecture and the arts of stone carving, woodwork, ceramics, inlay, glass work, carpets and kilims, metal work, furniture, calligraphy, and bookbinding.

THE CALIPHATE. The position of caliph in Islam has changed over time. Originally the word seems to have meant not only the successor and the vicegerent of the Prophet Muhammad, but also in general those who were blessed (Sura vi.165; xxxvii:26). As the Islamic armies acquired wealth and power in the early years, the title of their leader took on greater political meaning. With the court ceremonies came an additional aura of awe.

The first four caliphs are recognized as orthodox by Muslims; each was the commander of the Faithful. Their authority was over temporal matters; they were not the spiritual imam. Abu Bakr (632-634) was Muhammad's immediate successor. He was followed by Omar (634-644); then Othman was caliph (644-655); then Ali (655-661). After Ali's death there was a revolt and Ali's son Husain was murdered. The caliphate went from the Omayyids (descendants of Omar) to the Abbasids (descendants of Ali) in the 8th century, to the Fatimids in Egypt in the 13th century. The Ottoman Sultan Selim I took the caliphate from the Fatimids in 1517. The Ottoman caliphate lasted through the Ottoman Sultan Abdülmecit II (1922-1924) who held merely that position.

In many countries, notably in Turkey, the system of the caliphate has broken down. Mustafa Kemal Atatürk, the founder of modern Turkey, abolished the caliphate on March 3, 1924. For the Turkish Republic the abolition of the caliphate made possible secular education and secular law.

MUSLIM SECTS. Muslim sectarianism is negligible, except for the division of Islam into Sunnis and Shiites. This division arose over who should become the caliph in the first century of the Islamic calendar. It is a convention to treat Sunni Islam as the norm because the vast majority of Muslims are Sunnis. Orthodox Sunni Muslims observe the standard of conduct exem-plified by Muhammad; they are those who observe the Hadiths. The Icma and Sunni toler-ation have preserved them from other serious variations.

The Whirling Dervishes

SHIITES. The essential distinction between Sunnis and Shiites at the outset was that Shiites believed that Ali and his successors were divinely ordained caliphs. They consider that his sons Hasan and Husain were martyrs. Shiites have many more festivals than Sunnis; there are also many more saints, more dervishes and more religious communities (*tarikats*). Although they believe in the unity of God, in the Prophet Muhammad and in the Koran, their practice of the requirements of Islam differs from Sunni practice. The largest concentration of Shiites is in Iran.

SUFISM. A Sufi is a Muslim who has devoted himself to the life of mysticism (*tasavvuf*). The British scholar Professor H.A.R. Gibb has contrasted them with the stern Sunni legalists (*ulema*), noting that from the beginning of Islam many people lived their daily lives in a spirit of devotion and saw in Islam a discipline of the soul rather than a legal ritual. Sufis have ranged from people of humble background to whom mysticism was a moral and an emotional experience to those of great intellectual power who found in it a profound truth and spiritual enlightenment. Over the years a number of Sufi orders (*tarikats*) have developed, centered around charismatic leaders.[13]

TARIKATS. Dervishes were members of various Muslim religious communities called *tarikats*. The word "tarikat" means "the road that leads to spiritual union with God." Usually the community was a mystical order. The tarikats started as collections of disciples around a revered religious leader. After the breakup of the Selçuk Empire at the end of the 12th century these tarikats acquired a more formal but still popular and humanistic structure. Each tarikat claimed its origin in a historic founder whose inspiration the members traced from the Prophet Muhammad through an unbroken line of saints. The religious services of the tarikats were called *zikir* (a mentioning of the name of God), the purpose of which was to fill one's heart with love and to bring the worshipper into mystical union with God. The Koranic reference to this is found in Sura xxxiii: 41: "Oh, Believers! remember God with frequent remembrance, and praise Him morning and evening."

In some of the services the religious exaltation has been described as howling, in some as dancing. In some there was a hypnosis that was demonstrated in particular feats such as levitation, clairvoyance, or, among the Rifa'is, as eating red hot embers without being hurt.

The members of the tarikats were often contrasted with those of the *ulema*

The Süleymaniye Complex

(scholars). The tarikats drew some of their membership from among the poor and from the trade guilds. They served as the support group for their community, and offered close companionship in a secret society. The ulema, on the other hand, represented the educated, legalistic and theological segment of society that looked down on the dervish orders.

In addition to these that are noted here, many other tarikats have been founded and have been important in the social and religious life of Turkish communities.

MEVLEVIS. [14] One of the great Sufi leaders was Celaleddin Rumi; he is known also as Mevlana (Lord). He lived in Konya in the 13th century and wrote a number of mystical poems including the *Mesnevi*. His followers are called Mevlevi Dervishes (or also Whirling Dervishes). The *sema* (whirling dance) of the Mevlevis is open to the public in Konya annually on December 17; the date commemorates the death of Mevlana.[15] In the whirling the dervishes describe their soaring spirit as the falcon flying towards God.

BEKTAŞIS. [16] Another Turkish tarikat is the Bektaşi order; its members are followers of the 13th century Hacı Bektaş Veli. Their center is in Hacıbektaş between Kırşehir and Kayseri. They believe in the Prophet Muhammad, consider Ali as their guide, and accept Hacı Bektaş Veli as their sheikh or *pir*. Bektaşis tend to be more worldly-minded than mystical. The most important ethic for them is that they must keep their word. They pray for Ali constantly and do not drink water for ten days during Muharrem (an act they see of cleansing themselves from the previous year's sins). They celebrate Nevruz as the birthday of Ali. At the height of the Ottoman Empire many Bektaşis were janissaries, but the janissary corps was abolished and the order suppressed in 1826. Bektaşis observe an annual feast in mid-August in Hacıbektaş.

SHIITE ALEVIS. One other tarikat that should be mentioned is that of the Shiite Alevis. They constitute almost one-third of Turkey's population. The Alevi order is one of the oldest in Anatolia. Alevis have at times rebelled against the abuse that they have suffered as Shiites for their nonconformity to Sunni practices. Alevis believe that Ali was a divinely ordained caliph. They also believe in the unity of God and in the coming of the *Mahdi* (the divinely guided one). Every Friday men and women gather at their place of worship. The *dede* (their leader) reads a Sura from the Koran, the musicians play, they read the *Miraçname* (an account of Muhammad's miraculous spiritual ascent to heaven on the 27th of Recep), and then they begin the zikir. The Alevis also hold a sema in which they pray facing each other rather than the direction of Mecca. Their prayers are in Turkish, not Arabic, and are accompanied by the music of stringed instruments. Instead of fasting during Ramazan, they fast three days in Muharrem. They also mourn for the early martyrs throughout the month of Muharrem.

TURKS AND ISLAM. At one time the Turks of Central Asia were Shamanists believing that good and evil spirits were present everywhere and that those spirits could be invoked by the magic of inspired priests.

For a while they showed some interest in Buddhism, Christianity and Judaism. Because of their contacts with Arab Muslims in the 8th century AD they began to learn about and to accept Islam. Scholars see, however, a continuing influence of Shamanism in some of the practices of the tarikat.

By the 11th century many of the Turkish feudal states in the Middle East had become Islamic. In Turkey the Selçuks were instrumental in converting the indigenous people; this conversion continued under the Ottomans who helped spread Islam throughout their wide empire.

Fifty years ago there were an estimated three hundred million Muslims in the world. Today that figure has risen to well over one billion. A little less than one-fifth of the world's population is Muslim; of this, over half live in Asia.

Much of the strength of Islam lies in its unity and its comprehensiveness. Permeating every aspect of life, it appeals as a simple, consistent and universal faith.

Aerial view, Sultanahmet Mosque otherwise known as the Blue Mosque

[1] This chapter is not intended as a definitive discussion of these religions; readers who wish to learn more might refer to the Suggested Readings at the end of the book, or to many other works on the specific traditions and on comparative religion.

[2] In several places the Koran acknowledges the validity of the revelations to the Jewish prophets and to Jesus (i.e. Suras iv: 161-163; vi: 92; xvii: 57).

[3] Several points of confusion need to be noted in listing the family relations: There are seeming duplications (Lud and the Lydians); there are names that are probably geographical or political rather than family. Probably some of the families intermarried; undoubtedly some moved around; some names may have been spelled several ways; some families lived so far from the writer or writers in Israel that not much was known about them (Riphath? Togarmah?). Not all of them got along peaceably with each other or kept perfect records. While Noah is accepted by both as their progenitor, Jewish and Arab identity as Semitic people did not develop until many generations later.

[4] The Aramaic language figured in the fight between Sennacherib of Assyria and Hezekiah of Jerusalem: When Jerusalem was under siege by the Assyrians in about 701 BC, Hebrew-speaking Assyrians appeared underneath its walls. They threatened the defenders saying that, if the city did not surrender, they would force its people to eat their own dung. The commander of Jerusalem shouted back, "Please don't use Hebrew. We don't want our soldiers to understand you. Use Aramaic instead." (II Kings 18:26)

[5] See p. 138 - 139.

[6] The empire ruled from Constantinople for 1100 years was called by it the Eastern Roman Empire; it is more familiarly known as the Byzantine Empire.

[7] The French Lusignans — themselves Crusaders — who controlled much of Cilicia and Cyprus (1192-1475) tried unsuccessfully to force this group of Armenians to give their allegiance to Roman Catholicism.

[8] The word "ecumenical" means "universal." Thus a Christian ecumenical council would be one in which representatives from every Christian community throughout the world would participate. The Western Church holds that this has not happened since 787. The Eastern Church believes that the last truly ecumenical council was in 451.

[9] Traditionally there are ninety-nine attributes, or "Beautiful Names" of God. These are repeated as a Muslim fingers a string of prayer beads. The string commonly has thirty- three beads plus a large end bead so that the Muslim goes through it three times. The end bead represents the comprehensive name, Allah.

[10] The use of the masculine pronoun to identify Muslims is imposed by the lack of a non-gender word in English.

[11] The Islamic Calendar (*Hicri Takvim*) started in AD 622. The first day of the year was accepted as the 1st of Muharrem (the 16th of July in the Gregorian calendar) rather than the 27th of Sefer 622, the day on which Muhammad started the Hegira from Mecca to Medina. The months of the Islamic calendar are Muharrem, Sefer, Rebiülevvel, Rebiülahir, Cemaziyelevvel, Cemaziyelahir, Recep, Şaban, Ramazan, Sevval, Zilkade, and Zilhicce. The Muslim year varies from 354 to 355 days; hence the season and the months do not line up, and there about 33 Muslim years to every 32 Gregorian years.

[12] The ninth of Zilhicce in 1997 is April 17th; in 1998 it is April 7th; in 1999 it is March 17th, and in 2000 it is March 15. In some Muslim countries the dates are not announced until the new moon has been seen for that month.

[13] See H.A.R.Gibb, *Mohammedanism, An Historical Survey*, Oxford University Press, 1950.

[14] See pp. 206-207.

[15] In İstanbul a *sema* can be observed on the last Sunday of each month from 5:00 to 7:00 pm at the Galip Dede Tekkesi (Mevlevi Dervish and Classical Literature Museum) at the south end of İstiklâl Caddesi on Galip Dede Sokak.

[16] See pp. 188-190.

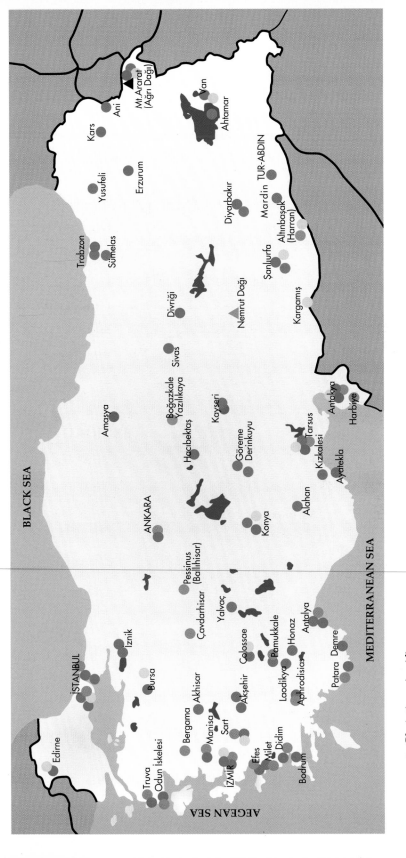

Map of Turkey indicating the locations of religious sites

BLACK SEA

AEGEAN SEA

MEDITERRANEAN SEA

Edirne
İSTANBUL
Truva
Odun İskelesi
İznik
Bursa
Bergama
Akhisar
Manisa
Sart
İZMİR
Efes
Milet
Didim
Bodrum
Akşehir
Colossae
Laodikya
Pamukkale
Aphrodisias
Honaz
Antalya
Patara
Demre
Çavdarhisar
Yalvaç
Pessinus
(Balllhisar)
ANKARA
Hacıbektaş
Boğazkale
Yazılıkaya
Sivas
Divriği
Göreme
Derinkuyu
Kayseri
Alahan
Konya
Kızkalesi
Ayatekla
Tarsus
Antakya
Harbiye
Amasya
Trabzon
Sümelas
Yusufeli
Erzurum
Kars
Ani
Mt.Ararat
(Ağrı Dağı)
Van
Ahtamar
Diyarbakır
Mardin TUR-ABDIN
Altınbaşak
(Harran)
Şanlıurfa
Nemrut Dağı
Kargamış

Christian significance
Muslim significance
Jewish significance
Pagan significance

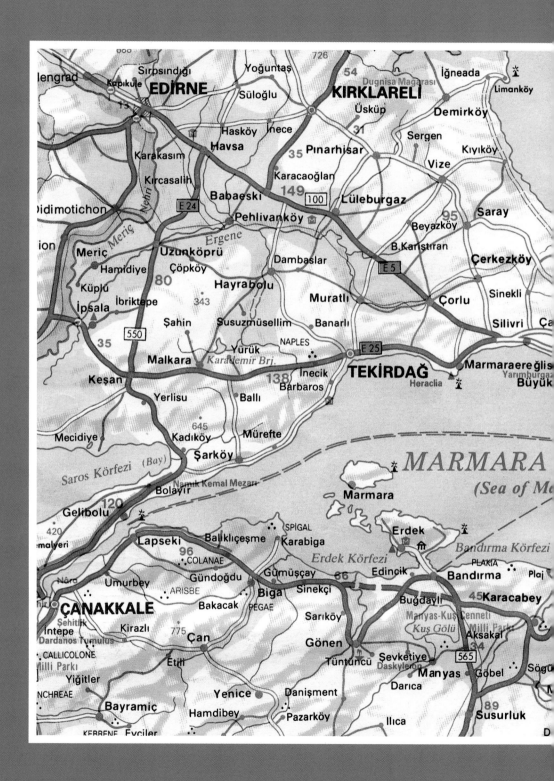

The Marmara and Thrace

The region of the Marmara and Thrace is the two-way funnel between Europe and Asia. Edirne on one side of the funnel in Europe and Bursa on the other side in Asia have been capitals of an empire, and İstanbul at its neck holds pride of place in the cities of the world.

*Aerial view,
the Blue Mosque
(in the foreground) and
St. Sophia*

THE MARMARA AND THRACE

Bursa (Prusa)
İznik (Nicaea)
Kadıköy (Chalcedon)
Üsküdar (Chrysopolis, Scutari)
Anadolu Kavağı, Yuşa Tepesi (Genoese Castle, Giant's Hill)
İstanbul (Byzantium, Constantinople)
Adalar (Princes' Islands)
Edirne (Hadrianople)

BURSA - PRUSA

Bursa has been considered one of the most delightful places on earth. Its multitude of religious buildings and its native son Süleyman Çelebi (author of the *Mevlidi Şerif*, see p. 85) distinguish it in religious terms.

It is renowned for its royal mosques, for its markets of spices and a covered bazaar where many local specialties may be found: cutlery, towels and, particularly in the Koza Han (the Cocoon Caravansary) the still-beautiful Bursa silk (Bursa's market area includes a collection of caravansaries) , and for its proximity to Uludağ (Bithynian Mt. Olympus), a winter ski resort and a summer hiking center. It was the hub of the Turkish silk trade in the 16th century and the automotive industry in the 20th. The city and its environs stretch along the northern foot of Uludağ about 90 km southeast of İstanbul. It is surrounded by orchards of peaches, chestnuts, quinces, olives and cherries, and by fields of tomatoes and onions. Its streams are fed by runoff from the mountain snows, and its highways are lined with factories.

Bursa was founded by King Prusias I of Bithynia around the end of the 3rd century BC, hence its name. It became part of the Roman Province of Bithynia in 65 BC, and then a minor city in the Eastern Roman Empire, overshadowed by the rivals, Nicaea and Nicomedia. Goths in the 3rd century, Arabs in the 8th and Persians in the 10th century battled here. In the 11th century Selçuks, Crusaders and Byzantines fought over it until finally about 1326 the Ottoman Turks under Orhan Gazi took it and made it their capital. Tamerlane pillaged the city in 1402, and before it returned to Ottoman rule it was sacked by the Karaman tribe from Konya.Very little is left of the old city. Parts of the old wall of the citadel can be found, and perhaps some of the gates identified. The foundations of the Eski Kaplıca (Old Baths) on the corner of Çekirge and Acemler Caddeleri may be Byzantine; the baths themselves date from the reign of Sultan Murat I (1359-1389). Marbles worked by Byzantine stonemasons — capitals and columns — were used in decorating this building, as they were in Yeni Kaplıca, the Muradiye Medresesi, the tomb of Orhan Gazi, and the small mosque of Ömür Bey, among others.

Most of the hotels in the Çekirge region of the city have their own thermal/mineral baths.

There is an old story of a ruler who left his beautiful young daughter near Bursa at one of the thermal springs, expecting her to die of a wasting disease.

When he returned he found her in radiant good health, thanks to the healing

_The royal mosques
of Bursa reflect the
years when this city
was the capital of
the young Ottoman
Empire in the 14th
century._

effects of the water. Justinian's wife Theodora visited the springs in the 6th century bringing 4,000 courtiers in her train; Süleyman the Magnificent came here to the Kükürtlü and Yeni Kaplıca baths to relieve his gout in the 16th century; and Atatürk was here in the early 20th. The popularity of the thermal baths was highest in the late 19th and early 20th centuries when members of the European royal families were joined here by artists and writers like Pierre Loti. Such hotels as the Çelik Palas, with its sumptuous marble bath, reflect the style of that period.

More than one hundred mosques dot the city. Several unusual qualities distinguish the **Hüdavendigâr (Murat I) Mosque** from other Bursa mosques. One of the oldest mosques of the city, built between 1366 and 1386, it was the first Ottoman mosque complex to include a number of buildings for community social services. It had a bath, a public kitchen, a children's school, plus a fountain, toilets, a convent for traveling dervishes, and a _medrese_ (religious school). Rooms on the main floor were set aside as the dervish quarters, while on the next floor there were sixteen medrese cells. The combination of these two in a mosque is strange because the dervishes leaned towards a liberal interpretation of religious tenets while the students of religious law tended to be conservative. It has been suggested that the sultan put them together so he could keep an eye on both. Another anomaly in the building is a small, domed room directly above the _mihrap_ (prayer niche) that has a window that looks down onto the main central hall.[1]

Ulu Cami (the Great Mosque), completed in 1399, is Bursa's most impressive mosque from the outside because of its size. Inside, the twelve great columns supporting twenty domes are intended to create a sense of God's omnipotence and grandeur. The building seems airy in spite of its size because of the central marble pool and ablution fountain and because of the light that comes in from above it and through the windows in the domes. The _minber_ (pulpit), made of carved walnut, is one of the finest of such work.

Three buildings make up the Yeşil complex: **Yeşil Cami** (Green Mosque), **Yeşil Türbe** (Green Mausoleum) and **Yeşil Medrese** (Green School). They were built by or for Sultan Mehmet I who died in 1421. The interiors of both the mosque and the mausoleum are covered with beautiful green and dark blue tiles, some laced with gold. These tiles were the work of ceramists from Tabriz. The medrese is now the Museum of Turkish and Islamic Arts, housing displays of Ottoman weapons, calligraphy, a room decked out with a circumcision bed, and a number

_Interior of Ulu
Cami, Bursa_

of the Karagöz puppets (see p. 85). The proportions and the simplicity of these buildings make them outstanding Ottoman buildings.

The **Mosque of Yıldırım Bayezit** is on one of the spurs of the mountain, east of the Gökdere valley. It is a Bursa-type mosque; ceramic tiles which decorate the exterior mihrap have a thunderbolt design; similar designs have been carved on the interior arches. The design is appropriate because *yıldırım* means thunderbolt in Turkish. Yıldırım Bayezit got his nickname from the speed with which he was able to move his armies around. He was the father of Mehmet I and the man whom Tamerlane defeated and captured in the battle for Ankara in 1402.

The Green Mausoleum, Bursa

Bursa was the home of **Süleyman Çelebi**, the author of the most famous of all Turkish poems, the *Mevlidi Şerif*. He wrote it in 1409 as an inspired counter to a certain religious leader who asserted that Muhammad deserved no more regard than any other prophet. He and his family lived in Bursa and he may have been an advisor at the court of Sultan Bayezit I. He became the chief *imam* (Muslim priest) of Ulu Cami about the time that Tamerlane captured Bayezit in 1402 in Ankara. He died and was buried at the mosque in 1421.

The *Mevlidi Şerif* is sometimes called "The Birth-song of the Prophet." For Turks the poem is the source of their emotional understanding of the birth of Muhammad and of his miracles. It is chanted publicly and privately thousands of times a year in homes and mosques throughout Turkey. No observance of the Night of Power omits it; few families would let their dead rest beyond 40 days without reciting it. Its appeal is not only a popular one, it also holds its place in Turkish literature because of its artistic beauty.

Bursa is supposed to have been the home of the Ottoman Empire's beloved wits, Karagöz and Hacivat, who appear as puppets in the shadow plays each night during *Ramazan* (the month of fasting) and at circumcision parties. The puppets are made of camel skin; their colors show through on the screen behind which they act. Hacivat played the role of the educated, worldly-wise, self-righteous opportunist; Karagöz was the ordinary, unpretentious man, always able to turn a difficult situation to his benefit. The two capitalized on human weaknesses to fuel their ridicule. Like the commedia dell'arte in Europe, their plots were dependent on the current situation, but they were more given to slapstick solutions than the European theater. While this shadow play is related to similar plays in the Far East, the popular version of the Turkish origin is that a 13th century mason, Hacivat, and a blacksmith, Karagöz, were working on a mosque for Sultan Orhan in Bursa. But they were such clowns that they interfered with the work and at last the Sultan executed them. Once they were gone the Sultan regretted his hasty decision, so his sheykh, a man named Küşteri, reincarnated them in the puppets.

Shortly after a disastrous 17th century naval battle, a puppeteer gave a Karagöz show to Crazy Sultan İbrahim in which a galley and a merchant ship fought beneath a cliff. İbrahim was so pleased at the outcome that he made the puppeteer his Grand Admiral. The actor wisely declined the dangerous honor.

IZNIK - NICAEA

The town of İznik on the east shore of Lake İznik is the ancient Nicaea. Nicaea was the venue for the first and the last Ecumenical Councils (see pp. 66-7), meetings of representatives of all Christian churches. Legend has it that it was founded by the god Dionysus who taught its people how to grow grapes; many vineyards still surround it. Lysimachus named the town he had just taken in 316 BC for his wife Nikaia. Walls that were stormed by Arabs, Crusaders, Byzantines and Ottomans, by Tamerlane, and, lastly, by the Greeks in the 20th century still enclose most of the present town.

One of its famous native sons, Hipparchus of Nicaea (flourished 146-126 BC), was an astronomer who made a catalog of 1080 stars visible to the naked eye. He may have learned his knowledge of astronomy from the work of his predecessors in the schools of Harran and Edessa (Şanlıurfa). He originated scientific geography by inventing the means of establishing the location of a point by intersecting lines of latitude and longitude. He also used parallax to estimate the size of the moon and its distance from the earth.[2]

*One of the gates to
the city of İznik*

Dilemmas posed by the advent of Christianity to the Roman rulers of this region are evident in Pliny the Younger's correspondence with the Emperor Trajan. Pliny lived here when he was the Roman governor of Bithynia, and perhaps died here at the end of his two-year term (AD 111-113). He wrote to Trajan for advice on what to do about the Christians in his province. Trajan advised mercy, but demanded allegiance to his authority.

Pliny reported that he had questioned people accused of being Christians and ordered their death sentence as traitors only if they stubbornly persisted in refusing to worship the statues of the emperor and the gods, and to revile Christ. When Pliny forbade their meeting for such a service the Christians complied, but they persisted in what he called their "base and excessive superstition." Although he had put to death those who were adamant in their faith, Pliny was concerned that their numbers were swelling. Trajan replied that Pliny had done the right thing in examining the cases carefully. He said he did not want Pliny to harry the people, and he insisted that anonymous charges should not be considered.

At the main crossroads of İznik is the **Museum of St. Sophia.** This is the building in which the Seventh — and last — Ecumenical Council was held in 789. In ruins, the building's past history includes its foundation at the time of Justinian, its conversion into a mosque about 1331, restoration of the mosque by Sinan after fires in the 15th and 16th centuries, increasing neglect, and then destruction in the fighting between Greece and Turkey in 1922. Each spring the truncated minaret is home to a family of storks with their nest.

The First Ecumenical Council was held in Nicaea in 325. That

First Council took place in Constantine's palace on the shore of the lake. Stones from his palace can be seen submerged in the water on the southwest corner of the city, but it is hard now to make out any shape to the building.

In the 16th century ceramists in İznik created the most beautiful tiles ever made in Turkey. In addition to the clarity of their colors and the artistic composition of the designs, the tiles are distinguished by a particular tomato red. Only the tiles produced in İznik between 1560 and 1620 have this red. An explanation for this is that the Iranian ceramists who knew the technique were moved from İznik to Rhodes in 1580; when those they had trained stopped working, the secret of the composition of the red was lost. Some scholars also think that the source of the color may have been exhausted in the end. In any case, this mystery is unresolved. These tiles decorate the walls of the Topkapı Palace, a number of İstanbul mosques and the Selimiye Mosque in Edirne. **The Archaeological Museum of İznik**, located in the Nilüfer Hatun İmareti, contains a good collection of them together with coins and sarcophagi.[3]

Unique Iznik tiles of the 16th century

KADIKÖY - CHALCEDON

Kadıköy, on the Asiatic shore and across the Bosphorus from what was once Byzantium and is now European İstanbul, claims in legend to be older than Byzantium. Byzantium's founders looked down on it, saying that those who had settled there were blind to have ignored the better site in Europe. However, many of its residents have preferred to live here because it is in Asia and therefore is closer to the holy city of Mecca.

The Church of St. Euphemia (probably located somewhere near the crossroads of Altı Yol) was the location of the Fourth Ecumenical Council (the Council of Chalcedon) in 451. This Council brought the decision against the Monophysites which divided the Armenian and Syrian Orthodox churches from the Latin (Roman) Catholic and Eastern (Greek) Orthodox (see p. 67). Stones from the ruined building were used in the 16th century in the Mosque of Süleyman the Magnificent in İstanbul.

İznik ceramics have been prized by collectors around the world. Museums in all the major cities display the dishes, vases, and tiles from this workshop which was in the center of the city.

Present-day Kadıköy is a bustling metropolis with an almost carnival atmosphere among its residents.

ÜSKÜDAR - CRYSOPOLIS, SCUTARI

Once the Asiatic port for all traffic, both commercial and military, between İstanbul and the far reaches of Asia, the interest religiously in Üsküdar is in the royal mosques founded by or for women and in the mosque of the Dönme community (see p.89). In Roman times the town was known as Chrysopolis, the Golden City, perhaps from the taxes collected here, perhaps also from the light that the evening sun reflects in almost burning gold on the windows of the houses. Another derivation of the name is that it came from the tomb of Chryses, the son of Agamemnon and Chrysis, the girl over whom Agamemnon and Achilles had a falling out during the Trojan War. The name "Scutari" is thought to refer to the word in Greek for shield bearers.

Off the usual tourist route, Üsküdar repays the visitor in unexpected ways. The view from the top of Çamlıca on a clear day gives a perspective to the whole city. Many things are less expensive here. Best of all, the Asian shore has a distinctly different feel than the European, being closer to the Anatolian heartland.

It was on the hill of Çamlıca above the landing where in 324 Constantine the Great defeated Licinius, the man with whom he had had to share the position of emperor. During the Fourth Crusade the Venetians camped in Scutari (1203) and launched their final attack against Constantinople. By Ottoman times Üsküdar had become distinguished for its immense Muslim cemetery with its forest of shady cypress trees. In Üsküdar the Ottoman armies under the sultans from the 15th through the 17th centuries mustered to begin their campaigns south and east.

During the Crimean War (1853-1856) wounded soldiers were hospitalized in the **Selimiye Barracks** in Haydarpaşa. There they were nursed back to health by Florence Nightingale, the British founder of modern nursing. Her room in the Barracks is now the **Florence Nightingale Museum**, open every week day. (Haydarpaşa is both a ferry stop and the Asiatic terminal of the Berlin-to-Baghdad railroad.)

Of the royal mosques in Üsküdar, all were built either by or for a woman. Two of them are the work of the architect Sinan: the **İskele Camii** (1547/48), built for Süleyman's daughter Mihrimah Sultan, and the **Eski Valide Camii** (1583) built for Nur Banu Sultan, the Italian Jewish wife of Sultan Selim II. The Eski Valide is considered one of the most pleasing of Sinan's works. The **Çinili Cami** (1640) was founded by Kösem Mahpeyker Sultan, the mother of Sultan Murat IV and Sultan İbrahim. Its walls are covered with pretty tiles. Gülnuş Sultan is the Queen Mother honored by the **Yeni Valide Camii** (1710) built by Sultan Ahmet III. Sultan Mustafa III built the **Ayazma Camii** (1760/61) to honor his mother Mihrimah Sultan. (The one other royal **mosque** on the Asian shores of the Bosphorus, that of **Beylerbeyi**, was built in 1778 by Sultan Abdülhamid to honor his mother Rabia Sultan.[4])

One rather plain mosque in Üsküdar, the **Bülbül Deresi Mescidi**, and the cemetery with it are reserved for members of the *Dönme* community (converted Jews). These Dönmes are descendants of a group touched in the middle of the 17th century by a

View of Üsküdar as seen from the European side

remarkably charismatic leader. **Sabbatai Zebi** (1626-1676), a mystical rabbi, believed that he was the Messiah. With his not inconsiderable gifts he attracted a large following among his fellow Jews. In Persia they refused to till their fields or pay their taxes because they believed that his appearance signaled the end of the world. From Hamburg, Amsterdam and London his followers sent huge sums of money to support his cause. After living

for a while in Jerusalem, he returned to Smyrna in the fall of 1665 where he was greeted with delirious enthusiasm. People expected him to restore Israel to Jerusalem and to announce the millennium in 1666. The public disturbances attracted the attention of the authorities and he was put in prison in Abydos (east of Çanakkale). His confinement in prison did not greatly diminish his appeal. Many people from around the world visited him bringing their business. The business also profited the rest of the Jewish community in Çanakkale which then gained prominence in international commerce. When Zebi was brought before the sultan in 1666 he chose apostasy to Islam rather than martyrdom. The effects on his followers were shame and despair. While most of them reverted to their original faith, a group centered then in Thessaloniki also became Muslim converts and continued to respect his inspiration. Their members have long made quiet but impressive contributions to the intellectual life of Turkey.

YUŞA TEPESİ - GIANT'S HILL,
ANADOLU KAVAĞI - GENOESE CASTLE

Two places of interest because of their long history as religious sites are near the northern end of the Bosphorus on the Asiatic side. **Yuşa Tepesi**, a grave and a mosque high on a hill north of Beykoz, is a place of pilgrimage for Muslims who count it holy and believe that the water from the well in front of the mosque has healing powers. The huge grave (about 18 m long) is reputed to belong to Yuşa, or Joseph, Dede; earlier it was called "the Bed of Hercules." Justinian built the **Church of St. Pantaleimon** here on top of a pre-Christian Temple to Jupiter. The grave itself is thought to date back to the Neolithic Period.

A bit farther north is the fishing village of Anadolu Kavağı, a good place for a seafood meal. The **Genoese Castle** on the hill is the place in legend where Jason built a Temple to Zeus Ourios (Zeus of the Favorable Winds) for helping him find the Golden Fleece. The base of that temple is in the British Museum. The Temple to Zeus was one of twelve here, each dedicated to a god of Olympus. Collectively they were known as The Heiron, or The Holy.

The temples attracted hordes of pilgrims who lavished gifts on them. Darius (? 521-486 BC) is reported to have been one of them; he sat for a while at the Heiron contemplating his accomplishments, perhaps before his defeat at the Battle of Marathon.

Cicero talks about the temple -- could he have been a tourist? King Prusias I held this hill briefly in the 2nd century BC. Around AD 1350 the Genoese strengthened the fortress that was here. Their arms of flowered crosses are emblazoned on the doorways. With its mate on the European side the two fortresses commanded the northern entrance to the strait. The view from the hilltop is as dramatic today as it was for Darius and Cicero.

Passenger ferries are conveniently scheduled so that people who wish to enjoy the good fish dinner offered in the restaurants in Anadolu Kavağı can go and come at the proper times. Those who walk up the hill can also explore a 14th century castle.

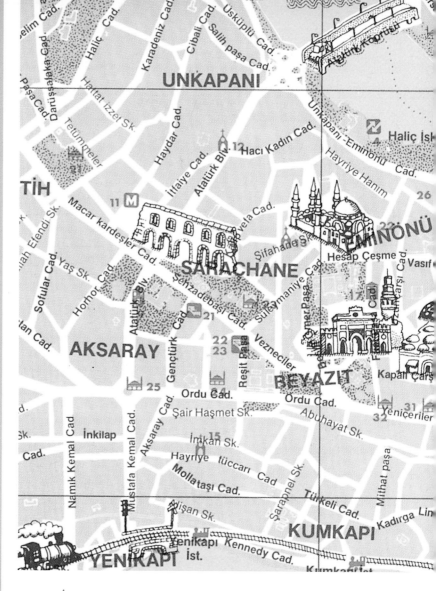

Several meanings are used to explain the name of the Golden Horn, the estuary separating old İstanbul from the newer city. Most obviously, its shape is similar to a cornucopia. Some have said that the Horn is golden because of all the treasures people have thrown into it to keep them from the invading armies. With this in mind, foreign companies have sought permission -- unsuccessfully -- to dredge the bottom and profit by what they find. Others have seen a more poetic meaning in the golden colors of the sunset sky glinting off the waters of the Horn.

İSTANBUL - BYZANTIUM, CONSTANTINOPLE

İstanbul holds an unsurpassed concentration of places of religious interest and importance. From sites touched by mythology, to the world's masterpieces of St. Sophia and the Mosque of Süleyman the Magnificent, to such a simple demonstration as the sign in Ortaköy that celebrates the community of Jews, Christians and Muslims living in harmony together, İstanbul has always been an intermediary. Its residents have been heretical, syncretistic, byzantine, rank and contentious. They have been imperious and expedient, both religiously and politically. Taking all these into consideration, on balance their contributions to Western civilization are incalculable and their city has been a bridge, a go-between, an agent of geography and in human exchange.

Greater İstanbul bridges the continents of Europe and Asia. It includes the old city within its 5th century walls and then in increasingly wider perimeters Karaköy, Beyoğlu, both shores of the Bosphorus, Üsküdar, Kadıköy and beyond taking in the European and Asian shores of the Sea of Marmara and the Princes' Islands. The city is continuing to grow in area and population.

The first written records about the Bosphorus speak of a leader named Byzas and his followers who had come in 667 BC from Megara to occupy the thumb of land, now called the Seraglio Point. Descendants of these Byzantines and later colonists from Rome honored their emperor by changing the city's name to Constantinople in AD 330. From that time on for 1100 years (except for the brief Latin occupation from 1204 to 1261), it was the capital of the Eastern Roman Empire and an exemplar of civilization to the Western world.

"*...though every other city goes through its times of power and then of ruin, only Constantinople appears to have the immortality that will last as long as there are people here.*"

--Pierre Gilles,
The Antiquities of Constantinople, c.1560

Artist's rendering of the plan of Greater İstanbul featuring the Bosphorus

Like many medieval cities, Constantinople was enclosed behind a series of military walls.

Like most late 20th century cities, İstanbul is encircled by an expanding multitude of homes hastily thrown up by the flood of people coming from more rural areas.

Conquered by the Muslim Turkish Sultan Mehmet II in 1453, the city became the capital of the Ottoman Empire, a position it held until the Turkish Republic was proclaimed in 1923 and the capital was moved to Ankara. While its political situation is changed, İstanbul continues to influence the whole country.

Geographically İstanbul is usually divided into four parts for the purpose of describing the historic sites most tourists want to see. These enclose many of the Byzantine and Ottoman monuments. **1)** The old city is the European thumb of land within the 5th century AD walls that circle from the Seraglio Point on the southeast along the Golden Horn, cross the peninsula between Ayvansaray and Yedikule, and return along the Sea of Marmara. **2)** The "new city" lies on the European side of the Bosphorus north of the Golden Horn. **3)** Asiatic Greater İstanbul includes Kadıköy on the Sea of Marmara and stretches north along the Bosphorus. **4)** The Princes' Islands in the Sea of Marmara are also a part of Greater İstanbul.

Seven hills are used by geographers to describe the regions of the old city. The **First Hill** includes the Topkapı Palace, St. Sophia and the Blue Mosque. The **Second Hill** takes in the Covered Bazaar, the Burnt Column and the Nuruosmaniye Camii. The

Third Hill is the land of İstanbul University plus the Süleymaniye Külliyesi (the complex of buildings with the mosque of Süleyman the Magnificent at the center). The **Fourth Hill** is crowned by the Mosque of Fatih Sultan Mehmet II, and the **Fifth Hill** by the Mosque of Selim II. The top of the **Sixth Hill** is at the Edirne Gate of the city walls with the Mihrimah Camii rising prominently there. The **Seventh Hill**, once the place of kitchen gardens, is the least defined, being the slope from Millet Caddesi to the Sea of Marmara. The Haseki Hürrem Külliyesi is here, and at the far western edge the Museum of St. John the Baptist of Studion.

Residences line both sides of the narrow Bosphorus, and ferries ply back and forth between Europe and Asia. This strait is probably the world's busiest international shipping lane. Both the Princes' Islands in the Sea of Marmara and the Black Sea towns north of İstanbul have popular bathing beaches.

Constantine transported so many art objects from Rome to Constantinople that one of his disgruntled senators complained that the only thing he'd left undisturbed was the cemetery.

PAGAN SITES

Remains of pagan sites of worship in the city limits of İstanbul are not commonly identified as such. One of the oldest is the bronze **Serpentine Column** in the Hippodrome that was once in the Temple to Apollo in Delphi. Made from the shields of the fallen Persians, this column commemorated one of the first battles for independence. Names of the Greek states who united to defeat the Persian invaders at the Battle of Plataea in 479 BC are engraved on the base (now hidden in the dirt). There used to be three serpents' heads; the only one left is in the İstanbul Archaeological Museum. The column is only one of many art objects that Constantine the Great took from Rome to embellish his new city, following the tradition of his Roman predecessors who had helped themselves to whatever caught their fancy around their world.

There is the story of a Column of Venus (is it the **Kız Sütunu** in Aksaray?) that had the reputation of embarrassing girls who pretended to be virgins. The column, or maybe censorious Venus, called up a mischievous wind to toss the girls' skirts above their heads if they ventured near. The **Column of the Goths** in Gülhane Park is thought to date about AD 268 or 279, but it was a war memorial to a victory against the Goths, not a religious site. The foundations of St. Irene (in the First Court of Topkapı Palace) are on a Roman Temple to Aphrodite. An old black and white mosaic exposed in the floor of the building may be from that temple.

The Serpentine Column on the left; Obelisk of Theodosius (brought from Egypt) on the right

The **Burnt Column (Çemberlitaş)** was part of Constantine's political maneuvering to please both the pagans and the Christians in his city. He built into the foundation of the column and a small chapel at its base a number of religious items symbolically meaningful at the time to both groups: a wooden figure of Pallas

Athena that Aeneas had carried from Troy to Rome, Noah's ax with which he hewed the timbers of the Ark, the rock that Moses struck in the Wilderness to produce water, and the crumbs gathered after Jesus had fed the five thousand. At the top of the column was a statue of Constantine crowned with the rays of the sun god, while a piece of the True Cross that his mother St. Helena had found in Jerusalem was enclosed in the statue itself. The statue stood until it was toppled during a storm in 1105; the authenticity of the other items is debatable.

Various current *ayazmas* (holy springs) probably have pagan identities. The Roman Catholic **Church of St. George in Galata**, rebuilt after a fire in 1731, is thought to be on the site of the Temple to Aphrodite Pandemos which Bishop Pertinax dedicated to St. Irene in the 4th century AD. Among the people remembered by their tombstones here are the mother and the grandmother of the two brothers Andre de Chénier, the French poet martyred in 1794, and Marie-Joseph de Chénier, the playwright. These men were born in Galata (today's Karaköy).

Long before Sultan Süleyman filled in the **valley of Dolmabahçe**, the south side of the slope was the site of a Temple to Apollo, one of the places along the Bosphorus where Jason stopped to pay his respects. Crusaders charged up the hill here in 1203 in their attack on Constantinople. By some accounts, this was where Mehmet the Conqueror's soldiers began their highway of greased logs over which they dragged their ships one night so they could attack the city on its soft underbelly of the Golden Horn.

The narrow point of the Bosphorus between Rumeli Hisar and Anadolu Hisar is by tradition the place where Darius's engineer Mandrocles led the army of 700,000 men safely across the water in 500 BC. Darius is said to have watched the exercise from a rock throne that had been hewn for him where the **Rumeli Hisar** castle now stands. In the valley behind the castle was one pagan temple, and on the hill was another to Hermes. The village was called Hermaion because of it. Some of the marble from those temples

Rumeli Hisar, the Bosphorus and the Asian side

was worked by Sultan Mehmet the Conqueror and his generals into the castle in 1452, as was a stone cannon ball placed on the south side of the Rose Tower facing Constantinople. The hill is still sacred, now as a cemetery for a few of Mehmet's soldiers who died to conquer the city and for a number of more recent Muslim saints. The castle enclosure has been used as an outdoor theater for summer plays since 1953. Among the plays performed here is Shakespeare's *Macbeth*. Soldiers in their heavy army boots have again dashed along the curtain walls, whooped down through the audience and brandished their branches from a local "Burnham Wood."

CHRISTIAN SITES

For anyone interested in Byzantine church history and church architecture, İstanbul is unequaled as the place to study and appreciate it.

At the end of the First Ecumenical Council[5] in Nicaea (325), Constantine ordered a delegation of bishops to accompany him to the town of Byzantium. This was the place that he had picked for his new capital, after having considered and rejected Alexandria Troas among other locations. Taking a church already in existence, Constantine enlarged it and dedicated his first cathedral to St. Irene (Divine Peace). It remained the city's cathedral until 360 when the first St. Sophia (Divine Wisdom) was dedicated. From then on the two buildings were identified as one Great Church (*Megala Ekklesia* in Greek); they shared much of the same history over the years. St. Irene was the cathedral again from 404 to 414 when St. Sophia had been destroyed. Burned to the ground in the Nika riots in 532, both churches were rebuilt by Justinian. St. Irene suffered damages from fire in 564 and from earthquake in 740.

St. Irene Museum, exterior

The Church of St. Irene was dedicated to Divine Peace. During its first centuries it was the focus of several religious riots. During the Ottoman Empire, as one of the buildings inside the Topkapı Palace walls, it was used as an arsenal.

St. Irene is important in Christian history as the setting of the meetings of the Second Ecumenical Council in 381. Unlike the other Byzantine churches in İstanbul, St. Irene was never converted into a mosque. For years under the Ottoman Empire it was first an arsenal and then a military museum. Now some of the classical music concerts of the yearly İstanbul International Festival are held here. Other than on those evenings, one must apply to the Ministry of Tourism in Ankara for permission to gain entrance to it.

St. Irene is interesting as a church building because it shows a transition in type from a basilica (an oblong building used as a court and having a semicircular apse at one end) to a cruciform church with a central nave flanked by two transepts. In St. Irene, the transepts are defined inside the structure by columns rather than in the exterior outline of the building as in the true cruciform church. A few of the capitals on the columns carry monograms of Justinian and Theodora similar to those in St. Sophia. The apse has the only surviving Byzantine *synthronon* (the tiers of seats for the bishops) in İstanbul.[6] (It makes an excellent riser for a chorus today.) Underneath it is a passage that the bishops could have used to get from one side to the other without crossing in front of the altar.

For both Christians and Muslims, **St. Sophia** is holy ground. The name, St. Sophia, means holy wisdom. When Sultan Mehmet II took the city in 1453 this symbol of profound knowledge and sovereignty became the prime mosque of his capital. Recognizing its historic and universal importance, the Turkish government made it a public museum in 1935.

The museum of St. Sophia (Ayasofya Müzesi) appears to many visitors to be more like an echoing barn than a place of worship. In spite of that, its esthetic proportions, its size, its antiquity and its history have challenged architects, theologians, generals, historians, novelists, artists and politicians to admire, to study and often to covet it. The closer one looks at it, the richer becomes one's appreciation of the building and the people who have added to its history.

In addition to the current protective scaffolding, inside the nave you will notice the expanse of the building, and your eyes will be drawn to the dome which rises 56 meters above the floor. Its diameter is about 32 meters; the irregularity of its circle was caused during the reconstruction when the dome was replaced and heightened after it fell. Four huge piers stand at the corners of the 31 m ^{2} central area and lead up to four arches. Those blend into the graceful pendentives used to solve the architectural problem of balancing a dome on top of a cube. Between the piers, columns of red porphyry and vert antique help support the galleries and the semi-domes. Inscribed in the marble floor you can see small X's that mark the plumb line of each of the ribs of the dome.

St. Sophia's columns are all thought to have come from pagan temples around the Mediterranean. Eight of green serpentine, now under the arches of the nave, may once have stood in the Temple to Diana in Ephesus. Eight more of red Egyptian porphyry on the sides of the nave are supposed to have been in the Temple to the Sun in Baalbek.

The six large disks with the names of God, of Muhammad, and of the first caliphs and imams punctuate the angles of the domes. These were installed in the mid-19th century by the architect Fossati who was charged by Sultan Abdülmecid with restoring the building. (Another account dates them to the work of a certain calligrapher İbrahim in 1650.) The patterns in the marbles of the revetment were made as the blocks were sliced and then placed side by side. Many sightseers entertain themselves imagining faces and animals in these patterns.

If you have been impressed by the size of the nave from the ground, you may be even more amazed at the size and the height of the dome as you look at them from the galleries. Take a minute as you reach the north gallery to look down its length and see in the elliptical arches startling evidence of the speed with which the building was constructed. The arches lean outwards showing the plastic quality of the cement when the heavy dome was added.

Some of the graffiti in the balcony make footnotes to Byzantine history. Scratchings on one of the north walls show the outline of a sailing ship. They hint at a long, boring service. On the balustrade of the south balcony are Nordic runes cut there perhaps by a 9th or 10th century Viking who served in the emperor's army. The east wall of the balcony is decorated by rather crude mosaic portraits of several royal figures. Two of them represent the Empress Zoe (1028–?1054) and her husband. Her husband's face was changed from her first, Romanus III (whose death she arranged), to her second,

St. Sophia, interior

Michael IV (whose nephew deposed and exiled her and whom she subsequently blinded), to her third, Constantine IX (who outlived her).[7]

The finest of all the mosaics is in the south gallery. An early 14th century work, it is called the Deisis, a common Byzantine grouping with Christ, flanked by Mary and John the Baptist on either side. Even as a fragment this is a masterpiece of the artistic expression of pathos and compassion.

St. Sophia as seen from the sea

In its day the monastery of **St. John the Baptist of Studius** (near Yedi Kule — the Seven Towers) was a mighty force in the Byzantine Empire. Its abbots ranked next in importance to the bishops of the Eastern Orthodox Church; its scholars were renowned as Byzantine historians. The church of the monastery was founded by the patrician Studius (for whom it is named) in 463. Basilical in shape, the aisles of the nave are marked by columns with Corinthian capitals; the mosaic pattern of the floor is largely intact.

The discipline associated with the monastery of the Studion was severe. Those who had not been received into the fellowship or who were under some punishment were not allowed into the nave; those attending church who were infidels were relegated to the galleries. But the monks themselves were subject to even stricter measures. Each week they had to shed their clothing in a central heap and then reclaim by chance whatever piece was at hand, regardless of its size. Any monk caught moping or bewailing his fate was set to intoning 500 *Kyrie eleisons* and performing 150 genuflections a day. Any monk who greeted his mother with a kiss was excommunicated for 50 days. If a copyist made a mistake in his work he was reduced to a meal of dry bread. (The other monks considered fried vegetables once a day to be a feast.) The monastery was the home of several great Byzantine hymn writers. It was also the home at the end of the 8th century of Abbot Theodore, the prelate who not only fought to preserve iconography but also had the courage to denounce the immorality of the court. He was beaten, blinded and banished by the emperor, but continued to be the voice of conscience of the monastery until his death in 826.

After 1453 the Studion continued briefly as a Christian institution; however, by the end of the 15th century it had been closed and the church had been converted into a mosque known as İmrahor Camii. The mosque was so damaged by an earthquake in 1894 that it was abandoned. Now in ruins, it is the oldest Christian building standing in İstanbul and is protected as a museum.

In the 11th century three emperors sought refuge in the Studion. Michael V tried to flee from an enraged mob only to be torn off the altar and blinded. Isaac I Comnenus believed himself mortally ill and no longer able to rule. He and his wife were quietly buried here. Michael VII, called the Starver for having made wheat so expensive people couldn't buy it, was forced into exile because of his disastrous economic policies.

The new Patriarchal House of the Greek Orthodox Patriarchate in İstanbul (above) and its main entrance (below)

The **Church of St. Sergius and St. Bacchus (Küçük Ayasofya Camii)** was built by Justinian and Theodora in 527 before they rebuilt St. Sophia. It is interesting to architects for its ribbed dome, for the capitals that have the monogram of the founders, and for the difference in the axes of the rectangular outer wall and the inner octagon. Its ceiling is interesting as a precursor to St. Sophia where pendentives were used successfully to bridge from the rectangular base to the circular dome.

Justinian intended the building as thanks to the two saints who appeared in a dream to the Emperor Anastasius and interceded to save his life. The building later saved the life of Pope Vigilius who had angered Justinian. Justinian had summoned Vigilius from Rome to his palace to settle a dispute over the nature of Christ. Vigilius refused, partly on theological grounds, partly knowing that the dispute was over supremacy in church authority, Rome or Constantinople. He fled from the palace barely ahead of Justinian's soldiers, made it to the church, and grabbed the altar railing. The soldiers stormed in and tugged at him until the railing came crashing down on all of them. Justinian finally granted him his life, but kept him prisoner for seven years. The Roman church was not as pardoning, and the conflict over power added to the rift between the Orthodox and the Catholic churches.

Frescoes originally on the walls of a side chapel of the **Church of the Kyriotissa (Kalenderhane Camii)** depict the life of St. Francis of Assisi. These were painted about 1250, twenty-five years after St. Francis's death, by Franciscan missionaries.[8] The monks had made use of the Latin occupation of Constantinople (1204-1261) to establish their order; they have been active here ever since. Their paintings predate the work of Giotto in Assisi by almost fifty years. These have been removed from the chapel and may now to be seen in the İstanbul Archaeological Museum.

The **Church of St. Mary of the Mongols** (c. 1261) is the only church that has belonged to the Greek Orthodox community since before the Conquest. The woman who reputedly founded it was the widow of Hulagu, the Mongol khan. When he died, his widow became a nun in the convent associated with this church. There is an 11th century portable mosaic called the Theotokos Pammakaristos displayed in the building.

Theodore Metochites, to whom we owe thanks for the art of Kariye Camii, was considered to be a mediocre poet, an unscrupulous public servant, and an insufferable bore. All that is insignificant in relation to the masterpieces that he funded.

The **Church of St. Savior in Chora (Kariye Camii)** is located close to the city walls at Edirne Kapı. The mosaics and frescoes for which it is famous were designed and executed between 1315 and 1321. The man who commissioned them, Theodore Metochites, is pictured in the lunette over the door into the nave. His soaring hat indicated his position as chief minister of state. The theological themes which follow through all of the decorations are those of Christ as the Land of the Living and those of the Blessed Virgin as the Home of the Uncontainable. The mosaics in the inner narthex picture the life of the Blessed Virgin; those in the outer narthex are of Christ and his ministry. The frescoes in the side chapel, the mortuary chapel, represent the Last Judgment, Heaven and Hell and the Resurrection.

Part of the artistry of the mosaics and the frescoes of Kariye Camii lies in the human details: The serving maid who prepares the bath for the baby Anne (Mary's mother) tests the water to be sure it is the right temperature. The faces of the girls who had competed with the Virgin Mary for yarn to weave the purple temple veil show jealousy and scorn. As Joseph leads Mary home from the temple he has turned around to be sure she is following, and her skirts flap around her legs as she hurries to keep up. One of the souls being conducted to hell by the devil turns wistfully to look back while another is politely offering for his friend to go first. The expression in the face of Jesus as he stands in judgment is one of patient suffering and infinite care for the whole of creation.

The **Church of the Virgin Pammakaristos (Fethiye Camii)** is partly an 11th and partly an early 14th century building. Between 1456 and about 1590 it was the patriarchal church of the Greek Orthodox community. Under Sultan Murat III it became a mosque, and the Patriarchate moved to its present location in Fener. The side chapel of the church (open with special permission from Ayasofya) contains mosaics equal in artistry to those in Kariye Camii.

The **Greek Orthodox Patriarchate** moved to Fener in 1601 and dedicated the newly restored **Church of St. George** at that time. The church was rebuilt in 1720. A relatively small building, it houses relics that have been treasured for centuries. There is the coffin of St. Euphemia whose church in Kadıköy was the location of the Fourth Ecumenical Council, and an 11th century portable mosaic icon similar to the one in St. Mary of the Mongols. On the right hand side of the church is the ivory-inlaid throne of the patriarch, thought by some to have been the throne of the 4th century St. John Chrysostom in St. Sophia (though more probably it is a 14th century work). The Ecumenical Patriarch who resides here is His All Holiness, the first among equals of the Greek Orthodox ecclesiastical community. At Easter many pilgrims gather in the church and its courtyard to take part in the midnight service which he leads, and to greet each other with the words, "Christ is risen; he is risen indeed."

Zoodochus Pege, (Balıklı Kilise, the Church of the Fishes**)** in Silivrikapı, has been the place of burial for the Greek Orthodox patriarchs for generations. During Byzantine times the emperors and their court came here to the sacred spring for relaxation. Then in 1453, according to the legend, a priest of the church exclaimed that he believed it as impossible for the city to be

Fearless and incorruptible, St. John Chrysostom (the golden-tongued) dared to criticize the licentiousness of the empress Eudoxia and her court. Trumped-up charges accused him of treason and he was exiled to Anatolia. His sermons are still studied for their picture of the time and for their grace and eloquence.

The Kariye Museum, exterior

Over 100 Christian churches representing many different sects are scattered around the city. On Sunday their bells ring out calling the congregations to worship.

captured as it was for the fish he was frying to jump out of the pan. Gold fish now swimming in the pool of the spring are reputed to be direct descendants of those half-cooked fish that escaped from the priest's frying pan. The spring did not stop flowing, but under the Ottoman rule the buildings around it went to ruin until early in the 19th century the sultan ordered the church restored. The paving of the courtyard is gravestones that are marked with pictures of their owner's occupation (a tailor's scissors and a measuring tape, for instance) and are inscribed with the Karamanlı script, the Greek alphabet adapted to write Turkish words.

Among other buildings in İstanbul that are interesting because they were Byzantine churches are the following, listed by date. They were converted into mosques after the conquest.

Monastery of Constantine Lips (Feneri İsa Camii), AD 907,1259-1282
Church of the Myrelaion (Bodrum Camii), ? late 10th century
St. Theodosia (Gül Camii) ? late 10th century
Church of St. Theodore (Kilise Camii), ? 10th - 12th century
St. Savior Pantepoptes (Eski İmaret Camii), c. 1085-1090
Church of the Pantocrator (Zeyrek Camii), c. 1120
St. Andrew in Krisei (Koca Mustafa Paşa Camii), c. 1284

Frescoes in the side chapel of the Kariye Museum

A most unusual building is that of **St. Stephen** located on the Golden Horn and belonging to the Bulgarian Orthodox community. This is a Gothic-type structure built in 1871 entirely of cast iron. All the decorations, including the apparent marble revetment on the inside are iron. The story is that the sultan gave permission to the community to build their church if they could complete it within one week. The pieces were cast in Vienna, floated down the Danube and assembled here, obviously in record time. A double was cast and built in Vienna, but it did not survive the bombing of World War II.

In the 15th century the **Armenian Orthodox Patriarchate** was in the **Church of Surp Kevork (Sulu Manastır)** in Samatya. Sultan Mehmet II recognized its Patriarch as the head of a separate *millet* in one of his acts shortly after he conquered the city. The building had been built in 1031 by the Emperor Romanus III, the aged senator who married his predecessor's daughter Zoe (see St. Sophia, p. 96). He was buried here as was a later, also aged, Emperor Nicephorus III whose accession to the Byzantine throne was gained with the help of the Selçuk Turks. Surp Kevork served as the patriarchal church until 1641.

Today the Armenian Orthodox Patriarchate is in Kumkapı; the church is called **Surp Astvadzadzin (the Holy Mother of God)**, built originally in 1645 and replaced by the present one in 1913.

This is the building in which each new patriarch is enthroned, attended by prelates from other Armenian sees, and from other churches such as the Coptic Orthodox and Syrian Orthodox that are held in communion with the Armenian Orthodox church.

Another ancient Armenian church is located in Balat on the Golden Horn. This is the **Church of Surp Resdagabet**. An 18th century building, the property has belonged to the Armenian community since the 17th century. The cathedral church of the Latin (Roman) Catholic community is **St. Esprit** in Elmadağı. It is a 19th century building, having been built in 1846 and become the cathedral in 1876. During World War II the Papal Nuncio here was Angelo Guissepe Roncalli who became Pope John XXIII in 1958. Several other Catholic churches have interesting details: **St. Benedict** in Karaköy was dedicated in 1427. When Sultan Süleyman made moves to convert it into a mosque, King Francis I of France intervened and gained for it the status of the French ambassadors' chapel. Suffering from the fires that repeatedly devastated Karaköy, the Grand Mufti in the 17th century granted it the right, previously permitted only to mosques, to have a lead roof. The keep over the bell has survived from the 15th century, as has the pillared entrance off the main Kemeraltı street. The rest is 18th or 19th century reconstruction.

Not all of the places of Christian worship in İstanbul are buildings that pre-date the 17th century. The **Syrian Orthodox** community dedicated its new **Church of St. Mary** in Tarlabaşı, built of stone from Tur Abdin, in 1963. **St. Mary Draperis** on İstiklâl Caddesi is an 18th century church. Among its possessions is an icon of the Virgin Mary. **St. Louis** within the grounds of the French legation dates from 1831; it is served by Franciscan fathers who preserve the tradition of the monks who painted the frescoes of St. Francis in the Church of the Kyriotissa in 1250. **St. Antoine**, also on İstiklâl Caddesi, is the largest of the Catholic churches in the city. It was built in 1913.

Services are held regularly for the Anglican community in **Christ Church**, dedicated in 1868 in memory of the men who had served in the Crimean War. The Union Church of İstanbul, a nondenominational Protestant community, meets in the **Dutch Chapel**, a building of stone walls thick enough to withstand the Galata fires. It is dated about 1705; it served both as the ambassador's private chapel and, in its basement, as a prison for Dutch citizens. The hoops in the walls to which the prisoners were chained were removed about 1962.

In all, over a hundred churches, Catholic, Orthodox, Protestant, serving many different language communities, have active congregations in İstanbul.

Pope Paul VI conducted mass in St. Esprit in 1967 after he and Patriarch Athenagoras mutually annulled the 11th century anathema (formal ecclesiastic curse) against their churches. Pope John Paul II also conducted mass here in 1979.

One of the most outstanding mosaics of Kariye depicting the assumption of the Virgin Mary

St. Antoine Church

MUSLIM SITES

Evliya Çelebi says that Eyüp's grave was identified with an inscription on a square stone of vert antique, and that when it was opened the body was found wrapped in a saffron-colored shroud.

The earliest Muslim presence in İstanbul is evidenced in the grave of **Eyüp al-Ansari**, a companion of the Prophet Muhammad, entrusted by him to be his standard bearer in battle. He had welcomed Muhammad on his flight from Mecca to Medina; in honor of that the Prophet's tomb was built on the site of Eyüp al-Ansari's house in Medina.

Eyüp al-Ansari (also known as Eyüp Sultan) and his army attacked Constantinople hoping to fulfill the prophecy of the Prophet that one of his followers would conquer Constantinople. He died during the siege (674-678) and was buried just outside the walls. According to the 17th century writer Evliya Çelebi, that grave was found at the time that Sultan Mehmet II was besieging the city in 1453. In respect to his predecessor Mehmet built a mosque in 1458 beside the grave in the village now named for Eyüp on the Golden Horn. Thus the mosque is the most holy in İstanbul for Muslims and one of their most holy anywhere in the world. The present building dates from 1800, the first having suffered from time and earthquakes. During the years of the Ottoman Empire the new ruler came to Eyüp soon after he was proclaimed sultan. Here he was girded with the Sword of Osman in a ceremony similar to the crowning of a king. (Osman was the first sultan of the Ottoman dynasty.)

The **Eyüp Camii** has a different atmosphere than that of the other mosques of the city. It is quieter and more reserved. Many of the worshippers have come here from some distance. The courtyards are shaded by plane trees where hundreds of pigeons and smaller birds perch. Occasionally a stork winters over here, fed on grain and *simits* (sesame rolls) by the admiring visitors. The walls of the inner courtyard are covered with patterned tiles, while in the center is a large ablution fountain. The mosque plan is an octagon inside a rectangle. The walls are a white stone; they and the windows give the interior an airy feeling.

The *türbe* (mausoleum) of Eyüp Sultan is lined with blue and white tiles. The sarcophagus is protected by a silver screen that

People making wishes at the Eyüp Sultan Mosque

was made by Sultan Selim III. Many others presented gifts to the türbe and mosque including Sultan Mahmut II who worked the embroidery on the covering of the sarcophagus and Adnan Menderes, prime minister from 1950 to 1960 who gave the green carpet.

On the first Fridays of the months of the Arabic calendar, people who had special prayers would give some small bit of their clothing to the muezzin (the man who gives the call to prayer). He would display these from the balcony of the minaret while he was giving the call to prayer. When he descended he would return the bits to their owners. Also during the call to prayer people whose business was not going well and young girls who were engaged would turn on the water faucets on the four corners of the iron fence around the large plane tree in the inner courtyard and leave the water running. Those behind them would turn the water off and then turn it on again.

Whirling Dervishes in the Galata Mevlevihanesi in İstanbul

The area around the mosque is considered holy ground; many people have wanted to be buried within the hearing of the call to prayer from its minarets. Among those buried in the cemetery which stretches up the hill beyond the mosque are the Grand Vizier Sokollu Mehmet Paşa (he commissioned the bridge over the Drina at his home in Visegrad, a scene of recent fighting in the former Yugoslavia[9]), Melek Ahmet Paşa (husband of Sultan Murat IV's daughter Kaya Sultan) and a number of Grand Muftis. Of the sultans, only Mehmet V, who died in 1918, is here, but several of the sultan's wives are, including Mahfiruze Sultan, the mother of Sultan Osman II.

An additional interest in the area of Eyüp, the **Piyerloti Çayevi** on the hill above the mosque affords a good view of the city to the east. An attractive place in which to relish a cup of Turkish coffee or tea, this is where the 19th century novelist Pierre Loti enjoyed his *keyif* (pleasure in life) and perhaps found inspiration for *Aziyade* and *Les Désenchantées*.

Loti's career as a naval officer took him to many parts of the world. A romantic, he was a master of description, but his style palls now for readers expecting more action and less musing.

Arap Camii in Karaköy has been a mosque since the 15th century, although one legend assigns it an earlier date of 715. That legend gains credence in the fact that the Muslims had more than one mosque in Constantinople before the conquest. The present building dates from 1327 when the Dominicans built it and the square belfry (now the minaret). At that time it was dedicated to St. Paul. It is a plain, long, narrow building. It was converted to a mosque before 1481. When it underwent a restoration between 1913 and 1919 a number of the Christian tombstones with their armorial bearings were uncovered beneath the paving and removed to the İstanbul Archaeological Museum. In spite of its use

Artist's rendering of Mimar Sinan's portrait

Reputed to be the daughter of a Russian priest, Roxelana was presented as a slave to the sultan. Süleyman fell in love with her at once, and she replaced his first concubine in his affections. A fight between the rivals ensued, and while Roxelana lost the fight, the first woman lost her residence in the harem. The jealousy continued until Roxelana secured the succession of one of her sons to the throne.

as a mosque and the many conflagrations in Karaköy, it retains much of its original character.

Another old site on the north side of the Golden Horn just south of the beginning of İstiklâl Caddesi is the **Museum of the Mevlevi (Whirling) Dervishes**. This is the **Divan Edebiyatı Müzesi (Museum of Ottoman Palace Literature)**. Musical instruments and manuscripts related to these dervishes can be seen here, and during the summer İstanbul International Festival there are performances of the dervish service. A public *sema* (religious service) is performed here every last Sunday each month, accompanied by the Sufi music.

Over three hundred buildings — religious, commercial, public, private — were built in İstanbul by **Mimar Sinan**, the Chief Court Architect from 1538 to 1588.[10] Sinan was a Christian conscripted into Sultan Selim I's janissary army sometime before 1520 when Selim died. Recorded as the son of Abdülmennan, he was taken from his village of Ağırnas (now called Mimarsinan) a short distance east of Kayseri. As one of the *devşirme* (conscript), and as the slave of the sultan, he was taught Turkish, military arts, arithmetic, statesmanship, Islamic law and religion. The janissary training was difficult; it was strict. But everyone knew that each slave had the possibility of rising to a position of power: governor, general, admiral, vizier. Each slave was also taught a trade; Sinan's was carpentry.

The early 16th century was a time when the Ottoman Empire was expanding. Many soldiers were needed, and Sinan rose quickly through the ranks. As in all armies, the corps of engineers was called on frequently to build roads, bridges, canals, and fortresses. Sinan must have sawed a lot of lumber, pounded hundreds of nails, and hit his thumb more than once during those years. A story credits him with helping build the ships that carried the Ottoman cannons across Lake Van during the Two Iraqs campaign in 1534. Another says that he was in charge of building a bridge across the River Prut. His work attracted the attention of Sultan Süleyman who awarded him the position of Chief Court Architect. From then on, for fifty years Sinan's genius had free scope to express in architectural terms the grandeur and majesty of the empire that Süleyman and his son, Selim II, ruled.

Sinan's first commission in İstanbul was the **Haseki Hürrem Sultan complex** between Millet and Haseki Caddeleri which he built for Süleyman's wife Roxelana (Hürrem Sultan). It included a mosque, a hospital, a primary school, a public kitchen and a *medrese*. It is the third largest such complex in the city. Although the mosque seems squeezed because of the limits of the property and the encroaching buildings, the medrese and the hospital show

Sinan's developing skills. Columns in the medrese have the detail of carved snakes, perhaps referring to Asclepius and Galen. Some have thought that because the hospital was founded by a woman it was intended originally for women; it now is a general hospital.

Shortly after the Haseki Hürrem complex was finished, Süleyman's oldest son Mehmet died of smallpox. Grieving for the one he had chosen to succeed him, Süleyman ordered Sinan to build a suitable memorial. This is the **Şehzade complex** which Sinan considered the work completing his apprenticeship, and which the court found a resounding success. Part of that success was that Sinan had made both the inner and the outer shape of the mosque meaningful and pleasing. While the walls are plain except for the windows, Sinan decorated the minarets with carving on the lower shafts. A number of the members of the royal family are buried here in the courtyard in addition to Mehmet. They include his crippled brother Cihangir, his brother-in-law Rüstem Paşa (who married Süleyman's daughter Mihrimah), his daughter Humaşah Sultan and his granddaughter Fatma Sultan.

The mosque Sinan built for **Rüstem Paşa** in İstanbul is in a crowded market section not far from the Spice Bazaar. To enter it one must duck into a dingy flight of stairs that leads to the upper level courtyard. Structurally and economically, it is supported by the many shops on the street. The whole setting is in keeping with its founder's personality. Rüstem Paşa was parsimonious. When his father came to İstanbul, he let him beg in the streets rather than help him. He sold anything that might bring income to the palace including the vegetables and fruit from the palace yard. However, the mosque itself is a gem. While the design is simple, its fame is in the 16th century ceramic tiles fired in the İznik kilns. Carnations, hyacinths, pomegranates, artichokes, roses, snails and tulips everywhere make a heavenly garden on all the walls.

Sinan's masterpiece in İstanbul is the **complex of Sultan Süleyman, the Süleymaniye**. Built in seven years from 1550 to 1557[11], the mosque continues to represent in architecture the elegance, the power and the mastery of Sinan, of Süleyman and of Islam. Here the balance of mass, line and height culminate in the architect's inspired interpretation of a place of Muslim worship.

The Süleymaniye Mosque, one of the masterpieces constructed by Architect Sinan

Sultan Ahmet I grew up under the shadow of an older brother Mahmut who he expected would execute him the minute he inherited the throne. Mahmut, however, was implicated in a plot to overthrow his father Sultan Mehmet III, and therefore was executed himself. Ahmet was given less than a year to reassess his fortunes before Sultan Mehmet died and he came to power. He was barely 14 years old.

Everything about Süleyman's mosque is majestic. The courtyard, punctuated by the four graceful minarets and the marble fountain, and the main door lead into the immense main room. An arabesque of lamps hangs overhead, colossal columns support the towering dome, a rug patterned with places marked for worshippers stretches out to the distant mihrap. Quiet grandeur and reverence and awe are almost palpable.

Sinan labored in the building of the mosque himself. More than once when Süleyman came to inspect he found his architect out of reach on the scaffold above him. A story goes that Süleyman was so impatient to have his mosque finished that he kept pressing Sinan for a date. At last Sinan gave in, quoting a day that seemed to Süleyman too good to be true. Sinan then scurried around hiring everyone he could find, gypsies and nomads included. At the dedication, right at the promised time, Süleyman gave Sinan the key with the recognition that he had earned the right to enter first.

Sinan died in 1588, the Grand Old Man whose influence dominated Ottoman architecture for another century. Much of the skyline of İstanbul today is defined by his work and that of his protégés. Considered in his time to be the master of the Masters, his tomb is in the shadow of the Süleymaniye, a building that belongs as much to him as to his sultan.

The architect of the **Blue Mosque (Sultanahmet Camii)**, Sedefkâr Mehmet Ağa, was one of Sinan's students. Built for Sultan Ahmet I between 1609 and 1617, and located close to Topkapı Palace, it is the most popular for many people. In silhouette the domes and six minarets of the Blue Mosque stand out on the Seraglio Point as the focus of the city. The marble-lined courtyard is almost the same size as the interior; a covered portico runs almost unbroken around all four sides. In the interior of the mosque one's attention is drawn to the elephantine piers that support the dome, the low, clear windows that flank the east side, and the pervasive color of the tiles and the frescoes which gives the

The six minarets of the Blue Mosque

mosque its English name, "the Blue Mosque." Sultan Ahmet was less interested in his empire being known for its military gains than in its dedication to Islam, a stance, coupled with his attachment to his harem, that made him unpopular with his viziers. He was so eager for his mosque to be completed that he often became one of the workmen and was there on Fridays to hand out the pay himself. Perhaps he was wiser than he knew: he died of typhus the year after his mosque was dedicated.

Sultan Ahmet started the custom of illuminating the night sky with lights hung between the minarets of the Blue Mosque so as to form words. Called *mahya*, in his time the lights were oil lamps suspended in order to trace the words from a wire stretched across the distance. The trick was not only to carry all the equipment up the dark minaret stairs and out onto the balcony, but also — often in a wind and driving rain — to light and arrange the lamps quickly enough that the first one would not have burned out before the last one was in place every night. Today the greetings such as "Welcome Ramazan" are written in electric lights, and the muezzin has only to flick a switch.

During the Ottoman period when the sultan was the caliph, the religious head of all the Sunni Muslim community, a camel caravan started from the Blue Mosque each year on the 12th of the Muslim month of Recep, two months before the month of Ramazan. It carried the sultan's gift of the new covering of the Kaaba in Mecca.

Several frequently-visited later mosques show the influence of baroque architecture. **Nuruosmaniye Camii** (the name in English means "the light of the Ottomans") near the entrance to the Covered Market was built in 1755. **Nusretiye Camii**, named by Sultan Mahmut II to celebrate his victory over the janissaries in 1826 was built by the Armenian architect Kirkor Balyan. (Another member of the Balyan family built the Palace of Dolmabahçe.) A third mosque of this period is **Lâleli Cami**, dated between 1759 and 1763. Its name refers to the tulips (*lâle*) which were a craze in the early 18th century.

Yeni Cami (the New Mosque) in Eminönü was commissioned in 1597 by Sultan Ahmet's grandmother, Safiye Sultan. (Safiye Sultan was a Venetian; her father was governor of the island of Corfu when she was kidnapped and sent to become the favorite of Sultan Murat III.) The first architect of Yeni Cami was Davut Ağa, another of Sinan's protégés. Davut Ağa had hardly started the work before he was executed for heresy.

The second architect of Yeni Cami was Dalgıç Ahmet Ağa. His sobriquet of *dalgıç* (the diver) recognized the contribution he made to one of the main problems of the building: In the late 16th century the region of Yeni Cami was a swampy slum where Karait Jews (a non-orthodox community) lived. The Jews were moved to

The Byzantine emperor Constantine XI Dragases tried to stave off the Turkish conquest by getting help from the West. He even agreed to a union between the Greek Orthodox and the Roman Catholic churches. Catholic mass was celebrated in St. Sophia on December 12, 1452, but the union was rejected by the people who cried that they preferred the Muslim turban to the pope's tiara.

Hasköy up the Golden Horn, but the swamp continued to interfere with the work on the mosque. Dalgıç Ahmet Ağa solved this by building stone piers reinforced with iron in a series of bridges on which the mosque still sits. The founder Safiye Sultan died in 1605, the construction was stopped, and the Jews moved back. In 1660 Turhan Hatice Sultan, the mother of Sultan Ahmet's grandson Sultan Mehmet IV, took up the project and saw it to completion in 1663. In order for her to be able to keep a close eye on it, the first part finished was the long, separate ramp and her royal pavilion on the southeast side of the building. Grimy now from the heavy air pollution, Yeni Cami and its dependencies transformed the area. It came to be known as much for the mosque as for the customs security office located there. That office was called in Turkish the *gümrük emini*; the square in front of (*ön* in Turkish) the office continues the designation of "in front of the security": *Eminönü*. There are over 400 mosques in İstanbul, all of them under the General Directorate of Pious Foundations (Vakıflar Genel Müdürlüğü).

Topkapı Sarayı (the Palace of Topkapı), was begun by **Sultan Mehmet II** in 1459. (He reigned from 1451 to 1481.) This was the time in Europe when France and England were recovering from the Hundred Years War (1337-1453), when Gutenberg invented the printing press (the first dated paper was issued by the Pope against the Turks in 1451), when the importance of a united loyalty to the Holy Roman Empire was giving way to the nation states, and when the Italian Renaissance was at its height.

In a way, Mehmet was a Renaissance man himself. He was a scholar and a humanist, encouraging scientific studies, endowing many benevolent and educational institutions including İstanbul University, and through a socio-political arrangement called the *millet* (religious nationality) system giving legal standing to the disparate communities of his empire. With the stability that dates from his reign, came the economic and cultural developments of the 16th century.

When Mehmet's father Sultan Murat II died in 1451, Mehmet was a youth of 19. He had one burning primary goal, which he couched in religious terms, to conquer the capital of the Christian Eastern Roman Empire, Constantinople, for the glory and the authority of the Muslim Ottoman Empire. This had been attempted many times before by wiser and more seasoned generals than he, and he had among his closest advisers men who told him in public many times that he could not be successful.

Having carefully studied the city's defenses, Mehmet realized that he would need some extraordinary offensive tactics. Among those that he used, three are referred to over and over in both contemporary and later descriptions of the siege. The first was the fortress he built at Rumeli Hisar on the Bosphorus that helped him control access to the city from the sea. The second was the huge cannon, cast by the Hungarian Urban, that could hurl 540 kg balls a distance of 2 km. Using it and other smaller cannons, Mehmet kept up a bombardment of the walls for over 50 days. But the third and most unexpected tactic was the transport of his naval fleet over an oiled corduroy that stretched from the Bosphorus up and across the Galata hill and down into the Golden Horn. This move outflanked the Byzantines who had thought their iron chain at the mouth of the Horn to be insuperable. Besides the military advantages these tactics gave him, they also contributed to the psychological warfare against the defenders.

The main battle began in the early morning of Tuesday, May 29, 1453. Before evening Mehmet's soldiers had planted the Turkish flag on the walls and swarmed into the city, the last Byzantine emperor had died, and Mehmet had ridden through the streets as Conqueror.

For the Turks (and for their Muslim coreligionists) the conquest of Constantinople gave them a majesty and a prestige that confirmed them as a world power. Having now united the Ottoman holding in Anatolia and Europe, Mehmet was quick to use his power to extend his empire from the Danube to the Euphrates.

A poet (he wrote an entire collection -- *divan* -- of about 900 poems), a man of tolerance (he enabled the Greek Orthodox and the Armenian Orthodox communities to continue the practice of their religions) and artistic interests (he protected the Christian mosaics of St. Sophia with a cover of whitewash and he commissioned the Italian Gentile Bellini to paint his portrait), still his more salient characteristics are those of a vigorous, decisive *gazi* (warior), fighting on behalf of Islam for his empire, alert to his time, to the dangers, the challenges and the pleasures of the empire he had founded.

The **Palace of Topkapı** was the residence of the sultans until the 19th century. It includes in its multiplicity of displays one building set aside for some of the most treasured of all Muslim mementos associated with the Prophet Muhammad. The Pavilion of the Holy Mantle **(Hırka-i Saadet)** is on the northwest side of the Third

Sultan Mehmet the Conqueror after Gentile Bellini's portrait

Mehmet built Topkapı -- which was called "the New Palace" -- to be his administrative center. His residence was in another palace (since lost) on what is now the gounds of İstanbul University.

The Pavillion of the Holy Mantle, (above), the Tower of Harem, Topkapı Palace Museum (below)

Court, opposite the rooms devoted to the treasury. The supranational religious and historic significance of the relics has been recognized by the Turkish government in making the pavilion open to the general public.

These Muslim relics include the swords belonging to the Caliphs Abu Bekir, Ali, Omar and Othman. There are the large wooden gutters from the Kaaba, one of the doors, and a gold shield that once covered the black meteorite of the Kaaba. In another room items that are more personally connected with Muhammad include hairs from his beard, one of his teeth, and his seal. Protected by glass and grillwork are the most holy of the relics, his sword (embellished by Sultan Ahmet I), the flag which his standard-bearer Eyüp carried for him into battle, and his cloak or Holy Mantle which he gave to Kaab bin Züheyr, a follower who wrote a poem eulogizing him. The sultans continued to carry this Holy Standard into battle into the 17th century. The Holy Mantle was unwrapped and displayed to the sultan's family and the high officials once a year on the 15th of Ramazan. (Even the cloths that had been used to clean it were considered sacred souvenirs.) These items came into the possession of the sultans in several ways: the hairs of the Prophet, the keys of Mecca and Medina, the sword of the Caliph Omar and the Holy Mantle were brought from Cairo by Sultan Selim I. Some other pieces were gifts. The Holy Standard was taken by the janissaries in their capture of Damascus in 1595.

Three museum buildings are clustered close below the Harem in the Fifth, or outer, Court of the Topkapı Palace. These are the İstanbul Archaeological Museum, the Museum of the Ancient Orient and the Tiled Kiosk. The **Tiled Kiosk (Çinili Köşk)** was built as a pavilion by Sultan Mehmet II the Conqueror in 1472; it is the oldest standing secular Ottoman building in İstanbul. Its name comes from the mosaic faience on the walls both inside and out. Ceramic ware representing all the periods of the Ottoman Empire is displayed here.

The largest of the museum buildings, the **Archaeological Museum**, contains among its treasures the 4th century BC **Alexander sarcophagus**. This marble sarcophagus is covered with high reliefs representing scenes from the life of Alexander the Great. They include a leopard hunt and perhaps the Battle of Issus (333 BC). It was found in Sidon in 1887 by Hamdi Bey, the first director of the museum. Another treasure is the gold Schliemann found in **Troy** and gave to the Turkish authorities.

Three items of religious interest, particularly in Jewish history, in the Archaeological Museum have come from Palestine: The smallest is a piece of stone carved with the oldest known Hebrew writing. This was found by chance in the excavation at **Gezer**; apparently it is a child's lesson about the seasons: One month was for harvesting flax (March?), one for summer fruit (July). Its date is the 10th century BC. Next in size is the inscription from the **Siloam** tunnel in Jerusalem. King Hezekiah made this tunnel in order to connect the spring water of Gihon with the Pool of Siloam (2 Chron. 32:2-4; Isa. 22:8-11; 2 Kings 20:20). His intent was to supply the residents with water throughout the siege that he expected during the attack on the city by Sennacherib (701 BC). The inscription records the excitement of the men tunneling from the two directions through the bedrock and finally hearing the blows of each other's axes. The third and largest stone is one of many that were set around the outside of the **Temple in Jerusalem** to mark the limit beyond which no non-Jew was permitted to approach the holy ground. Its inscription is in Greek rather than Hebrew so that no Gentile could plead that he did not understand the prohibition.

Opened first in 1896, the Archaeological Museum recently has acquired several new wings and modernized many of its displays, including one especially for children.

The Alexander sarcophagus

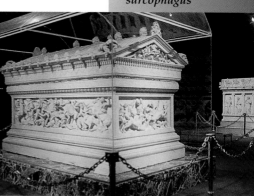

One of the newest additions to this museum is the collection of **frescoes** from the Church of the Theotokas Kyriotissa (Kalenderhane Camii, see p.98). The frescoes were painted during the years the Latins occupied Constantinople (1204-1261) to illustrate the life of St. Francis of Assisi. Thus they predate the work of Giotto.

The **Museum of the Ancient Orient** in the same courtyard specializes in pre-Islamic objects. One of these is the record of the Treaty of Kadesh in which the Hittites and the Egyptians promised to keep the peace bet-ween them; the date is about 1285 BC. This copy was found in Hatussas. Other items include Mesopotamian pottery 7,000 years old.

The Tiled Kiosk

Details of Ottoman life, including carved stone, woodwork, ceramics, glass, calligraphy, illuminated Korans, old kilims and folk art can be seen in the **İbrahim Paşa Museum** across the Hippodrome from the Blue Mosque. This museum is world-famous for its collection of very old carpets (15th century Selçuk) and very large palace carpets.

Since the 1950s a number of mosques have been restored or built, including one in Şişli, a conventionally designed building, and one at the ferry landing on Heybeliadası, a more modern concept.

JEWISH SITES [12]

The Jewish presence in İstanbul dates back at least to the Byzantine period when there was a synagogue in Balat on the Golden Horn that had been built by Jews from **Ohrid** in Macedonia. Later, during the time of the Ottoman Empire other Jewish families from Macedonia built the Kastoria, Saloniki and Ihtipol synagogues. Balat became the Jewish quarter of İstanbul.

At the time of the Spanish Inquisition in the late 15th century when many Jews were welcomed to the Ottoman Empire they built the Geroush, Neve-Shalom Messina, Tchana and Monties synagogues. According to Evliya Çelebi, in the 17th century there

Ortaköy Etz Ha Haim synagogue together with the Ortaköy mosque

was also a large Jewish community in Hasköy. Some of those people were the Karaits who had been moved from the Yeni Cami area by the sultan.

Two synagogues served the Karait sect, one of which is still functioning.

By the turn of the 20th century the whole country was experiencing a severe economic depression. Those Jews who remained in İstanbul moved to newer districts of the city. Of the original synagogues in Balat, only the Ohrid remains and is functioning. It was restored most recently in 1955. A magnificent chandelier hangs from the central dome.

Among the other synagogues now active are the **Çorapçı Han** in Sultanhamam, founded by Russian Jews in the late 19th century; the **Neve-Shalom** at Tünelbaşı that was the scene of a tragic terrorist attack in 1986; the **Ashkenaz** on Yüksekkal-dırım; and the **Or A Hayim** synagogue and hospital in Fener. The **Şişli Beit Israel** synagogue is a recent building having been dedicated in 1952. The **Kuzguncuk Beit Yaakov** and the **Ortaköy Etz Ha Haim** synagogues have roots in the

Byzantine period. These two share their neighborhoods with churches and mosques. There are recent synagogues on three of the Princes' Islands, Burgaz, Heybeli and Büyükada.

PRINCES' ISLANDS - ADALAR

The Princes' Islands include Kınalı (Prote), Burgaz (Antigone), Kaşık (Pitta, Spoon), Heybeli (Khalke), Büyük (Prinkipo), Yassı (Plati), Sedef (Terebinthos), Tavşan (Nyandros), and Sivri (Oxia). In Byzantine times the Princes' Islands were both a place of welcome retreat for monks and of miserable exiles for numerous members of the royal family. Each has had its monasteries, convents and churches; each has some bit of cruel or heroic Byzantine history associated with it. One of three Byzantine women who ruled in their own right, the Empress Eirene in 802 was deposed and exiled on Büyükada; she had previously sent her granddaughter to the convent named for her. Another, the Empress Zoe (see p. 96), banished by her husband's nephew, was in this convent briefly in 1041 before the people of Constantinople demanded her return. The wife of Emperor Alexius I, also called Eirene, voluntarily exiled herself to the convent here in 1115 in order to be near Alexius who was dying in a monastery. Between 1929 and 1932 Leon Trotsky lived as a political exile on this island.

The **Monastery of the Holy Trinity** on Heybeli was founded in 857. Although nothing of that institution is left, there are the buildings of the Greek Orthodox school of theology on the same location. Closed in 1971, the school still functions as a library known for its Byzantine manuscripts. The grounds of another monastery on Heybeli are now used by the Turkish Naval Lycée. The harbor of Burgaz is dominated by the Greek church of **St. John the Baptist**. The cell beneath the church floor is believed to be where Bishop Methodius was immured for seven years in the early 9th century for preaching in favor of icons. Armenians on Kınalı worship in the **Church of Kirkor Lusavoriç**. The ruined **Monastery of St. Ignatius** on Tavşan was named for the Patriarch Ignatius who was incarcerated here by the 9th century Emperor Michael III the Sot. All of the islands are favorite vacation places in the summer.

EDİRNE - HADRIANOPLE

Capital of the Ottoman Empire for 80 years, and favorite of many sultans, Edirne is distinguished by its royal buildings, of which Selimiye Camii is considered Sinan's masterpiece.

The largest of the cities in European Turkey outside of İstanbul, Edirne is located where the Tunca and Arda Rivers join the Maritza (Meriç). The splendor and variety of its mosques, and the presence of the largest synagogue in the Balkans mark it in religious terms. The name of the city comes from the Emperor Hadrian who founded Hadrianople here in AD 125. Two hundred years later, one of Constantine the Great's acts of derring-do was to jump into the Maritza, urging his soldiers to follow him across and defeat his rival Licinius.

Valens, for whom an aqueduct in İstanbul is named, attacked a group of invading Huns and Avars in Hadrianople in AD 278. (This is the first time that Huns come to notice in European

Selimiye Camii

history.) Although Valens probably started with the advantage, his Roman army was completely destroyed, and he died that night, perhaps in a set fire. The defeat opened the land south of the Danube to invasion and settlement by these people.

Sixty years later Attila the Hun was in Edirne harassing the emperor Theodosius II. Although Attila has been known in history as a ruthless bully, he must have had other qualities because Honoria, the granddaughter of Theodosius, begged him to marry her.

Among the Crusaders who marched through Hadrianople was Frederick I, nicknamed Barbarossa for his red beard.

Hadrianople was taken by the Ottomans in 1361 by Murat I who then made it his capital and called it Edirne. (Their previous capital had been Bursa.) His great grandson Murat II did much to shape the city. Murat II so much wanted to retire and live quietly there that he turned his government over to his 12-year-old son. Two years later he was forced to take it back, but on Murat's death that same son, Mehmet II, proved his father's confidence in him by capturing Constantinople.

After Sultan Mehmet II moved his residence and capital to Constantinople, Edirne remained a favorite retreat of the sultans and their court. They used it as the staging place for military expeditions into the Balkans and as a summer residence. The sultans' palace was on an island in the Tunca River. The island was considered a paradise and was beautifully kept up throughout the time of the empire. Each June it is now the place of the renowned Kırkpınar greased wrestling contest.

The **Jewish synagogue** in Edirne, built in 1906 but now unused, was once the largest in the Balkans; it had the third largest seating capacity of any in Europe. Their community reflected the commercial importance of Edirne on one of the major east-west trading routes.

Four important mosques were built while Edirne was the capital of the empire, and one just after the capital had moved to İstanbul. A fifth royal mosque, the Selimiye, is the masterpiece of the 16th century architect Sinan.

The **Hüdavendigâr** or **Yıldırım Camii** is the oldest of the city. It was built toward the end of the 14th century by either Murat I (known as Hüdavendigâr or Conqueror of the World) who had captured Edirne, or by his son Yıldırım Bayezit I. The mosque is one of the few outside İstanbul that used the foundations of a ruined church on which to be built. The floor plan is a cross; on either side of the entrance on the east are rooms for the dervish convent associated with the mosque.

The **Eski (Old) Cami** is part of the history of the time between 1402 when Tamerlane defeated and captured Bayezit I and 1413 when Bayezit's son Mehmet I regained the throne. The mosque was started in 1402 by Bayezit's son Süleyman Çelebi. Another son Musa Çelebi contributed to it, and Mehmet I finished it in 1413. Like Ulu Cami in Bursa, the central area is covered with many domes. The square pillars and the walls are marked with strong, bold arabesques and Arabic inscriptions from the Koran. Each of the central domes is built differently: The first at the entrance sits on squinches; the entrance was probably once lighted by an open,

The very popular Kırkpınar greased wrestling competition held annually in early summer is a kind of religious festival marked by prayers and age-old rituals. Contestants are urged on by drummers and zurnacıs (pipers playing instruments similar to oboes) in their struggles which may last for hours.

The Ortaköy Mosque with the Bosphorus Bridge in the background

The floral designs of the tiles in the Muradiye Camii reflect a theme of six stars circling around a central sun. They are one of many examples in Islamic art of geometry, combined with floral patterns, symbolizing the infinite starry heaven.

circular window in the center of the dome, similar to the one in the Bursa mosque. The second dome sits on pendentives. The third is on Turkish triangles.

Sultan Murat II built the **Muradiye Camii** in 1436 first as a hospice for Mevlevi Dervishes of which he was a member. He changed it into a mosque soon after. Intricate designs on the blue and white hexagonal ceramic tiles around the mihrap are accented with turquoise colored triangles. The building has been quite damaged by earthquakes this century.

Üç Şerefeli Cami (the mosque with three balconies on the southwest minaret) has an oblong prayer hall and a larger oblong outer courtyard. It was built by Murat II between 1437 and 1447. The minaret with three balconies (from which the mosque gets its name) is the second tallest in the former empire. Three separate inside staircases lead to the separate balconies. The other minarets are distinguished by their designs: spiral (*burmalı*), diamond (*baklavalı*) and ribbed (*çubuklu*).

The **Bayezidiye Külliyesi** northwest of the center of Edirne and across the Tunca River was for its time the largest charitable organization in the world. Built in 1488 by Sultan Bayezit II, it included, beside the mosque, two hospices where traveling dervishes were welcomed with free meals for three days, a hospital, an insane asylum, a medical school, a bakery and a soup kitchen. The sick were treated with musical concerts and the fragrance of flowers. For many years the complex was in disrepair, but it has recently been restored and the University of Thrace holds some classes here.

The **Selimiye Camii** (built in 1575 for Sultan Selim II) that soars above the city is the building that Sinan counted his crowning work. Viewed from the outside, there is a balance and a rhythm in the silhouette of the outer courtyard with the four graceful minarets and the dome of the mosque rising with supporting semidomes like cumulus clouds. Inside, the sense of light and space are conveyed both by the many windows and by the great arching dome. The complexities of mass and space and detail, of proportion and line and color are so harmonized that the total effect is a unity.

The shafts of the four minarets are fluted; each has three balconies supported with Selçuk-like stalactite brackets (corbels). Those on the north have three separate staircases. On special occasions a

Mural tiles in Muradiye Camii

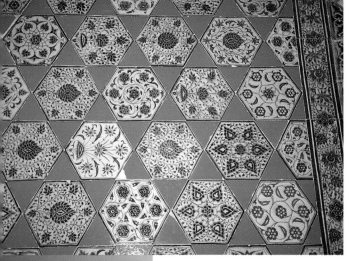

number of muezzins might give the call to prayer antiphonally from these balconies.

Unlike any of Sinan's other mosques, this one has a small ablution fountain in the center under the single dome. In its placement it echoes the plan of much earlier mosques such as the Ulu Cami in Bursa where the main fountain is in the center of the mosque and is open to the sky. The fountain and its water symbolize God's mercy (*rahmet*). (*Rahmet* is one of the Turkish words for "rain.") The muezzin's gallery acts as a canopy to this fountain. Carved low on one of the marble pillars of the gallery is a small tulip that hangs upside down. Perhaps a gardener who owned the land previously asked to be so remembered; perhaps a stonemason wished to remind the worshipper who chanced on it that in old Turkish the words for "tulip" (*lâle*) and "God" (Allah) are written with the same characters. Whatever the thought behind it, this is the stuff of legend, of remembrance and of inspiration.

In the Selimiye Sinan took Ottoman architecture to its climax of balance, monumentality, and unity.

[1] The Hüdavendigâr mosque is typical of the Bursa-style, or eyvan (recess) or inverted T mosque with a central hall beyond which is the deep eyvan. The cross-bar of the T is made by cells or convent rooms on either side of the central hall. Under the dome of the central hall, which originally was open to the sky, was a small ablution fountain. The Muradiye Mosque in Edirne (see p.116) is an even clearer example of this type. Notice that the dome of the Hüdavendigâr is supported by Turkish triangles, not by pendentives (as is the case in St. Sophia in İstanbul) or squinches (Eski Cami in Edirne).

[2] Parallax is the apparent shift in the place of an object due to a shift in the point of view. This is the phenomenon seen when you hold a finger in front of your face and close first one eye and then the other. The finger seems to move relative to the background. The distance of this shift is relative to the distance of the object from your eyes.

[3] Nilüfer Hatun was the wife of Orhan Gazi (1324-1360). The story is that Orhan's father Osman Gazi (from whom the Ottomans take their name) was invited to a wedding of a neighboring Byzantine prince. The plot was that he would be trapped and murdered by the groom's family. Forewarned, he arrived, overwhelmed his attackers, and carried off the bride, Holifera, whom he married to his son at once. Renamed Nilüfer, she became the mother of the next sultan, Murat I. She was known for many philanthropies of which this soup kitchen was one.

[4] The title of "Sultan" comes before the name of the man who held the position. It follows the names of his wives who bore him sons and also the names of his daughters.

[5] See pp.66 - 67 for a discussion of the Ecumenical Councils.

[6] Compare this with the restored synagogue in Sardis.

[7] In about 1040 Constantine IX took over the protection of the Armenian capital of Ani north of Mt. Ararat. This was an attempt to save Ani from Selçuk inroads. However, it meant that the border of the Byzantine Empire confronted that of the invading Muslims. Thirty years later in 1071 at Malazgirt this confrontation led to the decisive battle between the Selçuk leader Alp Arslan and Constantine's successor Romanus IV Diogenes who had been forced to defend his eastern territory. Romanus lost and the Selçuk armies continued west through Anatolia.

[8] St. Francis had journeyed to the Holy Land in 1219-1220, and was interested in missionary work to the Muslims, but there is no record of his visiting Constantinople.

[9] A historical novel by Ivo Andric, *The Bridge on the Drina*, focuses on events centered for three hundred years around this bridge. The book was written in 1945; for it Andric received the Nobel Prize in literature in 1961.

[10] Mimar is the Turkish word for architect. Sinan was so consummate an architect that his name is synonymous with the profession.

[11] St. Peter's cathedral in Rome took its builders the whole 16th century to complete.

[12] People wishing to visit a synagogue should check with the travel agent to learn if special permission is required to enter the building because of security arrangements for foreigners.

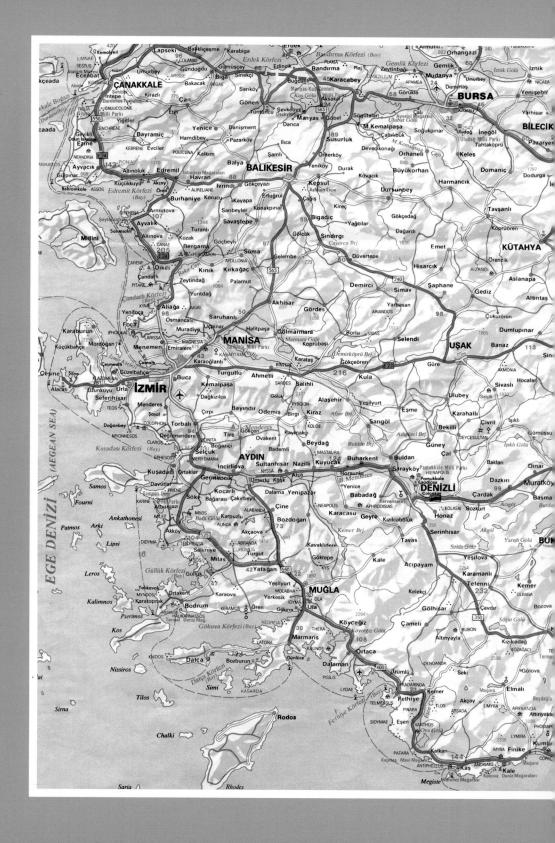

Aegean Turkey

Recreation, international business, archaeological exploration, ecology, history, tourism, scenic beauty, agriculture -- Aegean Turkey has it all. Here, easily available, are miles of golden sandy beaches, a pleasant climate, a fertile land, access to markets for commerce, and sites such as Troy and Ephesus where the imaginations of visionaries like Homer and St. Paul were kindled.

2nd Century AD
Synagogue,
Sardis

AEGEAN TURKEY

Truva (Troy)
Odun İskelesi (Alexandria Troas)
Behramkale (Assos)
Bergama (Pergamum)
Akhisar (Thyatira)
Manisa (Magnesia-ad-Sipylus)
Sart Köy (Sardis)
Alaşehir (Philadelphia)
Laodikya (Laodicea)
Pamukkale (Hierapolis)
Honaz (Colossae)
Dinar (Celaenae, Apamea)
Geyre (Aphrodisias)
İzmir (Smyrna)
Sığacık (Teos)
Klaros (Claros)
Selçuk (Ayio Theologos)
Efes (Ephesus)
Meryemana
Davutlar (Panionium)
Güllübahçe (Priene)
Milet (Miletus)
Didim (Didyma)
Bodrum (Halicarnassus)

Aegean Turkey has always been attractive. It has a natural beauty; its climate is warm; its land is fertile; its seas abound in fish. Uncounted numbers of people have lived and loved here for centuries, nor has the attraction of their work diminished. Each of the places had some salient quality that drew people — water, a hill that could be defended, crossroads, ore, a legend — and affected the kind of community it was.

TRUVA - TROY

Troy is the home of legend. Acknowledging that, for many visitors not steeped in Greek and Latin classics, Troy is a disappointment. It is small. The modern wooden horse at the entrance is an obvious tourist gimmick. So few weapons have been found in the rubble around the walls that one is forced to wonder if there ever had been a war at all. Even with a map and the posted signs it is hard to make sense of what little the archaeologists have left here. The Skamander River (Küçük Menderes Çayı) in the distance where Achilles almost drowned is little more than a muddy ditch. Where is the off-shore island the Greeks could have hid their ships? In spite of all these drawbacks, a visit to Troy can be a profound experience, over and over.

The very disappointment leads to questions: Why is so much changed? Why are

*Heinrich Schliemann was born the son of a poor German pastor. Forced to earn a living at a young age, he worked as a grocer's assistant and then as a cabin boy. On his first voyage he was shipwrecked. Doggedly determined to become a linguist, he memorized all of the **Iliad** in the original Greek. He also learned at least six other languages. Happening to be in California when that state joined the Union, he became an United States citizen. By the time he was 35 he had made himself a wealthy man, whereupon he turned his talents and his fortune to archaeology. Besides Troy, he excavated Mycenae and several other less successful places. He was contemplating further digging at Troy when he dropped dead on the street in Naples at the age of 68.*

there so many levels of habitation? Who were these people and what happened to them? What tragedy, what magic pervades the hill? What is truth here?

One's first impressions of Troy are the low hill, the walls, the excavations. There are house walls, temple platforms, theaters, city gates, and the long gash that Heinrich Schliemann cut hoping to prove with Priam's gold that Homer's story was history. Perhaps the history is here, but Schliemann's gold is not. A small fraction of that treasure is in the İstanbul Archaeological Museum; the bulk is divided between the Pushkin Museum in Moscow and the Hermitage in St. Petersburg. One has to imagine the engineering feat of tugging the wooden horse into the city, and the fear of the Greek soldiers hiding inside it that the Trojans might accidentally tip the whole thing over.

As for the archaeologists' history, of the thirty levels of habitation, **Troy I** is an Early Bronze Age settlement, sometime between 3,000 and 2,500 BC. **Troy II** was inhabited from about 2500 to 2200 BC; it was an imposing city with a well-furnished palace. This was the level from which Schliemann took the treasure that he claimed had belonged to King Priam, the ruler at the time of the Trojan War. Troy II was destroyed by a huge fire which is in keeping with Homer's story.

However, archaeologists now believe that the Troy of the *Iliad* is level **VI** or **VII**, when the Trojan culture was at its height. This city seems to have been destroyed by an earthquake, not by sack or conflagration. While this conflicts with the story as told by Vergil in the *Aeneid*, it may confirm another interpretation that Poseidon, the god of the sea (as in the story of the monster who engulfed Laocoon and his sons), was both the creator of horses (as in the story of the trick played on the Trojans) and the one responsible for earthquakes. Probably the Sea Peoples who invaded the Aegean region about 1200 BC added to the ruin of the city in those years.

By the time of the later **Troy VIII** there was a large Temple to Athena (since destroyed by archaeologists) that was visited in turn by Xerxes (5th century BC) who sacrificed 1000 oxen, by Alexander the Great (4th century BC) who traded his armor for some he thought belonged to the Trojans, and by Julius Caesar (1st century BC) who thought that he was a descendant of King Priam through Aeneas. Some of the items from the excavation and some from other excavations in the area are displayed in the **Çanakkale Museum**.

But Troy is something else besides a place where men fought to recapture a girl who had allowed herself to be kidnapped. It is the place where the merchant, Heinrich Schliemann, redefined the functions of myth in history. Beyond this, Troy represents the tangible evidence of an old story about people with all their failings and their greatnesses, that, thanks to Homer's genius, has set the standards for Western literature ever since.

Homer's story was not a history of the Trojan War; he assumed that his listeners knew it as well as he did. Nor was it the story of the capture of Troy. Rather, he portrayed the conflict between two friends (Agamemnon and Achilles) that led many people, both innocent and guilty, to dishonor and death. Homer saw the tragedy in the cause, in its inevitable effect and in the suffering.

While the gods of Olympus appear on the surface to be manipulating the actors as puppets, Homer drew each human as a real person responsible for his or her behavior, and the gods did not change their characters. The *Odyssey* began with Zeus's wrathful commentary, "Look how mortals are always blaming us gods for their misfortunes. In truth it's their own wickedness that brings them even more suffering than any we might devise." The actors on both sides of the story rose to heroic stature. Even Helen, who seemed to escape the tragic consequences, acknowledged her guilt and the irony of her position when she said to her brother-in-law Hector, "I wish I could comfort you. You bear the greatest burden to undo the evil which my blindness and Paris's has caused. For this our punishment will be eternal dishonor in the poets' songs."

Troy is not the place of a famous temple as is Didyma or Pessinus, nor a recently rediscovered civilization as is Boğazkale. Its gods and goddesses do not have strange unpronounceable names, nor has its language disappeared, although the people to whom its fame is due lived here about the same time as the Anatolian Hittites. Rather, like the sculptures and jewelry that are left from these other sanctuaries, it is the intensity of the artistry that stirs us; it is the intensity and the humanity of the *Iliad* and the *Odyssey*, even when the Trojan War was thought to be merely myth, that has preserved it. Homer's gods were no more ethical than Telipinu was; they no less symbolized natural phenomena than the Weather-god or Cybele did. Rather, it has been Homer's epic, so inspiring that it has been considered sacred, that has made Troy in itself a religious site.

Recitations of Homer's poetry became the test of rhapsodists at religious festivals by the 6th century BC. "Rhapsody" meant "the stitcher of verse": The contenders were assigned sections so that the whole epic would be heard and so that the contenders would not all recite only their favorite parts. Someone was in charge of telling them when to come in, and there was also a law passed allowing them to have prompters.

Treasure from Troy, the Museum of Archaeology, İstanbul

ODUN İSKELESİ - ALEXANDRIA TROAS

Once a city with tall buildings, Alexandria Troas was a major port on the Aegean and it was visited twice by Paul. Constantine the Great thought briefly about making it his capital of the Eastern Roman Empire. He chose wisely in not doing so. It was most accessible both to trade and to plun-

Luke is thought by some to be the author of both the Gospel of Luke and the Book of Acts. He may also be the person referred to in the Letter to the Colossians (Col.4:14) as "the beloved physician." Timothy became Paul's young companion when Paul was in Lystra. His mother Eunice and his grandmother Lois were Christian Jews; his father was a Gentile.

der. The few ruins that stand up now above the thistles witness to the neglect of the centuries.

Alexandria Troas was founded about 300 BC by Antigonus I, one of Alexander the Great's generals. His successor, Lysimachus, changed its name from Antigonia in order to honor Alexander and to identify its location on the Troad. A major benefactor to the city in the 1st century AD was the orator Herodes Atticus who gave the city the **baths**, the ruined walls of which are about all that are left. As Constantinople grew, so Alexandria Troas declined; its dressed stones were plundered to build the new capital.

The city's importance in religious history comes from the visits by Paul on his missionary journeys. On his second journey Paul had wanted to go north into Bithynia, but instead he and his companion Timothy were deflected to the Aegean Coast. In the night a Macedonian appeared to Paul calling him to cross the Aegean to Neapolis (Kavala) and Philippi. This is noted as the inspiration and beginning of the spread of Christianity into Europe (Acts 16:7-12). Perhaps it was here that Luke joined Paul in his journeys. The evidence is that the account in Acts changes at this point from "they" to "we" (cf. Acts 16:8, 10).

Paul was in Alexandria Troas again for a week as he returned from Macedonia on his third journey. This time he had so much to say to his friends that they stayed up all night. Eutychus, one of his young listeners, was sitting in a window, perhaps to get some fresh air because there were a lot of lamps burning. Around midnight he went to sleep in the stuffy room and fell out, landing on the ground three stories below. Paul ran down, examined him, and found to everyone's relief that he was still alive (Acts 20:5-12). The incident was only a brief interruption in the discussion that continued until after sunrise.

BEHRAMKALE - ASSOS

Assos is a southern port on the Çanakkale peninsula and as such was a stop-over for Paul. Perhaps its name derives from *Isij* meaning "the rising sun." Later Isij became "Asia," first for the southern shore of the Çanakkale peninsula, then for the coastal

Temple of Athena, Assos

region. For several hundred years Assos was ruled by "tyrants" (a term meaning at that time rulers who had absolute sovereignty). Tyrants were not necessarily cruel or self-seeking men as the title has come to suggest. Instead, one who tried to be just was the Tyrant of Assos in the 4th century BC, a eunuch named Hermias. Hermias had studied in Athens at the Academy under Plato. While there he

had become a close friend of Aristotle who followed him to Assos when Plato died. Aristotle married Hermias's adopted daughter Pythia and moved to Macedonia where he taught Alexander, the young son of King Philip, for eight years. The friendship between Aristotle and Hermias came to a tragic end when Hermias and the residents of Assos were captured by the Persians and massacred in about 344 BC. Aristotle's *Ode In Praise of Valor* was written in memory of his friend.

Remains of buildings on the peak of Assos dating from the time of Hermias and Aristotle include a 6th century BC **Temple to Athena**, a **marketplace**, the **city walls** and a **council chamber**. There are also the ruins of a later theater and a 14th century mosque. The walls of the acropolis were carefully and skillfully built. The Temple to Athena is unusual because of its mixture of Doric and Ionic architecture.

Paul passed through Assos on his way between Alexandria Troas and Miletus at the end of his third missionary journey. From Assos he sent a message back to Carpus in Alexandria Troas asking him to forward his cloak and notebooks. His friends had taken a boat from Alexandria Troas while Paul had traveled overland. He met them in Assos from whence they sailed together across the ten kilometers to Mytilene.

Acropolis, Pergamum

The picturesque port Behramkale provides access to the ancient city of Assos at the top of the hill and the amenities of a number of modern hotels, restaurants, and recreation facilities.

BERGAMA - PERGAMUM

Pergamum's religious interests lie in its pagan temples, in its place as the site of one of the Seven Churches, and in its role in the history of western Asia Minor. From its acropolis its kings controlled a major crossroads in the 3rd century BC. Its kings eventually ruled Aeolia, Ionia, the Troad, Phrygia and Caria.

They showed their power both as successful generals and as patrons of the arts. Under them the city accumulated one of the largest libraries in the ancient world. It was so extensive that jealous Alexandria, which had the monopoly, tried to curtail the number of volumes in its library by putting an embargo on the export of papyrus. The king was unwilling to give up his interest, so he resorted to having his books copied on skin. Skins do not roll up the way papyrus does, but they do make pages that can be used on both sides, an advantage over papyrus that eventually made them the preferred material. The kings also built magnificent public buildings that were faced with sparkling white marble. Pergamum with its temples, theater, library, palace and agora on the acropolis was a striking city when viewed from afar. Its

*The name "Pergamum" is related to the word **pyrgos** meaning "castle." The same word shows up in such place names as the island of Burgaz in the Sea of Marmara and the city of Lüleburgaz between Edirne and İstanbul.*

When Alexander the Great's general Lysimachus died in 281 BC, his wealth devolved to Philetaerus. Valued at 9,000 silver talents, it was enough for Philetaerus to build a number of temples, buy the friendship of his neighbors, and establish a dynasty that lasted through four succeeding kings.

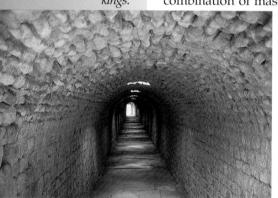

Asclepion at Pergamon

Karl Humann was directing the construction of a railroad linking İzmir and İstanbul when a workman happened to show him a fragment of frieze from the Altar to Zeus. Recognizing its importance, he turned his efforts to recovering what was left of the whole.

location and the buildings make it still an attractive tourist center.

The largest building on Pergamum's acropolis is the **theater** which can seat 20,000 people. The pitch of the hill and the thermal currents of air are such that no one in the audience would ever have had difficulty either seeing or hearing what happens on stage. The excellence of the acoustical engineering of the Hellenistic builders can easily be tested if one person in the orchestra speaks in a normal voice while others listen from the top row of seats. Above the theater is the **Temple to Trajan and Hadrian** (now being restored in white marble by German archaeologists) and next to that are the ruins of the small but famous **library.** The Pergamenes' library was estimated at 200,000 volumes.

King Attalus I of Pergamum (who had worked hard to accumulate the library) faced a serious problem in 230 BC of a demoralized army that was afraid to defend the eastern border against the raiding Gauls. Attalus solved it with a resort to a combination of mass psychology and sleight-of-hand. By secretly imprinting the words, "Victory for the King!" on the liver of an animal that he was preparing for sacrifice, he inspired his men to defeat the Gauls who previously had been invincible. The emotion of that battle still lives in the statue of the *Dying Gaul* now in the Vatican Museum in Rome.

Eumenes II followed Attalus I. Eumenes used his wealth to build the **Altar to Zeus**. The friezes on the outside walls depict a mythological battle between the gods and the giants which are among the most beautiful sculptures of their kind. (They are in the Pergamon Museum in Berlin; a small copy of the Altar is in the Bergama Museum in the center of town. Karl Humann was the German engineer who initiated the excavations of Pergamum when he discovered this temple in 1878.) Attalus II, brother of Eumenes II, succeeded to the throne in 159 BC. Among the events of his reign was his fight with King Prusias of Bithynia, the man who had befriended Hannibal in 183. Attalus III, nephew of Attalus II, reigned for five years. His scholarly interests turned to medicinal and poisonous plants which he tried out on condemned criminals. When he died his ministers were shocked to learn that he had willed his whole country to Rome.

The large **Red Basilica (Kızıl Avlu)** on the Selinus (Bergama Çayı) at the edge of present-day Bergama was probably a temple dedicated in the 2nd century AD to Serapis and maybe also to Isis and Harpocrates. Later the central part was used as a church. Today one of the towers is a mosque. Gravestones in the yard in front of the building are inscribed with Hebrew characters.

Southwest of the city is the medical center, the **Asclepion** with its temple to the god of medicine, Asclepius. This center was next to Epidaurus on the Peloponnesus in its high reputation for healing. Asclepius was usually represented with a snake coiled around his staff; the snake which sheds its skin was a symbol of rejuvenation and of prophecy. A marble capital has been set in the center of the present grounds, its twining snakes reminding visitors of the origins of the doctors' caduceus.

The famous physician and prolific writer, Galen, was born in Pergamum and practiced medicine here in the 2nd century AD. Among his patients was the rhetorician Aelius Aristides whose moving report on the earthquake of AD 178 that destroyed Smyrna inspired the Emperor Marcus Aurelius to rebuild the city. Aristides also recounted his dreams and visions that he had while he was under the treatment of sleep (he called it "incubation") in the Asclepion. One of the common cures was a mud bath; Aristides took this cure in mid-winter and described it with such enthusiasm that it would seem he enjoyed ill health. Doctors at that time also used another kind of hydrotherapy in their treatment of patients: Patients were led through the cool tunnel to the round building while above them priests chanted soothingly, and under them they heard the purl of rippling water. Galen started as doctor to the gladiators; his skill was such that soon the Roman emperors were going to him.

In the valley between the Asclepion and the acropolis is one of the few **amphitheaters** in Anatolia. This one was built across a stream which could be blocked when the performance included a sea battle or a fight with crocodiles. Amphitheaters (completely enclosed theaters) were used for wild beast fights; such baiting of animals was a Roman pastime. Animals were either set against each other or against people. At first the entertainment involved only a few animals, but as people grew to enjoy the bloody spectacle, more were added; there is a record of as many as 11,000 animals killed in a single celebration during Trajan's reign. The prelude to the main fight was a hunt which involved the hunter's skill in trapping an animal that was not dangerous enough to kill the man but that was nimble and clever. One such chase was for ostriches. The Emperor Domitian added a new quality to his games when he employed dwarfs and women as his gladiators.

Pergamum's place in religious history is largely because of the paragraph addressed to its Christian believers by John in the Book of Revelation (Rev. 2:12-17). He characterized Pergamum as the place where Satan was enthroned. Some people have thought that to be a reference to the Temple to Zeus which was on the acropolis. Some steps from the foundation were left *in situ* when it was sent to Berlin. John saw a group he called the Nicolatians as an additional threat to the believers. Who these people were is not

Statue of Nike, the Museum of Bergama

The double vaulted Roman tunnel that still carries the Selinus river under the courtyard of the Red Basilica can be seen near the southwest corner of the building. Roman bridges on both sides of the tunnel continue to carry traffic.

Concerts and plays presented in the small theater of the Asclepion were also part of the therapy for the patients.

The Temple to Zeus commemorated the defeat of the Greeks by the army of Attalus I. It was built by his successor Eumenes II. The theme of the frieze is the triumph of order over chaos.

Akhisar is still largely what it has always been-- an agricultural center. Among its crops are cotton and grapes.

The ancient name, Thyatira, meant "the city of Thya"; perhaps that is a reference to the sun god of the city, Tyrimnos.

Akhisar

clearly known. John condemned them for adultery and for eating food that had been sacrificed to pagan gods. John also promised a white stone and hidden manna to those who repented of their false beliefs and immoral behavior.

Known in Hellenistic and Roman times as Pergamum, Bergama holds a variety of interests for tourists today: ancient ruins and modern rugs, perhaps a play in the theater, and many stories of how its residents overcame their enemies. The popular hand-made Bergama and Yağcıbedir rugs, now made with natural dyes, can be found in many shops lining the main street. Also on the main street is a good, small archaeological and ethnographic **museum** where there is the replica of the Temple to Zeus along with other statuary.

AKHİSAR - THYATIRA

Located on the main road between İzmir and Bursa, Akhisar is a modern city with little of historical or archaeological interest visible to tourists today. It appears in guide books mainly because it is the old Thyatira, the site of one of the Seven Churches of Asia (Rev. 2:18-29). The ancient ruins you can see are a short section of a **colonnaded street**, a **temple** (perhaps to Apollo), and walls of a **church**. They are enclosed within an area of a small city block in the middle of Akhisar.

John's criticism of Thyatira in Revelation was related to the prophetess Jezebel. Whether she was a real woman of that name or whether he intended her as a symbol of licentiousness, John saw the challenge to Christianity which Thyatira represented as a moral decay among the members. To those who refused to compromise with their ideals he promised "the star of dawn" and "authority over the nations."

About forty years previous to the time that John wrote those words to the congregation in Thyatira, Paul had met one of the merchants from there when he arrived in Philippi. This was on his second missionary journey. The merchant was Lydia, a woman dealing in expensive purple cloth.[1] Under Paul's influence she and her whole household became baptized Christians. Lydia probably was well off; she insisted that Paul and his companions Timothy and Luke (who presumably was with them) should stay in her house in Philippi (Acts 16: 13-15). Perhaps her influence helped the church grow in Thyatira. By the end of the 1st century there must have been a sizable community there for John to have chosen it as one of his seven.

MANİSA - MAGNESIA-AD-SYPILUS

A natural **rock formation** on the southwest edge of the city of Manisa is identified with the legend of Niobe, the mother who must weep for all eternity because Apollo and Artemis killed her twelve children. The profile of her face can be imagined from the road, but from close up her features become only large, rough stones.

Gymnasium, Sardis

Two stone reliefs in the Manisa area are Hittite work, evidence of their influence on the Aegean coast. One, the **Taş Suret**, probably the seated Mother Goddess, was incorrectly identified with the Niobe legend for a long time. It is on the eastern edge of the city on the road to Turgutlu. The second relief is at the **Karabel** pass where a stone warrior defends the road. Perhaps a similar soldier was once stationed on the other side of the road.

The old name of Manisa was Magnesia-ad-Sipylus. The high iron content of the stone of Mt. Sipylus (Manisa Dağı) which rises above Manisa makes it magnetic. This property was common knowledge to the Greeks and Romans who called it the Magnesian stone from which the English word "magnet" is derived.

Alexander the Great came through Magnesia in 333 BC. The city was held by the Selçuks in the 14th century; their Prince Saruhan is remembered in the name of a neighboring town. Manisa was the provincial capital in Ottoman times, and several of the Ottoman sultans served as governors here when they were the heirs-apparent.

Sultan Süleyman built the **Valide Complex** (1522) to honor his mother who had lived here with him when he was governor of the province. Included in the complex is Manisa's largest mosque, the Sultan Camii. In the square in front of it a local festival of spicy candy, the Mesir Bayramı, has been celebrated the last Sunday of April since the 16th century. The candy is concocted from forty-one different spices; local people say it is like the ambrosia of the gods. They also hint that it might be an aphrodisiac.

The **Muradiye Camii** (1586) was built by Sultan Murat III. It is thought by some to have been planned by the architect Sinan. Next to it is the **Archaeological and Ethnographic Museum** located in the old *imaret* (soup kitchen) and *medrese* (school) of the mosque. Mosaics from Sardis are displayed here, along with items that date back to the Bronze Age.

On the slopes part way up the mountain is the 14th century **Ulu Cami**. Judging from the Byzantine capitals on its columns, the mosque apparently incorporates parts of an earlier church.

When Sultan Murat II tired of the responsibilities of governing his empire in 1444, he abdicated in favor of his 12-year old son Mehmet and retired to Manisa. There, in its gardens and in the company of a mystical dervish community, he hoped to find peace of mind. Two years later he was called back to İstanbul. This time he sent the boy to Manisa to gain an understanding of authority. Mehmet was resident in Manisa when he became sultan in 1452.

SART KÖY - SARDIS

The partially restored synagogue and the ruins of temples and churches mark the importance of Sardis as a religious site. Beginning in the 6th century BC Sardis was the terminus of the main east-west Royal Road. As the capital of Lydia it was the commercial center of the western Mediterranean well into the 1st century BC. On the main highway east from İzmir, now surrounded with rich farm land, Sardis owed much of its power to the gold that its kings took from the Pactolus (Sart Çayı) stream that comes down out of Mt. Tmolus (Bozdağ). The Lydian empire included almost all of western Anatolia.

2nd century AD synagogue, Sardis

The history of Sardis is told with many anecdotes by Herodotus.[2] One of its first kings, Gyges, was forced by the queen to kill his predecessor and marry her. Gyges carried on diplomatic relations with the Assyrian Emperor Assurbanipal (669-627 BC). This occurred during the time that Judah was a vassal state of Assyria and its merchants were busy throughout the Empire. Thus while there are no references in Herodotus or in the Bible to Jewish merchants in Sardis, it seems reasonable that they may well have been working there at the time. In the Old Testament Sardis perhaps appears as the place called Sepharad where there were exiles from Jerusalem (Obad. 19). These may have been people who had left Jerusalem after the Temple was destroyed in 586 BC. Or they may have been slaves who were sold to the Lydians by one of Nebuchanezzar's ministers, Nabuzaradan (II Kings 25:11-12).

Croesus was the king of Sardis from 560 to 546 BC; his name is still synonymous with wealth. However, overconfident because of his wealth, Croesus mistook the power of the Persian Empire which had replaced that of the Assyrian. Challenging the Persian

Cyrus the Great, he was defeated and captured in his citadel in Sardis in 546. From then until the time of Alexander, Sardis was a Persian satrapy. By the 6th century BC Lydians had made important innovations in music with the seven-string lyre and in finance with gold and silver coinage guaranteed by the state for its standard value. Sardis also contributed the game of dice to the world's entertainment market.

A **main street** of ancient Sardis parallels the present highway. A number of shops once opened onto that street — a paint shop and a hardware shop have been identified among them. To the north of them are one of the two synagogues and the gymnasium complex, both partially reconstructed in recent years by people contributing to the Sardis American Excavation Fund.

The reconstructed **synagogue** shows some of its original splendor and has several unusual features: It was originally a wing of the gymnasium; it was made into the religious center in the 3rd century AD, possibly with the help of the Emperor Lucius Verus. Its long, narrow shape comes from its previous use. It also is the largest known synagogue from this time outside Jerusalem. That, its frescoes and its mosaics suggest a large, well-established and successful Jewish community in Sardis. More familiar is the semicircular bank of facing seats for the elders at the west end; this feature was carried over into church architecture, as can be seen in the Church of St. Irene in İstanbul.

Across the highway are the **stadium**, **theater** and **market place**. In the so-called **House of Bronzes** opposite the synagogue excavators found so many pieces of bronze that are religious in character that they think the house may have been the residence of a priest.

The **Temple to Artemis**, built in about 334 BC at a time of regional prosperity, is at the foot of the peak and near the stream. Even in its ruined condition it is one of the most impressive buildings of antiquity. Of the original seventy-eight columns that surrounded the temple, two still are topped with their Ionic capitals. Reconstructed several times, the final building (a double temple) of AD 150 is about 50 m wide by 100 m long. In the northeast corner is a small, possibly 4th century AD **church** in poor condition.

A short distance southwest of the Temple to Artemis, on the bank above the stream, archaeologists have recently discovered the city's gold refinery. Not far from it are the ruins of a pre-7th century AD **church**.

In the Book of Revelation (Rev. 3:1-6), John stated that Sardis needed to wake up. He complained that their acts did not live up to their reputation, that they did not finish what they started. But he held out the hope to those who were not polluted that they should have robes of white. White was the color then of righteousness and immortality.

Aesop, the storyteller, is supposed to have lived in Sardis and been part of the court of Croesus. Probably many of his stories were already going the rounds, but he gave them his own twist. One account says that he was murdered because he embezzled money from Croesus. Another, according to Plato, is that Socrates amused himself in prison by turning Aesop's fables into rhyme.

ALAŞEHİR - PHILADELPHIA

The temples in Philadelphia and the festivities connected with them were so attractive that the city was nicknamed "Little Athens."

Philadelphia was somewhat off the main east-west highway that went to Sardis. For a 1st century colporteur carrying John's letter to the Seven Churches it would have been about a two-day ride from Sardis; the 64 km now can be covered by car in less than a hour. Like Sardis, it was on the north slope of Mt. Tmolus. It was founded by King Attalus II of Pergamum in the 1st century BC to protect his empire from Phrygia. Attalus had the title of "Philadelphus" because he was loyal and loving toward his brother Eumenes who had been king before him. Images of both of them appear on his coins. This new city which was the border post for Pergamene soldiers took his attribute of brotherly love for its name. It was surrounded by a **wall**, a part of which (perhaps Byzantine in date) runs along the road on the northeastern side of the city. Like most military border posts, it was not a major city.

Alaşehir

During the reign of Tiberius (AD 14-37) Philadelphia twice suffered from major earthquakes. It was rebuilt several times afterwards, thanks to the help of the emperors; in gratitude the people built temples to Tiberius, Caligula and Vespasian. Those temples created enough tourist business that the people did not give up their paganism. The martyrdom of some Christians from Philadelphia aroused the crowd in the stadium in Smyrna to call for the trial and martyrdom of Polycarp (?AD 152).

During Byzantine times Philadelphia was the seat of a Christian bishopric. Its significance in Christian history was because it was the place of one of the seven church congregations addressed by John in the Book of Revelation (Rev.3:7-13). Although one of the Seven Churches, Philadelphia was the least distinguished; it was the only one about which John had no real criticism. He characterized it as having been given an open door. It has been suggested that this is a reference to the border post. He told the Christians not to let anyone take away their crowns and promised that those who were victorious would become pillars in God's temple. The only evidences of Christianity in Alaşehir now are the ruined walls of an **11th century church** in the Beş Eylül district. It was the seat of a Greek Orthodox archbishop into the 19th century, and the title is still maintained in the church. Recent excavations on the hill above the city have uncovered a small **theater** and some of the citadel walls. The Roman temples have completely vanished. The **Şeh Sinan Camii** and a caravansary date from the 14th century. There is also a **covered market** here, and the ruins of a **mosque** built by Sultan Bayezit I in the same century. Alaşehir today is a city supported largely by the agricultural produce of the surrounding farms: grapes, cotton and licorice. It also has business in producing leather and textiles.

Philadelphia was only one of many cities whose citizens were massacred by Tamerlane in the early 15th century. Part of the wall he made with the corpses at one time was in the library of the Lincoln Cathedral in England.

LAODİKYA - LAODICEA

The site of another of the seven churches addressed by John in the Book of Revelation (Rev. 3:14-22), Laodicea is on a low hill between Denizli and Pamukkale and on the south bank of the Lycus River (Çürüksu). Ruins of **theaters**, a **gymnasium**, a **stadium**, and several other **public buildings** stand up above the wheat fields or the weeds, depending on the season. The city was intersected by main trading routes running east-west and north-south. As a commercial center, it had a large Jewish community. When Hadrian visited it in AD 129 it was at its height and called itself "the metropolis of Asia." Strabo, the 1st century geographer, reported that Laodicea was known for the unusually soft black wool from its sheep.

For John in Revelation, the Christians of Laodicea were neither hot nor cold and because of their indifference he wanted to spew them out of his mouth. This reference has made scholars wonder if John was thinking about the hot springs of Pamukkale only 7 km farther away. His promise to the Laodiceans who would respond to his lesson was that they would join the Spirit in the great feast.

Although it can only be speculation, it is striking to note that John chose details about each of the seven churches which applied specifically to the one he addressed. Had he visited the places individually? Or — as many believe — did he choose the seven to represent the whole Christian community and the challenges he saw facing it? To all the Christians who were faithful he promised a final seat on the heavenly throne.

Ancient Pamukkale pool (above), travertine terraces of Pamukkale (below)

Close to Laodicea was a once-famous medical school that was associated with a temple to Men-Karou, the moon-god.

PAMUKKALE - HIERAPOLIS

Ruins of several temples and the remarkably well-preserved Martyrium of Philip in Pamukkale draw visitors who are interested in religious sites.

Pamukkale ("the cotton castle" of white travertine terraces) is perhaps the best known of the hundred or so hot springs or spas (called *kaplıca*) in Turkey. Each has been analyzed for mineral content, radioactivity, and the beneficial effects of its waters for specific diseases.[3] The small pool at the Turizm Motel in Pamukkale, in addition to being good for gall bladder and kidney diseases, is attractive because even in a snow storm bathers in the warm bubbly water can paddle from a sunken marble column to a partially submerged capital. The spectacular calcium and other mineral deposits at Pamukkale and nearby Karahayit have been formed by the rivulets of hot waters that bubble up out of the earth along this edge of the mountains; they are evidence of continuing volcanic activity here.

The earliest literary references to Hierapolis — its Roman name —

are from the 2nd century BC, raising the question of whether the hot springs developed about that time due, perhaps, to an unrecorded earthquake. It seems unlikely that a place so striking and so pleasing should have gone unnoticed if it had been there previously. In Roman times it was a fashionable spa; the springs attracted the people for their curative powers. The large **Roman bath** is now part of the museum of Hierapolis. Nearby is the **sacred pool** enclosed by the Turizm Motel.

Next to the **Temple to Apollo** was the **Plutonium**, a shrine honoring the god of the underworld. It still discharges danger-ously noxious fumes. A large **cemetery** lies northwest of the sacred pool. Between the temple and the cemetery are the ruins of a **basilical church**. Some distance up the hill is the **Roman theater**, recently partly restored. In the 4th century AD the orchestra was closed up enough that it could be flooded and mock sea battles staged there. Even farther up the hill archaeologists have ex-cavated a cruciform building thought to be the **Martyrium of St. Philip**. To the disappointment of the excavators, his grave has not been discovered. Philip lived here after the Apostles scattered from Jerusalem.

Fifty years ago Pamukkale was rarely visited by foreigners. The sacred pool was marked only by a rickety wooden hut teetering above the grass at one end. Not until 1957 did Italian archaeologists begin to study the ruins, and not until after that did the tourist industry develop.

HONAZ - COLOSSAE

Colossae lies about a mile below the present village of Honaz on the north slope of Honaz Dağı and about 18 km east of Denizli. Of the sites described in this book it is one of the least rewarding to a casual tourist, but a walk from Honaz to it might give a hint of rural Anatolia as Paul experienced it. Its place in Christian history is because of a 1st century AD letter addressed to it that was included in the New Testament.

In the 5th century BC Colossae was a major commercial center on the trade route from Sardis to Konya. It lost its importance by the 1st century BC when Laodicea was founded. It, along with Laodicea and Hierapolis, was destroyed in the earthquake of AD 60. The cities of the area declined in the 7th and 8th centuries AD under the pressure of Arab invaders. Later the Byzantines and Selçuks fought over it. The remains of a **theater** are still discernible, along with a few other buildings; but the site has not been excavated and is rarely visited. Colossae was famous for the dark red wool cloth that carried its name, *colossinum*.

The Letter to the Colossians, attributed to Paul, was probably written about AD 60 or 65. The grammar and the vocabulary of the letter have called into question Paul's authorship. However, it

---

Philemon was a Christian of some wealth and standing in Colossae to whom Paul wrote a letter. Paul hints that Philemon had treated his slave, Onesimus, badly. Perhaps because of the injustice, the slave had run away. Paul grew to see Onesimus as his son while he was in prison, and sent him back to Philemon with the request that Philemon should now recognize his former slave's worth. Church historians note that sixty years later the bishop of Ephesus was a man with this same name.

High Priests of Aphrodite, Aphrodite Hall, Aphrodisias Museum

could be that he asked one of his companions to put his thoughts into words and then gave his mark of approval by adding a note at the end in his own hand. From various references in the letter, it would appear that some of the Christians in Colossae were Jews (Col. 2:11, 16, 21); and that Paul had not visited the city (Col. 1:4; 2:3). Rather, he had heard about the group from Epaphras and from Onesimus who apparently was from Colossae (Col. 4:9). Paul was in prison at the time (Col.4:3), possibly in Rome. It also appears that Paul had become reconciled with John Mark (Col 4:10) after their disagreement in Perge some years before. Others mentioned in this letter include Timothy (whom Paul had met in Lystra), Luke (thought to be the author of Acts which details many of Paul's journeys), Aristarchus who was in prison with him, and Tychicus whom Paul had asked to carry the letter. Paul also made reference in the letter to the Christian community in Laodicea.

DİNAR - CELAENAE, APAMEA

Dinar is located on the main road from İzmir to Konya. It is also at the crossroads of that road and the north-south road from Antalya to Afyon, Kütahya and Eskişehir.

Ancient Dinar was Celaenae where Xerxes the Great had a palace. Xenephon reported that Cyrus the Younger under whom he served filled the palace grounds with wild animals. (In those years lions and tigers commonly roamed Anatolia.) Renamed Apamea, according to Strabo it was one of the important commercial centers in the 4th century BC. Business here was under the control of the Italians and the Jews. One of the beliefs of the resident Jews was that the highest mountain behind the city was Mt. Ararat. Philip of Macedon used that tradition by adding the mountain to the coins he struck after he included Apamea in his conquests.

Dinar now is an agricultural town; it suffered from a serious earthquake in the fall of 1995.

GEYRE - APHRODISIAS

Aphrodisias is well off the main highway between İzmir and Denizli, about 35 km from the turn near Kuyucuk. It is in the pretty valley of a small tributary of the Menderes River near the town of Geyre which used to be located on top of it.

Temples, a **bishop's palace**, a **theater**, a **huge stadium**, **baths**, a **council chamber** and, above all of these spectacular finds, a great quantity of beautiful statuary distinguish Aphrodisias as one of the most attractive ancient cities in Anatolia. The earliest finds go back to about 5800 BC. During the Roman Period there was a major school of sculptors at Aphrodisias producing masterpieces of white and blue-gray marble that were sent throughout the

The war in which Xenephon fought for Cyrus was occasioned by Cyrus's desire to supplant his older brother Artaxerxes as king of Persia. With an army of Greek mercenaries, he attacked his brother and was killed in October 401 BC. This left the Greeks stranded in Persia, from where under Xenephon's leadership they forced their way through the winter across eastern Anatolia to the Black Sea.

Temple of Aphrodite and Tetrapylon in the background, Aphrodisias

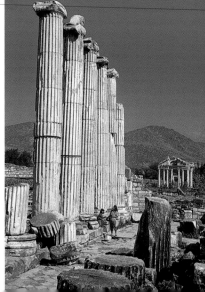

Roman world. The artists' workshop with their unfinished sculptures has been uncovered and some of their work put on display. Aphrodite, the city's patron goddess who symbolized fertility in the Greek and Roman Periods, was related through the city's first known Akkadian name, Ninoe, to the Assyrian goddess Astarte, the symbol of motherhood. The connection seems to be that Ninoe was the same goddess of love and war. Ninus was the legendary founder of Assyria. As a symbol of fertility, Aphrodite bore a similarity also to Cybele and to Artemis.

Aphrodisias flourished as an important religious and agricultural city, but it was also known as a center for the arts, letters and other intellectual and scientific pursuits.

One of the unique and most interesting buildings in Aphrodisias is the **Sebasteion**, a complex dedicated here to Aphrodite, but also a place where the Roman emperors were worshipped as deities. This structure, built in the first part of the 1st century AD, memorialized the Emperors Octavian, Tiberius, Gaius, Claudius and Nero. Scenes from mythology (Bellerophon and Pegasus, the Three Graces) were interspersed with statues of members of the imperial family (for instance, one of Nero's mother as Tyche in the act crowning him).

The **Temple to Aphrodite**, dating from as far back at least as the 7th century BC, was converted into a Christian basilica in the mid-5th century AD. At that time a large statue of the goddess was mutilated to fit into part of the new wall. The church ceased to be used after the 12th century when the Selçuks took over the region.

A modern, airy **museum** at Aphrodisias is a fitting tribute to the work of Professor Kenan Erim who conducted the excavations here from 1969 until his death in 1990. As a tribute to him, he was buried next to the Tetrapylon, the monumental gateway to the Temple to Aphrodite. Generously supported by the National Geographic Society, he was given its Centennial Award in 1990 for his lifetime of work on this city.

İZMİR - SMYRNA

İzmir is the third largest city in Turkey and the main center for exports. It was the site of the second church scolded by John in Revelation, and the home of the martyred Polycarp. A number of synagogues function as places of worship for the Jewish community. Tourists who stay here find it a useful center from which to explore the whole Aegean region. In addition, there is much to see in İzmir itself.

The history first. A port on the deep İzmir bay, many of its residents have probably always been merchants. The first settlers about 2000 BC seem to have lived in the **Bayraklı** region on the northwest side of the bay. There may have been some Hittite influence at that time. According Ekrem Akurgal, the archae-

---

Residents of Aphrodisias were slow to renounce their paganism. In spite of the imperial decree in the 4th century AD banning it, only in the 5th century did they convert the Temple to Aphrodite to a Christian church.

*The English Society of Dilettanti, a group of people who delighted in the fine arts, was founded in 1733/34. Because of their travels, its members called the attention of European scholars to their findings of classical art in Anatolia. Aphrodisias, Priene, Smyrna, and Cnidus are described in their volumes on **Ionian Antiquities**. Smyrna was the base from which they explored the region.*

ologist who has directed these excavations, the site was a small peninsula that jutted out into the bay. A well-built 7th century BC Temple to Athena was found here; capitals from the columns appear to have been decorated with a tulip design. Artifacts from the excavation are on exhibit in İzmir's **Archaeological Museum**. Ionians took the town in the 9th century BC. By the 7th century its place on the trade routes between Lydia and the west gave it great power and importance in its competition with Miletus and Ephesus. According to Herodotus (who was born just south in Halicarnassus in the 5th century BC), Lydians conquered Smyrna in the 6th century; it declined for 200 years thereafter.

İsa Camii, Selçuk

Alexander the Great moved the city from the Bayraklı location to the slope of **Mt. Pagus (Kadifekale)** in 334 BC. Smyrna was part of the Pergamene Empire from 190 BC until Attalus III willed it to Rome when it became part of the Province of Asia. Romans in Smyrna were slaughtered in the "Asian Vespers" carried out by King Mithradates IV of Pontus in 88 BC when he is said to have killed 80,000 expatriates in the province. There was a large Jewish colony in Smyrna at the turn of the Christian era, and one of the earliest Christian churches was established here.

Under the Eastern Roman Empire Smyrna's leading place in commerce was taken over by Constantinople. It went back and forth between Turkish and Byzantine rule. For a while the Knights of St. John held part of it before Tamerlane took it in 1402 and massacred almost everyone. He was quickly replaced by Turkish rule. After World War I and the subsequent occupation of Aegean Turkey by the Greeks, in 1922 as the Turkish army advanced on the city a great fire broke out which for three days raged through most of the Frankish, Armenian, Greek and Sephardic Jewish sections.

Ancient Smyrna was considered the most beautiful of the cities of the Roman Province of Asia. Many of its public buildings were faced with white marble. Its natural surroundings of mountains, water and fields agreed with the Greek ideal of proportion. It had the advantages of the sea coast for trade, the plains for agriculture and the mountains for respite from the summer's heat. Unlike the Ephesians, the Smyrnaeans won the struggle to keep their harbor from silting up by diverting the Hermus River (Gediz Nehri) to the northwest. Its most famous native son is Homer; he is thought to have been born near the river Meles, perhaps the small Halka Pınar stream that empties into the west end of the bay. (The island of Chios also claims him as its native.)

A few ruins from the Hellenistic or Roman city of Smyrna are visible in place: the excavated market underneath the **Kadifekale** fortress, a very short stretch of **Roman road** near the crest of Eşrefpaşa Caddesi and the **Roman aqueduct** in Buca. Kadıfekale itself on the top of Mt. Pagus is medieval in date.

Smyrna figures in John's Book of Revelation (Rev. 2:8-11) as the

The city of old Smyrna as it existed before Alexander the Great has been excavated by Ekrem Akurgal and John Cook. In the 2nd millennium, when the area was under attack by the Sea Peoples, its residents were in close contact with both the Hittites and the Trojans.

The Christian congregation in Smyrna in the 1st and early 2nd centuries probably stemmed from the sizable Jewish colony resident there.

place of the synagogue of Satan. John tells the Christians that they are about to suffer for their faith, but he also says that those who are faithful unto death will gain a crown of life.

While there is no record of any visit by Paul to Smyrna, probably he was in the city at least once or twice because he was resident in Ephesus for over two years. There was a lot of traffic between the two cities. If, as is thought, he traveled overland part of the way on his journey from Ephesus to Macedonia after the riot of the silversmiths, it would be logical for him at that time also to have visited the Christian communities in Smyrna, Sardis, Thyatira and Pergamum.

The **Roman agora** is a small open square about halfway between Kadifekale and Konak. A line of thirteen columns of the west stoa are still capped with their acanthus capitals. In the 2nd century AD there was an Altar to Zeus in the center of the agora. Statues of Demeter (goddess of agriculture) and Poseidon (god of the sea) stood side by side, perhaps the two main deities of commerce for the Smyrnaeans. This was the government center of the city; the law courts were here and a number of stores. The agora was a two-story area, and the vaulting of the lower level shows how carefully it was built to withstand İzmir's frequent earthquakes. One corner vault is unique because it is supported by five ribs. What can be seen today is part of the reconstruction financed by Marcus Aurelius after the devastating earthquake of AD 178.

The **main road** of Roman Smyrna probably followed Gazi Osmanpaşa Bulvarı past the western side of the agora and Eşrefpaşa Caddesi up the hill. At the top of that hill, about where the city gate might have been, a short stretch of that road serves as cobbled pavement for a weekly open air fruit and vegetable market. The tiered seats of the Roman stadium could be seen fifty years ago on the slope below Kadifekale. The stadium was the large sports arena for the city and the main outdoor center for public gatherings such as those that celebrated religious holidays.

Ignatius is one of the "Apostolic Fathers," a group whose writings were not included in the canon of the New Testament. Rather they became authorities on church practices because they had known Jesus's close associates. Ignatius was a fervently religious person. His letters glorified martyrdom, and were used by later churchmen to reject heresy and strengthen the position of the bishop.

By the turn of the 2nd century there was a large enough congregation in Smyrna to support a bishop. Of the early Christians, **Polycarp**, the fourth Bishop of Smyrna is known as one of the first Christian martyrs. He lived between about AD 65 and 155.

The earliest literary reference to Polycarp is in a letter addressed to him by the Bishop of Antioch, Ignatius, and sent from Alexandria Troas about 110. The letters Ignatius wrote during his journey to Rome (under Roman guard) are a main source of information concerning the organization of the early church, including the position and the responsibilities of a bishop.

About 40 years later Polycarp traveled to Rome to discuss with the Western Christian leaders the question of when Easter should be observed. Both sides were fully conscious that the issue combined theological and political aspects. Polycarp had been chosen by the Eastern community because he had known those who knew first-hand the original traditions (possibly Philip, Onesimus, John the writer of Revelation and others). Therefore he carried the weight of authority. The political issue that was tangled in the religious one was which center would dominate, East or West. The prelates resolved the question by agreeing that it was acceptable to be diverse. They could observe Easter on different days and still be in communion. In evidence of this and of their respect for each other, Polycarp accepted the honor of celebrating mass in Rome. He also met his pupil Irenaeus, who happened to be there at the time. Shortly after, when Polycarp returned to Smyrna, he was arrested by the Roman governor and tried in a public gathering in the stadium (located on the hill below Kadifekale).

When the governor Statius Quadratus tried to get him to temporize, Polycarp replied heatedly, "If you vainly suppose that I will acknowledge Caesar as sovereign, and if you pretend you don't know who I am, listen plainly: I am a Christian. For eighty and six years I have served Jesus Christ and he has done me no wrong. How can I blaspheme my King?" This was high treason, and for his crime Polycarp was burned at the stake.

Polycarp wrote several letters, but only the one to the Christians in Philippi has survived. It is almost as short as the short letters in the New Testament, but it is valuable because he mentions both the letters of Paul and of Ignatius. It also is important in tracing the early history and practices of the Christian church. Polycarp is revered for his clear understanding of the uncompromising demands of faith and for his utter lack of self-interest.

Today's central market in İzmir (the **Kemeraltı Çarşısı**) is a labyrinth of streets and alleys with major stores and pushcart venders all competing to sell their merchandise. It is a noisy, crowded, colorful area of everyday Turkish life. Here you can find dozens of kinds of olives and pickles, dried fruits and nuts, Turkish rugs, cheap plastic toys, circumcision costumes, television sets, all cheek by jowl with each other. Also here are five Ottoman mosques, the **Hisar Camii** (1597), the **Şadırvan Camii** (1637), the **Hacı Hüsmen Camii** (1651), the **Kestane Pazarı Camii** (c. 1650) which has the *mihrap* from the **İsa Bey Camii** of Selçuk, and the **Kemeraltı Camii** (also called the **Hacı Mehmet Ağa Cami**i, 1672). A 17th century caravansary in the market, the **Kızlarağası[4] Hanı**, has the reputation of having been the place of the slave market during the Ottoman Empire.

The **Kültürpark** occupying the main area of the 1922 fire is a recreation center and the location of the **International Fair grounds**, the **İzmir Archaeological Museum**, the **Ethnographic Museum** and the **zoo**.

A mere listing of the synagogues in İzmir gives an indication of the strength of the Jewish community. The **Aydınlı** (or Shalom)

*Smyrna was ravaged by Tamerlane in 1402 when he massacred almost everyone there. The Ottoman sultan Mehmet I took it in 1415. It was the base for work by the Society of Dilettanti, led by the British Consul John Cleland (who later wrote the novel **Fanny Hill**).*

İzmir has been known for its exports of figs, raisins, tobacco, cotton, olive oil, valonia oak, steel and textiles. The expatriate and minority communities have played major roles in its commercial life.

İzmir is a convenient place from which to explore many places with historical references. To the north along the coast are Cyme (once the biggest and best city of Aeolia), Pitane (today's Çandarlı, birthplace of Arcesilaus, disciple of Plato and head of the New Academy in Athens), and Phoceae (Eski Foça, site of a summer folklore and music festival). West from İzmir, the wine of Clazomene (on the peninsula at Urla İskelesi) was highly valued by the Romans.

Synagogue is one of six mentioned by the historian Rabbi Escapa. Also called Kaal de Abasho, it became known as the Aydınlı Synagogue when Jews from Aydın moved to İzmir. Having been damaged in a major fire in 1841, it was rebuilt that year. The **Bikour Holim Synagogue** is so named to commemorate the time of an epidemic when the hospitals of the city were so full that the synagogues were used to house the sick. It was built in 1724 by Solomon de Ciavez. The **Giveret (Signore) Synagogue** is thought to have been built originally by a Portuguese woman, Dona Gracia (Mendes) Nasi. A painting of that building hangs on the wall. It was rebuilt after the 1841 fire by Moiz Yerushalmi. The **Beit Israel Synagogue**, located on Mithatpaşa Caddesi, was built in 1905; it is the most active of the İzmir synagogues. In addition to these, there are the **Algazi,** the **Ez Hayyim** (or Beit Hillel, built in the Palaci family home), the **Rosh Ha Ar**, the **Hevra** and the **Shaar Ha Shamaim** (the Gate of Heaven) synagogues.

The **Bornova** region of İzmir (where Ege University is located) was developed because Frankish merchants wanted to escape from the heat of summer in the center of town and from the recurring plagues of both cholera and pirates. The houses they built were mansions with black and white pebble mosaic walks, marble columns and beautiful gardens. Their commute to work was speeded by a special train; the engine of that line is permanently stationed as a museum piece beside the main street.

Among the many churches of İzmir, three stand out. One is the Anglican **Church of St. John** in Alsancak which serves many of the English-speaking community. Another is the Catholic **Cathedral of St. John the Evangelist** built between 1862 and 1874. The third is the Catholic **Church of St. Polycarp**. The original building was founded by a gift from the stern French Cardinal Richelieu in 1625; the present structure was built in 1929.

SIĞACIK - TEOS

One of Anacreon's typical poems inspired an 18th century English drinking song. Its music, written, by John Smith, is sung now in the United States to the words, "Oh, say can you see by the dawn's early light..."

Teos is on the Aegean Sea southwest of İzmir; its Temple to Dionysus was important in pagan times. It is little but fields of grains and lentils interspersed with marble columns. The slope that rises gently from the sea, the green trees and fields, the view of offshore islands make Teos one of the most attractive of the ancient sites on the Aegean. It was supposed to have been founded before the 10th century BC and to have prospered early in its history.

Two literary men came from Teos, the 6th century BC poet Anacreon and the 1st century BC bibliophile Apellikon. Anacreon is known for his lyrics celebrating old age, love, spring, and wine and song. Apellikon bought Aristotle's library and tried to save the pages that had suffered from being stored in a damp place. Unfortunately, mistakes were made as they were copied, and, likewise unfortunately, much of it was later lost in Egypt.

Teos came into fame as an artists' colony in the 3rd century BC. Members of its artists' guild traveled around the Greek-speaking world to add their names and their talents to the glitter of the various music and drama festivals. Although by the 1st century the artists had fallen into disrepute as swaggering rowdies, Mark Anthony thought that their production was appropriate entertainment for Cleopatra who was staying in Priene. Of the ruined buildings, the **theater** and the **Temple to Dionysus** stand out. The theater is nestled against the southern side of the hill looking out to sea. (When it was in use the stage building probably blocked the view for the dignitaries who sat in the front rows.)

The temple in Claros suffers from the same problem that the Temple to Diana in Ephesus does, and also the three temples in the Letoon: Since their foundations are below the water-table, they would need to be pumped out constantly in order to be above ground.

KLAROS - CLAROS

Claros is almost due south of İzmir and something more than a kilometer from the sea. It is on the side of a stream bed off a road from Değirmendere to the sea.

The **oracle of Apollo** in Claros was known to Homer, making it at least as old as the 8th century BC. But although the oracle was wise enough to have warned that Helen would cause trouble for everyone, the site was apparently not important until the time of Alexander the Great. The ruins presently visible are from the 4th to the 1st century BC. Parts of huge statues of Apollo, Artemis and Leto are lying here. Apollo was represented seated; his statue would have been between seven and eight meters high. The two goddesses were similarly large.

The chamber for the oracles was beneath the Temple to Apollo. Excavators found a well there that they believe was the source of the water that the prophets drank.

Like Didyma, Claros was only a temple site and never a city; the nearest cities were Colophon (about 12 km north up the Ales River near Değirmendere) and Notion (about 2 km south on the sea). Unlike Didyma or Patara, the prophet here was a man. For him to deliver his prophecy all he needed to know was the name of the client; he didn't ask what the concerns were. His seance always took place at night when he entered the sacred cave and drank the noxious waters. Perhaps the best-known of the Clarian oracles was the one encouraging Alexander the Great to move the residents of Old Smyrna from its location in today's Bayraklı to the slopes of Mt. Pagus — today's Kadifekale. Another warned the too-popular Germanicus, and when he was poisoned soon after, suspicion pointed at the emperor Tiberius.

One wonders how this prophet was chosen: The Roman historian Tacitus says he was usually a man from Miletus. (Did Miletus have a corner on the market of supplying prophets and prophetesses?) While his mutterings were interpreted as poetry, he himself was illiterate. It was the responsibility of others to make his words meaningful. Pliny commented that the priests and scribes of Claros had lifetime appointments, but that the prophet lasted only a year in the position. Was that as long as the person could survive the fumes?

Sığacık

*Foundations of the
fortress on the hill
north of Selçuk date
from the attack by
Goths in AD 263.
With the several
later Arab attacks,
residents from
Ephesus moved to
Selçuk, taking with
them a lot of stone.
The Cathedral was
situated so that it
also was part of the
defense system. Not
all of the fortress is
open to the public,
but the site affords a
good view of the
countryside.*

People from as widely distant places as Great Britain and Russia came to Claros to learn what this oracle could tell them. As a pagan site Claros was active well into the Christian era; it was destroyed in the end not by angry churchmen but by an earthquake. The ruins now are usually at least in part under water from the stream of the valley, making excavation difficult.

SELÇUK - AYIO THEOLOGOS

In the 6th century AD the port of Ephesus had become impossibly clogged from the silt of the Cayster River (Küçük Menderes) and the town itself was a malarial swamp. Therefore its residents moved about 4 km east to the higher ground near the cathedral church which the Emperor Justinian and the Empress Theodora were building. The church was located at the traditional grave of John, the writer of Revelation. From that church and the writer, the town took the name of Hagios Theologos, "the holy word of God." In time the name was softened to Ayiotheologo and Ayasuluk. While the Selçuk army did not take the town from the Byzantines when it attacked in 1090, the town did eventually become the capital of the Muslim Aydınoğulları emirate in 1348, and in the next century part of the Ottoman Empire. Its name was officially changed to Selçuk in 1914. Now on a main highway from İzmir to Denizli, several places in Selçuk are worthy of attention.

The first is the **museum**. The best quick introduction to Ephesus is here. Statues, frescoes, mosaics, coins and household items are displayed in the six rooms and the courtyard. Among these are a fresco portrait of Socrates, a small bronze boy riding a dolphin, a Roman sundial, terra-cotta theater masks, a small ivory statue of an eunuch priest with a twinkle in his eyes, a gladiator, busts of Roman citizens and bronze crosses. The most famous and most striking statues are the two bigger-than-life marble statues of Diana with rows of oval objects — breasts? eggs? — cascading down her front. (Note that these were made a hundred years after Paul condemned their manufacture.)

John is believed to have lived in Ephesus before and after his exile on the island of Patmos. There is a question about which John it was who lived in Ephesus because the earliest references talk about three different men of the same name. However, whoever it was who wrote Revelation, he scolded the Ephesians (Rev. 2:1-7) saying that they had cooled in their early faith. To inspire them to repentance he held out the promise of the fruit of the tree of life.

The Ephesians were the first congregation of Christians John addressed; the others in order were Smyrna, Pergamum, Thyatira, Sardis, Philadelphia and Laodicea. John seems to have known specific details about each of them, but there is no evidence that he had been to all of them in person. Perhaps the number seven influenced the choice of these congregations as symbolic of the

*Statue of Diana, the
Selçuk Museum*

entire community. It is thought that each of them had a sensitive, distinguishing characteristic that John wanted to speak to, and, in singling them out, to warn others of those dangers. It is also possible that their relative locations made a route around which church-related information circulated. Each was about a two-day ride by horseback from the one before.

The Cathedral of St. John, Selçuk

The 4th century historian Eusebius tells a story about John having converted a young boy to Christianity before his exile on Patmos. When he returned, he learned that the boy not only had reverted to paganism, he had become a notorious brigand. An old man, John set out by himself into the hills around Ephesus where after some difficulties he found and rescued his ward.

The **Cathedral of St. John** was on the hill above the city. It has been partly reconstructed thanks to a gift from the people of Lima, Ohio; its new marble gleams in the sun. The building was in the shape of a cross and was covered with six domes. Under the central dome was the tomb of John; that has a marble marker today. Like other churches that Justinian and Theodora built, the capitals of the supporting columns were incised with their monograms. The baptistery with the keyhole-shaped font is north of the nave. When Christianity became the state religion, the crowds who once flocked to the Temple to Diana turned their attention to this cathedral.

On the field below the church, between Selçuk and Ephesus and lost under mud and weeds, is a stump of a column, all that is visible of the famous **Temple to Diana**, one of the Seven Wonders of the World. During Hellenistic and Roman times the Temple brought thousands of pilgrims and suppliants from around the Mediterranean; it was big business for Ephesus.

A 6th century BC Temple to Artemis/Diana was destroyed in the 4th century by Herostratus, a lunatic wanting to make a name for himself. It was rebuilt almost at once, the first made entirely of marble. Alexander the Great wanted to help in the project, but he was turned down by the Ephesians with the excuse that one god should not make an offering to another. The new temple was a large building, a little more than 55m wide by 115m long. (Compare this with the size of St. Sophia in İstanbul of 70m wide by 75m long.) By Pliny's account it had a forest of 127 columns. While much of the floor of the temple was taken up by the pedestals of those columns, still a large crowd of priests could have gathered inside for a communal religious service. Since descriptions of pagan worship concentrate on what the priests or the initiates were required to do, probably the general public expected

An 8th century temple dedicated to the Mother Goddess Cybele was the earliest temple on the site of the famous Temple to Diana. Like it, the subsequent temples were in a swamp which engineers struggled to control by digging drains. The positioning of so important a building in so troublesome a spot begs several questions. If the intent was for it to be prominent, why not put it on top of Mt Pion? Or were there property rights that dictated its location? Was there a sacred fountain here? Or was it only the inertia of tradition that kept it here?

Women have long exercised considerable influence in Ephesus. According to early Greek writers, Amazons were among its first residents. Its guardian deity was the Mother/Virgin goddess, known by Roman times as either Artemis or Diana. The most contentious issue in the Third Ecumenical Council was over whether Mary should be called "theotokos" ("Mother of God") or not.

to stand in attendance outside on the marble steps. Special occasions must have attracted extra crowds.

Between the Temple to Diana and the Cathedral of St. John is the classically beautiful **İsa Camii** that was built in 1375. Its founder was İsa Bey, the son of Mehmet Bey who was the Emir of Aydın at the time, and whose capital was in the city of Selçuk. The door of the mosque is decorated with black and yellow marble; inside the floor is a geometric pattern of marble squares. The windows show the same careful, intricate carving as the Alaettin Mosque in Konya.

EFES - EPHESUS

Gleaming white with marble, offering a full range of business and entertainment opportunities, Ephesus rivaled Rome in its magnificence. For pagans, the glorious Temple to Diana drew the crowds. Today the marble street where Paul walked and the theater where he faced a rioting mob call forth the most attention. The most important commercial center in western Anatolia, probably over a quarter of a million people lived here at its height in the Roman and early Byzantine Periods. Even its ruins are impressive.

Ephesus began as a port on the mouth of the Cayster River (Küçük Menderes); it became one of the leading cities of the world linking the western end of trade routes in Anatolia with the rest of the Mediterranean. The commercial banks of Ephesus, which controlled the banking of western Anatolia and which handled the foreign exchange, are considered to be the institutions where banking as we know it today originated.

Four times the public buildings that the citizens built honoring Roman emperors earned Ephesus the cherished title of "Temple Warden." One of the Roman governors of the Province of Asia, Gaius Julius Celsus Polemaeanus, so favored the city that he chose to retire here rather than in Rome. The **Celsus library** was started by his son Gaius Julius Aquila who also held the position of Roman governor. Celsus was a lover of books and was accorded the unique honor of being buried, not only within the city but, more, in the vault of his own library among his books.

Temple to Hadrian, Ephesus

The Austrian archaeologists who have worked in Ephesus for over a century have uncovered an impressive amount of the city and restored parts of a number of buildings. Thus with a modicum of imagination, people visiting Ephesus today can visualize the city when it was the capital of the province. The library of Celsus, the **Temple to Hadrian**, the **Baths of Scholasticus**, the **brothel**, the **public toilets**, the **Temple to Serapis**, the city **council chambers** near where the city's eternal flame burned, and the **east gymnasium** are only some of the buildings to be seen and marveled at.[5]

For many Christians the best-known building in Ephesus is the large **theater** where a 1st century AD silversmith attempted to stir up a riot to get rid of Paul who was damaging his business of making images of Diana. Now more a trinket than a cult figure, Diana is back on sale near that same theater.

In the plain to the north of the colonnaded street is the **Double Church** where in 431 the Third Ecumenical Council members fought over orthodox Christian belief. It is a long, narrow building, probably originally not a church. It might have been an educational institution, perhaps even the Hall of Tyrannus where Paul lectured during the noon hours when the building was usually empty. This is pure speculation: Neither the Hall nor the synagogue that Paul attended have been identified as such.

Ephesus with Celsus Library in the background

Paul preached and taught in Ephesus for over two years. During that time he sent Timothy and Erastus to Macedonia to continue the missionary work there. The fact that Paul was effective in Asia is proved in that the silversmiths, led by Demetrius, feared that if they did not stop him they would soon be completely out of work. He and his companions, Gaius and Aristarchus, were dragged into the theater to defend themselves. It is interesting to note that the town clerk was able to quiet the mob with an appeal to reason; the clerk reminded the would-be (and probably hoarse) rioters of their responsibility as law-abiding citizens.

The names of several other early Christians are recorded as residents of Ephesus. Among them are the eloquent Apollos with whom Paul associated himself, saying that he planted, that Apollos watered, but that God gave the growth (I Cor. 3:6). A couple, Priscilla and Aquilla, established a house church in Ephesus (I Cor. 16:19); perhaps Aquilla did well in the profession of tent-making that he shared with Paul. In the 2nd century one of the bishops of Ephesus was Onesimus; while that name became common for bishops to use, this particular man could have been the young runaway slave whom Paul adopted when he was in prison. That story appears in Paul's letter to the slave's owner Philemon appealing for pardon (Phil. 10-21). The daughters of the Apostle Philip lived in Ephesus, according to the historian Eusebius.

In the account in the Koran of the Seven Sleepers (Sura xviii, The Cave), the youths were guarded by their dog Katmehr. His name was sometimes added as a seal on a letter to insure its safe arrival.

A small stone building high up on the west corner of the city wall is pointed out as **Paul's prison.** The story — probably apocryphal — goes that he wrote the Letter to the Ephesians from this place. This building was not a prison, and there is much question over whether this letter was written by Paul or by one of his disciples.

Virgin Mary's Home

On the east side of Mt. Pion, the hill of Ephesus, to the right as one approaches the Magnesian Gate from the highway, is the crude **Cave of the Seven Sleepers**. The legend associated with this is that of young men who escaped religious persecution by sleeping a miraculously long time. It is similar to the story of the cave of Eshabıkehf near Tarsus. This one became a place of Christian burial just outside Ephesus; graffiti found here date from the years that Crusaders marched through Ephesus.

MERYEMANA - VIRGIN MARY'S HOME

About three miles away in the forested mountain above Ephesus is Meryemana, a modest stone house. This is now a sanctuary where according to the belief of people of many religious faiths, the Virgin Mary lived her last days. The tradition is that John brought Mary to Ephesus after the death of Jesus, in keeping with Jesus's admonition to John to care for his mother (John 19:27). (The conflicting tradition is that she died on Mount Zion in Jerusalem.) Also, John being a common name, it is difficult to establish which man is being referred to in the traditions. Both Pope Paul VI in 1967 and Pope John Paul II in 1979 have celebrated mass here. Many people congregate at this sanctuary every August 15 to observe the Feast of the Assumption of the Virgin. The foundations of the house are old; they may date back to the 1st century; the rest of the building may be 6th century. It was first identified in 1818 by an Austrian peasant, Anne Catherine Emmerich, who saw it in a dream exactly as it was found. The setting is beautifully peaceful, encouraging reverence and contemplation.

DAVUTLAR - PANIONIUM

Twelve cities, not all on the mainland, were original members of the Pan-Ionian League: Chios (Sakız Adası), Clazomene (north of Urla), Colophon (Değirmendere), Erythrea (Ildır), Ephesus (Efes), Lebedus (Gümüldür), Miletus (Milet), Myus (Afşartepe), Phocaea (Foça), Priene (Güllübahçe), Samos (Sisam Adası) and Teos (Sığacık). Smyrna (İzmir) joined the League at a later date. The League was a political union; its members were not obligated to come to the help of each other if one was attacked, but they did meet together in council at the Panionium. This was a sanctuary sacred to Poseidon, the Earth-Shaker. It was located northwest of Priene on the northeast corner of the Dilek Peninsula near today's Güzelçamlı. Apparently there never was a large temple here, but rather an altar for the sacrifices to Poseidon and a council chamber.

Davutlar is part of the national park system of protected forests.

It also boasts a new spa, the Davutlar Termal Tesisleri, which promises with a spacious indoor pool, treatment for rheumatism, high blood pressure, diabetes and skin diseases.

GÜLLÜBAHÇE - PRIENE

Priene has the theatrical stage setting of an almost sheer cliff as the backdrop, a long narrow stage, and, in place of the orchestra, to the southwest a view out across the plain to the Aegean Sea. In Byzantine times Priene was the seat of a Christian bishopric; the basilica's pulpit and the base of the altar stand in place near the theater. Pagan temples, including one to Alexander the Great, are found throughout the site. Originally Priene was a port city located on the sea. It moved to its present location in 350 BC. What is now Lake Bafa was a bay extending between Priene and Miletus 50 km inland to Heraclea-under-Latmus.[6] As the Meander River brought more and more silt into the flood plain, both Priene and Miletus lost their harbors and their importance. Priene was never a large city, but it was responsible for managing the Panionium, the place of the Pan-Ionic Temple to Poseidon and the council seat of the Panionium League. (The Panionium was just over the mountains to the north.)

The ruins of the Hellenistic city suggest that its residents liked precision: The main streets run east-west; the side streets are perpendicular to them like a grid. Those side streets had to be stepped to accommodate the slope. There were four houses to a block, while public buildings took up one, two, or three blocks. The **bouleterion** (city council) and **prytanaeum** (administrative building) occupied one block. The bouleterion was an almost square building with seats for 640 people on three sides. Among the images on the altar (a single, rectangular block of marble) were bulls' skulls holding garlands of laurel. The bulls recall the Hittite worship of bulls as symbols of virility.

The **Temple to Athena** is the oldest and most important build-ing to be seen in Priene. It was begun by Pytheos (c. mid-4th century BC), the architect who also built the Mausoleum in Halicarnassus. Pytheos wrote a text book on architecture using this temple as the model; the book was the standard work for centuries. Alexander the Great contributed to the completion of the temple in 334 BC (after his similar gift had been refused by the Ephesians), and later it was dedicated jointly to him and to Athena. Although the sanctuary of this and all other temples was off limits to everyone except the temple staff, the steps and the colonnaded area were favorite places for people to stroll. From the Priene temple there was a refreshing view of the sea.

Besides the Temple to Athena, among the other interesting buildings are a **gymnasium**, a **Christian archbishop's basilica** and the **theater**. An altar to Dionysus occupies the center of the front row of seats in the theater and at the west corner of the orchestra is

Priene's most famous native son was the philosopher Bias (fl.c.570 BC). In the face of an enemy attack on the city when everyone was fleeing and taking all their possessions with them, someone saw him leaving without anything. On being questioned about where his things were, Bias answered, "But I do have my valuables; I'm never without them."

Priene

Thales of Miletus (640-546 BC) holds the distinction of founding Greek geometry, astronomy, and philosophy. In geometry he showed that by knowing the precise relationship between different parts of a figure, the unknown part could be determined. He used this, for instance, to find the height of an unknown object by comparing its shadow to the shadow of a known object. The excitement caused by his correct prediction of the sun's eclipse probably started the Greeks on their scientific inquiries. In philosophy he sought to find a unity in the origin of things. (He also thought that magnets had souls because of the attraction they exerted.)

the base of a water clock. The clock is an unusual addition: It is thought that the plays were not timed, but the theater which was also used for large public meetings needed the clock to tell the speaker and his listeners that his time had run out. High above Priene, on Mt. Mycale, is the acropolis. The man who commanded the troops stationed there was required not to leave during his four-month term. The stadium, located on the lower edge of the city, had seats only on the north side since the south side falls off steeply.

MİLET - MILETUS

Miletus in ancient times was a port at the mouth of the Meander River (Menderes Nehri). Thus it was the hub of the traffic between the inland centers of Phrygia and those of Egypt, Italy, Greece and its colonies. It lay across the bay from Priene. (That bay has since shrunk to the inland.) As a most important city on the Aegean coast, Miletus had its share of pagan temples, then churches, and later mosques. Paul said good-by to his friends and his work in Asia near the lions that still guard the former harbor. By the 5th century Miletus had developed a system of writing that the people of Athens adopted. This then became the standard Greek alphabet. Although leveled by the invading Persians in 494 it became a major city again in the Roman Period. The streets of Miletus were arranged on the pattern of a grid like those of Priene.

Excavations at Miletus show that its settlement began about 1500 BC. Homer some time before 800 BC talked about the Milesians who fought for the Trojans. Milesians are credited with founding colonies on the Dardanelles, the Sea of Marmara and the Black Sea. It was the birthplace of several philosophers, among them Thales (who predicted the eclipse of the sun in 585 BC), Hippodamus (who organized towns on a grid of crossing streets) and Anaximander (who invented the sun dial). The 6th/5th century historian Hecataeus who was the first to write a methodical account of Greek myth and tradition was a native son, as was the 4th century poet and musician Timotheus who upset the musicians of Sparta and Athens by adding extra strings to the lyre.

The religious center of Miletus was the **Delphinium** located just east of the harbor stoa. Here worshippers conceived of Apollo Delphinius particularly as a protector of sailors and — in the form of a dolphin — as a lover of music.

The most distinguished woman of the eastern Mediterranean in the 5th century BC was the beautiful courtesan Aspasia who came from Miletus. Aspasia was the teacher of rhetoric to Socrates; she was also the mistress of Pericles whose tears in court were all that saved her once from a charge of impiety. That gave fuel to Aristophanes who accused her of being behind all of Pericles' political actions. Pericles got a law passed that made their son his legitimate heir. She was an early champion of women's rights, criticizing the restricted behavior and education imposed on her sex. The wealthy, socially-proper Athenian Thucydides ignored her in his *History*, but Socrates paid her the tribute of quoting the funeral oration that she made honoring those who had died for their country.

Paul visited Miletus in the spring — perhaps AD 57 — as he completed his third missionary journey (Acts 20:15-38). For Paul and for his listeners, many of whom had come from Ephesus, it was an emotional visit. They were close friends; they had gone through many ordeals together as Paul reminded them. Paul was looking forward to a time of more great trial for himself personally and for the church as a whole. He expected to be thrown into prison; he expected that the church would be attacked by people who wanted to distort the truth. He might have lingered with them and they most certainly regretted saying good-by to him, but he was in a hurry to get to Jerusalem before Pentecost (in Paul's time it was 50 days after the first day of Passover).

Theater of Miletus

Two stone lions that guarded the entrance to the harbor had been in place for over two hundred years when Paul took leave of his friends and boarded his ship. The harbor is gone, but the lions are there today.

Miletus was a proud and important city; the extent and the wealth of the ruins record its strength. Its splendid **theater** seated at least 15,000 people; of the ruins it is now most prominent in projecting some sense of the grandeur of the city. An inscription on the 5th row of seats indicates this area was reserved for "God-fearing Jews." There are also a city **council chamber** which had seats for 1,500 people in its auditorium, a large 2nd century BC **stadium**, three **market places**, a **synagogue** near the old harbor, a 5th century AD basilical **church**, and a **Temple to Serapis**. One of the market places was the largest anywhere in its time. The gate of this market has been reconstructed in the Pergamon Museum in Berlin. Built by Faustinia, the wife of Marcus Aurelius, the Baths remain one of the better preserved buildings from the Roman Period. The **Mosque of İlyas Bey**, finished in 1404, south of the south marketplace, is an excellent example of the artistry and architectural skill of 15th century builders.

Medusa head, Didyma

The cult of Serapis, a god of the underworld, was originated by Ptolemy Soter about 290 BC when he stole a statue from Sinop on the Black Sea. Ptolemy's intent was to give the Egyptians and the Greeks a symbol they could worship together. Serapis was a god of healing whose oracles came in dreams. By the time of Hadrian (AD 117-135) the cult was popular around the Mediterranean.

DİDİM - DIDYMA

Didyma was the main place of pagan worship for the people of Miletus. A sacred road stretched the 20 km between the two, its final length marked by statues of lions, priests and priestesses.

Ancient historians record that long before the Ionians settled in the area in the 19th century BC Didyma was a sanctuary in a grove of trees — probably bay or laurel — beside a sacred spring. While some of the early houses and shops have been unearthed showing that a few people did live here, Didyma was never a more populous town than it is today. Rather, most people who worked

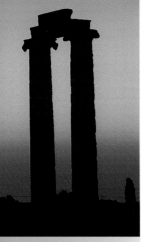

Temple at Didyma

When Croesus was defeated by Cyrus (546 BC), Cyrus honored him by allowing Croesus to send the chains with which he had been bound to the Delphic oracle. This was his reproach to the oracle for her having misled him in the prophecy of the downfall of an empire. The Delphic priestess retorted that even a god could not escape destiny, that Apollo had kept Sardis from being captured for three years, and that anyway Croesus should have been smart enough to ask which empire.

in Didyma lived in Miletus; Didyma was tied administratively and financially to Miletus. By the 6th century BC the sanctuary, the **Temple to Apollo**, was one of the most important and most impressive religious sites in Anatolia.

Like other temples, this one existed because people who came to it believed that here they would find answers to their pressing problems. One of the early inscriptions — from about 600 BC — records that the prophetess told some supplicants that it was all right for them to follow their father's profession of piracy. The prophetess was consulted for political or economic advice, and thanked appropriately when the advice had helped. Herodotus reported that the Egyptian King Necho gave his armor to this temple in gratitude for his success at Magdolus (presumably the Battle of Megiddo — located southeast of today's Haifa — where he defeated Josiah — 2 Kings 23:29). Further evidence of the temple's importance is that King Croesus heaped a huge amount of gold (including his wife's jewelry) on it equal to his gift to the Temple to Apollo at Delphi in Greece. This was in spite of the fact that the Delphic oracle passed the test of guessing his riddle correctly while the Didymaic did not.

The bronze cult statue of Apollo Philesis (Apollo the Affectionate) which stood in the center of the inner recess of the temple was made about 500 BC. When the Persians defeated Miletus in 494 BC they went on to destroy Didyma and to carry off this statue to Ecbatana (Hamadan in Iran). Following that disaster the temple suffered almost two hundred years of inactivity until Alexander the Great became interested in it. He found this statue in Persia and sent it back to Didyma. (The statue has since disappeared; if it was typical of 6th century statues, it probably represented the god in a rather stiff position standing formally, looking straight ahead rather than in the graceful pose of the 1st century BC Apollo of the Belvedere). Alexander's general and successor, Seleucis, ordered the rebuilding of the temple; the Milesians and then the Romans continued to work on it for six hundred years without ever completing the job. The influence of the Greek builders can be seen in the Ionic plan of the temple and the Corinthian capitals; that of the Romans is in the designs on the bases of the columns in the outer row on the east side. The Medusa head, one of several which made up the frieze above the outer row of columns, was thought to have been crafted by sculptors from Aphrodisias in the 2nd century AD.

Worship at the Temple to Apollo began with the supplicants performing a ritual ablution at the well east of the building. They then sacrificed an animal (often a goat) at the altar. If the sacrifice seemed propitious, they went on to ask their question of a priest who transmitted it to the prophetess. Then they waited to get their answer from the priest who had turned the delirious mutterings of the prophetess into doggerel. Usually the answers could be interpreted several ways.[7]

At the height of the temple's activity when the place was crowded with worshippers the rites must have consumed the better part of the day. Temple grounds were often shady parks with places for picnics. The temples where the Muse of prophecy could be invoked boasted museum items, exotic animals, trophies from famous battles, and curiosities — much like today's museums. (The word "museum" means "pertaining to the Muse.") The prophetess at Didyma was required to fast for three days before she inhaled the stupefying fumes. Possibly the duties were passed around among several women; possibly the position was not for life.

The great festival of Didyma was an athletic and cultural event and took place every four years. The races were held in the stadium immediately south of the temple. Spectators sat on the long rows of the temple steps. Perhaps there is a hint of the long wait between the racing events in the graffiti of crude squares for games of dice scratched on the steps. Some of the cultural events of the festival were held in Miletus, but in spite of the large theater there, it was in Didyma that the tragedies were played. This should not be surprising: One theory holds that tragedy was a religious ceremony growing out of the "dithyramb," the religious hymn celebrating the events in the story of the god Dionysus.

Didyma continued important into the 4th century AD. Diocletian (AD 284 - 305) consulted its oracle for advice on what to do with the rising power of Christianity, and Julian the Apostate (361-363) ordered that the chapels built at Didyma to honor Christian martyrs should be razed. The end to the temple as a pagan worship center came in 385 when Theodosius I forbade "the detestable consultation of oracles."

The sacred spring at Didyma went dry after the Persians destroyed the temple. A century and a half later when Alexander the Great was approaching, the spring began to flow again. Such a portentous event moved the oracle to prophesy that he would win the Battle of Arbella (Erbil in Syria). In thanks, Alexander ordered a new temple to be built. Work on it continued into the 4th century AD, until the Christian emperor Theodosius I forbade pagan divination.

BODRUM -- HALICARNASSUS

Bodrum's interest in Christian history is in its link with the Crusaders through the Castle of St. Peter. In Hellenistic times it was the Mausoleum, one of the Seven Wonders of the World, that attracted visitors to Halicarnassus, as it was then called. Most stately of such monumental tombs, the Mausoleum was built in the 6th century BC by Artemesia to honor her brother/husband King Mausoleus. The tomb — long since gone — was famous as much for its size as for its marble statuary. Some of the beautifully carved marble from it can be seen in the British Museum in London. A small part of a frieze has recently been uncovered and is now in the **Museum of the Mausoleum** of Halicarnassus.

Today it is the **Castle of St. Peter** that is the first building in Bodrum that catches the attention of visitors. This Crusader fortress, perhaps the best preserved of any in Asia, is on a small hill attached to the mainland by a man-made isthmus.

The Crusaders' Castle , Bodrum

The reconstruction of Queen Ada, the Carian Princess, Bodrum Museum

The Knights of the Order of the Hospital of St. John of Jerusalem (the Knights of Rhodes) date their beginning to a hospital established in Jerusalem when that city first became a place of Christian pilgrimage. It was maintained by Benedictines and then by Augustinians. With the Crusades, the Order came under the protection of European royalty. Expelled from Jerusalem in the 14th century, the Knights moved their headquarters to Cyprus, to Rhodes, and then to Malta.

Although the Knights Hospitallers of St. John of Jerusalem had been stationed in Halicarnassus since 1304, it was Tamerlane's capture in 1402 of their Castle of St. Peter in Smyrna that made them strengthen the castle in Halicarnassus. With their main fortress on the island of Cos not 20 km away, the two together made the Hospitallers an effective sea power. The construction and remodeling of the buildings of this fortress continued until 1523 when it was taken by Süleyman the Magnificent. But more than the Ottoman seizure, it was the invention of gunpowder that outmoded this castle and its kind.[8]

Like everyone else, the knights used the building materials they had at hand, notably in this case the marble from the ruined Mausoleum. Their work and their particular areas within the castle were organized by linguistic groups (*langue*), each group building its own tower. The English, the French, the Italian and the German towers are identified with the coats of arms of the knights. A number of the towers also can be dated because of these arms. The arms of Francesco Boxolles of Castile carry the date of 1474; those of Fra Constantius Opertus of the Italian langue show 1505-1506. The several coats of arms on the English tower present an impressive historical record of the many noble families (prime among them is that of King Henry IV) whose sons served here. [9]

The chapel of the castle and a building adjacent to it are now the **Bodrum Underwater Archaeology Museum**. This museum houses the finds from both the land, such as 9th century BC sarcophagi and Mycenean period vases, and from underwater excavations directed by George Bass. Oğuz Alpözen, curator of the museum, has created a number of modern displays including that of Queen Ada, the Carian Princess. This can be seen in the Ace Tower where there is a replica of the banquet hall built in 355 BC by King Mausoleus in Labranda. Labranda was the sacred temple area of the main city of Mylassa (Milas), some 15 km to its north. Queen Ada, the sister of Mausoleus, is shown here, her facial reconstruction realized by the Manchester University Art Department.

Of the underwater finds, there are the permanent amphorae exhibit, the glass wreck, and the display of 14th century BC copper ingots shaped like stretched animal skins. There are seals, carved ivory boxes, a gold chalice, and blue glass ingots. In the Medieval Gallery, located on the lowest level of the French tower are items brought up from an 11th century AD Islamic ship. Another rich collection is in the Gallery of Glassware that is displayed in a dark, dramatic setting.

The gallery underneath the French and Italian Towers houses a coin and jewelry exhibit. This is the first museum to use coins to present a comparison between the buying power in the ancient world and in ours. Among the many ships that have been found on the sea floor near Bodrum is one from the early 7th century AD.

Underwater excavators, directed by Dr. George Bass, have brought this one to the surface and partially reconstructed it as part of the Bodrum museum exhibitions.

Bodrum can be described as a town of white houses with colorful flowers. It offers a unique experience for outdoor lovers: swimming in warm waters, sun bathing, yachting, scuba diving, surfing, good seafood and shopping. For many tourists, Bodrum is also the place from which to put out to sea for a week or so on a "Blue Voyage." Sailing, sunbathing, swimming, snorkeling, and exploring the many ruins along the coast combine in an unforgettable vacation. Or, the attractions may be a landlubber's relaxed life-style of basking on the nearby beaches all day and partying all night at one of the many discos or restaurants.

Shopping is a delight in Bodrum. Locally made blue beads, original leisure clothing, handmade leather sandals, painted T-shirts and dresses, handcrocheted wares, costume jewelry, hand-painted cushions and porcelains with Bodrum designs are among the specialty shopping items of the town.

Bodrum's many craftsmen, the boat builders, have a special place. Boats built in Bodrum have an international renown.

Bodrum's lively, friendly and bohemian atmosphere makes it the meeting place of the art community of Turkey.

The well-known Turkish author, "the Fisherman of Halicarnassus" (Cevat Şakir Kabaağaç) made his home in Bodrum after he was sent into political exile in 1925. His stories attracted an artistic colony; succeeding generations have increasingly emphasized the social arts of pleasure.

Artist's rendering of Cevat Şakir Kabaağaç

---

[1] The cloth and the color referred to were so expensive that it was reserved for use by royalty. The purple dye came from some of the mollusks (mainly *Murex brandaris* and *Murex trunculus*) of the Mediterranean; getting enough of them to make the dye was difficult. It was used for the priests' robes in Israel (Exod. 25:4) and for Solomon's seat (Song of Sol. 3:10). Jesus was clothed in regal purple when the soldiers struck and mocked him. For the Byzantines, the designation of "born in the purple" (*porphyrogenitus*) was given to an emperor whose father had been reigning when he was born. Purple still indicates the church office of a bishop.

[2] Herodotus reports that Lydia sent a colony to settle Etruria in Italy about 800 BC. This apparently was one element in the Etruscan civilization which also seems to show ties to the Urartian civilization and art of eastern Anatolia.

[3] For instance, the waters of the Baths of Agamemnon in İzmir will help rheumatism and gynecological problems. Those of Davutlar, south of Kuşadası, are reputed to relieve the pains of rheumatism as well as general stress and tension. While some of the springs are mostly mud baths, the more popular ones have large swimming pools. The Bursa and Yalova spas are visited by people with rheumatism and skin diseases. Other baths can be found south of Ankara at the Kızılcahamam Kaplıcası, near Çeşmealtı at Şifne, in Simav at the Eynal Kaplıcaları, at Ilıca (Harlek) north of Kütahya, and at Gönen southwest of Erdek. The temperature of the water as it comes out of the earth for these baths ranges from slightly less than body temperature (Pamukkale) to close to boiling (Karahayıt near Pamukkale and the Kükürtlü Kaplıca in Bursa).

[4] The Kızlarağası was the Chief Black Eunuch in charge of the sultan's harem.

[5] More details of the buildings, the statues and the friezes are on display in the room devoted to Ephesus in the New Hofburg Museum in Vienna.

[6] Heracleia-under-Latmus (Kapıkırı) is associated in Greek legend with the story of the handsome sleeping shepherd Endymion whom the moon goddess Selene seduced.

[7] This happened to Croesus who was told by the Delphic oracle that his planned encounter with the Persians would end with the downfall of a great empire. He thought that meant that he would defeat the Persian empire. Instead, he lost his own.

[8] The combination of saltpeter, sulfur and charcoal to make gunpowder took place in the mid-14th century. It was some years later that guns and cannons could be cast strong enough to withstand the explosion.

[9] See Evelyn Kalças's study, **Bodrum Castle and Its Knights**, Birlik Matbaası, Bornova, İzmir, 1976.

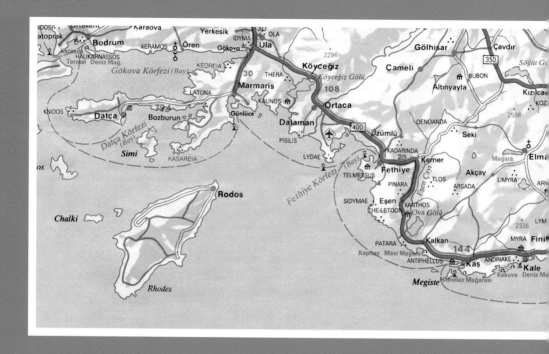

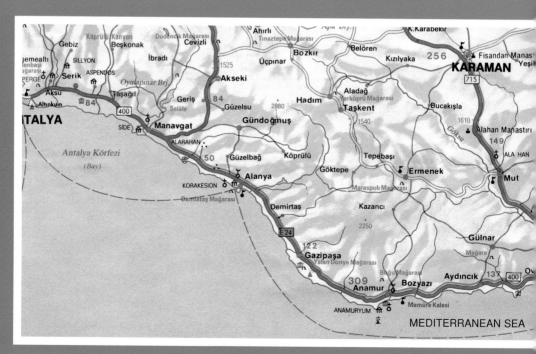

Mediterranean Turkey

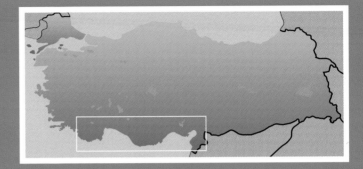

Year- round recreation, historic sites, spectacular scenery -- southwestern Turkey has it all. Washed by the Mediterranean's warm turquoise waters, the coast is a choice destination for vacationers .

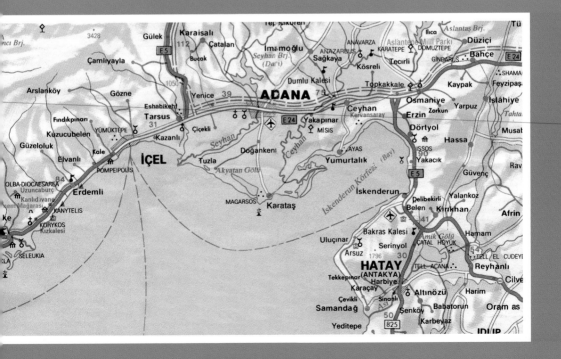

MEDITERRANEAN TURKEY

Knidos (Cnidus)
Fethiye (Telmessus)
Patara
Kınık (Xanthus)
The Letoon
Demre (Myra)
Antalya (Attalya)
Belkıs (Aspendus)
Termessus
Chimera
Perge
Side
Alanya (Coracesium)
Anamur (Anamurium)
Ayatekla
Silifke (Seleucia ad Calycadnum)
Uzuncaburç (Olba/Diocaesarea)
Kanlıdivane (Kanytelis)
Kızkalesi (Corycos)
Cennet, Cehennem (Heaven and Hell)
Alahan
Tarsus
Eshabıkehf
Karatepe
Antakya (Antioch-on-the-Orontes)
Harbiye (Daphne)

KNİDOS - CNIDUS

The history of Cnidus parallels that of many of the coastal cities. Only a land-fall for Paul, it is the Temple to Aphrodite that identifies the religious importance of the site. After the Persians had defeated the Lydian kingdom in 546 BC, they turned south to Caria. Threatened by the Persians in 546 BC, the Cnidians started to carve a canal to isolate themselves from the mainland. The Persian army arrived before their work was done, so they were forced to submit to Persian rule off and on until the time of Alexander the Great. By about 360 BC they had moved their city from present-day Datça to the tip of the peninsula.

Although Cnidus is best reached by boat from Marmaris or Bodrum, the sea around it has always had a reputation for being treacherous when the northwest wind blows, and many boats have sunk in these waters. Cnidians built a causeway between the mainland and the small adjacent island almost as soon as they moved here. This gave them a double harbor, one safe against the northwest wind, one against the southeast.

The boat carrying Paul to Rome sought to put in at Cnidus before she turned out into the open Mediterranean. However, the winds prevented a landing, and the boat continued on a very rough crossing to Cyprus.

Cnidus was an important commercial city in the 4th century BC; it was also the home of a well-known medical school. Among its famous native sons were the mathematician Eudoxus, and the architect Sosistratus who built the lighthouse of Alexandria, the Pharos.

Cnidus now is better known for the circular **Temple to Aphrodite** where a nude statue (long since lost) sculpted by Praxiteles (c. 370-330 BC) contributed to the esthetics of the rites of love. The statue had been sculpted for Cos, but when those people saw that the goddess was nude they rejected it. Bought by the Cnidians, it attracted many tourists in addition to the art critics, the curious and the covetous. One of those interested was King Nicomedes of Bithynia who wanted it so much for his own city that he offered to pay all the debts of Cnidus. Many of the other artistic works from Cnidus are in the British Museum.

FETHİYE - TELMESSUS

Fethiye, the ancient Telmessus, played its part in Christian history as a Crusader stronghold. Today it is a port city on the east side of the large Bay of Fethiye. Almost completely rebuilt after the destructive earthquake of 1957, there is little left from its past. From Fethiye it is a short drive to **Ölüdeniz** (Dead Sea), a shallow lagoon almost completely enclosed by a long sandy hook, ideal for swimming and sun bathing. In the heat of summer the resins from the wild flowers of the maquis myrtle, sage and rosemary make that drive fragrant.

The 4th century BC **rock tombs** of Telmessus are on the southeast side of the city. Apparently they imitated the typical Lycian wooden houses of the time. Some may have been tombs of priests or priestesses since they have temple façades with simulated Ionic columns. That of Amyntas even has imitation nails carved into the stone. The Christian congregation in Telmessus was important enough that it was represented at the Fourth Ecumenical Council in Chalcedon in AD 451.

*Lycian rock tomb
in Fethiye*

On the acropolis are walls of a **medieval castle** probably built in the 12th or 13th century by the Knights of St. John, the same group that built the Castle of St. Peter in Bodrum. A small **museum** in the center of the city has a few items from the archaeological sites of the region, the most valuable of which are trilingual stelae from the Letoon.

PATARA

Patara was a major port at the mouth of the Xanthus River (Esen Çayı) until it silted up and turned into a marsh, plagued with mosquitoes and malaria, much like Tarsus and Ephesus. Patara's lost Temple to Apollo and its association with Paul and St. Nicholas connect it with religious history.

Triple-arched gate, Patara

The buildings now visible there include the city's **triumphal triple arch** (c. AD 100), the **theater** (intruded upon by shifting sands), the **granary of Hadrian**, some small **temples**, **baths** and a small **basilica**. Alexander the Great was here; Ptolemy II held it for a while; and Brutus was here during his Lycian campaign (42 BC). Its harbor was one of the largest and best on the Mediterranean coast. Its coast now is known for the sandy beach that stretches seemingly on forever.

The Temple of Apollo at Patara equaled that of the famous temple on the island of Delos in the reputation of its priests. People believed that Apollo lived on the island in the summer but spent the sunny winters in Lycian Patara. The prophecies of the Patara temple were considered to be as accurate as those of Delphi in Greece, although none were of enough import to be reported by the ancient historians. Probably the temple was large and beautifully decorated, but little can be said about it now because it has not been discovered. Nor have the spring nor the vaporous chamber where its prophetess would have had her revelations. According to the historian Strabo, the founder of Patara was the son of Apollo and the nymph Lycia, a daughter of Xanthus. Other equally mythical founders are credited, including a Spanish girl who was carrying a "patara" — a bowl — of cakes that she intended to give to Apollo. She dropped it and the bowl floated ashore here, giving the city a reason for its name. The myth does not say why she was Spanish or what the city was called before her bowl turned up.

Scenes on Greek vases give some ideas of the shape of the boats in which Paul may have traveled. Finds from the wrecks located in underwater archaeology such as are displayed in the museum in Bodrum reveal more of the life of the sailors and their dependence on favorable winds.

Patara figures in Christian history several times. It was a port of call on Paul's third missionary journey when he and Luke stopped here enroute from Miletus to Jerusalem. They may have transshipped here from a small coastal vessel to one that could brave the open seas of the Mediterranean.

Patara was the birthplace of Nicholas (c. 300 AD) who became first the Bishop of Myra, then figured in the legend of the three girls who were saved from prostitution by his anonymous gift of gold (the origin of the sign of three balls on a pawn shop). Some centuries later he was transformed into Jolly Old St. Nick. Into the 15th century Patara was a stop on the route of pilgrims from Europe to Jerusalem.

Pillar tomb of Xanthus

On the southwest entrance to the theater of the Letoon are a row of masks similar to masks found at other theaters such as Myra and Side. Among the characters here are Dionysus, a satyr, and a comic old woman. The use of masks to identify characters is probably distantly connected to the masks that appear in the frescoes of costumed priestesses in Neolithic Çatal Höyük.

KINIK - XANTHUS

Xanthus is located dramatically high above the Xanthus River (Esen Çayı). Two of Homer's heroes are from here, Lord Sarpedon and faultless Glaucos who came from the distant, whirling waters of Xanthus. One of the most heart-rending stories of history, told by Herodotus (I: 176), is of the defense of the city against attacking Persians about 540 BC. When the Lycians realized that they would lose, the men collected their wives, children, slaves and all their other possessions, locked them in the citadel, set fire to it, and then sallied forth to die every man fighting against the enemy. This gruesome story was repeated in 42 BC when Brutus attacked the city trying to get enough money to pay for his fight against Mark Anthony and Octavian. But the present power and romance of Xanthus are largely in its monuments, almost all of which are in the British Museum in London. Some few pieces are in the İstanbul Archaeological Museum, some fewer are still *in situ*. Those in London, dating between the 6th and the 4th centuries BC, were carried there around 1840 by Sir Charles Fellows. More recently the French archaeologist Henri Metzger has worked here. The **Nereid Monument** (only the base is in Xanthus), the **Harpy Tomb**, the **Lion Tomb** and the **Pavaya Tomb** are best seen in London, although plaster casts now replace some of the monuments in Xanthus. Also to be seen on the site are a **Roman theater**, the Lycian **acropolis**, the 5th century BC **Inscribed Pillar** (covered with still undeciphered Lycian), a Byzantine **monastery** on the Roman **acropolis** and a Roman **archway**. The monastery may be on the site of an earlier Roman temple.

THE LETOON

About 5 km west across the Esen Çayı from Xanthus is the **Lycian shrine** dedicated to Leto. In myth, Leto was the dark-robed, gentle wife or mistress of Zeus and the mother of Apollo and Artemis. In one account she was chased by jealous Hera until she gave birth to the twins on Delos; in another the birthplace was at the source of the Xanthus River (Esen Çayı). One story says that shepherds angrily refused to let her drink from a fountain when she was thirsty; she turned them into frogs in punishment, and as frogs they continue to croak angrily in the Letoon. Another story says that wolves helped her find the Xanthus River. In thanks to them she named the country Lycia: Lykos in Greek means wolf. When Niobe presumed to pride herself over Leto for her six sons and six daughters, Apollo and Artemis killed them and left Niobe to turn to stone on Mt. Sipylus (Manisa Dağı).

Interior, Church of St. Nicholas

Three adjacent **temples** have been excavated, the largest, a 3rd century BC building, being consecrated to Leto. Near these a 4th century BC inscription written in Greek, Lycian and Aramaic has been found, one which may help unlock the Lycian language. A public **fountain**, a 4th century AD **monastery**, and a good-sized Hellenistic **theater** are here; some of the inscriptions and statues are in the local museum; some are in the Antalya museum.

Demre is not a seaport, nor is Myra which is even farther inland. The port now is at Andriace, 3 km to the south. Here there are a good sandy beach for swimming, and also, in summer, boats that go to Kekova for a day of unsurpassable swimming.

DEMRE - MYRA

Demre is the village between Kaş and Finike which identifies the site of the ancient Myra. In Roman times Myra was on the sea. It was the port where Paul and his companions Luke and Aristarchus changed ships on their way to Rome in about 60 AD.

St. Nicholas is supposed to have been born in Patara about 300 AD; as an adult he became the Bishop of Myra. While his name is still a familiar household word, his fame does not rest on his great theological wisdom (as did many of his contemporaries' renown like Basil and Gregory). Rather he is known for his miracles; he continues to be loved because he cared for people in need. He is the patron saint of Greece and of Russia, and the protector of children, scholars, merchants and sailors. People fearful of being robbed when they are traveling seek his help.

Little is known for certain about St. Nicholas. He is supposed to have been persecuted by the Emperor Diocletian and kept in prison because of his faith; later he is supposed to have been present at the First Ecumenical Council in Nicaea. In old pictures he is often shown standing in a tub with three boys. According to legend these boys were murdered and concealed in a tub of salt belonging to their butcher. Nicholas restored them to life and health. Legend also says that he surreptitiously gave three sisters enough gold for their dowries to save them from lives of sin. This may be the origin of giving presents in secret on the eve of December 6th — his day.

Double harbor, Cnidus

*Yivli Minare,
Antalya*

The importance of St. Nicholas spread in several different forms. In the 11th century people from Bari stole the remains found in his tomb and carried them back to Italy, arriving there on May 9, 1087 when the town put on a big celebration to welcome them. The townsfolk built a new basilica in Bari to commemorate that event. About the same time, English people had a custom of electing a Boy-Bishop on St. Nicholas's Day. He was dressed up in the bishop's robes and paraded around the town blessing all the people. He had possession of the cathedral of his town; he and his fellows officiated at all the church ceremonies except mass for three weeks until the Feast of the Innocents on December 28. The custom lasted in England until it was abolished during the reign of Elizabeth I in the 16th century. In Germany a similar custom continued until 1799.

The 11th century **Church of St. Nicholas** in Myra has recently been refurbished; a church service there on December 6th celebrates his memory. In addition to the church, Myra/Demre is interesting also for the **Roman theater**, and for the **rock tombs** cut into the cliff above the theater. Of them, the Painted Tomb, a "house type," has scenes of a family engaged in various activities.

ANTALYA - ATTALYA

During the spring months, Antalya offers the chance to ski in the mountains and swim in the Mediterranean on the same day. The mountain ski resort is at Saklıkent almost due west of Antalya in the Beydağları.

Antalya nestles at the northern end of a gulf against the high Lycian mountains (Beydağları). Paul sailed from Antalya about AD 48 on his return to Antioch-on-the-Orontes after his first missionary journey. To the west and north of the city the mountains rise precipitously out of the Mediterranean Sea. East, a broad plain stretches beyond along the coast to Alanya; it is a farmland producing much of Turkey's citrus fruit and early summer vegetables.

Antalya was founded by Attalus II, King of Pergamum between 160 and 139 BC; it was called then Attalya. When Attalus III gave it to Rome, it joined Cilicia, Pamphylia, Lycaonia, Isauria, Pisidia and Cyprus as a province. The whole region suffered from both a series of corrupt governors and an infestation of pirates. At last under Pompey in 67 BC the pirates were suppressed. Cicero, who was governor in 51 BC, was instrumental in restoring justice in its administration. During his time Galatia and Cappadocia were also under his protection. The Emperor Hadrian visited Antalya in AD 130, and the **triple-arched gate** on Atatürk Caddessi was built to commemorate him. The city does not figure in history again until the 12th century when it was a transfer point from ship to caravan for the Crusaders' supplies. Under Sultan Bayezit I in the late 14th century it became part of the Ottoman Empire.

Items that date from the earliest history of Anatolia are in the **Antalya Museum**. Included in them are Stone Age small flint scrapers and flint knives used for harvesting grain, and bones from animals that were alive in the Paleolithic Age but have since become extinct. These came from the Karain cave southwest of Antalya. There are 7th century BC Phrygian bronze cauldrons and iron arrowheads, Hellenistic jewelry and 2nd century AD statues of gods from Perge (including a Zeus and a head of Artemis above a crescent moon). A 6th century AD raised pulpit from a church with the relief of the Angel Gabriel marked by the word "Allah" in a corner is evidence of its use several centuries later in a mosque.

Aerial view, Aspendus, the best preserved Roman theater in the world

There is a statue of Sabena, the wife of Hadrian and another of Plancia Magna, a major benefactress of Perge. The first room of the museum is devoted to ways to attract children and help them relate to the objects in the displays.

The tall **Yivli Minare** (fluted minaret) near Cumhuriyet Caddesi is one of the symbols of Antalya. This was part of a Selçuk mosque complex built by Sultan Alaettin Keykubat in 1230. The mosque replaced a Byzantine church, and the complex included a *medrese* (religious school); only the minaret now shows the fine quality of Selçuk workmanship. Another Selçuk building, the **Karatay Medresesi,** is a short distance down the hill from the clock tower. The medrese is used as a school building for classes in Turkish classical musical instruments. One other old building, the **Kesik Minare Mosque** was first a Roman temple, then a Byzantine church, then an Ottoman mosque, and now is a burned-out ruin.

The coast both south and east of Antalya is a paradise for those who enjoy aquatic sports. The many excellent tourist facilities and the long season have made it a top vacation center.

Famous Döşemealtı carpets come from a town about 20 km north of Antalya. They are characterized by a ground of deep red with patterns worked in dark blues and tans. A "latch hook" design that makes a kind of stylized tree is typical in the borders, and the center commonly contains three large medallions.

BELKIS - ASPENDUS

Early in its history Aspendus was a port city; its river was deep enough to accommodate the largest ships of the time. The inland location had been chosen to give the residents protection from pirates by preventing them from escaping quickly into the open sea. A Roman bridge over the river is ruined, but the 13th century Selçuk **bridge** continues to be used.

The outstanding structure in Aspendus is the **theater**, standing in almost perfect condition since it was built during the time of the Emperor Marcus Aurelius (AD 161-180). Even part of the carved frieze on the stage building is in place. A statue of Dionysus, patron god of theaters, decorated the base. Above the highest row of seats is a vaulted gallery that could have given protection to some in bad weather. Perhaps the theater was built to seat about 15,000 people; twice that many squeeze in today. A 3rd century AD **basilica**, built first as a law court on one side of the agora, was later converted by Christians into a church. Bases of some of the columns in the nave remain showing how and where the roof was supported. A **stadium**, a **public fountain**, a **council chamber** and a **public bath** are among the other ruins that have been excavated.

TERMESSUS

The distinguishing feature of Termessus is its location. The climb from the parking lot to the site is up a rather steep, rough path. The difficulty of reaching it has always been part of its defense and of its attraction. From several of its buildings, particularly the **theater**, there is a spectacular view of the sea in the distance and far below. Nearby is a well-preserved council chamber. Most of the other buildings are partly hidden under a tangle of shrubs and vines. Beyond the theater are a **Temple to Zeus** and another to **Artemis**. The Temple to Zeus was supported in part by fines levied on people who robbed the local graves, as inscriptions on sarcophagi in the necropolis request.

CHIMERA

On the side of a mountain a few kilometers northwest of Olympos and about 65 km southwest of Antalya is the natural phenomenon of a fire which has burned there for perhaps 3,000 years. The fire is visible at night from out at sea; its size has varied over the centuries though today it is not a spectacular site. The hole from which the flame issues is small and scarred. The place was a **sanctuary to Hephaestus**, the god of fire. The ancients recognized this fire as evidence of volcanic activity on the coast.

The Chimera was a mythological animal. It was represented by Homer as having the heads of a lion and a goat, the body of a lion, and a snake for a tail. In legend, Bellerophon was sent on the dangerous task of slaying the Chimera which he accomplished mounted on his magically winged Pegasus. In one story he won the hand of the king's daughter for his deed; in another he became so cock-sure of himself that he expected Pegasus to fly him to heaven. He fell off, but Pegasus did get there and was given the honor of bringing Zeus his thunder and lightning — an idea perhaps related to the electrical storms created by volcanic activity.

The wild plants of the Mediterranean coast are among the earliest that people domesticated:grapes figs, blackberries, olives. Other trees also characterize the landscape: cypress and Aleppo pine (used in shipbuilding), plane (çınar, which Xerxes liked so much he decorated them with gold baubles), carob (the seeds were the original jeweler's "carat" weight), sumac (the seeds are used as a red spice), pomegranate (a symbol of fertility), and storax (a source of incense).

Termessus theater

PERGE

Perge is almost next door to Antalya, being a short distance east and only 2 km off the main road.

Perge is one of the cities that Paul visited with Barnabas and his cousin John Mark on their first missionary journey in about AD 47 or 48. It was in Perge that John Mark left the others to return to Jerusalem. Whatever the reason for the difference of opinion, Paul continued to hold John Mark's desertion against him, but his uncle Barnabas did not. (Since to Christians Paul, Barnabas and John Mark are Fathers of the Church, it is hard to think of them at this time as young men, and subject to occasional hasty judgments.) John Mark did not accompany Paul on the second missionary journey; instead he and Barnabas went together to Cyprus while Paul went with Silas into Anatolia (Acts 15:36-41). Perhaps Paul and John Mark were reconciled later for Paul includes greetings from a Mark to Philemon (Philem. 24).Perhaps also John Mark is the author of the Gospel of Mark, presumed to be the first of the Gospels to be written. However, Mark has been a common name, so it is not possible to say for sure that these were the same man.

According to an inscription uncovered in Perge, its residents believed that their city had been founded by the Greek heroes of the Trojan War. Not heroes, but soldiers anyway, a theory equates the marauding Sea Peoples with those who sacked Troy, brought the downfall of the Hittite Empire, and continued down the coast to invade Canaan about the 12th century BC.

Among the people who are known from antiquity, Alexander the Great led his army through Perge in 333 BC. Apollonius of Perge (born c. 262 BC) was a mathematician whose work on conics identified parabolas, ellipses, and hyperbolas. He was an astronomer (probably also an astrologer) whom Ptolemy credited with the theory that the motion of the planets was a series of epicycles, and that the earth revolved around the sun.[1]

Perge, like Ephesus, is interesting because it is a city typical of its region in the years of the 1st and 2nd centuries AD. It was a

Gaius Verres was one of the Roman magistrates best known for their mismanagement of the provinces. In 80 BC he was responsible for the district of Perge which, with the governor of Cilicia, he plundered mercilessly. Being pardoned for that because he gave evidence against his superior, he went on to become governor of Sicily where he canceled contracts, imposed outrageous taxes, and stole private and public works of art. Cicero presented the charges against him, and he was banished to Massilia in 69. He lived in exile until 43 BC when Mark Anthony, who wanted some of his art treasures, had him condemned to death.

Stadium of Perge

Both in 78 BC and again in 76 BC Julius Caesar tangled with pirates in the eastern Mediterranean. He was captured by them the second time, but treated his captors with studied contempt while he waited for his ransom to come. Having promised them that he would return to crucify them, he did exactly that as soon as they released him.

prosperous city then: A system of large public fountains, and the canal through the center of town helped lower the summer heat. There are a large **theater** (seating the same number of people that the one in Side did), an equally large **stadium**, and a handsome double set of city **gates**. Under the direction first of Arif Müfit Mansel and then of Jale İnan, excavations of these, of the **marketplace** and of the **baths** have brought to light both some of the customs and history. From a number of inscriptions here it is thought that a woman, Plancia Magna, was a 2nd century BC magistrate of the city and one of its benefactors.

During the Hellenistic period when the theater was built, the stage was decorated with reliefs showing the life of the patron god of the theater, Dionysus. Dionysus was honored each spring because he was the god of fertility; it was believed that drama itself evolved out of the merrymaking during his festival. In time that holiday entertainment came to be a contest for the best plays and was a time when city notables were honored. The Romans modified the seats around the orchestra probably by the 1st century AD to allow for a screen that would protect them from the gladiatorial fights with wild beasts that they found more exciting than the plays of the Greek theater.

SİDE

The very popular Mediterranean port of Side (pronounced See-deh) lies 66 km east of Antalya. Everything and anything a tourist might want in a summer holiday can be bought here.

Among the recent additions to the interest in Side is the partial reconstruction of the **Temple to Apollo** on a small peninsula near the ancient harbor. This and the **Temple to Athena** next to it were 2nd century AD buildings. The restoration of the Temple to Apollo has been financed by Mrs. Jean Friendly in memory of her late husband Alfred Friendly. The Friendlys, frequent visitors to Side for 30 years, founded the "Friends of Side" to finance the archaeological work on the site. East of the temple are the ruins of a 5th century Christian **basilica.** Ninth or 10th century additions of another smaller church were made next to it. The buildings were used into the 19th century.

Side was an important port on the Mediterranean from the time it was founded about the 6th century BC until the 7th century AD when Arab raiders destroyed it. A fortified city, some of the walls that surrounded it are still visible. It has come to life again in the last twenty-five years as a fashionable recreation center.

Roman engineers brought Side's water through tunnels, channels, and an **aqueduct** from about 30 km inland. The arches of the aqueduct are the first ruins of the flourishing 1st century city that visitors now see. Perhaps Side was Paul's port of call on his first missionary journey.

The statue of Nemesis, the goddess of revenge, in a niche in the imperial palace in Side

Inside the walls and between the main gate and the east gate are the ruins of a 5th century Byzantine **basilica** and bishop's residence. This general area of Side has not yet been excavated.

Besides the many present-day tourist enterprises, Side is interesting for its old **theater**, **marketplace**, and good modern **museum**. The theater, in its heyday one of the best in Anatolia, seated up to 15,000 people

The imperial palace in Side

— a suggestion of the population of Side and its environs that would have required so large a facility. In the museum (originally the 5th century AD bath complex) are marble statues (the Three Graces, Hercules, and Hygeia with a snake), sarcophagi, amphorae and a number of inscriptions written in the language of Side that has not yet been deciphered. Much of the material here is from the work of the archaeologists, Jale İnan and the late Arif Müfit Mansel.

Side's main market backed up against the stage building of the theater. This was the social and business center of town, and where the slaves — many of whom had been captured by the local pirates — were bought and sold.

Side was founded on a narrow peninsula that could be defended against mainland attacks by its fortified wall that stretched across the base of its triangle. Its harbor presented different problems for those who wished to enter it. The sands which now make the beach attractive filled in the harbor so frequently that the job of dredging it became proverbial for any unremitting, thankless expense. Not only that, the skill required of the sailors to negotiate a safe entrance was so great that the citizens turned out to cheer them in.

ALANYA - CORACESIUM

The rhinoceros nose of Alanya, a rocky promontory on the sea, identifies it from miles away. Two sandy beaches stretch east and west of the rock, and inland the Taurus Mountains rise to snowy heights. Alanya has become a tourists'paradise with year-round sun, boat trips for hire, yacht facilities, a cave to explore, discotheques, every kind of food from simple Turkish dishes to American fast-foods, and a wide range of hotels.

Separate from the modern, bustling town, the castle area of the headland is interesting for its history and its old buildings. Alanya (or Coracesium, the "rookery," as it was known in antiquity) was a pirates' lair until the Roman general Pompey defeated them in a sea battle in 67 BC. A few years later Mark

Wines at the turn of the first millennium would have seemed strange to palates today: People then thought that drinking wine straight was uncivilized, so they mixed it with honey and water. They added spices, or boiled it, or treated it with plaster of Paris to improve its intoxicating effect. The first containers were hides that had been rubbed with oil or resin to make them waterproof. (The resinous quality is still there in the retsina of Greece.) Some also thought that the practice of mixing sea water with wine made it sweeter.

Just west of Alanya the cave of Damlataş ("the dripping stone") sparkles with thousands of stalactites, mineral formations deposited by the underground water.

Anthony gave the region to Cleopatra because she wanted the lumber from its trees for her ships. Wood continued to be an important export from Alanya into Ottoman times.

Alanya was the port city of the Sultanate of Iconium which controlled much of central Anatolia from the 11th to the 14th century. The Red Tower, an orange-colored octagonal brick tower on the water's edge, was built in 1226 by Sultan Alaettin Keykubat I to help in the defenses of the harbor. It was his winter capital, and he named it Alaiye, the origin of its present name. That year he also built the wall that rises from the Red Tower and encircles the steep hill. His palace was on the highest point of the citadel; some of the walls of it still survive.

Two religious buildings are located on the citadel. One is the shell of a 10th or 11th century Church of St. George in the inner fortress. The second is a 16th century Ottoman Mosque of Süleyman that replaced an earlier Selçuk mosque. The attractive museum of Alanya contains both archaeological and ethnographic displays pertinent to the general area.

ANAMUR - ANAMURIUM

Anamur is on the most southern point of Turkey, about half way between Alanya and Silifke. Two separate areas near the present city of Anamur are of interest to tourists. South and west of the city are the ruins of ancient **Anamurium**.

Red Tower, Alanya (above); Mamure Castle, Anamur (below)

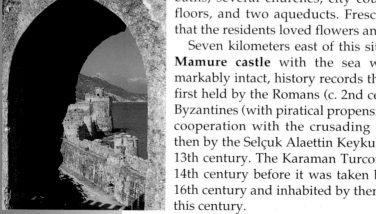

Recent excavations have helped define the theater, several baths, several churches, city council chambers, mosaic floors, and two aqueducts. Frescoes in the tombs show that the residents loved flowers and pet animals.

Seven kilometers east of this site is the large medieval **Mamure castle** with the sea washing its walls. Remarkably intact, history records that this fortification was first held by the Romans (c. 2nd century AD), then by the Byzantines (with piratical propensities), the Armenians (in cooperation with the crusading Lusignans of Cyprus), then by the Selçuk Alaettin Keykubat who rebuilt it in the 13th century. The Karaman Turcomans added to it in the 14th century before it was taken by the Ottomans in the 16th century and inhabited by them into the early years of this century.

SİLİFKE - SELEUCIA AD CALYCADNUM

Silifke was founded by Alexander's general Seleucis I in the late 4th or early 3rd century BC. On the Calycadnus (Göksu) River, it was a Crusader stronghold in the 12th century AD and was visited by Frederick I Barbarossa as he led the proud army of the Third Crusade south. But on the 10th of June 1190 Barbarossa drowned in the river a short distance upstream from the castle, and the army fell apart without its leader. A good view of the city can be had at the **castle (Camardesium?)**, but visitors should be warned that it is riddled with pitfalls.

In Silifke itself there is a 2nd century AD **Temple to Zeus**, a Selçuk period **Ulu Cami**, and a pleasant, small **museum** with a good Persian and Byzantine coin collection.

AYATEKLA

A short distance south of Silifke are the ruins of a large **basilica** noted on the road signs as Meryemlik or Ayatekla. This was the 5th century church of the nunnery begun by the 1st century convert to Christianity, Thecla.

Thecla is the heroine whose story appears in the apocryphal *Acts of Paul and Thecla* that was popular in the 2nd century. Thecla was from one of the better families of Konya where she first fell under the spell of Paul's preaching. Unusually attracted to him and his message, she became one of his most devoted converts. Against the customs and dictates of propriety of the time, she tried to follow him by disguising herself in men's clothing. Her mother accused her of being a Christian and she was tried and condemned to be burnt at the stake. A timely rain put the fire out, whereupon she was turned over to the mercies of the wild beasts. Those she likewise overcame miraculously. Barred by Paul from accompanying him in his missionary work, she moved south to Silifke where she established her nunnery, gaining fame throughout the area as a nurse and as a Christian missionary herself. (Her story makes one wonder what influence she had on Paul's criticisms of women who tried to speak out in church.)

Kız Kalesi, Silifke (above), basilica, Ayatekla (below)

Zeus had many names by which he was worshipped. Among them are "the Protector of the Hearth," "the god of Thunder," and "the Averter of Flies."

UZUNCABURÇ - OLBA/DIOCAESAREA

Uzuncaburç is about 35 km north and high above Silifke on the Kırobası road. Founded by Seleucis, it is presently a place to which people from the coast can escape for relief from the summer heat. Of the ruins visible, besides the **theater**, the **monumental arch**, and the **colonnaded street**, there are two temples, one to Zeus Olbius and one to Tyche. The **Temple to Tyche**, the goddess of fortune, was the 1st century AD gift to the city by a citizen, Oppius, and his wife Kyria. Alexander the Great's general Seleucis built the **Temple of Zeus Olbius** in the 3rd century BC. The temple priests had political control of the city and the surrounding region. The building is interesting because it is the earliest known Anatolian Corinthian-type temple.

The castle in the sea at Kızkalesi is in better condition than the one on land. There is a small church sitting in the middle of the keep. Good swimmers can reach it easily, and also there are frequent boats there during the summer season.

KANLIDİVANE - KANYTELIS

Lying about 4 km off the main road and half way between Ayaş and Limonlu, Kanlıdivane is marked by a large **crater** in the center of the town. The crater is part of the general geologic structure of the region with much of the limestone having been hollowed by underground streams. The south wall of the crater has a strange 3rd century BC relief of four female and two male figures, possibly priests. It must have taken some unusual engineering to protect the workmen as they carved into the sheer stone. Stories tell of condemned prisoners being thrown into this hole. There is a basilica **church** from the Byzantine Period, and a small unidentified **temple**.

KIZKALESİ - CORYCOS

About a third of the way between Silifke and Mersin is the old port of Corycos, marked now by the romantic, **double castles** which guarded the entrance to the harbor, and by the plethora of tourist accommodations.

Crusaders and their Armenian cohorts built the double castles, one on the beach and the other 100 meters out in the sea, in the 12th century. The two were once connected by a causeway; now the connection is made by boat or by swimmers. As with many such stranded castles, the distant one was reputedly the prison of a beautiful princess whose handsome lover unintentionally caused her death (of course the romantic story says that it had been foretold) by the present of a basket of fruit in which a snake lay hidden. The name of the castle, Corycos, is supposed to be related to the word for saffron because of the quantities of the yellow fall crocus which once grew wild around its walls.

CENNET, CEHENNEM - HEAVEN AND HELL

Two large, deep depressions in the limestone earth a short distance from Kızkalesi are known locally as Heaven and Hell. Perhaps it is both symbolic and reassuring that, while the descent into Hell is quite difficult, the path to Heaven is well-trod. **Hell** was considered by the ancients to be, in all truth, one of the entrances to the underworld, while the stream that rushes with a great roar just out of sight at the far end of the cavern of

Alahan

Heaven was thought to be the Styx. Heaven also was the place where the monster Typhon held Zeus a prisoner. Zeus finally got the better of him, but not before Typhon begot the Chimera and a number of ill winds including the typhoon which still carries his name. A small 5th century Byzantine **church** sits just at the entrance to the cave of Heaven.

12th century Crusaders' fortress

ALAHAN

A Byzantine monastery is hidden a short distance off the main highway between Silifke and Konya, and about 20 km north of Mut. The buildings with their elaborate relief sculptures are on a terrace that has a spectacular view over the Göksu River valley and the mountains to the north. Alahan is a collection of two basilical churches and monastic buildings. Only since about 1975 have tourists been able to approach it except on donkey-back.

The earlier of the churches — named the **Church of the Evangelists** by the archaeologists — is a 5th century building. The title comes from the symbols of the evangelists on the main door. In addition, among the stone carvings are the four beasts of the Apocalypse, St. Gabriel standing on top of a bull (thought to represent his triumph over Mithraism), and St. Michael above two Phrygian women (maybe the triumph over the pagan Mother Goddess Cybele). Christ's head held up by angels adorns the doorway. The dome of the apse still has bits of red, green, blue, turquoise and gold tesserae that composed a mosaic painting. This is the first building you see as you approach the monastery from the parking lot.

Beyond it are the **baptistery** with its cruciform font, the **refectory**, **kitchens** and **monks' cells**. The 6th century **East Church** — also basilical in form — is at the far end of the site. It is in a better state of preservation than the Church of the Evangelists because part of its walls was carved out of the living rock of the hillside. It, too, is decorated with animals and abstract motifs.

TARSUS

Paul's birthplace of Tarsus is one of the oldest settlements in Cilicia. Excavators, including the late Hetty Goldman, working on the mound rising in the northwest quarter of the city have un-covered evidence of settlements here in the Chalcolithic (fourth millennium BC), Early Bronze, Hittite, Hellenistic and Roman periods. Some of those finds are in the **Adana Museum**, some in the **Tarsus Museum**, a building originally used as a theological school.

Among the famous people of Tarsus is the name of Sit Aleyhis-

Gold and silver tesserae were made by gluing the metallic leaf between two layers of glass. This kept the metal from wearing off. The metal was spread on a tray of glass about 12 cm in circumference. The tray was then heated. A second layer of molten glass was poured on top and pressed so that it bonded to the first. A diamond or a glass cutter's wheel was used to break the glass into small cubes, usually about half a centimeter square.

The Tarsus museum is in the 16th century Kulat Paşa Museum near the center of the city. Among the items there is a figure of a man entwined with a snake. While neither its date nor its original location is known, it may be part of a local legend: East of Tarsus between Adana and Ceyhan is a striking, medieval castle called Yılan Kalesi (Snake Castle). A snake in the coat of arms above the entrance helps perpetuate its name. In Kurdish the castle is named for Shah Maran (the king of the snakes). This shah may have been a real person who lived here doing good and charming the snakes, most of which have disappeared.

selam, otherwise known locally as Adam's son Seth; he is reputedly buried in a mausoleum on the eastern side of Ulu Cami. A somewhat later, and likewise legendary, burial is that at Dönük Taş of Sardanapalus (or Assurbanipal), the Assyrian king who is sometimes credited with founding Tarsus in about 820 BC. The Emperor Julian the Apostate was buried in Tarsus after his defeat in his battles with the Persians in 364. (The place of that grave is no longer known.) The Emperor Trajan also died here, and his heir, Hadrian who was with him, assumed the power.

Alexander the Great marched through southern Anatolia in 334 BC enroute to his lightning conquest of the East. He stopped long enough in Tarsus to catch what was almost his death of cold swimming in the Cydnus River (Tarsus Çayı). When his empire was divided, the southern Anatolia portion fell to his general Seleucis Nicator. In 66 BC the government of the province of Cilicia — and of Tarsus as the capital — passed from Seleucid administration to that of Rome. Mark Anthony made it a city free of some taxations, perhaps because he had been captivated by one of the age's more popular flirts, Cleopatra, who sailed into Tarsus to meet him with all her flags flying. Later Octavian gave it some important commercial immunities.

The city has changed hands many times. Harun ar-Rashid settled his Abbasid soldiers in Tarsus in 787. Tarsus became a Byzantine holding thanks to the First Crusade, then a Selçuk annexation, and then a part of Lesser Armenia, dependent upon the support of the controlling Crusaders.

The most famous person associated with Tarsus in religious history is **Paul the Apostle**. Paul was born a Jew of the tribe of Benjamin in Tarsus about AD 10 and spent his early years here. His father was a Roman citizen; Paul inherited that citizenship and its rights (Acts 21:39). Probably he grew up speaking both Hebrew and Greek at home, and probably he learned the trade of tentmaking from his father. While still a youth he was sent to Jerusalem to study with Gamaliel, a leading Jewish theologian. Paul was one of the Pharisees, a group of scholarly, influential Jews characterized in the New Testament as zealous observers of the law. While in Jerusalem Paul persecuted members of the new Christian community and was present when Stephen was stoned (Acts 7:58). Continuing his intent to stop the new group from spreading, Paul went to Damascus. Shortly before he arrived, he was struck blind with the vision of Jesus who called him to witness to the Gospel (Acts 26:4-18). From then on his life was devoted to that mission.

Paul was back living in Tarsus when Barnabas recruited him to work with the church in Antioch-on-the-Orontes. He and Barnabas made a brief trip to Jerusalem to take relief supplies to famine-stricken people. Soon after (perhaps in AD 47), Paul,

Barnabas and John Mark started on their first missionary journey which took them to Crete and then back to the mainland.

Paul is described in *The Acts of Paul and Thecla* as a small man. He was bald; his eyebrows were heavy, his nose was hooked, and his legs were crooked. He complained about some undefined serious physical ailments, but only to underline his devotion to his calling.

Paul made two subsequent missionary journeys through western Anatolia (with two years spent in Ephesus) and into Greece before he went to Jerusalem about AD 57. Paul's intense advocacy of Christianity put him several times in danger of his life from outraged crowds. Jewish people from the province of Asia who saw him in Jerusalem caused a riot charging him with bringing Gentiles into the Temple. He lived under police protection for two years until, claiming his right as a Roman citizen, he demanded that the charge of a capital crime against him be heard by the emperor. With a Roman guard he set sail (Acts 27:1); the passage started out stormy and got worse, ending with shipwreck on the coast of Malta. When the winter storms subsided, Paul continued on to Rome where he preached for two years (Acts 28:30-31). Tradition says that because of his faith he was martyred in Rome during the reign of Nero.

Tarsus originally was a seaport on a lagoon at the mouth of the Cydnus River. But, during the reign of Justinian in the 5th century, the course of the river was altered in a vain attempt to save the city from periodic flooding and to stave off the demise of Tarsus as a port. (The Tarsus waterfall is part of this man-made channel.) The lagoon, no longer flushed out by the river, silted up and the area of the old Tarsus harbor became an almost impassable, malaria-ridden swamp. Into the 10th century Tarsus was a hideout for Arab pirates. Since then the coast has gradually moved farther and farther out into the Mediterranean Sea.

Like much of southern Anatolia, Tarsus was a Crusader holding from 1100 until 1362 when the Selçuks and the Mameluks took over the region. That control passed to the Ottoman Turks upon the capture of Egypt in 1516 by Sultan Selim I. French forces occupied Cilicia briefly from 1918 to 1921. The most striking evidence of the Hellenistic and Roman wall of Tarsus is the west city gate called popularly either **Cleopatra's Gate** or St. Paul's Gate. It does not date from either of their lifetimes. Only some of the stones in its construction may have been in the gate which those two people and their contemporaries could have used. The walls were built and rebuilt by the Byzantines, the Arabs, the Armenians, and the Turks, and then — except for this one gate — torn down in 1833 by the Egyptians.

The foundations of **Ulu Cami** and the north wall of the mosque appear to have been part of the Church of St. Peter, the

Tarsus was one of the centers of Stoic philosophy and learning. Among the teachers were Chrysippus (282-206 BC), the second founder of the Stoic school, his pupil Zeno of Tarsus, Athenodorus Cananites (c.74 BC-AD 7) who taught Augustus, and Athenodorus Cordylion (d. c. 45 BC) who became a librarian in Pergamum and who was so intent upon Stoicism being right that he cut out the the passages in Stoic writings that he did not like. Theologians have tried to trace some influence from Stoicism in Paul's letters.

Both Christians and Muslims have perpetuated the legend of the Seven Sleepers. In Arabic Eshabikehf means "the Companions of the Cave." The seven boys' names are found in different forms: Malchus (Mesliha), Maximilianus (Mislina), Martinianus (Mernus), Johannes (Yemliha), Dionysius (Debbernus), Serapion (Shazzernus), and Constantinus (Kefestatyus). These were often inscribed on talismans for protection against evil.

Their famous dog's name is recorded in the Koran.

date of which is not known. The minaret of the mosque carries an inscription giving 1362 as the year that it was built, while the present mosque was built in 1579. The mosque is similar in plan to the Umayyad Mosque in Damascus. The date of the mosque clock tower is 1895.

Some traditions are associated with an old structure known as **St. Paul's Well**. Numerous people believe that the water from the well has healing properties, but there is no firm evidence to connect it in any way with Paul or his family.

Presently a structure dating from Roman times, the tall, rectangular building called **Dönük Taş** (the revolving stone) may have originally been a palace, a temple, a gymnasium or a tomb.

Other Roman remains have been found in Tarsus. For example, the foundations of the Tarsus American Lycée[2] are on top of vaults that probably were part of a Roman or Hellenistic hippodrome. Just across the street from it, in the garden of the Misakımilli primary school, are the remains of banks of seats of a **Roman theater**.

ESHABİKEHF

About 20 km east of Tarsus in the foothills of the Taurus Mountains is a **small cave** which has long been a place of pilgrimage for Moslems. It is visited commonly by people who are enroute to Mecca on their pilgrimage for the Festival of Sacrifice.

The legend connected with Eshabikehf is that this is the cave in which the Seven Sleepers hid. Their story is supposed to have begun during the reign of the Emperor Decius (240-251) when Christians were persecuted. The boys hid here to escape the Romans who would have executed them for treason. Miraculously, they slept until the persecutions ended years later. During the whole time they were guarded by their dog Ketmehr. The legend is reported in the Koran as an example of God's care for those who are faithful (Sura XVIII: 8-26). (A similar legend attaches to a cave on the north side of Mt. Pion in Ephesus.)

The entrance to the cave is next to a modern mosque just off a road between Tarsus and Namrun. Tradition says that the person who squeezes through the narrow keyhole near the entrance scrapes all his sins off and leaves them behind him. Rags tied in and around the cave show how many people have sought relief from their troubles here.

KARATEPE

When the Hittite kingdom fell to the new wave of Indo-European invaders about 1180 BC, a few Neo-Hittite centers survived. One of these in Cilicia was Karatepe (about 90 km northeast of Adana), the Hittite **summer palace** of King Asitawanda about 720 BC. The site is now in a pine forest overlooking the Ceyhan River and its dam. Its excavators have been the late Bahadır Alkım, the late Helmuth Bossert, and Halet Çambel.

What is left of Asitawanda's palace are large slabs of rock with reliefs of light-hearted scenes of musicians and banqueters entertaining the king. Like the spirit of humor and revelry that appears in the mosaics from Daphne and Antioch, the reliefs uncovered at Karatepe show a human — almost vulnerable — side of the Hittites. Photography of the finds is not allowed because they have yet to be published, but the quality of the reliefs — although they are crude — makes them memorable. Along with the ever-present Hittite lion guards, there are sphinxes and attendants carrying spears at the entrance. Two duck-like vultures stand threateningly over a smaller rabbit in another scene while below them two cats dance upright, each holding a hand and each with a paw on the shoulder of a dwarf. Farther on is a mother standing by a date palm nursing a very large child. The mother's dress looks like it is of knitted material; the artist had made an attempt to show the way the material would stretch around her body contours. Rows of Arameans bringing meat and drink and Assyrians playing cymbals, pipes and lyres seem to be entertaining the king, perhaps the last of his family, who sits at his ease enjoying the feast and the attention.

Church of St. Peter, Antakya

Karatepe and the rest of the kingdom was ultimately taken over by the Assyrians. For archaeologists, the importance of Karatepe is that here they discovered a bilingual Phoenician text which had helped them unlock the hitherto unreadable Hittite hieroglyphics.

ANTAKYA - ANTIOCH-ON-THE-ORONTES

Antioch -- where Christians were first named -- is a city on both banks of the Orontes River (Asi Nehri), the surrounding hills and the generally mild climate make the site an attractive one. The Orontes River begins in the Beqaa Valley of Lebanon and flows north through Syria until it reaches the southern side of the Amanus Mountains (Nur Dağları) where it turns sharply west. Its broad, fertile valley has determined the traffic of traders and armies south and north through Syria and to the coast for thousands of years. In Arabic and in Turkish the name of the river, the Asi, means "rebellious;" some say this is because it flows away from Mecca, others because it seems to flow uphill contrary to the Tigris and the Euphrates. Its total length is 568 km, and it carries a lot of water, but the rapids in the mountains between Antioch and the Mediterranean coast keep it from being a navigable stream. Antioch has a reputation for spectacular electrical storms and flash floods. In Hellenistic times, one of the tributaries feeding into the

Many impressive castles and fortresses may be found in the Çukurova area. Besides those mentioned in the main text, they include Anazarbus (dating from the 1st century BC), Hierapolis Castabala (also known as Bodrum, dating from the 4th century BC), Sis (a 12th century AD site currently called Kozan), and Toprak Kalesi (the Crusader fort of Til Hamdoun).

Orontes at Antioch was nicknamed Onopniktes — drowner of donkeys.

Antioch was considered part of Syria under Roman administration; the same designation was kept under the Ottoman Empire. As one of the actions taken by the League of Nations when it juggled borders in the Middle East, a plebiscite was held in 1939 to determine to whom the population of the Hatay wished to give allegiance; that vote went to Turkey. Today there are strong Arabic and Aramaic influences in the Turkish language that is spoken here.

The earliest settlements located in the Amuq Plain (Amik Ovası) are from the Neolithic Period. This is the rich valley of the Orontes River east of Antioch. Palaces of the Bronze Age have been unearthed in Tel Açcana showing that this was an important location controlling trade and traffic between the interior of Anatolia and the Mediterranean coast. The region was part of the Hittite Empire (c. 1900 - 750 BC), and as such there were Hittite settlements on the Orontes River. South of Antioch near Yayladağ on Mt. Casius there was a Hittite temple which continued into the Greek period to be a place of pilgrimage for sailors, evidence of the perceived power of the site.

The control which the location of Antioch affords over the approaches to it from all directions, the abundant supply of water, the fertile plain, and the protecting mountains have contributed to its strategic importance for the many armies that have fought for its possession ever since Alexander the Great's general, Seleucis Nicator, founded it in 300 BC. An earlier city had been started by another of Alexander's generals, Antigonus, who placed his city on the Karasu River northeast of the present site. That city was shortly abandoned when Seleucis trounced Antigonus, and then was used merely as a supply center of building materials for the new one. Antioch's name, however, did not come from that general, but from Seleucis Nicator's father, Antiochus (one of many in the Seleucid family to bear that name).

Antioch was known for its beauty, both natural and man-made. Capital of the Seleucid empire and then of the Roman province of Syria, it was a political, a commercial and a cultural center. Many palatial estates lined the roads leading out of the city; several bridges spanned the river (one Roman bridge in the center of town is still in use), and among the public buildings were a theater, an aqueduct (partially visible), a circus, and various places of worship. Into the 20th century Antioch was concentrated on the left bank of the Orontes. The Seleucid kings' palace was on an island in the river. That palace, and the island itself, have long since disappeared, perhaps in one of the many destructive earthquakes that have shaken the region, or perhaps because of the rebellious river itself.

Some of the musical instruments that are played today are little different from those played in biblical times. Bronze cymbals, long-necked lutes, trumpets, drums, wooden flutes, and reed instruments were common even before 2000 BC. The examples found in excavations are often only simpler kinds of today's instruments. What rhythm was used is not known, but in Mesopotamia at least one of the scales was like the Western major scale. In addition to Psalms, there are hymns recorded in other books of the Bible, as in II Samuel 22 and 23, Matthew 1: 46-55 (the Magnificat), and Revelation 4:11.

*(Notice the musicians in the **Hatay Museum** mosaics.)*

The Hatay Museum, located on the right bank of the Orontes River, holds the richest, most varied collection of Greek and Roman mosaics in Turkey. Almost all were floor mosaics, bits of marble, glazed ceramic, colored stone, or glass, set into a lime mortar; almost all illustrate some mythological story. Animals, sometimes comically misshapen, sometimes drawn with the eye of a scientist, cavort around the gods and goddesses. One almost intact panel shows a dramatic "Boat of the Psyches" with the god Eros urging the group on. In another, a collection of a lion, a boar, a panther, an eagle and other animals -- all smiling -- listens entranced to the music of Orpheus. In a third, a sad-looking goddess of the sea is accompanied by fish, octopuses and shrimp while young boys ride on dolphins across the border. Other items in the museum are from the much earlier Mitanni, Assyrian, Hittite and post-Hittite periods (15th-6th centuries BC) found in local excavations. These include basalt altars, lions and cult objects. At the turn of the Christian era the population

*A number of artificial mounds (**tel**, **höyük**) dot the countryside. Some are the remains of ancient cities; some others were once guard posts built up to give soldiers the advantage of height when watching the roads.*

Roman mosaics of Noah's ark and animals, the Hatay Museum.

of Antioch was a mixed one. The city was a military base for the Roman army in its struggles against the Persians of Mesopotamia. Many people from Asia passed through it on their way to Rome: Juvenal, the Roman satirist, commenting on this said that the Orontes had become a tributary of the Tiber. Also among the residents there was a sizable and an influential Jewish community. Followers of Jesus who fled to Antioch from Jerusalem in about AD 35 found their welcome with them.

Tradition has it that Peter was the first to establish a church in Antioch; this belief is based on the references in Acts 9:32 and in Galatians 2:11. When Barnabas was sent shortly thereafter by the Jerusalem church to Antioch he encountered an enthusiastic community. Needing a helper, he went up to Tarsus to get Paul to join him. Together they worked in Antioch for some time before they started off on their first missionary journey. It was to identify this large group as distinct from the rest of the Jewish congregation that they were given the name "Christian." Antioch served as the home base for Peter, Paul and Barnabas; shortly it became the third most important

*For help in understanding Jewish and Christian beliefs and history, scholars turn to several collections of religious writings that are not in the Bible. These include the Apocrypha (works "hidden" from full acceptance), the Pseudepigrapha (works that may have been written by people other than those to whom they were attributed), and the writings of the Apostolic Fathers (early Christians who had known the Apostles). Among these that have been referred to in this book are **1st Maccabees, The Acts of Paul and Thecla,** and **The Letters of Jesus and Abgar.***

bishopric (after Jerusalem and Rome) in the developing church.

Antioch apparently was not a typical 1st century Jewish community, even prior to Peter's arrival. In some of their synagogues the Jewish community had been using Greek in the service rather than Hebrew or Aramaic, and reading from the *Septuagint*, the earliest Greek translation of the Old Testament (translated perhaps about 288 BC). Before the refugees from Jerusalem arrived in Antioch there were a number of Antiochene Gentiles who had already been attracted to the high moral qualities of Judaism and to the Judaic concept of God. They were not converts to Judaism, nor were the men circumcised, but they were encouraged in their leanings by the Antiochene Jews, and they also presented fertile ground for planting the seed of Christianity.

One of the earliest differences among the Jewish Christians of Antioch was over the question of circumcision. The conservative group held that according to Mosaic practice only those who had been circumcised could be saved. Faithful to a vision which he had received, Peter already had baptized the Gentile Roman centurion Cornelius, his family, and his relatives, and had eaten a meal with them, both acts in contravention of Mosaic practice which prevented such association. Barnabas and Paul also believed that the gift of the Holy Spirit as evidence of God's acceptance of a person was stronger than circumcision. Thus they were chosen to present the views of the Antioch church to the elders and apostles in Jerusalem, an act which they accomplished successfully.

These details suggest that this diasporic group was less conservative than the Jews of Jerusalem who stuck rigidly to their customs and beliefs. The details are among the evidences used to explain in part why the Christian community moved from Antioch rather than from Jerusalem into the Gentile Greek- (and then Latin-) speaking Western world.

The third bishop of Antioch was Ignatius whose seven letters, written as he was enroute to martyrdom in Rome in AD 110, are among the earliest non-biblical church documents in existence.

The left bank of the river is the old section of the city. Its narrow, cobbled streets and houses with inner courtyards behind blank walls are reminiscent of a city several hundred years ago. The Eastern Orthodox community meets in the Church of St. Mary here on Hürriyet Caddesi. The Mosque of Habib Hassan, also in the old section, was originally a church. A short distance east near the road to Aleppo and up the slope of the hill is a grotto known as the Church of St. Peter. Crusaders besieging Antioch in 1098 identified this as the place where early Christians met secretly. They found a buried sword which they believed was the one Peter used to cut off the soldier's ear when Judas approached Jesus on the Mount of Olives. Tunnels behind the altar lead off, perhaps as escape routes through the mountain. The floor mosaics inside may be from the 4th or 5th century AD; the façade dates from 1863. Mass is celebrated here on various occasions, notably yearly on the feast of SS Peter and Paul, June 29.

HARBİYE - DAPHNE

A shady grove of cypress and laurel trees, white ribbons of waterfalls, caroling nightingales and blackbirds — this was the woods sacred to Daphne located about 9 km south of Antioch. Its pretty setting calls to mind the myth of Apollo's unrequited love for the nymph Daphne. Also in myth it was here that Paris gave the golden apple to Venus. In history it is reputed to be where Mark Anthony married Cleopatra.

Alexander the Great's successor Seleucis I (312 - 280 BC) built a Temple to Apollo in the early 3rd century BC. Later there were other temples to Artemis, Aphrodite, and Isis. Antiochus IV (196 - 164 BC) built a Temple to Zeus and a stadium where the Olympic Games were held.[3]

Daphne's pleasant climate (in contrast to Antioch which is hot and muggy) drew the wealthy Antiochenes to build their homes here in the suburbs. Many of the mosaics displayed in the Hatay Museum — scenes from mythology such as Paris and Helen, Narcissus, Medea, Apollo and Daphne — were originally the floors of those houses.

By the time of the Romans, Daphne had declined and was known mainly for its licentiousness. When the Emperor Julian the Apostate wanted to worship here in AD 363 he found that Daphne was the Antiochene Christian cemetery. The Temple to Apollo was in ruins, and Julian was greeted on its steps by only a pale old priest who had no richer sacrifice to offer than one of his own geese. Julian ordered the Temple rebuilt, but in the night someone set a torch to it. In retaliation, he executed some of the churchmen, closed the cathedral in Antioch, and probably would have carried out more far-reaching repressions had he not died soon thereafter in battle against the Persians near the Tigris River. Rumor had it that one of his own Christian soldiers murdered him.

Nothing beyond the woodland atmosphere of Daphne remains today. The park and its restaurants are still popular with the local people. The temples are gone; the grace and the power of the splashing rivulets have been transmuted by the dam above the spot into hydroelectric power for the region.

Mosaics such as those from Daphne were made of porphyry, variously colored marbles, and glass. The floor was carefully pounded hard and even. A 15-25 cm bed of stone, dry rubbish and lime was laid on top, and then a slightly thinner bed of mixed lime, crushed brick and water was added. The pattern was drawn with a pointed instrument and the tesserae laid in place while the matrix was still soft. Lime, powdered white marble and water were poured over it and brushed into all the cracks. When it had dried and set the mosaic was polished.

---

[1] It took until the time of Kepler and the invention of the telescope in the early 17th century for European astronomers to catch up with him.

[2] The Tarsus American Lycée was founded as St. Paul's Institute in 1888 by an American missionary, Dr. Thomas Christie.

[3] Antiochus IV was the ruler who tried to suppress Judaism, thus provoking the Maccabaean revolt. He is reviled in the Book of Daniel (Dan. 11: 21-32).

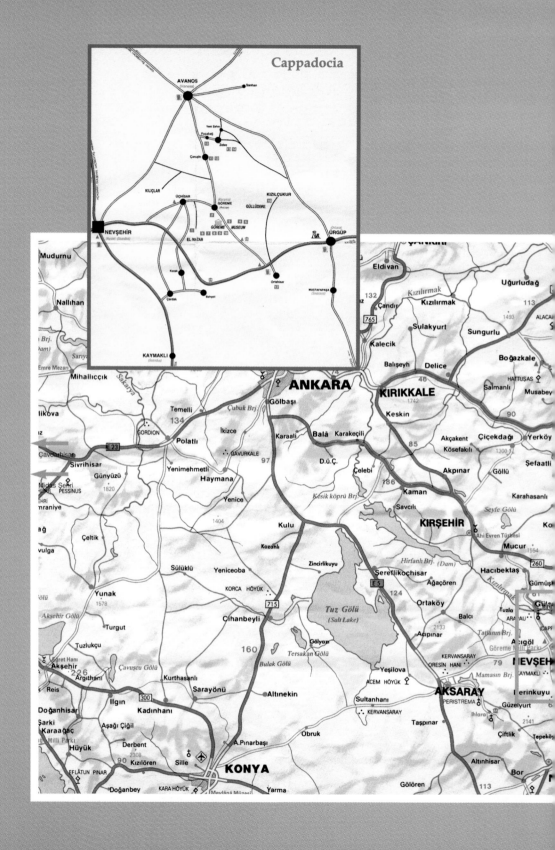

Central Turkey

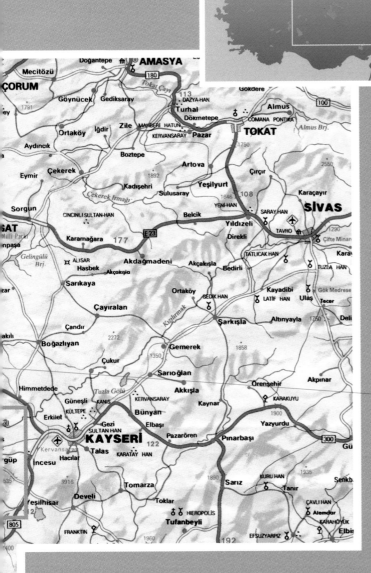

The heartland of the modern Turkish Republic is the high central plateau. The past and the present of the art and religion of Asia Minor can be found here. Around the capital of Ankara are the Fairy Chimneys of Göreme, the Whirling Dervish museum in Konya, the Stone Age city of Çatalhöyük, and Yalvaç where St. Paul preached his first sermon.

Frescoe,
St. Vasilios
Mustafapaşa

CENTRAL TURKEY

Ankara (Ancyra)
Boğazkale (Hatussas)
Yazılıkaya
Alaca Höyük
Hacıbektaş (Morimene)
Kayseri (Caesarea)
Kültepe (Kanesh)
Hierapolis (Comana)
Cappadocian Churches: Göreme, Çavuşin, Soğanlı
Derinkuyu, Kaymaklı
Sivas (Sebaste)
Tokat (Comana Pontica)
Amasya (Amaseia)
Yassıhöyük (Gordium)
Ballıhisar (Pessinus)
Midas Şehri
Çavdarhisar (Aizanoi)
Konya (Iconium
Çatal Höyük
Yalvaç (Antioch-of-Pisidia)
Akşehir (Philomelium)

ANKARA - ANCYRA

Situated in approximately the center of the country, Ankara was chosen to be the capital of the Turkish Republic in 1923 because it symbolized the break between the Ottoman Empire whose capital had been İstanbul and the new Republic. Its central location also made it less vulnerable to attack from its borders. The choice was one of many ways in which the first president, Mustafa Kemal Atatürk, defined the character of the country. It was a Turkish village of about 20,000 people in the early 1900s; today more than five million people live in this modern metropolis.

The government in Ankara balances the resources of the country, coordinating the largely agricultural east with the industrial west; it helps shape the responses of Turkey to its neighbors: to Russia, the Arab states, Greece, Armenia and Georgia; more distantly it relates to the European community, the Turkic republics, and to the United States, Israel and Japan.

Ankara was on one of the main Hittite thoroughfares; its old citadel sits on a sharply defined hill above the gorge of the Bent Deresi, a tributary of the Sakarya (Sangarius) River. The city is about half way between that river and the other main river of north central Turkey, the Kızılırmak (Halys). The Hittites knew it as "Ankuwash"; the Phrygians called it "Ankyra" (in Phrygian *ank* means gorge); at the time of the Romans it was "Sebaste Tectosagum," a capital of the Celtic tribes ruled by King Deiotarus.[1]

The **citadel** dominates the skyline of old Ankara. Its Byzantine walls are

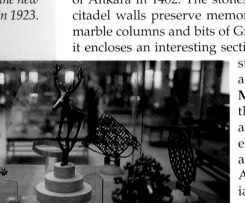

Because of its central location, Ankara was chosen by Atatürk to be the capital of the new Republic in 1923.

The Museum of Anatolian Civilizations, Ankara

The Synod of Ankara held in AD 314 ordered the Church to tolerate the marriage of deacons, and safeguarded the right of congregations to challenge the appointment of a bishop.

probably on foundations from the Hittite period. Harun ar-Rashid, the Abbasid ruler, besieged it unsuccessfully in 797 and again in 806. Crusaders captured it in 1101 from the Selçuks, and the Mongol ruler Tamerlane defeated the Ottomans in the Battle of Ankara in 1402. The stones that have been used to repair the citadel walls preserve memories of the city's past; they include marble columns and bits of Greek and Selçuk inscriptions. Today it encloses an interesting section of old buildings with handcraft stores and restaurants scattered among the homes. Close by is the **Museum of Anatolian Civilizations**, the museum above all others that attracts visitors to Ankara. Remodeled in 1968, with its collection of artifacts, particularly from the Stone Age through the time of the Phrygians, this is one of the outstanding museums of the world. Wall paintings and statues from Çatal Höyük (6,500 BC); bronze standards of sun bursts and deer, gold bracelets and crowns from Alaca Höyük (2,000 BC); huge stone reliefs of warriors and sphinxes from Carchemish (800 BC); and some small personal objects, mirrors, seals, buttons, and vases, all these bring to life the range of artistic skills of the Anatolians. Not only items showing their religious practices (cult objects, reconstructed rooms) but also examples of what amused them (from Kültepe a double vessel of human figures whose mouths are open wide enough to please any dentist) help round out this remarkable treasury.

Among the Christian lore are reports that Peter visited Ankara and that later Paul did so also. The reports are based on two things: Paul traveled through Galatia (Acts 16:6), and he addressed his letter to the Galatians to people in this region. Into the 19th century the Keçiören district was largely Jewish; there was also a Church of St. Paul that stood there until the end of that century. The present Ankara **synagogue** was built in 1840 and restored in 1902.

Several old Selçuk mosques are found not far from the museum. The Selçuks took the town first in AD 1127 and maintained their influence until 1243. Their buildings include the **Alaettin Camii** (?12th century), the **Ahi Şerafettin** (or Aslanhane) **Camii** (also Selçuk), and the **Ahi Elvan Camii** (14th century). These Ahi mosques were built by members of a guild of leather craftsmen centered in Kırşehir. Their priests, the Ahibabalar, were powerful as religious leaders, merchants and governors throughout Anatolia — including Ankara — between the 14th and 18th centuries.[2]

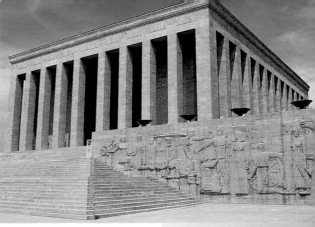

The Ottomans captured Ankara first in 1354, and then again in 1360. It remained under Ottoman control from then on, except for an interlude following Tamerlane's defeat and capture of Sultan Bayezit I in 1402. The foundation of the **Hacı Bayram Camii** dates from the years after Sultan Mehmet I reclaimed the throne, but the main building is 17th or 18th century. A tradition associated with the Hacı Bayram Camii says that one who visits it on first arriving in Ankara will return many times.

Abutting the Hacı Bayram Camii are the walls of the **Temple of Rome and Augustus**. From the 5th century AD to the 15th, the temple was used as a church. After the Ottomans took over it became a *medrese*. Its walls carry — almost intact — in Latin and Greek the official account of Caesar Augustus's accomplishments. That inscription had once existed in bronze on Augustus's tomb in Rome as well, but until the Flemish ambassador Ogier Chisolm de Busbecq happened upon it, recognized what it was and recorded it in 1555, it had been lost to the world.[3] Part of the Latin text has also been recovered in Yalvaç in the vicinity of Akşehir, and part of the Greek text has been found in Uluborlu north of İsparta. This is one of the very few contemporary records of the early Roman Empire that confirm the events reported in the Bible: It states that Caesar Augustus ordered the census that is a reference for the date of the birth of Christ.

Atatürk's mausoleum (above), Hacı Bayram Camii, Ankara (below)

In the new part of Ankara some other buildings are of note: the **Ethnographic Museum**, the **Independence Museum** (where the first members of the Grand National Assembly ratified the Treaty of Lausanne), the **Opera House**, the current **parliament buildings**, the new **Kocatepe Camii** and the **presidential residence** on the Çankaya hill.

Atatürk's mausoleum, the **Anıt Kabir**, stands alone, massive and bold, a statement of the strength and stability which were part of his legacy to the nation. It was dedicated in 1953. On one wall is carved part of his speech on the 10th anniversary of the Republic. Facing it is his exhortation to Turkish youth to preserve the independence and future of their country.

BOĞAZKALE - HATUSSAS

Boğazkale (the current name) means the citadel at the pass. It is an accurate description of the situation of Hatussas, the stronghold-capital of the Hittite Empire from about 1750 to 1100 BC. Located about 150 km east of Ankara, Hatussas was probably chosen for its strategic location on an easily defended hill in the center of the

Genesis 23 records Abraham's purchase from Ephron the Hittite of the cave of Machpela in order to bury his wife Sarah. The cave became the burial place of Abraham himself, and of Isaac, Rebecca, Jacob, and Leah. Machpela is in the city known today as Hebron. Scholars are puzzled at how and when Hittites could have been in control of land so far south in Canaan, but perhaps this gives us some indication of the wide-ranging influence of the Hittites.

empire. It sits between two rivers and near the crossroads of two ancient trade routes.

The Hittites were an Indo-European people whose kingdom at its height included much of Lebanon, northern Syria, east to the Euphrates, west possibly as far as the Aegean Sea and north to the southern slopes of the mountains that edge the Black Sea. They challenged Egypt and Assyria for control of central Syria. They may have participated in the Trojan War. There are biblical references to them: Ezekiel calls the mother of Jerusalem a Hittite (Ezek. 16:3,45); that may or may not be a metaphor. Heth, one of Canaan's sons in the Table of Nations (Gen.10:15) is the presumed ancestor of the Hittites. Isaac disapproved of his son Esau because Esau had Hittite wives (Gen. 26:34-35). Uriah, one of King David's soldiers, was a Hittite (II Sam. 11-12). (The Bible doesn't say what nation Uriah's wife Bathsheba belonged to.)

For centuries the Hittites were lost to history until in the late 19th and early 20th centuries scholars became curious about inscriptions in a previously unknown language found at such widely separated locations as Aleppo, Babylon and Boğazkale. Their interest was spurred when one of the thousands of tablets they found in the **king's archives** in Boğazkale turned out to be the Hittite copy of the treaty between Pharaoh Ramses II and King Muwatallis. This was the agreement they had made following the Battle of Kadesh in about 1290 BC; the Egyptian copy of it was known and somewhat discounted.[4] As more and more tablets were translated, the importance and power of this kingdom became evident.

Other buildings include several **temples** including a large one to Teshub, the Weather-god, with a large stone basin carved on two sides with lions, a **palace**, **houses** and the **fortifications**. The walls are punctuated by towers and gates. The **King's Gate** (early 14th century BC) on the southeast side is distinguished by the relief of a war god. The original of this relief is in the Museum of Anatolian Civilizations in Ankara; this is a copy. The long, corbeled exit, **Yer Kapı**, is guarded by two sphinxes; a short distance beyond it at the top of the hill at the **Lion's Gate** two stone lions (late 14th or early 13th century BC) bare their teeth at all (including any evil spirits) who wish to enter their gate past them.

King Suppiluliama I (c 1380 BC) stands out as the ruler under whom the Hittite Empire became a major power. Before him, the Hurrians (related to the Mitanni) were the strongest power controlling the northern area between the Tigris and the Euphrates. Suppiluliama defeated them taking over their land and going on to further enlarge his own kingdom south toward Damascus and west toward the Aegean. Thus the Hittites became rivals of the Babylonians and the Egyptians. The Battle of Kadesh (c. 1290 BC) on the Orontes River was important because in it Suppiluliama's grandson Muwatallis defeated the Egyptians.

Seal impressions of Hattusili III and Queen Puduhepa

One of the generals in the battle was Hattusilis III (c. 1289 - 1265), the brother of Muwatallis. On his way back to Hatussas, Hattusilis stopped at a Hurrian temple to the goddess Ishtar to offer his thanks to her for saving his life. A "goddess" appeared to him during the ceremony; apparently she was Puduhepa, the daughter of the High Priest, whom Hattusilis then married. On Muwatallis' death the succession passed to Urhi - Teshub who proved to be a weak ruler. With the help of **Puduhepa**, Hattusilis easily overthrew him. From then on husband and wife reigned together. Their history is told in the annals of Hattusilis, in some court records, and in a relief-portrait of them on a rock face above the Yenice River at Fıraktin southeast of Develi.

A natural sanctuary, the sense of worship is enhanced by the physical setting of Yazılıkaya.

Puduhepa was a remarkable woman: She was a busy mother, a faithful wife, an active international diplomat, and, even though as a Hurrian she was a foreigner, a successful queen of the Hittites. She and her husband had at least five children who married well. Two of their daughters became queens in Egypt. Puduhepa was a religious leader, and with her son, Tuthaliya IV, she was a cultic reformer who introduced Hurrian beliefs into the Hittite religion. She supported her husband's politics when he challenged Urhi-Teshub for his kingship, and she prayed — apparently with success — for the goddess Ishtar to restore him to health. (His feet hurt.) She may have become priestess in her childhood home because she had an uncanny ability to heal. She conducted her own correspondence with Pharaoh Ramses II, who complimented her on how well she wrote. She was the judge in a trial involving an international incident and she decided in favor of the Ugarit foreigner who proved that the Hittite captain of his ship had deliberately wrecked it. She worked tirelessly caring for the needy, listening to their problems and helping them get food and clothing. It seems likely that Puduhepa would have attracted as much attention when she appeared in public as any queen does today. Perhaps she walked with regal dignity. Probably she had a decisiveness and energy.

Yazılıkaya

YAZILIKAYA

Two kilometers northeast of Hatussas is Yazılıkaya (the inscribed rock), the **sanctuary** of the Hittite Empire. Few temples show in such detail the rituals and the beliefs of the worshippers. It was a great gallery of the Hittite pantheon, a shrine built using an open-air natural rock cleft for the inner sanctum. Temple structures protected the immediate access to the shrine. The west wall of the rock gallery is decorated with **reliefs** of gods who appear to be in procession to the north central spot, and the east wall has reliefs of goddesses likewise in procession. On the north wall are the Weather-god standing astride two submissive mountains and the Sun-goddess balanced on a lion greeting him.

Hacıbektaş

Their hands are raised almost in a toast. Also here in stone relief is the moving representation of the god Sharruma embracing King Tuthaliya IV (1250 - 1220 BC). Close by is the relief of a huge sword decorated with crouching lions that appears to have been plunged like Excalibur into the rock. Probably Yazılıkaya was where the festival of the new year was celebrated each spring. Perhaps also it was where Tuthaliya IV, one of the last of the kings of the empire, was buried.

ALACA HÖYÜK

In close proximity, Alaca Höyük (about 20 km from Boğazkale) was an important center from the Early Bronze Age (c. 3000 BC) through the Hittite. From the tombs archaeologists have recovered beautifully wrought cult items such as bronze standards, gold bracelets, diadems and pitchers, and an iron dagger. (Iron at that time was a more precious metal than gold.)

A visit to Alaca Höyük begins at the **sphinx gate** of the city. Two sphinxes guard the entrance, while on the right hand rock a double-headed eagle adds its protection.[5] On either side of the entrance are copies of reliefs showing the king and queen, some acrobats and jugglers, and the Sun Goddess. (The originals are in the Ankara Museum of Anatolian Civilizations.) Walls of a **temple**, a central **plaza** and the **graves** where archaeologists Remzi Oğuz Arık and Hamit Koşay found the gold are identified with markers. One of the bas reliefs found here shows the Weather-god in the shape of a bull.

Contrary to conventional practice of using squared stones for straight walls, the builders of the wall of Alaca Höyük at the Sphinx Gate painstakingly carved each stone to fit into the curves of its neighbor. This seeming bit of whimsy may be reflected in the informality of the relief of jugglers and musicians at that entrance.

HACIBEKTAŞ - MORIMENE

Located between Kayseri and Kırşehir, Hacıbektaş is famous as the burial place of Hacı Bektaş Veli, the patron saint of the Bektaşi dervish order. According to tradition, Hacı Bektaş Veli lived in the 12th century; his birthplace or his early education was in Khorasan (northeastern Iran) from where he came to Anatolia, living in Kayseri, Kırşehir and Sivas. Eventually he settled in the village now named for him. By uniting the Shi'ite groups who had survived a Babai[6] revolution in the 13th century he planted the seeds of the Bektaşi order. The mystical order which is associated with his name grew rapidly, accepting members from all religious backgrounds, particularly Muslims and Christians. Its syncretistic rites and dogmas reflect the features of this mixed community. Bektaşis hold as the center of their faith a trinity of God (*Allah*), the Prophet Muhammad and the Caliph Ali. In their services when new members are initiated they distribute wine, bread and cheese — reminiscent of Christian communion. Women participate in the services unveiled.

The walled Bektaşi **lodge** (*tekke*) in Hacıbektaş is now a museum and a place of prayer. The grounds include fountains, the 1367 Meydan Evi (House of the Central Court), a kitchen with great cauldrons, a bakery, a bath, living quarters, and a meeting room where the "fathers" of the order (sitting on furs — *post* — designated for each one) meet together in the evenings. Here also are the tombs of Hacı Bektaş Veli and Balım Sultan. Balım Sultan is the "Second Pir" or Master who is credited with the actual founding of the order by the end of the 15th century. He set its rules and regulations. Bektaşis continue to make a pilgrimage here in mid-August every year.

The town of Hacıbektaş was known as Morimene in ancient times. It was a site of a famous and well-attended sanctuary to the god Venasa who had attributes similar to those of Zeus and who was represented by an eagle. It also was the reputed burial place of an early Christian martyr, Charalambos.

During the early years of the Ottoman Empire, the Bektaşis were a powerful political influence; the sultan's elite army, the janissaries, were Bektaşis. After the Ottoman government became inclined toward the Sunni sect, the Bektaşis lost their political influence. The fact that the janissaries were almost all Christian recruits helps to explain some of the Christian — and heretical — stigma attached to them. The Bektaşis wore a distinctive costume including a white headdress supposed to have originated as the sleeve which Hacı Bektaş Veli cut from his robe to honor a disciple. Brutally suppressed for their rebelliousness by Sultan Mahmut II in 1826, the order revived by the end of the century, but then along with all dervish orders, it was outlawed in Turkey in 1925. Although the janissary corps was abolished, *Bektaşilik* has spread to the Balkans where it continues to be active, particularly in Albania.

There are two branches of Bektaşis, one in the Balkans whose members hold that Hacı Bektaş Veli was a bachelor, the other in Anatolia whose members say that he was married. Those in Anatolia have merged with the Alevis.

The Bektaşis' white headdress has four or twelve folds symbolizing the "four doors" as their basic rule. The *Sheriat* (Islamic law) Door introduces the observance and the obedience to the rules of Islam. Those who enter the *Tarikat* Door find a method of moral and spiritual training. (*Tarikat* thus came to mean a community, usually monastic, of those who shared a special moral and spiritual discipline.) Those who enter the *Hakikat* (Truth, Reality) Door learn the secrets of the universe, the true nature of God and God's absolute beauty. They will love and help others. The *Marifet* (Skill, Spiritual Knowledge) Door opens a person to a knowledge of God through contemplation. The individual will be cleansed and will reach a mystical unity with God.

Bektaşis are known for their mystical poetry and their sweet-

*Each janissary unit (an **orta**, consisting of between 100 and 500 men) had its own soup cauldrons which were guarded by officers. If the officers let the cauldrons get lost in battle they were disgraced and the entire unit could no longer take part in public ceremonies. The janissaries' signal of revolt was to overturn their cauldrons. By the reign of Sultan Ahmet III (1703 - 1730) they had become un-governable. During his 28 years they overturned their kettles and set fire to İstanbul 140 times.*

"We regard no one's religion as contrary to ours. True love is born when all faiths are united as one."
--Yunus Emre

tempered humor. They are a free-thinking and tolerant community. Probably their influence on the Turkish government can still be traced in the reforms of the Atatürk period and in the still-prevalent religious moderation.

One of the greatest and most humble poets of Turkey was a Bektaşi, **Yunus Emre** (d. 1321). A native of the region around Bolu, he is the earliest poet to use the language of the common people. Yunus Emre began as an unlettered villager. According to one story, he first came in contact with members of the Bektaşi order when he appeared at their lodge to beg for a cartload of wheat. True to their mystical turn of mind, the dervishes offered him a choice between bread for the body and bread for the soul. Thinking first of his starving family, he chose the wheat, but after he had started home he repented of his choice. He was welcomed back at the lodge by Hacı Bektaş Veli himself, but was told by him that the search for this kind of bread was a search for his spiritual guide.

Yunus Emre became a disciple of the Bektaşi teacher and hermit Tapduk Emre and for forty years was his silently submissive servant. Finally Tapduk Emre asked him why, out of all the sticks of wood he had cut and brought from the forest, there had never been a crooked piece. Yunus Emre replied that there was no virtue in anything crooked, either in this world or the next. At that Tapduk Emre said, "You have served your time." Thereupon Yunus Emre began to speak his hymns that still sing in the hearts and minds of Turkish people. Probably he was influenced in his thought by the mystical philosophy of Celaleddin Rumi, but his poetry has no formal polish and uses no Persian conventions as does Rumi's work. Nor are there the affectations common to the language of the divan (Ottoman court) poets. For that reason his 14th century poetry is more easily understood today than even the more recent 19th century Ottoman court poetry. He expressed his idea of life in a rhymed couplet: "I am not here on earth to stride,/ Love is the mission of my life." Tradition says that Yunus Emre traveled to Mecca, Damascus and Gaziantep; tradition also says he was buried in Mihalıççık north of Sivrihisar. Many other places also claim him: Karaman, Çay, Bursa, and Tuzla near Erzurum among them. Yunus Emre's philosophy is a love for all mankind grounded in his love for God. Through the depth of his religious experience he could say that the meaning of the Law, of the Gospels, of the Koran is God. "Wherever you are, there is God; we have found him everywhere." As evidence of the lasting appeal of his work, it has inspired Adnan Saygun, a 20th century Turkish composer, to write the *Yunus Emre Oratorio*.

Artist's rendering of Yunus Emre's love for everyone

KAYSERİ - CAESAREA

Selçuk, Ottoman and Armenian religious buildings stand in Kayseri. It was also home to St. Basil and St. Gregory. Known in Byzantine times as Caesarea or as Caesarea Mazaca, it went back and forth among the Selçuks, Byzantines, Turcomans, Mongols, Crusaders and Mameluks until Sultan Selim captured it and made it part of the Ottoman Empire in 1515. Its commercial history is reflected in the reputation of Kayseri's shrewd businessmen.

The dark gray basalt **citadel** in the center of the city was built by the Selçuks in the early years of the 13th century. Behind the imposing citadel walls is the **bazaar** of the city. Here and in other shops around the city the local Bunyan and Yahyalı rugs are sold. Most of the buildings of interest to tourists in Kayseri are from Selçuk time: Built in 1286 by Sahip Ata (the philanthropist who also built the İnce Minareli Medrese in Konya), the **Sahibiye Medresesi** with its elegant Selçuk doorway is in the center of Kayseri. Across the street from the citadel is the **Mahperi Huand Hatun Külliyesi** (Mahperi Huand Hatun Complex, 1238). The **Gevher Nesibe Sultan Medresesi** operated as a medical school, hospital, and insane asylum from 1206 to 1890. A museum now, its library is a research center for students from the medical faculty of Erciyes Universty. The **Kayseri Archaeological Museum** (a modern building) is a short distance off the main street leading to Talas. Items from Kültepe and its neighboring Assyrian Karum are displayed here. The largest mosque in the city, the **Ulu Cami** (Great Mosque), is also a Selçuk building, perhaps incorporating in its foundations an earlier church building. There are a number of free-standing mausoleums (*kümbet*), including the **Döner Kümbet** (? 1276) which is decorated with winged leopards, a griffin, and a double-headed eagle, and the **Sırçalı Kümbet**. One mosque is Ottoman: The **Kurşunlu Cami**, a Sinan building dated 1585, stands in the Atatürk Park.

In early church history Kayseri was an important bishopric. Two early church leaders lived part of their lives here. The first was Gregory the Illuminator who is reputedly the founder of the Armenian Orthodox Church. As a young child Gregory was taken by his nurse to Caesarea about AD 257 because his father had killed the reigning king of Armenia and the soldiers were after revenge. In Caesarea Gregory was brought up a Christian. On reaching maturity he disguised himself and returned to Vagarshapet (Echmiadzin in Armenia) to serve Tiridates, the son of the king his father had murdered. But when Tiridates insisted that he worship pagan idols, his family identity came out and the king threw him into a dungeon where he languished for fourteen years. In the meantime, Tiridates fell in love with a beautiful Christian nun, Ripsime. When she refused him, he killed her and then went insane. According to legend, Tiridates released Gregory because of a vision which promised that the prisoner could cure

Two architectural developments took place in Anatolia under the Selçuks. They picked up the local preference for stone rather than brick which they had been using for their buildings in Persia. They also built religious schools separate from the mosques. An early example of a school adjoining a hospital is Cevher Nesibe Sultan Külliyesi, indicating that teaching and practice went hand in hand here. There is a similar example in Divriği.

Basil was able to interpret Christianity to bring together both the mass of people who accepted it in their dying hours as a way to get to Paradise, and the sophisticated elite who embraced it for their own personal mystical ecstasy. His life exemplified the everyday discipline of following the teachings of Christ.

his madness. Not only did Gregory heal the king, he converted him to Christianity. Although married, Gregory became a bishop about 290; his son Aristaces was one of two bishops representing Tiridates at the First Ecumenical Council in Nicaea in 325. Gregory helped Tiridates destroy the last vestiges of paganism and establish Christianity as the state religion. Thus Armenia claims to have become a Christian nation before the time of Constantine. Besides that, Gregory helped the king ally his country in the 4th century with the Graeco-Roman Empire which brought a Hellenizing influence briefly to the region. After the Council of Chalcedon (451), the Armenians broke with Constantinople over the issue of the nature of Christ. (The Armenian heritage is evident in Kayseri in the **Church of St. Gregory the Illuminator**, restored in 1885.)

The most famous native son of Caesarea was Basil the Great (330-379). Other members of his family were also leaders of their time: His sister Macrina and his two brothers, Gregory of Nyssa (Patriarch in 381) and Peter of Sebaste, were important in church affairs; his brother Naucratius was a jurist. An eager student, Basil studied theology in Constantinople and Athens before he became a clergyman. Having also studied monasticism in Syria and Egypt, he set out to reform the church in Cappadocia. He wrote a new liturgy that is still used. He established the monastic Rules of Basil that demand obedience, personal poverty, chastity, and self-denial along with prayer, fasting and work. These rules controlled the monastery of St. John of Studion in Constantinople in the 9th century; they have been influential in the Eastern Orthodox Church in Russia and in the monasteries on Mt. Sinai and on Mt. Athos. Basil built a philanthropic institution outside Caesarea where the poor and the sick were fed and nursed. His political power he used to help defeat the Arian heresy and to lead the Church to make the "iota" of difference between the doctrine of **homoiousios** (Jesus the Son and God the Father are similar but not of the same substance) and **homoousios** (the two are consubstantial).

KÜLTEPE - KANESH

Of the Hittite towns, the first major one was Kanesh or Nesa, known today by its Turkish name of Kültepe ("Ash Hill" in English — a reference to a fire perhaps 4000 years ago). Kültepe is about 20 km northeast of the center of Kayseri on the road to Sivas. It was a commercial center where Assyrian traders sold imported tin and cloth goods to the local residents and received gold and silver in return. These foreigners lived outside the main city in their "karum" (a trading outpost or enclave).

The earliest history of the Kayseri region was written around 1900 BC by Assyrians on small clay tablets. More than 15,000 tablets have been found revealing human details in the early commerce between Anatolia and Mesopotamia. Archaeologists

Paşabağ, Zelve, Cappadocian Valley

suggest that written language was at that time the sacrosanct province of Assyrian priests. As Hittites traders themselves, they comprehended the sovereign power that written language possesses. Thus the Hittites' history -- at first brief speeches attributed to their gods -- developed from this religious contact.

Kanesh disappeared, probably in some catastrophic event, perhaps in a battle between two rival Hittite princes in about 1850 BC. The people fled in haste, leaving their records to be found by archaeologists. What little was left of Kanesh was built over after the Phrygians had leveled it in about 1200 BC. By the Roman period its citizens had deserted it for the more prosperous city, Caesarea/Kayseri, to the south. There are the remains of **houses** from the time of the Assyrian merchants where the tablets were found at level II. At level I b, which was occupied about the time of Hammurabi of Babylon, the houses were built very closely together. Both these levels can be seen from Excavation area I.

HIERAPOLIS - COMANA

An unexcavated city of Cappadocia, Comana, was a site of a sumptuous temple from the time of the Hittites through that of the early Roman emperors. It is located about 40 km south of Pınarbaşı and 10 km northwest of Tufanbeyli. Records show that the brother of the Hittite King of Carchemish, King Shar-Kushukh (c. 1320 BC?), happened to die there while he was worshipping the goddess of war, Ma-Bellona. About two hundred years later the Assyrian King Tiglath-Pileser I attacked the city and left a record of his success on a copper plaque on the citadel. Strabo reports that 6,000 people were employed in the solemn service of the temple during his life (about 63 BC - AD 24). Its head priest ranked next to the king in honors. The importance of the **temple** continued into Christian times.

Cylindrical stones about 5 cm long with a hole lengthwise through the center were carved in minute detail. These were used as personal seals on the clay tablets to identify the individual Assyrian merchants in Kanesh. The seals might show a god or goddess, animals, battle scenes, and geometric figures. A similar personal seal is found in the biblical story of Judah and his daughter-in-law Tamar (Gen. 38).

CAPPADOCIAN CHURCHES: GÖREME, ÇAVUŞİN, SOĞANLI, AND OTHERS

This region of a haunting, almost imaginary landscape, has a beauty found in few other places. Like a badlands, the topography is a product of erosion which is still going on and which reminds one of the power of natural forces. In addition to the usual tourist sites around Göreme, many other valleys are honeycombed with caves. Some were once used for pagan worship; some were the retreats of Muslim mystics. But large numbers are the rock-cut Christian churches and monasteries decorated with works of major artistic and historic importance.

The relatively soft volcanic tuff that overlies the region of Cappadocia around Nevşehir came from the nearby Mt. Erciyes. This is an extensive region of odd, conic forms of gray-yellow rock, some topped with off-angle hats, and many more than 15 m high. When the tuff is exposed to air it hardens, making it ideal for people to hollow out rooms of any shape or height, since the walls and ceilings do not need supports. In Turkish these cones have been poetically called **Peri Bacaları** — Fairy Chimneys.

In the long distant past the residents must have lived in natural caves, later digging into the tuff in whatever size and shape they found useful to them. Their techniques of excavating remained the same for hundreds of years. They used masonry only when they wanted to extend a space or when they needed a retaining wall. In general they made their rooms rectangular. Access to the upper rooms of the caves was sometimes through a narrow chimney that went up the middle of the cones. In place of a ladder, notches for hand and toe holds were cut into the chimney wall, similar to some seen in southwestern Native American dwellings.

The 3rd or 4th century people who carved churches may have come as anchorites wishing to withdraw from secular life. They may have been inspired by their contemporary Basil the Great who founded the ascetic Basilian monastic order. Those who

Frescoes of Elmalı Kilise, Göreme

lived here were called "troglodytes," a word meaning "cave dwellers." None of the churches has a specific, defining architectural style. Rather, their sculptors/builders repeated the free-standing forms they knew, seemingly without reflecting on structurally useless elements such as columns.

In part influenced by the unique geography of the area, the monastic communities of Cappadocia were unusual in that, unlike the community on Mt. Athos in Greece for instance, they mingled with the neighboring secular communities. The monks do not appear to have rejected these neighbors or felt a need to disguise themselves, in contrast to other nearby communities whose members at times fled underground.

Göreme Valley

Over 3,500 rock churches have been identified in the area. A number of symbols appear throughout, pomegranates (signifying eternal life), birds (paradise), lions, snakes, vines, and the obvious crosses. It is thought that the artists commonly based their iconography on cartoons from books that were copied or passed around (codices, some of which are preserved in libraries such as the Vatican in Rome). Thus there is a similarity in style between the frescoes in Cappadocia and those in Trabzon or in Constantinople. (The similarities carry over into the European tapestries of the same period. Perhaps there is a relationship between these frescoes and the work of the 17th century Spanish painter El Greco.) Almost never were the faces shown in profile, which necessitated an occasional awkward pose. Many other details are worth taking time with: The use of angels' wings, the drape of clothing, the costumes, the combinations of colors and the use of light are only a few.

The Fairy Chimneys of Cappadocia are a striking example of how geography and human habitation have worked together, and how geography has influenced people's imaginations. Perhaps the fact that the art has survived is not only because of the isolation that the region has enjoyed, but also because of the respect and awe which the geography helps evoke.

The main development of the community began at the end of the iconoclastic period (843). Many narrative paintings date from the 10th and 11th centuries. (It should be noted that the use in the frescoes of only symbols and geometric designs does not necessarily mean that the painter was an iconoclast refusing to represent the human figure.)

The churches usually visited include most of the following.

The **Kokar Kilise** in Ihlara (a late 9th century church) has a scene of shepherds playing bamboo ney-like flutes while below them are attentive, stylized sheep. The **church of St. Eustace** (970-1148) in Göreme shows the Flight of Elizabeth with her pursuer holding a drawn bow. On either side of her are two graceful trees.

A striking representation of the Last Judgment can be seen in the 11th century **Yılanlı Kilise** also in Ihlara. The band of scenes at

Near Zelve is a collection of cones identified as the Monk's Valley. Some of the caves in these cones were general meeting rooms. One particular cone is called St. Simeon's because of an inscription on the wall invoking the 5th century Syrian stylite. On the ground floor was the monk's chapel. The two upper floors were his living quarters. Not only the altar but also the fireplace, his bed, and even his pillow were carved from the stone.

the top shows Christ seated between two angels. Twenty-four elders stand in formal attendance on the ceiling, each holding a book with a letter of the alphabet. In the second band are the Forty Martyrs of Sebaste. The third band is a composite of souls being judged. On the right side are four women who represented lust, disobedience, slander and the abandonment of children; they are being punished by snakes. Stretching across the lowest scene is a large, three-headed dragon-snake, each mouth of which is swallowing a person. It is ridden by a devil and is about to swallow the next soul who is weighing his deeds in a basket held by an angel. (The symbol of a snake here does not appear to represent healing as it did for doctors in the 1st century.)

The frescoes of the **Kılıçlar Kilise** are from the early 11th century. Scenes of the Journey to Bethlehem (Mary sits side-saddle), the Nativity, the Crucifixion and the Death of Mary are on the ceiling of the larger nave; portraits of ten martyrs are on the other. The faces are individual, and many of the men wear jeweled clothes.

The three hundred years of paintings from 900 to 1200 represented in the **Old and New Tokatlı Churches** are often used for illustrations of Cappadocian art. Because of the styles and colors used, the frescoes in the crypt and the front part of the church are dated about 920; those in the apse were added when the building was enlarged at the end of the 10th century and then painted again. In a dramatic moment in the scene of the Magi in the ceiling of the nave, one man holds his hand up to shield his eyes from the vision he has seen above.

The later 11th century period shows a classical Byzantine style. Many of the churches in Göreme fall near or in this period. In addition to its frescoes, the 11th century **Karanlık Kilise** is a good example of how the architects gave the exteriors of the buildings a familiar church design with an artificial façade. An even more distinctive church-like effect can be seen in the 11th century **Kubbeli Kilise** at Soğanlı where the chimney peak was carved to represent the conical roof and drum of a church. The details of fake cornice and brickwork were added to complete the impression.

*Yılanlı Kilise,
Ihlara Valley*

In the ceiling above the entrance to the **Elmalı Kilise** (1190-1200) there is a scene of the Ascension. Each of the faces of the Apostles in this was carefully drawn to show the individual character.

The late 13th century **Church of St. George** at Belisirma reflects some of the political situation after the Selçuks became the dominant power in central Anatolia. The church was founded by the Emir Basil Giagoupes and his wife Thamar (Thamar incidentally is a girl's name from the Black Sea region). The inscription naming them also names the Byzantine Emperor Andronicus II (1282-1328) and "the most high and most noble Sultan Mas'ut," the Selçuk ruler from 1284 to 1295. That the patron saint of the church is St. George, a figure venerated by both religions, is consistent with a policy of recognizing Christian and Muslim interests.

Customs, beliefs and history can be traced in these churches. Frescoes in the **Dovecot Church** in Çavuşin commemorate the pilgrimage of the Byzantine Emperor Nicephorus Phocas II (963-964) to this monastery. Illustrations of *Aesop's Fables* are found in the 11th century **Monastery of Eski Gümüş** near Niğde. A fresco in the 13th century **Church of the Forty Martyrs** at Suves (Şahinefendi 20 km south of Ürgüp) shows the men standing naked on the ice. (Notice the unusually well-developed musculature in the men's knees.)

The influence of much earlier Anatolia can be discovered here also. The figure of a stag that crowned a Hittite standard reappears in the **Soğanlı Kilise** in Güzelöz in the Soğanlı valley. This is a pre-iconoclastic representation of the vision of St. Eustace. Here the stag stands on a rocky height, a cross added in the center of his pronged horns. Features common to Zeus were transferred to pictures of Christ as can be seen in **Church No. 2** at Güllü Dere. Such pagan residues troubled the orthodox churchmen, and one of their chroniclers, Theophanes, warned that a painter had been cursed with a withered hand because of his blasphemy.

Whatever their symbols, and however naive or sophisticated they were, the artists intended to represent eternal truths, usually in ways that were disturbing even for their time. Often the faces are portraits that allow us today to see back to these medieval artists' understanding of character. For many present-day visitors, the rock churches of Cappadocia have a surrealistic charm. The stories the frescoes illustrated are often unfamiliar; the faces, the shapes and the colors are uncommon; the defacements ugly, and the hanging columns eery. Nevertheless, the place as a whole is both fantastic and evocative. Surely those medieval residents must have hoped that their art would last and that they might communicate powerfully to an age they never would have imagined.

St. Eustace is known in church history for having established monasticism in Anatolia in the 4th century AD. He was a Roman officer who saw the vision of a cross between the horns of a deer that he was hunting. A convert to Christianity, he became a martyr because he refused to worship Caesar. Besides reference to him in the church in Güzelöz, he is pictured in the fresco in the Church of St. Eustace in Göreme holding a bow and arrow aimed at Jesus and Mary.

*Sultan Keykâvus I
was one of the
players in the very
complicated
political history of
Anatolia
that involved the
Selçuks, the Greeks,
and the Arabs
between the 12th
and the 15th
centuries. He made
peace with Theodore
Lascaris (Greek
emperor of Nicaea
after the Latins took
Constantinople in
1204). Then
Keykâvus went on
to extend his empire
by capturing Sinop
(1214) and with it
the Emperor of
Trabzon, Alexius I
Comnenus. He
forced Alexius to
pay tribute to the
Selçuks and to serve
in his army.*

DERİNKUYU - KAYMAKLI

Many **underground cities**, burrowed into the tuff similar to the churches in Göreme, were places of refuge where people have hidden themselves and their families from invaders. So far thirty-six are known, among them those in Derinkuyu and Kaymaklı.

In Derinkuyu the underground city extends several kilometers with small rooms and larger central squares where streets cross. Large millstone-like rounds of rock held in crevasses at the side of the streets at strategic locations could be rolled down the inclined grooves to seal off the passages. Father Guillaume de Jerphanion who was in the region in the first years of the 20th century reported talking to people who remembered how they — like their ancestors — had fled into the ground when the Egyptians had invaded Anatolia in 1832.

The most recent tunneling appears to have been in the 10th century AD when Christians escaped into the earth to avoid the Arab invaders. Elaborate systems of ventilation, storage rooms, churches and connecting passages within the layers — perhaps as many as eighteen levels, some of which are more than 85 m down into the ground — are still being discovered.

Entrances to these cities were located some distance from the main shaft and disguised to prevent casual discovery. The vents also were disguised as much as possible. In addition to the military protection these afforded, they were also valued for their refuge from the extremes of weather: As visitors today notice, because of their insulation they are cool in summer and evenly warm in winter. Xenephon described such a city in eastern Turkey during a blizzard where he and his weary soldiers were welcomed and taught to wrap their horses' hoofs against the snow and ice. He also reported that people entered the caves by means of ladders and that they raised various livestock — poultry and goats — underground.

SİVAS - SEBASTE

Sivas lies almost due east of Ankara on the Kızılırmak (Halys River). In addition to its being an agricultural center, it is famous for its handwoven rugs, carpets and kilims.

Some of the most beautiful examples of Selçuk stone carving are found on old medreses in Sivas. They are the **Şifaiye Medresesi** (1217/18) and three built in 1272: the **Çifte Minareli Medrese**, the **Gök Medrese** and the **Burucuye Medresesi**. Marco Polo, who was here shortly after these buildings had been finished, called the city one of the glories of Anatolia.

The earliest of these buildings, the Şifaiye Medresesi, was built by the Selçuk Sultan Keykâvus I. Rather than being a school as the name "medrese" suggests, it was used as a hospital. The stone doorway is bordered with carved lions and bulls, intended as symbols of the sun and the moon. The *türbe* of its founder is to the right of the *eyvan* (alcove). The Mongol governor of Sivas in 1271/72 is thought to have built the Çifte Minareli Medrese which was once a school of theology. Its name comes from its graceful, twin minarets that are decorated with patterned bricks and shafts of turquoise tiles. The doorway is decorated with unusually delicate high reliefs on the stones. The Gök (or Blue) Medrese (named for the turquoise tiles of its minarets) was founded by Sahip Ata, the man who also built a famous medrese in Konya. The doorway, like that of the Şifaiye Medresesi, is beautifully carved. A short distance away, the Burucuye Medresesi was built by a certain Muzzafer who was from the town of Burujerd in Iran. Like almost all the other Selçuk buildings, the entrance is defined with intricately carved stalactites. Another building, older than any of these, is the **Ulu Cami** built in 1197 by Kızıl Arslan bin İbrahim.

Not far from Ulu Cami, the mound of **Toprak Tepe** has been identified by archaeologists as what is left of a Hittite town.

In Christian history, Sivas was known as Sebaste,[8] the place of the Forty Martyrs who lived during the time of the Emperor Licinius (308-324). (Note the frescoes in several churches in Cappadocia that tell their story.) These forty young men who refused to worship the emperor and the Roman state were forced to stand naked on a frozen lake until they died.

Two years before the Battle of Ankara, the Mongol leader Tamerlane besieged and conquered Sivas in 1400. Of its 100,000 inhabitants, he is said to have buried 4,000 alive as an example of what he intended to do to others who resisted him. Its recent history is happier: Mustafa Kemal convened a congress here in 1919 which created the foundation for the government of the Turkish Republic; that building now is an **Ethnographic Museum** with costumes, military weapons and household implements.

Sivas enjoyed a period of peace during the Selçuk domination from the mid-11th century to the early 14th. On one of the major east-west routes, it prospered under its Selçuk Muslim rulers

TOKAT - COMANA PONTICA

About halfway between Sivas and Amasya is the small city of Tokat; in its older section there are several dozen buildings that date from the 12th to the 18th century. Among them is the Selçuk **Gök Medrese** (c. 1270). Once a medical school, it is now the **Tokat Museum**. Like other Selçuk buildings, the vault of the doorway is elaborated with stone stalactites. Besides the ethnographic items displayed, there are sarcophagi, statues, coins and other items from Roman, Byzantine and Selçuk

Çifte Minareli Medrese at Sivas, an exquisite example of Selçuk stone carving

*Comana Pontica
had close ties with
Hierapolis-Comana
south of Pınarbaşı.
Part of its fame was
because its cult
statue of Diana
supposedly was the
one that Orestes
and Iphigenia had
stolen when they
escaped from the
Taurians. Euripides
used the story of
their escape in his
drama,* Iphigenia
in Tauris. *Many
people in Comana
made a good living
from the licentious
celebrations of the
Mother Goddess,
Ma.*

times. Another building from Selçuk years is the still-used
bridge across the Yeşilırmak. The **Hatuniye Külliyesi** across
from the Gök Medrese was built by Sultan Bayezit II in 1485 to
honor his mother Gülbahar Hatun.[9] A 19th century Protestant
missionary, Henry Martyn, died and was buried in Tokat in
1812. The purpose of the school and hospital commemorating
his work in Hyderabad, India, is one of reconciliation among
peoples of all faiths. The ruins of Comana Pontica, the site of a
large pagan **Temple to Ma**, the Pontic incarnation of the
goddess Cybele, are a short distance north of town. Over 6,000
priests and their slaves served the goddess here during the
Roman Period. People left it when Christianity replaced
paganism. West of Tokat is a ruined **castle** overlooking the town
of Zela (Zile). This is the site of Pharnaces' defeat by Julius
Caesar in 47 BC which occasioned Caesar's laconic report to the
Roman Senate, "Veni, vidi, vici."

AMASYA - AMASEIA

Northeast of Ankara is the town of Amasya (Amaseia in Roman
times) sitting astride the Yeşilırmak (the River Iris). It was the
capital of the kings of Pontus, among them several named
Mithradates, between 301 and 63 BC. The geographer Strabo
(about 63 BC - AD 24), without whom we would know so much
less of the ancient world, was born here. From Ottoman times until
now Amasya has been a center of the silk trade.

The places to see in Amasya, besides the river and the old houses
overhanging it, are the old mosques, the old medreses, the tombs
and the citadel. Of the first two, the **Burmalı Minare** (twisted
minaret) **Cami** (1247) and the **Gök Medrese/Cami** (1266/7) are both
Selçuk buildings. The Mongols built the now-ruined **Timarhane
Medresesi** in 1308 as an insane asylum. The **Sultan Bayezit II
Mosque** (1486) was built by the grandfather of Sultan Süleyman the
Magnificent. Downstream on the right bank, the unusual octagonal
Kapı Ağası Medresesi (1488) has an open courtyard.

*At one time
Amasya was
famous for its silk
manufacture and
for its fruit,
especially its sweet,
crisp apples.*

There are Selçuk, Turcoman and Ottoman tombs in the city.
Each has been hollowed out behind the façade, but none has any
identifying inscription. Three **Hellenistic cave tombs** above the
old palace of the Pontic kings on the hill are puzzling: There is a
long tunnel next to them but no exit has been found to it. On that
hill, the ruins of towers and cisterns, parts of the curtain wall, and
a medrese remain from the years that the citadel was the stronghold of the city. By one account, the Eastern Roman Emperor
Romanus IV Diogenes who had been defeated by the Selçuks at the
Battle of Malazgirt (1071) was also defeated here by his countrymen
and put to death. Tamerlane also met defeat here, one of the very
few times this happened to him: He was unable to capture the
citadel of Amasya.

YASSI HÖYÜK - GORDIUM

Gordium, located on the Sakarya River near Polatlı, was a settled town from the Early Bronze Age (c. 3200 BC). Evidence of the earliest Phrygian invaders is mixed with Hittite remains. Gordium took over the primacy from the Hittite Hattusas and was the Phrygian capital until the Cimmerians invaded in the 7th century BC. According to legend, Gordius — for whom the city is supposed to be named — appeared at the city in a wagon as had been prophesied and was forced by the residents to be their king. A second element in the legend is an eagle that landed on his cart, adding its weight to his legitimacy. His wagon was put in the Temple to Zeus (or Cybele) in Pessinus with the new prophecy that the one who could undo the knot fastening it to the shaft would rule all of Asia. This was the knot that Alexander the Great is said to have undone by slicing through it in 333 BC.

The city of Gordium was surrounded by strong, high walls. Remains of the stone **city gate** to the east show that this entrance could have been protected by archers standing on three sides above it. On the floor of one of the large public buildings (a megaron) was found a **pebble mosaic** floor with geometric designs in dark red, blue and white stones. (Perhaps the patterns repeated the designs of rugs that were usually spread on the floor.) This is the oldest known example of a pebble mosaic (part of it can be seen in the museum here).

Gordium is now distinguished by a number of **burial mounds**, the largest of which has been reputed to be the grave of either King Gordius or King Midas, the son of Gordius and the goddess Cybele, again according to myth. It is about 300 m across and stands 53 m high. Because of 20th century graverobbers, the contents of the grave — bronze cauldrons, jewelry, ceremonial vessels, wooden tables — are now protected in the Ankara Museum of Anatolian Civilizations. The structure of the grave itself is of interest: the chamber was protected with wood logs and a gabled roof before the huge earth tumulus was heaped on top.

King Gordius is a semi-real figure; King Midas who ruled Phrygia from Gordium (or at least one of the people of this name) is somewhat more real. Midas lived from about 725 to 696 BC. He was the enemy of the Assyrian King Sargon II, perhaps because of the location of his kingdom through which most of the traffic had to pass in all directions. In Gordium he had a stranglehold on the commerce between Mesopotamia and the Aegean countries. King Midas's lasting fame was his worship of money. That gave him the reputation for having a golden touch so powerful that he destroyed even his little daughter. The gold that he is supposed to have washed off his accursed fingers was carried down the hills into the small Pactolus River (Sart Çayı) at Sardis from which two hundred years later King Croesus got his own riches.

Alexander the Great wintered in 334-333 BC in Gordium. From there in lightning moves he went on to occupy all of the eastern Mediterranean coast, routing the Persians, and leaving them without a port.

BALLIHİSAR - PESSINUS

The 19th century British archaeologist Sir William Mitchell Ramsay studied the geography of western Asia Minor in great detail. He was attempting to determine the routes that St. Paul might have taken on his missionary journeys. One of his unanswered questions was whether St. Paul traveled as far north as Pessinus. In his studies he was helped by the presence in many places of the Roman milestones that had not yet disappeared. Thus in his book, the Historical Geography of Asia Minor *(1890), he presents maps of the possible routes. Ramsay's studies were motivated in part by the questions of what distinguished Paul from a typical, well-educated Jew of the 1st century: How did his society influence him? Did contemporary events affect his career? What of the geography of the region determined his routes?*

Pessinus, now the village of Ballıhisar south of Sivrihisar, was a temple-state. That meant that the city existed because of the **sanctuary** dedicated to the goddess Cybele, the Great Mother. The ruins of the temple here seem to suggest that this one was built early in the 1st century AD, but the site reached its greatest influence earlier in the 3rd century BC when it was the religious center for the Phrygian state.

The fame of the temple reached beyond Anatolia to Rome when Rome was challenged by the Carthaginian general Hannibal in the Punic Wars. Hannibal had been nurtured by his family for one purpose: to conquer and humiliate Rome. His military stratagems, particularly his march over the Alps, greatly frightened the Roman senators. Believing that they needed supernatural help, the senators appealed to the oracles for advice. The Sibylline oracle's answer was that, if they brought the cult statue — a meteorite — from Pessinus to Rome, Cybele would protect them. In 204 BC envoys hurriedly approached King Attalus I of Pergamum for help. Wanting to ingratiate himself with this growing power, Attalus gave them the rock which they then incorporated in a silver statue to Cybele-Rhea on the Palatine Hill. Hannibal revenged himself against Pergamum when he defeated them at sea. His trick was to throw cauldrons of snakes into the enemy's ships. The Romans continued to pursue him until he committed suicide in King Prusias's castle near today's Gebze on the İzmit bay.

At first Roman citizens were forbidden to take part in the Mother Goddess services; the frenzy of those who participated was considered offensively immoral. Slowly the senators and then the general public began to use the spring festival as a time of great rejoicing. By the 2nd century AD the ceremonies included a baptism of the worshippers in the blood of bulls and rams (notice the similarities with the Mithraic cult). Cybele was herself represented seated between lions.

Pessinus is an example of the influence on a site of a defining element. It was not far from one of the sources of the Sakarya (Sangarius) River, and was on the east-west trade route, as were many other cities. But more important, as long as it possessed the meteorite it was unique. Its power began to disappear when the Romans took the stone, although the priestesses continued to maintain the temple for many years. In the end people had moved to the higher ground of Sivrihisar 15 km to the north.[10]

Because Pessinus was on the much traveled road between central Anatolia and the Aegean coast, and because in Acts (16:6-8) there is the statement about Paul's frustrated desire to go into Bithynia, it is suggested that he might have traveled through Pessinus on his second missionary journey. However, there is little evidence of Christianity here before the 4th century.

MİDAS ŞEHRİ - YAZILIKAYA

Because of a few letters in an otherwise undeciphered Phrygian inscription, a village south of Gordium is known as the City of Midas (Midas Şehri). Above the village are the ruins of a Phrygian settlement dated between the 8th and the 6th centuries BC. These ruins include several **tombs** cut down into the rock, several **altars**, a rock **throne**, defense **walls**, **reliefs** and **inscriptions**.

On the smooth, sheer northwest face of the hill the façade of a temple was carved with a precise interlocking geometric pattern surmounted by a false sloping roof. The roof repeats the shape found inside the tombs at Gordium. The façade stands about 17 m high and 15 m wide. The Phrygian inscriptions here contain the letters "MITA," misread originally for Midas but now known to refer to Cybele. At the base of the façade is a niche where a statue of Cybele may have been placed when religious ceremonies were in progress.

Midas Şehri

From an iron foundry that archaeologists discovered here they think that this temple was associated with the rites of metal working. Probably Cybele was invoked to bless the transformation of ore into metal and the use of the metal objects as weapons of war. Attention must have concentrated on the ironmonger priests who were caught between fear and hope as the metal was cast — fear that the casting might explode and kill them, hope that the weapons would be strong and not snap when they were wielded against the enemy. This foundry perhaps corroborates the biblical reference to the bronze vessels that Judah got from Meshech/ Phrygia (Ezek. 27:13) and to their weapons which spread such terror (Ezek 32:26-27).

From the coins of Aizanoi it appears that a statue of Zeus must have stood in the temple's main chamber. On the coins Zeus is holding a spear in his left hand; on his right hand he carries an eagle.

ÇAVDARHİSAR - AIZANOI

Aizanoi is of recent date relative to other Anatolian sites; it goes back only to the 1st century BC. In part because of this recentness, its **Temple to Zeus,** built during the Roman Period, is one of the most complete and best preserved in Turkey. It owes its present condition also to the fact that it has been off the mainstream of traffic; thus from it one can imagine what earlier temples may have been.

The temple is located on a slight rise on the edge of the village of Çavdarhisar on the Rhyndacus River (Koca Çay) between Kütahya and Gediz. The roof of the temple is missing, but most of the more than 20 m high walls and 16 of the original 52 columns are standing, along with the architrave. According to the inscription on the wall, it was built during the reign of Hadrian (AD 117-138), during which time the town of Aizanoi was at its peak. The basement, a barrel-vaulted room the length and breadth of the temple proper, was used at first for the worship of Cybele, the mother goddess who shared honors with Zeus in Aizanoi. No statue

A Greek legend says that the hero Perseus defeated the opponents of Hellenism near Iconium by holding up the head of the monster Gorgon and turning them into stone. From that event, the name of the village Amandra was changed to Iconium because of the icon (image) of the monster. The myth was repeated on the coins of the city dated during the reign of Hadrian (AD 117 - 138).

of Zeus has been found here, but there were some terracotta figurines of Cybele in the basement. Some of the statuary is currently in the field — originally the agora — in front of the temple. A larger-than-life marble bust of Cybele has been set below the front steps of the temple. During Byzantine times the town was a Christian bishopric; at that time the temple was used as a church.

Not far off are the ruins of a **theater** that faces a large **stadium**. A **gymnasium** and **baths** are near by, and a **meat market** whose walls boast a copy of Diocletian's edict in AD 301 setting maximum prices and maximum wages throughout the Roman Empire. Two Roman **bridges** across the river are still in use.

KONYA - ICONIUM

Konya is almost due south of Ankara; it has long been a crossing point for many trade routes. Today its definition is its importance as a place of Christian and Muslim pilgrimage. The central rise of the city, now the Alaettin Park, was occupied at least as early as the 3rd millennium BC. Hittites lived here, and then Phrygians, Lydians, Persians and Greeks held it until Attalus III of Pergamum gave it to Rome in 133 BC.

From the late 12th century for over a hundred years Konya was the capital of the Muslim Selçuk Empire.[11] The Selçuks as a distinct Turkish tribe came on the Anatolian scene in the mid-11th century, at first as raiders in the eastern region. Their main purpose seems to have been plunder, not territorial conquest. However, the confrontation in August 1071 between the Byzantine Emperor Romanus IV Diogenes and Alp Arslan at Manzikert (Malazgirt) changed the history of Anatolia. Within a few years the Selçuks and the Byzantines were cooperating against the Crusaders whom both saw as a threat. The Byzantine Emperor Alexius I allowed the Selçuk Süleyman to establish a holding in Nicaea (İznik) in 1081; Alexius also gave him certain rights in central Anatolia including the town of Konya.

The disintegration of the Byzantine Empire and the resultant splintering of the country can be seen in the growth of Selçuk power and the appearance of other Turcoman principalities, Danishmend, Saltuk, Mengüchek and Artukid. Byzantine power was largely confined to western Anatolia, part of Thrace and Macedonia, and southern Greece.

Before the end of the 12th century, Konya had become the Selçuk capital. At the beginning of the 13th century their Sultan Key-

Aizanoi

hüsrev had conquered Antalya, thus giving them an outlet to the sea. His son Alaettin Keykubat ruled from 1220 to 1237 at the height of the Selçuk Empire. His rule extended from the Mediterranean coast north throughout central Anatolia to Dorylaeum (Eskişehir) and in the south and east to include Malatya, Van and Kars.

The beautiful Selçuk buildings found throughout Anatolia date from these centuries. Bridges and caravansaries suggest the great amount of trade that was carried on and the prosperity of the Empire. The religious architecture included mosques, medreses and tombs, the most notable of which are the buildings in Kayseri, Sivas, Niğde, Divriği, Malatya and Konya.

Among the distinctive features of Selçuk art are the main entrances to their buildings. The entire stone doorways are deeply carved with elaborate geometric patterns and inscriptions from the Koran. The vaults tend to be triangular or ogive and have stalactite ornamentations. Often two minarets, fluted, marked with tilework or patterned bricks, flank the door. Occasionally there were human (or heavenly) figures, as in the case of the crowned angel originally on the gate of the Konya citadel (now in the İnce Minareli Medresesi), or the fabulous animals on the capital of the Gök Medrese in Sivas, or the stylized birds on the Ulu Cami in Divriği.

In the minor arts there are examples in a number of museums of their work in ceramics, bookbinding, metals, carved wood and illuminated manuscripts. The Selçuk influence continued when the Ottomans, also an Islamic, Turkic tribe, rose to power in the 14th century.

Two thousand years ago Konya was called Iconium; Paul preached here on his first missionary journey. Paul and Barnabas went first to the synagogue (the building has not been identified) as was their custom. There they spoke so effectively that they made many converts (Acts 14: 1-6). They stayed in Iconium for some time until they had gotten word that a group of Gentiles and Jews together were plotting to stone them, so they quickly moved on to Lystra (? Hatunsaray) and Derbe.

According to a story told in the 2nd century work, *The Acts of Paul and Thecla*, among the people whom Paul attracted was the daughter of a leading citizen of Iconium. The girl, Thecla, fell so deeply in love with Paul that she broke her engagement to her fiancé Thamyris whom her parents found more suitable. To their disgust, she declared that she had become a Christian. She was turned over to the city officials and condemned to be burned alive, but a timely rain put the fire out. She ran off to Antioch-of-Pisidia, following Paul and disguising herself as a man. There she was caught and exposed to a variety of wild animals such as snakes and bulls, from all of which she escaped unharmed. In view of Paul's remarks to the Corinthinans that women should obey the law and

Aziziye Mosque, Konya

The history of the Middle East from the 11th to the 14th century is colored in large part by the Selçuk rulers. The Selçuks were a Turkish tribe that came from central Asia. In 1055 one of their princes, Tuğrul Bey, took Baghdad from the Shiite Buyids and reestablished an orthodox Muslim as the caliph. A second prince, Alp Arslan, extended the Selçuk rule to the north, defeating the Byzantine emperor Romanus IV Diogenes at Malazgirt in 1071.

*Mevlana's
Mausoleum,
Konya*

*Muslim religious
music is most
commonly
performed in
connection with a
sema. It is mono-
phonic. During a
Mevlevi rite the
group of players
(called a* **mitrib
heyeti***) will use a
rebab (3-stringed
instrument), several
neys (reed flutes
with 7 nodes),
tanbur (6-stringed
instrument), two
pairs of kudums
(small double
drums), and a pair
of zils (finger cym-
bals). The singers
are called the
ayinhan. Mevlana
himself was an
accomplished rebab
player.*

keep their subordinate place (I Cor. 14:34), one is tempted
to conclude that Thecla not only was a real person but also
that Paul was not comfortable with her. The early church
repudiated this story but celebrated September 23rd in
honor of a woman who not only converted many people to
Christianity but who also was a miraculous healer of the
sick. The ruins of the basilical Church of St. Thecla are on
the point of land south of Silifke, where she is reputed to
have had her nunnery and hospital (see p.169).

Konya's renown today as a religious center is because of
its association with Celaleddin Rumi and the Mevlevi
Dervishes — the Whirling Dervishes. Their **tekke** and
museum are the focus of the city. **Mevlana Celaleddin
Rumi**, mystic, poet and humanist philosopher, lived here
from 1227 to 1273. On his death people of many religious
persuasions — Christians, pagans, Jews, Muslims — joined in the
funeral cortege. The order of his followers, the Mevlevi Dervishes
founded after his death by his son Sultan Veled, recognizes the
moral and esthetic imperatives of faith and their expression in love
which he envisioned for the whole world. Sultan Veled himself
was an important poet.

Mevlana's father was the respected philosopher and mystic,
Bahaüddin, who fled with his family from Afghanistan in about
1227. (Mevlana had been born in Balkh in 1207.) When they
arrived in Konya, the Selçuk Sultan Alaettin Keykubat welcomed Bahaüddin and on foot led his horse into the city,
indicating that even as sultan he recognized that spiritual
authority was higher than political authority. Mevlana found in
Konya a climate both of scholarship and of remarkable tolerance
that encouraged his budding mysticism. When he was 37 years
old he met Şemsüddin of Tabriz and, in the friendship that
blossomed, he came to realize that the secret of all existence is
love. Deprived of companionship with Şemsüddin for a time,
Mevlana turned to poetry to express the agony of separation.
After a short reunion, his friend disappeared, this time for good.
Accepting that he would not return, Mevlana embarked on a
mystical search for his true God.

At the urging of his disciples he wrote his masterpiece of
Islamic mystical literature, the **Mesnevi**.

For Mevlana, love was greater than any formal religion. He
spoke of searching for God in Christendom without finding him
on the Cross; of searching in Indian temples and finding Him
neither in idols nor in fire; of searching all over the Kaaba without
success; and finally of looking within his own self. He welcomed
everyone, regardless of creed, ethnicity, social status or past
behavior, at his shrine of hope and love. The traditional warm
Turkish hospitality still reflects this welcome.

Mevlana's invitation to all to join in his discipline is seen in his often quoted quatrain,

> *Come, come again, come! Infidel, fire-worshipper, pagan,*
> *Whoever you are, however often you have sinned, Come!*
> *Our gates are not the gates of hopelessness.*
> *Whatever your condition, Come!*

Mevlana compared the mystic's desire to be reunited with God to the sigh of the reed flute, the *ney*, used in Mevlevi services: The ney cries to return to its reed bed from which it was torn. The Mevlevi service (*sema*) is another expression of the soul's unending search for the unattainable: In the sema the whirling of the dervishes expresses the search for God in all directions. Their stamping is to crush selfishness under foot; their jumping is their attempt to rise to God. Bowing means the complete submission of one's soul to God. The position of the hands is important: The right arm is held upward toward God, the left downward to the earth; the two make a balance, the dervish freely transmitting to fellow humans all that he receives from God.

A Whirling Dervish

The dervish orders were abolished in 1925; the lodge of the Mevlevis and the tomb of Mevlana were turned into a museum. Now the date of Mevlana's death, December 17, is remembered every year in Konya with a week-long celebration of the *sema*.

When Mevlana was alive Konya was the capital of the Selçuk Empire. The prosperity of the city then is still evident in the Selçuk buildings: the **Karatay Medresesi** (a museum of ceramic tiles), the **İnce Minareli Medrese** (a museum of stone and wood carvings), the **Sırçalı Medrese** (a museum of tombstones) and the **Sahip Ata complex** (with sarcophagi of the founder and his family). The **Alaettin Camii** on the site of the **acropolis** of old Iconium and the **İplikçi Camii** are both 12th century buildings. The minbers of both the İplikçi and the Alaettin mosques are beautifully carved; that of the Alaettin is made of ebony. The **Şerafettin Camii**, the **Aziziye Camii** and the **Selimiye Camii** are Ottoman buildings.

Interior, Mevlana's Mausoleum, Konya

The **Museum of Archaeology** houses a few of the finds from Çatal Höyük and some Roman marbles. In the yard are two stones, one incised with the word Lystra, the other Derbe; no one is sure where they came from, but Lystra is thought to be the same as the Hittite Lusna. The museum's most valuable piece is a 3rd century AD sarcophagus decorated with reliefs of the labors of Hercules.

ÇATAL HÖYÜK

Çatal Höyük, a Stone Age site about 35 km southeast of Konya, is one of the earliest and best examples of an Anatolian community that was active in the Neolithic Period. It was on the edge of a river that flooded periodically. Out of its 32 acres, the one that was excavated in the 1960s had been inhabited from about 6800 to 5700 BC and showed ten successive levels of building.

The **shrines**, like the **houses**, were single-story mud-brick rectangular structures built on brick foundations. Sometimes one was built on top of the previous one. (Little of the structures is visible at the site today. The accumulated dirt of centuries preserved such things as mud brick walls. When they were exposed they crumbled under the attacks of rain and tramping feet.) Each shrine differed from the others, although the symbols found in each were similar. They were decorated with wall paintings, reliefs, figures (usually animal), and groups or rows of bull's

A rython from Çatal Höyük

horns. The paintings had some kind of religious significance. Because many were covered up and painted over with a cream-colored plaster it would appear that they may have been seen for only a short time (during a particular service?). Sometimes several layers of paintings were found. The paintings were of human figures, goddesses and hunting scenes with animals such as bulls, vultures, boars and bears in red, pink, brown, black and white colors. A reconstruction of the shrines can be seen in the Museum of Anatolian Civilizations in Ankara. Weird, striking paintings show people chasing vultures that have human legs; the vultures are attacking headless human skeletons. Perhaps they represent funerary rites that involved similarly costumed priestesses.

This religion apparently focused on the great human events of birth and death. The ceremonies were presumably observed to placate the supernatural forces, often in the face of inexplicable natural disasters. Sometimes the images of birth and death were painted on facing walls, sometimes the images were of many hands. Many of the images remain puzzling. In the wall paintings geometric designs suggest that these may have been copied from woven patterns (possibly *kilims*). Perhaps they were thought to carry occult powers: Hands and cross designs are still used in necromancy. (Hands also appear in the frescoes in the churches of Göreme and Ihlara.) Notice also the use of geometric design to outline and to define the areas of importance.

The bare bones of humans were found in graves beneath the houses in Çatal Höyük; probably to protect the health of those who continued to live in the houses, the flesh had been removed before burial. Children were buried in the center of the room; adults were buried under the shelves on the edges. With the bodies were also buried such items as daggers, necklaces, mirrors, baskets, wooden vessels and pottery.

As an interesting historical note, the oldest known landscape painting, one on the wall at Çatal Höyük, shows a town spread out in terraces something like the arrangement of the buildings found there. Overshadowing the town is a mountain from which four vents apparently spew out rocks at the same time. Archaeologists think that this records the eruption of a volcano, possibly Hasan Dağı about 130 km northeast, or the nearer Karaca Dağı. They think that the volcano was active about 6200 BC.

YALVAÇ - ANTIOCH-OF-PISIDIA

Yalvaç lies southwest of Akşehir and northeast of Eğirdir; it is not on the usual tourist route. The 1st century AD town of Antioch-of-Pisidia (on the edge of Yalvaç) was not either. It is sufficiently out of the way to raise questions first about why Paul went there, and second about where else he may have traveled. Possibly people he met in Konya attracted him to this Antioch; possibly there was a strong connection between its residents and those of the Antioch-on-the-Orontes. Possibly, since he did get to Antioch-of-Pisidia, he could have visited Ankara, Pessinus, Dorylaeum (Eskişehir) and other northern Phrygian and Galatian towns. But these are only speculation.

Antioch-of-Pisidia is thought to be originally a 10th century BC Phrygian town centered around the **Temple to Cybele**. Carved marble from this temple is scattered over the site. It was founded (or refounded) by Seleucis Nicator between 300 and 280 BC. (The founding of a city does not necessarily imply that it did not exist before; rather, it has also meant that someone provided the funds to maintain it permanently.) The residents were the local Phrygians plus Jews, Romans and Greeks, most of whom were settlers who had come from Magnesia-on-the-Meander.

Antioch-of-Pisidia today is a collection of ruins on the hill slope. A plan of the site shows the location of the main buildings that archaeologists found in the early 20th century. On the **acropolis** there was a **monumental arch** with a figure of Victory, a 2nd century AD statue. Archaeologists found here part of an inscription in Latin of Caesar Augustus's official acts, among which was a census. The text in both Latin and Greek is almost complete on the Temple to Augustus in Ankara.[12] Stones from a temple entrance, many carved with bull's heads, a **church**, a **basilica** and an **aqueduct** mark the old city. Some of the more interesting findings from the excavation which took place before World War II are in the **museum** in Yalvaç.

In 1210 the Greek emperor of Nicaea Theodore Lascaris captured the emperor of Trabzon Alexius I Comnenus in a battle with the Selçuk Turks near Yalvaç. Lascaris, the son-in-law of the emperor Alexius III (d. 1203) had fled from Constantinople after the Latins took the city in 1204. He established his state which included roughly the Roman provinces of Bithynia and Asia, and which lasted until Michael IX Palaeologus marched back into Constantinople in 1261.

Could the behavior of the women of Antioch have influenced Paul to say that women should not speak in meeting (1 Cor. 14:34)?

Paul and Barnabas visited Antioch on their first missionary journey, going to the synagogue on the Sabbath (the Jewish day of worship), and Paul was asked to speak to the congregation. In the Bible this is Paul's first recorded sermon. What Paul said about Christianity so interested his listeners that he had an overflow audience the next week. That crowd included many who did not regularly attend the service, and the members of the synagogue took violent exception to what Paul was doing. He berated them when they objected to the presence of the outsiders. Paul was following the custom of the Jewish congregation in Antioch-on-the-Orontes of welcoming Gentiles into the congregation. However, the Jews of this Antioch did not want either the strangers or the missionaries. Instead, leading Jewish women and city elders had Paul and Barnabas expelled from the city. In their anger these citizens continued to harass the missionaries wherever they went in Pisidia (Acts 13:14-52).

AKŞEHİR - PHILOMELIUM

Akşehir is located about 20 km by twisting road over the mountains north of Yalvaç. In the 2nd century AD there was an active Christian community here. These are the people to whom

Evarestus, a Smyrnaean Christian, addressed a letter giving his account of the death of Polycarp the year before. Although Akşehir is on an east-west road, it has not figured greatly in the history of Anatolia either before the 2nd century or after. Crusaders passed through it, as must have many other armies. There is a Selçuk mosque, **Ulu Cami**, and a *medrese* that is now a **museum**, but both have been much changed since they were built.

For many people, one of the attractions of Akşehir is an open-air **türbe** in the center of town. A lock on the grill in front of the türbe is no protection because it otherwise stands exposed on all sides. The joke is in keeping with the **grave of Nasreddin Hoca**, Akşehir's favorite son.

In the early 15th century Akşehir was the encampment for the Mongol terror Tamerlane following his victory at Ankara. By one account, his prisoner Sultan Bayezit I died here. But there is no record of Tamerlane having wreaked the kind of horrific vengeance on Akşehir that he did on Sivas or on İzmir. Rather, in the wit and wisdom of Nasreddin Hoca, he met his better here. Recounting on one occasion what he had enjoyed the previous week when he had

Artist's rendering of Nasreddin Hoca

been absent from Akşehir, Tamerlane listed the rampages of a mad dog and a bull, a murder, a hanging, a fire and a tornado. In response, a man in the audience lifted his hands praising God. Tamerlane wanted to know what there was in his account that could be blessed, to which Nasreddin Hoca replied that it was fortunate that Tamerlane had returned as he would now leave a few citizens in peace.

The old religious teacher with the huge white cloth wrapped in many folds around his felt cap who rode backwards on his donkey, Nasreddin Hoca is the beloved, much-quoted comic of the Middle East. He appears in a number of incarnations such as Djuha and Abu Ali in the Arabic countries; he is also known in Bosnia. The Hoca's basic character is that of a teacher and a Muslim. The body of anecdotes that has collected around him represents Turkish folk wisdom, wish-fulfillment and occasionally ribald buffoonery. At times the jokes are on him; often they are against the establishment. Always they are taken good-naturedly.

Once upon a time someone asked Nasreddin Hoca if God's will prevailed invariably. The Hoca thought a minute and then said, "Yes, in my experience. Otherwise I would have gotten my way once in a while."

Tamerlane was born in 1336 in Kesh, a town south of Samarkand. His life was one of many battles, both at home as he defended his position and abroad as he increased his holdings. He died on February 17, 1405 when he was beginning a campaign into China. His grandson Ali Yazdi characterized him as liberal, benevolent and illustrious, but then the boy had not been present during the massacres in Sivas. All Tamerlane's biographers agree that he was lame, but they do not tell whether he was born so or not.

[1] Deiotarus is remembered because he entertained Julius Caesar in 47 BC when Caesar was celebrating his lightning success against the Pontic ruler Pharnaces in Zile. The food at the banquet must have been tainted: Caesar got deathly ill and thereupon charged Deiotarus with attempted murder. Fortunately for him his good lawyer friend Cicero defended him and the case ended in acquital.

[2] The Ahis or craft guilds were both professional and religious fraternities whose origins apparently went back into the Byzantine Greco-Roman social structure. In the 13th and 14th centuries they were societies of young, celibate men grouped under a spiritual leader (a sheykh or *ahi*). According to the traveler Ibn Battuta, in 1333 the Ahis shared their earnings, cared for strangers by offering them food and shelter in their hospice, and were noted for their sober self-discipline.

[3] It was Busbecq also who sent the first tulip bulbs from Turkey to Holland.

[4] One of the first known written treaties, the Turkish government sent its replica to the United Nations. In translation it reads "... Behold, as for the relationship between the land of Egypt and the Hatti land, since eternity the god does not permit the making of hostility between them because of a treaty valid forever."

[5] That symbol of the double-headed eagle appears on the Selçuk sultans' emblems in the 12th century AD and on the Holy Roman Emperors' coat of arms in the 14th century.

[6] Babais were a Turcoman group who exercised considerable political and religious influence in 13th century Anatolia.

[7] Medreses, or religious schools, were at times also medical schools and hospitals as here, at the Beyazit Külliyesi in Edirne, and at the Şifaiye Medresesi in Sivas. The Selçuks licensed their graduates to identify their competence in practicing medicine.

[8] "Sebaste" is a title in Greek for the emperor.

[9] An Albanian by birth, legend also has it that Gülbahar Hatun was a French princess kidnapped for the sultan's harem.

[10] In addition to the temple at Pessinus, there were also temples to Cybele at Sardis (probably the Temple to Artemis), on Mt. Sipylus (Manisa Dağı), Cyzicus (near Bandırma), Erythrea (Ildır) and on the peak of Mt. Ida (perhaps today's Gergis).

[11] For studies of this confused period, see Claude Cahen's *Pre-Ottoman Turkey*, the *Cambridge History of Islam*, and the *Cambridge History of Iran*.

[12] Latin inscriptions are relatively rare in Anatolia; Latin was used in official government communications, but Greek was the language commonly spoken.

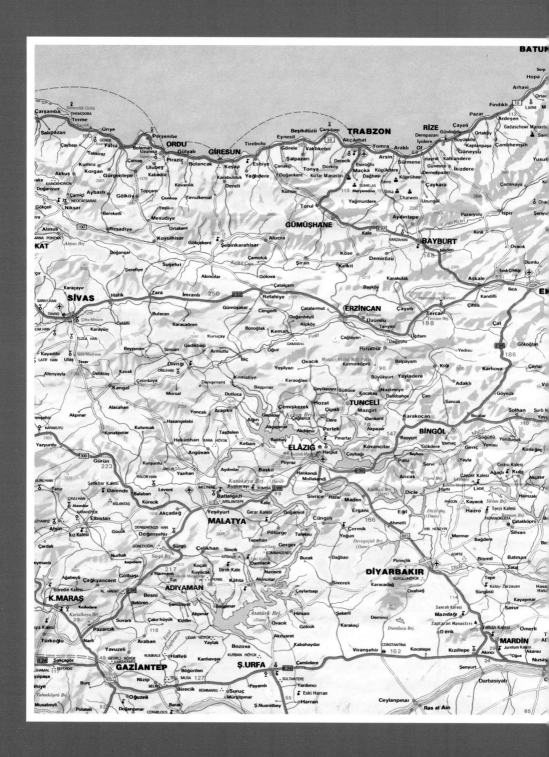

Eastern Turkey

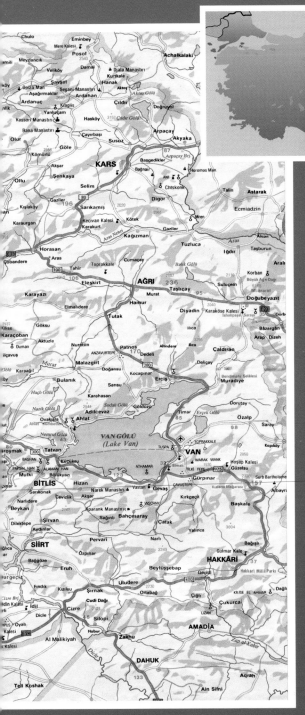

Spectacular and foreboding, the frontier region of Turkey has a magic of its own. Farmers and hotel keepers, guides and bank clerks, whoever they are, the people are warmly hospitable. Awesome river gorges, vast seemingly barren steppes, and towering mountains combine with magnificent buildings and dire tales, half-myth, half-reality, to cast a spell on all who travel to the East.

Sumelas Monastery perched on a hill in the Zigana mountains, Trabzon

EASTERN TURKEY

Nemrut Dağı
Kargemiş, Barak (Carchemish)
Malatya (Aspuzu)
Dicle and Fırat (Tigris and Euphrates Rivers)
Altınbaşak (Harran)
Şanlıurfa (Edessa)
Diyarbakır (Amida)
Mardin (Marida)
Tur Abdin
Cudi Dağı
Van (Tushpa)
Ahtamar
Malazgirt (Manzikert)
Ağrı Dağı (Mt. Ararat)
Ani
Erzurum (Theodosiopolis)
Kars
Yusufeli
Trabzon (Trebizond, Trapezus)
Sumelas (Meryemana)
Divriği (Tephrice)

NEMRUT DAĞI

Nemrut Dağı[1] — northeast of Adıyaman in south-central Turkey — is fascinating far beyond its significance either historically or religiously. **Colossal heads** — broken statues of gods, animals and King Antiochus himself — stare sightlessly out from three sides of a 50 m bare **tumulus** above the original 2100 m mountain. This is the place of the presumed grave of Antiochus I of Commagene, a megalomaniac who governed a small kingdom between the eastern edge of the Taurus Mountains and the Euphrates River between 62 and 38 BC. Commagene was only briefly an independent kingdom. It lasted between the years of the Seleucids beginning in 305 BC and the time when the Roman Emperor Vespasian took over the rule of the Province of Syria in AD 72. Its commercial values lay in its mineral resources and in its farming land, not in its citizens' military prowess.

Not much is known about Antiochus I beyond what appears in the inscriptions that he commissioned. He must have had enough money and enough manpower to build the tumulus which is 50 m high and 150 m in circumference. Perhaps it was too much of both money and slaves that made him think that he was if not immortal at least invincible: He backed the Parthians against Rome, was defeated and lost his throne. On his father's side he claimed to be a descendent of Darius the Great of Persia; on his mother's, of Alexander the Great of Macedonia. None of this is different from many others who have lived in Anatolia and have passed into anonymity.

His real claim to fame lies in the hauntingly macabre statues on this mountain, largely ignored by the outside world until about 1965.

The gods that he associated himself with seem to reflect his desire (and Alexander's) to combine the Eastern and Western traditions: On the east terrace of the tumulus are 8 to 10 m statues of Zeus-Ahura Mazda (the principal gods), of Apollo-Mithra-Helios-Hermes (the sun gods), and of Herakles-Artagnes-Ares (the gods of strength

Traveler Arnold C. Hanson carefully observing the giant heads on Nemrud Dağı

A hundred years before Megiddo (see next page), the fate of Carchemish had been held up as a warning to Israel by the prophet Isaiah. He called the Assyrian king Sargon II lawless and promised that his arrogance would be so punished that not even the chirp of a bird would be heard in his land (Isa. 10: 5-14).

and war) according to the inscriptions on each. They are unusual syncretistic representations. The inscriptions also detail sacrifices which were to be performed at dawn on the stepped incense altars in front of them. Present-day tourists often brave the chill wind on the mountain top because they wish to watch the dawn lighting the faces of the statues. On the west terrace Antiochus is shown in relief shaking hands with Apollo, Zeus, and Hermes in turn. Next to them is the relief of a lion (perhaps representing the Sun: in Mithraism the sun symbolizes fire) which wears the breastplate of the crescent moon. Stars and planets are also pictured on the slab; they have been interpreted as Antiochus's intent to preserve the date (thought to be 7 July 62 BC) when the Roman general Pompey put him on his throne and when the planets Mars, Mercury and Jupiter were in conjunction.

KARGEMIŞ, BARAK - CARCHEMISH

Atop a hill dominating what was once a major ford of the Euphrates River, Carchemish sits at the border with Syria. It was a fortified Hittite city; the friezes on its walls proclaimed its pride and its power. Conquered by the Assyrian King Sargon II (722-705 BC), little is visible today. Sculptures from the basalt gates and palace façades — battle scenes, lions, religious figures — were taken to museums, particularly the Museum of Anatolian Civilizations in Ankara. The sculpture of warriors, lions, horses and carts records something of the life in the 9th century BC. It shows what men wore in battle, how they used their weapons, what trappings were on their horses. Some of the lions became models for Greek artists. The mythological sphinx, a winged cat with a serpent tail and the double head of a hunting lion and a warrior, links Carchemish with Egypt. Also among the sculptures are elements of the *Gilgamesh Epic*.

Besides there not being much on the site to see, there is an additional reason not to linger casually here: Such a visit is guarded by armed soldiers because this is a border post where one might stray into a military trap. Visitors must stop at Barak and get one of the guards to accompany them to the ruins.

The importance of Carchemish in Jewish and Christian religious history is because of the attempted negotiations which occurred here in 609 BC between the Egyptian Pharaoh Necho and King Josiah of Judah (II Chron. 35:20,25). Josiah wanted to stop the Egyptians who were struggling with the Babylonians to control Syria. Necho tried to reason with him, saying that the Hebrews did not have a justifiable quarrel against him, but Josiah was determined to fight. Josiah was interested in both religious reform, getting rid of foreign influences, and in political expansion. It is thought that he did not want any outside power interfering in his domain. Josiah was killed that year at the battle of Megiddo. From the light of later history, this battle had an ironic outcome: Necho might have protected Judah although he defeated him then, but the battle so weakened him that he himself was defeated at Carchemish by the Babylonian Nebuchanezzar in 605. Nebuchanezzar went on to conquer Jerusalem and send the Hebrew people into exile.

MALATYA - ASPUZU

Malatya is a relatively new city, famous for its apricots in July. It is a possible starting point for a trip up Nemrut Dağı. Known in the 16th century AD as Aspuzu, the Ottoman sultans sometimes spent their summers here when they were on an eastern campaign. For tourists it is interesting because of its **museum** which contains items from the Chalcolithic Period (5000-3000 BC) through the Selçuk (11th to 14th centuries AD) and Ottoman (14th to 20th centuries) Periods. These came largely from the archaeological excavations at Aslantepe and Eski Malatya. Aslantepe is 7 km northeast of Malatya. An Assyrian and a Hittite settlement, it was part of the 13th century BC history of conflict between the Hittites and the Hurrians. Between the 11th and the 9th centuries BC it was the capital of a Neo-Hittite principality; this was the same time that King Asitawanda was holding court in Karatepe. Cimmerians destroyed it in about 657 BC. Its original name was Milit which became Malatya when people moved to the new site. A few traces of the **walls** are left; the large statue of the 8th century BC King Tarhunza is in the Ankara Museum of Anatolian Civilizations.

Megiddo, a site southeast of Haifa in Israel, controlled major trade and military routes, and as such was fought over frequently. The memories of those battles may have been the reason that the writer of Revelation chose its name as the symbol of the kind of cataclysmic vengeance God would exact from the world for its sinfulness: In Hebrew Armageddon *means* Mt. Megiddo. *(See* Rev.16: 13-21).

Bald ibis, Birecik

Eski Malatya, 12 km north of Malatya and identified as Battal-gazi, was known as Melitene. It was fought over by the First Crusaders, the Selçuks, and the Mongol terror Tamerlane among others before it became part of the Ottoman Empire in the early 16th century. The ruins of two old buildings, a 17th century **Mustafa Paşa caravansary** and a 13th century Selçuk **Ulu Cami** are of more than passing interest. The rear wall of the mosque still has some ceramic decoration.

Melitene, along with Tephrice (Divriği), was a center of the evangelical and heretical Christian sect of Paulicians between the 6th and the 13th centuries.[2]

In the Koran account, God commanded his angels to take seven handfuls of hard black mud and seven handfuls of sand from the earth. Then God made the rain to fall and soften it. But after the angels had kneaded it and God had shaped it into Adam, He let it alone for 200 years before He gave it life (Sura XV: 26).

DİCLE AND FIRAT - THE TIGRIS AND THE EUPHRATES RIVERS

In the story of Adam and Eve, the Bible describes the original perfect home of the human race where God planted a garden out of which four streams flowed, the Pishon, the Gihon, the Tigris and the Euphrates. The Koran parallels the biblical account. In the Koran, God promises that the gardens of Eden, underneath which there are flowing rivers, will be the resting place of the righteous. The identities of the Pishon and the Gihon Rivers are lost, but the names, Tigris and Euphrates, have been associated with two of the main rivers of Anatolia since as early as 2,000 BC. Both of these rivers rise in eastern Anatolia and flow south through today's Syria and Iraq into the Persian Gulf. In this "land between the rivers" (known also as "Mesopotamia," the fertile basin of the Tigris and the Euphrates), some of civilization's most important developments have taken place: for example, written language, codified law, and the concept of one God.

The two rivers have defined the routes of migrants, herders, traders and armies. They have marked boundaries. The places where they could be forded have determined the locations of cities. The ruins of palaces on their banks suggest the power and wealth of the people who have controlled these routes. Even today these

The Euphrates

rivers play a major role in Middle East politics, and it may be the control of their waters that will determine who dominates the land in the future.

The Tigris (called the Dicle in Turkish), is the shorter river; it carries a greater volume of water than the Euphrates by the time it empties into the Persian Gulf. The western source of the Tigris is Lake Hazar, located only a few kilometers south of the eastern shore of the Keban Dam. A number of more easterly streams drain the mountains south of Lake Van including the Bitlis Çayı which starts in the mountains west of Lake Van, and the Botan Çayı east of Siirt. Cuneiform inscriptions and reliefs are found at the sources and salient points along the banks. The western Tigris runs southeast to Diyarbakır and then through several new dams to Cizre, where it forms the border between Turkey and Syria. Southeast of Cizre, the Hezil Suyu from the mountains south of Lake Van defines the Turkish-Iraqi border for some miles until it joins the Tigris. In past centuries traffic on the Tigris south from Diyarbakır was managed on wooden rafts buoyed by inflated skin bags (called *kelek*). These cheap "camels" were broken down in Baghdad, the wood sold for lumber and the skins taken back to Diyarbakır to be used again.

Atatürk Dam

In its upper reaches, the Tigris is a swiftly-flowing stream; the Euphrates descends more gradually. For thousands of years irrigation ditches between the two rivers south of Baghdad have aided the agricultural development of the southern land of Mesopotamia. Both rivers have been dammed over the centuries, largely for agricultural purposes, but until now their flow was unregulated, causing either flood or drought across their basins. In the latter half of this century they are being developed along their courses for their commercial potentials of hydroelectric power.

The northern branch of the Euphrates, the Karasu, starts in the mountains east of Erzurum. It flows generally west past Erzincan and then bends sharply south not far from Divriği. Shortly thereafter its waters begin collecting at the Keban Dam. The southern branch, the Murat Nehri, begins in a number of streams that come together around Ağrı; it flows south to Malazgirt (where the Selçuk leader Alp Arslan defeated the Byzantine Emperor Romanus IV Diogenes in 1071). Just beyond Palu it joins the Karasu in the Keban Dam. As the Euphrates, it continues south through a series of dams including the Atatürk, the world's third largest earth-filled dam. It goes past Birecik which has always been an important ford in the east-west trade route. (Birecik has

According to Genesis, the source of the four streams was a single river. It watered the garden of Eden that God had planted "away to the east," and where God put Adam and Eve. Of the four streams, the Pishon encircled Havilah, perhaps today's southern Mesopotamia or Saudi Arabia. The Gihon encircled Cush, maybe a reference to southern Iraq. The Tigris flowed east of Asshur (Syria?). Presumably the Euphrates was so well-known that it did not need identification.

attracted attention from ornithologists as one of two places in the world where the bald ibis - *Geronticus eremita* - nests. In danger of extinction, these birds are protected by the Turkish government.) Continuing beyond Birecik, the Euphrates crosses the border into today's Syria at Carchemish.

The Southeast Anatolia Project (*Güney Anadolu Projesi* or *GAP*) in southeastern Turkey is a development project tapping these two resources for the provinces of Adıyaman, Diyarbakır, Gaziantep, Mardin, Siirt and Şanlıurfa. The planning of this project has been under the Directorate of State Hydraulic Works in the Ministry of Power and Natural Resources. Presently one of the less developed areas of the country, the project includes irrigation and hydro-electric power in addition to industrial, transportation and social development. Through efficient use of the region's resources the Turkish government's overall objectives are to raise the income levels by improving the economic structure, to increase the productivity and the employment opportunities, to enhance the assimilative capacity of the cities and to contribute to the nation's sustained economic growth and social stability. In the agricultural field, the hopes are that more land will be used for better and more diversified crops, that with the dams some agro-industries will develop, that there will be increased employment opportunities and that there will be enough crops grown and produced that some can be exported. Along with these national interests, Turkey is committed to supplying water at an annual average of 500 m^3 per second downstream to Syria and Iraq.

In developing agriculture, it is also hoped that GAP will aid in a higher level of education, income, and employment in the region thus contributing to a development of the entire country in terms of earnings, savings, foreign exchange and political stability. The plan covers a broad spectrum of irrigation facilities, farm mecha-nization, agro-chemicals, land tenure systems, pricing and market-ing. Animal husbandry (natural and artificial insemination), im-proved pasturage and feed and veterinary services are included, along with fisheries, afforestation, tourism and the related industrial developments (mills, gins, refineries, tanneries, construction materials, etc.).

Begun on November 4, 1983, the biggest of the dams is the Atatürk Dam at Karababa. Its reservoir capacity will be 48.7 billion m^3; its eight-unit power plant will have a 2400-megawatt capacity. It is the largest of all the structures ever built in Turkey. The Atatürk Dam complex includes a tunnel and canal system for irrigation purposes. The twin 26.4 km Urfa tunnels, currently the longest such tunnels in the world, will carry water from the Dam to the plain of Harran and beyond.

Turkey continues to work both on a just international access to the water and on the stature which this resource gives her.

Twenty-two dams and 17 hydroelectric power plants on the Tigris and the Euphrates Rivers are planned, with the expectation that 1,633,000 hectares of land will eventually be irrigated and 26 billion kWh of electric energy will be generated annually when the project is completed in 2005. With all of these, the amount of irrigated land in Turkey will be doubled and the electric power generated will increase 71 percent.

ALTINBAŞAK - HARRAN, CARRHAE

Harran is an important site for Judaism, Christianity and Islam because it is considered to have been Abraham's home when he heard God's call. Abraham, "the father of many nations" and "the friend of God," is held by the Jews, the Christians and the Muslims to be their patriarch. Historians put his date — assuming that he was an historical person — anywhere between 3,000 and 900 BC. The most commonly accepted date is sometime between 2,000 and 1,500 BC. A 13th century AD reference by the Arabic scholar Ali al-Harawi says that Abraham's sanctuary at Harran was called the Sanctuary of the Rock and that Abraham used to sit there when he tended his sheep. Al-Harawi also mentions that there was a small mosque on the site.

The Jewish and the Christian traditions hold that Abraham's father Terah led his clan in its migration from Ur of the Chaldees to Harran (Gen. 11:31). Harran is referred to as Aramnaharaim, meaning "the land of the Arameans of Two Rivers." The Aramean clan traced its ancestry to Noah's grandson Aram.

The distance between Ur of the Chaldees in southern Mesopotamia (once a thriving city with a long history) and Harran in today's southern Turkey presents a problem to some scholars. The location of Harran is less questioned than that of Ur because it is identified not only in Harran itself but also because it is referred to in tablets found in Nuzi in northeastern Iraq. Ur is not as certain. According to the prevailing theory, Terah and his clan would have had to make the thousand kilometer trek following the Euphrates

Terah's sons were Abraham, Haran and Nahor. Haran died before Terah, leaving one son, Lot. Lot went with Abraham when he migrated to Canaan. Later Lot's wife who looked back at the destruction of Sodom and Gomorrah turned to a pillar of salt (Gen. 19:1-26). Nahor, on the other hand, stayed in Harran. His granddaughter Rebecca became the wife of Abraham's son Isaac. Her father Bethuel was also from Harran. Nahor's son Laban was the greedy father of Rachel and Leah, wives of Jacob (Gen. 22-24).

Temple/university grounds, Harran

Harran was one of the cities that were destroyed by a coalition of Medes, Scythians, and Babylonians in about 661 BC (2 Kings 19: 12). A few years later its commercial life had recovered enough that Ezekiel listed it as a major Assyrian city dealing with Tyre in expensive cloth (Ezek. 27:23-24).

Jacob and Laban matched wits. Jacob contracted first to work seven years for Rachel. Laban substituted her dull-eyed sister Leah. Jacob agreed to work a second seven, at the end of which Laban let him marry Rachel. Desiring to return to Canaan, Jacob asked Laban for his wages. After Laban agreed to give him the black sheep from the flock, Laban hid them all. Because of Laban's many shady dealings, one is inclined to forgive some of Jacob's (and Rachel's!) guile when he stole away from Harran at last (Gen. 29-31).

northwest, the Balikh north and then the Cullab (a tributary of the Balikh) to get to Harran. It is a long, but not impossible, journey for nomads. However, there is a small minority opinion that presents evidence that Terah may not have traveled so far. These scholars suggest that Chaldea extended from the delta of the Tigris and the Euphrates on the Persian Gulf into northeastern Anatolia. With that, they add the early tradition that Terah's Ur was Urfa (or Edessa). The evidence is partly religious, partly linguistic: Religiously, Ur in southern Mesopotamia, Harran in southern Turkey and its neighbor Urfa shared the distinction of being important centers of the worship of the moon god Sin. In linguistics, the language of the early Chaldeans was Semitic and possibly Aramaic. "Laban," the name of Abraham's nephew, in Semitic meant "white" and referred to the moon god. In themselves these points neither prove nor disprove the location of Ur of the Chaldees, but they are some of the many threads that cross and recross here. By the 9th century BC Aramaic was the lingua franca of the Middle East. Parts of the Old Testament were written in Aramaic; one of its dialects is probably the language that Jesus spoke.[3]

Of the pre-Christian Syriac literature, a story about Sennacherib's wise and virtuous secretary, Ahikar, who eventually prevails over his wicked nephew, Nadhan, has been told and retold hundreds of times. The earliest known version of it is from the 5th century BC. It is similar to the 3rd century (or maybe 6th century) BC Book of Daniel and the 2nd century Book of Tobit. The 4th century BC Greek dramatist Menander also used its plot. It is referred to in the Koran, and it appears in the *Arabian Nights*.

Jews and Christians believe that Abraham was called on to sacrifice his son Isaac; Muslims believe that Ismael (the son of Rebecca's slave Hagar whom Abraham sent out into the desert) was the son whom Abraham would have sacrificed and with whom he founded his holy house. The three religions share a number of prophets and apostles besides Abraham.

The Koran reads, "We believe in God. We believe in what has been revealed to us through Abraham, Ismael, Isaac, Jacob and their tribes, to Moses and to Jesus, in what has been revealed to the prophets by God. We do not make a difference between any of them, and we submit ourselves to God." [4] This Islamic tolerance is part of the background of the coexistence of peoples of different faiths over the years.

On his death, Abraham's father Terah was buried in Harran. After Abraham heard God's call to found a great nation and to move to the land of Canaan, some of the members of his extended family remained in Harran.

When it was time for Abraham's son Isaac to take a wife, Abraham was concerned that Isaac should not choose one of the

Canaanite women. (The Canaanite religion was loathed because it was associated with the Weather-god Baal and the eroticism of a fertility cult.) Therefore Abraham sent his servant back to Harran to get a woman from his own tribe. This girl turned out to be Rebecca, one of Abraham's nieces. A similar story of recourse to the family in Harran occurred when Isaac's son Jacob had to flee from Esau's wrath because Jacob had cheated him out of his birthright. Back in Harran Jacob started looking for his cousin Laban. By chance Laban's daughter Rachel came up to water the sheep. Smitten, Jacob rolled the stone off the well for her and took his thanks in the form of a kiss. While Laban agreed to the marriage, he not only made Jacob work seven years before he could marry her older sister Leah, he also made Jacob work a second seven for Rachel who had been his first choice. It was a high price, but then Jacob probably was not in any hurry to go home and face Esau (Gen.27:41-29:30).

Halil ar-Rahman Mosque, Şanlıurfa

Today Harran is a small, partially walled village distinguished by a cluster of **bee-hive shaped houses**, a 13th century AD **fortress**, and the ruins of a **temple/-university complex**. In ancient times it was a prosperous city on the edge of the Fertile Crescent.[5] It had grown as a crossroads trading post on the routes that ran either north and south from the Halys River (Kızılırmak) and Malatya to Rakka and Babylon on the Euphrates, or east and west from Antioch through Aleppo to Nisibin (Nusaybin) and Cizre, and then down the Tigris to Nineveh, Baghdad and Babylon. Perhaps as many as twenty thousand people lived here at its height. Harran's water came from both the Cullab River and from a number of wells. The Cullab flowed from the Tektek Mountains north of Şanlıurfa past Harran and joined the Balikh River just across today's Syrian border. During the reign of the Abbasid ruler Harun ar-Rashid (AD 786-809) a canal was built to bring water from the Cullab into Urfa and divert it from Harran. Before the sack of Harran by the Mongols under Hulagu in AD 1259 the Cullab also supplied water to a string of villages; but all of these were cut off when Urfa took the water for its own uses. As for the wells, one known locally as **Bi'r Ya'qub** is by tradition associated with the stories of Rebecca and Rachel.

Religion in Harran and throughout Mesopotamia in the thousands of years before the Christian era was associated with the study of heavenly bodies. In Harran it centered on the worship of the moon god, Sin (who was also worshipped in Ur of the Chaldees). His temple here was perhaps the greatest in Meso-potamia. Its roof was made from the cedars of Lebanon; the ceiling and walls were covered with designs in lapis lazuli and silver.

Marcus Licinius Crassus got his wealth trafficking in slaves and buying up the property of condemned men. He agreed to the minor consulship of Syria because he expected to plunder it and its neighbors. But he was defeated at Harran in 53 BC by the Parthian general who put him to death by pouring molten gold down his throat.

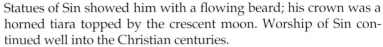

*Saladin lived from
1138 to 1193. His
name means "one
who honors the
faith." Proud and
courageous, he was
also gentle with
children,
impeccably honest,
and totally
committed to what
he considered was a
sacred cause.*

*Birecik and its
castle (above),
Crusaders' fortress
in Harran (below)*

Statues of Sin showed him with a flowing beard; his crown was a horned tiara topped by the crescent moon. Worship of Sin continued well into the Christian centuries.

The importance of the moon and of astrology/astronomy for the people of Mesopotamia can be inferred from the fact that their Magi (priests) studied in detail the phases of the moon, attempting to predict the future. It was probably from them that Thales of Miletus learned to predict the eclipse of the sun. The priests first defined the zodiac — the twelve constellations through which the sun seems to pass — as their interpretation of the meaning of the relation of the earth to the sun and the stars. The Mesopotamian observatories adjoined the temples, and in one puzzling account it seems that the priests even knew about the phases of Venus, though how they managed that with the naked eye no one understands.

The earliest book on astronomy dates from the time of the Assyrian ruler Sargon II (722-705 BC). The temple and the school at Harran probably contributed their full share to these scientific observations which eventually were transmitted to the West through the writings of the 12th century AD Jewish philosopher Maimonides. Maimonides was personal physician to Saladin, the brilliant Ayyubite Muslim commander during the Third Crusade who united Egypt, took Jerusalem back in 1187, and defeated Richard the Lionhearted at Jaffa in 1192.

Saladin's brother al-Malik al-Adil rebuilt the **fortress of Harran** in 1191 according to a 13th century geographer Ibn Shaddad. He reported that in the 10th century the fortress had been a Sabian[6] temple to the moon god before it was taken by the Muslims. The fortress is an irregular rectangle with parts of three of its four towers still standing. The stone piers of the southeast gate are decorated with pairs of dogs on each side. Those on the west are shepherd dogs, those on the east are hunters. The dogs crouch as though they are about to spring, but their heads are turned back, and they are restrained by chains. Their sculptors must have had a sense of humor because the dogs seem almost to be smiling. On the arch above them part of the Arabic inscription indicates that it was a quotation from Sura cxii: "God is one and eternal. He neither begets nor is begotten. None is like him." More inscriptions identify the rulers of Harran and help date the work. Ibn Shaddad also reported that two djinns made of copper were buried in the tower of Harran's water gate as talismans against snakes.

ŞANLIURFA - EDESSA

Şanlıurfa claims connections with Abraham and Nimrod, and with 1st century Christian missionaries. Its mosques reflect the Muslim presence here from the 12th century on. Perhaps it was the capital of a Mitanni kingdom in the second millennium BC. In the succeeding centuries Hurrians, Hittites and Assyrians must have been its rulers. In Chaldean, Abraham was called Orham which suggests some relationship to its Hurrian names of Callirrhoe, Orrhoe, and Osrhoene.[7]

Alexander the Great came through here in 333 BC; his inheritor and general Seleucis renamed the place Edessa, referring to a city he knew in Macedonia. It was called that through the time of the Crusades. "Urfa" harks back to the earlier name. Since the Turkish Revolution of 1923 it has acquired the distinguishing title of "Şanlı" — "Glorious" Urfa. The Abgar kings who ruled the country of Osrhoene beginning about 132 BC reacted against the Hellenic Westernization of their land as defined by the Seleucid kings of Antioch. In defiance they set about to develop their own Arabic civilization using Arabic as their language rather than Greek.

Two **late-Roman columns**, part of what is called the "Throne of Nimrod," rise prominently on the hill southwest of the city; one bears an inscription in Syriac concerning Queen Shalmat, but who she was has not been established. They, or two **pools** below them, may have been sites of a pre-Christian temple to Astarte. In this cult of Astarte, the Semitic goddess of love, the sun (Nergal) and the moon (Sin) were worshipped as twins and associated with the zodiac sign of Gemini. Some scholars have tried to associate them with the twins in the apocryphal Syriac book, *The Acts of Judas Thomas*. ("Thomas" means twin.) Written by "Judas-the-twin," the book is a justification of both celibacy and asceticism. It ascribes to the belief that this Judas was the brother of Jesus.

Şanlıurfa claims the distinction of being the birthplace of Abraham. One of its early names, "Hurri," which is thought to mean "grotto" or "fortress with a spring," is related to the legend that a cave under the citadel of the city is his birthplace. In Muslim tradition this was where Abraham rebuked King Nimrod and his subjects because of their worship of idols (Sura vi:74-79). For the insult and his refusal to follow the king's practice, Abraham was condemned to be burned. This story is echoed in rabbinical tradition. But God turned the fagots for the pyre into carp and the flames into two pools. These pools are considered sacred by the residents of Şanlıurfa, and the tradition makes it a place of pilgrimage for Muslims.[8]

The Christian influence in Edessa, according to the 4th century Christian historian Eusebius, began when King Abgar V (4 BC - AD 50) addressed a letter to Jesus asking him to come cure him of his leprosy. Perhaps his appellation "Ukkama" meaning "the

One tradition says that only one pool was formed when Nimrod threw Abraham off the citadel hill above Urfa. This pool (Birket İbrahim) is near the Mosque/Medrese of Halil ar-Rahman. A second pool there (Ayn-i Zeliha Birket) carries the name of the mother of Nimrod. Zeliha is also supposed to be the wife of Potiphar and the one who accused Joseph of attempting to make love to her (Gen. 39: 6-20).

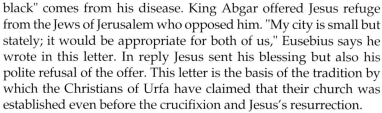

A cave in the Mevlid-i Halil Camii on Göl Caddesi southeast of the pools is held to be the birthplace of Abraham. Men and women who wish to worship there enter the cave through separate doors.

black" comes from his disease. King Abgar offered Jesus refuge from the Jews of Jerusalem who opposed him. "My city is small but stately; it would be appropriate for both of us," Eusebius says he wrote in this letter. In reply Jesus sent his blessing but also his polite refusal of the offer. This letter is the basis of the tradition by which the Christians of Urfa have claimed that their church was established even before the crucifixion and Jesus's resurrection.

The tradition continued with the 4th century *Doctrine of Addai.* When the early community began to spread out from Jerusalem, Thaddaeus (known in Syriac as Addai) was sent as one of the twelve apostles to Edessa. According to this account, Thaddaeus healed the king of his leprosy and witnessed to the Christian message. The 4th century Christian historian Eusebius, however, says that it was Judas, the son of Thaddaeus, who was sent.

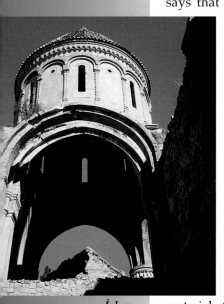

İşhan

Perhaps the latter part of this story is inaccurate only in putting the earliest date of missionary activity in the region before about AD 140, the time of the writer Tatian.

Tatian, a 2nd century AD resident of Edessa, wrote prolifically attempting to convert others to Christianity as he had been. In his efforts to convince his readers that the pagan view was indefensible he damned the absurdities of Greek mythology and the immoral behavior of the gods. He insisted both that people should have a freedom of choice and that evil comes from free choice, but at the same time he also believed that free choice can put things right again. The Church considered him to be a heretic on several counts, but, because the only contemporary statements about him that are still in existence come from his enemies, it is difficult to assess the truth. Tatian wrote a "harmony" (*Diatessaron*) of the gospels — a compilation of the material of the first four books of the New Testament arranged in a single narrative sequence. Not only did this work influence the text of the writings accepted as the Christian canon, it also established into the 5th century the basis of the biblical and theological vocabulary of the Syrian Orthodox Church. His work probably helped influence the divergence in belief between the Syrian Orthodox and the Eastern (Greek) Orthodox Churches.

Eusebius claims in his 4th century *Ecclesiastical History* that he had access to a document from the official archives of Edessa that supported the claim of Jesus's letter to King Abgar. That document has since disappeared, so it cannot be examined. Western historians doubt that there was such a letter and believe that the account of the first Christian king belongs to the 2nd century King Abgar IX. There is a similar account in the *Doctrine of Addai* of which a complete 6th century copy does exist.

The apocryphal *Acts of Judas Thomas* is thought to be a 2nd century AD Syriac work, written perhaps by Bardaisan, a friend of Abgar IX. Bardaisan was a poet who wrote many hymns, none of which except the *Hymn to the Soul* has survived.

King Abgar IX (AD 179-214) was a Christian, as is shown on his coins by a cross on his crown. He also encouraged the flowering of Arabic literature. Two buildings in Edessa were destroyed in a flood in the fall of AD 201. One was the earliest known structure built specifically as a Christian church; the other was the king's palace. In the 6th century Emperor Justinian dammed the stream to prevent the flooding and built a deep channel to the east of the city to draw off the surplus water.

In 978 a Christian Arab writer reported that there were more than 300 churches in Edessa, and a few years later another said that the cathedral of Edessa, long since gone, with its beautiful mosaic-covered, vaulted ceiling was one of the great wonders of the world.

Not only was Edessa an active center of Christianity, it became an important university city where a number of scholars translated original Greek works on theology, history, science, philosophy and mythology into Arabic. Many of these were lost to European scholars; some were destroyed when the library of Alexandria was lost.[9] It is largely thanks to the Edessene scholars having made the writings — particularly those of Aristotle — available to their neighbors that they were a link in the awakening of medieval Europe: Through the Arabic texts this rich literature was reintroduced to the West by Crusaders who were here in the 12th century.

Edessa was a prosperous city that more than one conqueror coveted. As an important city on the main Persian Royal Road between Susa and Sardis, it has seen many armies pass through its streets. The Persian Shahpur I was here in AD 260 and defeated the Roman Emperor Valerian whom he kept a prisoner for the rest of his life. He was followed by the Arabs, the Byzantines, the Selçuk Turks and the Armenians before the First Crusader Baldwin I of Boulogne captured it in 1098. Baldwin created a countship here which lasted until 1144 when the city was taken by the Muslim Imadeddin Zengi. That event so shocked the western Christian world that within three years the Second Crusade against Islam was set in motion. This Crusade had two major effects on subsequent events: First, the defeat of the Christians by the Ayyubite ruler Saladin in 1187 eroded the Muslim perception that Westerners were invincible, and second, the self-serving behavior of both the Eastern and the Western Christians added fuel to their distrust of each other.

Edessa profited in the Mongol invasion in 1260 which was led by Hulagu, the first king of Persia and founder of the Ilhanlar dynasty, who cut off the water supply of its rival Harran, thus destroying the irrigation system of the plain south of Edessa. About 150 years later it was sacked by Tamerlane. The city became part of

Urfa's title of "Şanlı" (glorious) was accorded it recently, about the same time that "Kahraman" (heroic) was added to Maraş. Both titles reflect the honor given to their citizens for their part in the Turkish Republic's history.

The walls of Diyarbakır are among the few man-made structures on earth that are visible from the moon.

the Ottoman Empire during the reign of Sultan Murat IV in 1637 and was the capital of the province of Aleppo. Its name reverted in time to "Urfa."

By repute, the oldest Muslim building in Şanlıurfa is from the 12th century: **Ulu Cami** ("Great mosque"), a red stone building on Atatürk Caddesi, was founded by Nureddin and patterned on the Great Mosque of Aleppo; its minaret doubles as a clock tower. (Nureddin was the ruler of Aleppo and Damascus.) The medrese (Islamic school) associated with it is thought to have been built by Saladin in 1191. Perhaps it occupies the site of the famous Christian cathedral. Other old buildings date back to the 13th century. Reflections of the religious complex of the **Mosque of Halil ar-Rahman** and of its medrese shimmer in one of the sacred pools associated with the memory of Abraham. Tradition says that anyone so sacrilegious as to eat the fish of this pool will go blind. The **Ridvaniye Camii** and its medrese and the **Abdurrahman Camii** and its medrese are from the 18th century. Not far from the pools is the old bazaar, a place whose crowded streets, whose goods and whose methods of manufacture, whose sounds and smells and hubbub, whose merchants, their costumes and their bargaining are reminiscent of the fabled romance of the old Ottoman Empire.

Crosses on Mor Gabriel

DİYARBAKIR - AMIDA

Diyarbakır, along with Harran and Şanlıurfa, must be one of the oldest continuously occupied cities of the Middle East. Once important, the Syrian Chaldean and Syrian Orthodox communities are overshadowed today by the city's Muslim institutions. The original part of the city on the **citadel** overlooking the Tigris is surrounded by sturdy **black basalt walls** whose foundations go back at least to Roman times. A military zone, the citadel is on the northeast corner of the walls. The 12th century **Hazreti Süleyman Camii** inside the citadel is open to the public.

When the walls were first built, these walls were pierced by the north-south and east-west roads that still intersect in the center of the city. The four main gates are these: To the north is the Harput, or Dağ, or Elazığ Gate, a formidable black tower. Above its door are carvings of two lions and a bird. South is the Mardin Gate which once had two arches. On the west is the New Gate, and to the east is the Urfa Gate. The latter is decorated with an eagle outstretched above a bull's head. Two winged dragons guard an inscription. A number of the towers in the wall also carry inscriptions including the Keçi, Yedi Kardeş, Nur, Evli Beden, and Melek Şah towers. It is possible, but not easy, to walk around the walls, although the circuit involves several detours.

Located at a ford on the Tigris, and at the northern end of the navigable stretch of that river, Diyarbakır had a long succession of rulers. In Roman times the city was known as Amida (later called Kara — black — Amida). The Roman Emperor Trajan was here in AD 115. For centuries as a border defense it went back and forth between the Persians and the Romans/ Byzantines. Its Christian community was represented at the First Ecumenical Council in Nicaea (325) by a bishop. Julian the Apostate who was fighting the Persians in 363 died near Diyarbakır, having been stabbed — according to rumor — by one of his own Christian soldiers.[10] In 638 the city was taken by the Arabs; shortly thereafter people from the tribe of Bakr settled in it, giving it the name of "the dwelling place (*diyar*) of the Bakr." It was part of the Ommayad and then the Abbasid holdings. Tamerlane captured it, to be followed by the Black Sheep (Kara-koyunlu) and the White Sheep (Akkoyunlu) Turcomans in the 15th century. Under Selim I in 1515 it became part of the Ottoman Empire.

A few streets north of the intersection of the main streets is Diyarbakır's oldest and largest mosque, **Ulu Cami** (Great Mosque), built by al-Malik al-Adil Shah, the Selçuk ruler in 1091. Two carved lions attack two carved bulls on the entrance to the mosque. The plan of the mosque is that of a great courtyard like the mosques of the Arab countries where the climate is hot, rather than like the more northern mosques which are covered with a dome. It burned in 1155, and was restored soon thereafter. Some accounts say that its foundations go back to 639, and that it had been a Byzantine church that was converted to a mosque when the Arabs conquered the city the year before. Thus, not only does this make it the oldest mosque in Turkey, it is also reputed to be the fifth oldest mosque in the world. The entrance to a 16th century caravansary, the **Hasan Paşa Hanı**, is directly across the street from **Ulu Cami**. The caravansary serves now as a market place, mostly for rugs.

The **Nebi (Peygamber) Camii** was built probably in the 15th century AD. Three other mosques were founded by men who had been *devşirme* conscripts. They were Ottoman governors of Diyarbakır and later became Grand Viziers: the **Hüsrev Paşa Camii**, the **Melek Ahmet Paşa Camii** and the **Behram Paşa Camii** (the largest mosque in the city). After İstanbul, Diyarbakır has the most religious buildings in Turkey.

Other mosques which should be noted are the **Citadel** or **Nasiriye Camii** (it and the Hazreti Süleyman Camii honor early Muslim saints and are places of pilgrimage for young girls), the 12th century **Zinciriye Medresesi** and the **Mesidiye Medresesi**, and the 16th century **Safa Camii** with its white minaret. The

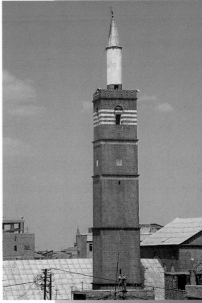

The square minaret of the 11th century Ulu Cami, Diyarbakır, the very first of the great Selçuk mosques in Anatolia

The older buildings in Diyarbakır - the mosques, the old churches, the citadel walls - give a sense of the power of the medieval or early Ottoman city. Like the Rüstem Paşa mosque in İstanbul, ceramic tiles completely line the lower walls of the Behram Paşa mosque (1572).

In the churches of Tur Abdin, people celebrate Christmas by lighting a fire of oak branches to remember the fire that the shepherds lit in Bethlehem to warm the baby Jesus. Legend also says that the Magi (wise men or astrologers) passed through here following the star. Could these Eastern Magi have been Mesopotamian sages from Edessa?

Sheykh Mutahar or **Kasım Padishah Camii** (1512) has a minaret that is balanced on four basalt columns that were carved from a single stone. While it is possible to walk under the minaret, local tradition has it that wishes come true for those who walk around the columns seven times.

Close across the street from the Kasım Padishah Camii is the **Surp Giragos Kilisesi**, the church of the Armenian Orthodox community of Diyarbakır. Members of the Syrian Orthodox community in Diyarbakır worship in the **Meryem Ana Kilisesi** (Church of the Virgin Mary). Those members of the Syrian Chaldean community worship in the **Keldani Kilise**.[11]

MARDİN - MARIDA

Mardin (known during the time of the Assyrian Empire as Marida) is a small city, mostly tawny brown in color, surmounted by a 15th century citadel (not open to the public). It was conquered by Saladin and later by Tamerlane. Against the escarpment and beneath the citadel is the stately **Sultan İsa Medresesi**. Dated 1385, the medrese is both a school of Islamic law and a museum containing archaeological items from the area such as Christian stone carvings from Midyat and from Hasankeyf. Other large stone carvings may be representations of Sumerian gods. **Ulu Cami** is an 11th century Selçuk building; its cylindrical minaret was damaged when the Kurds revolted in the early 19th century, but it has since been rebuilt. **Latifiye Camii**, a 14th century mosque, has a beautifully carved entrance. These two mosques are near the main square of Mardin. **Kasım Paşa Medresesi**, a 15th century school built by the Akkoyunlus, is some distance to the southwest of the center of the city; the 13th century **Artukid Şehidiye Camii** and the 14th century **Bab-üssür Camii** are to the east.

A number of the residents of the Mardin/Tur Abdin area are Syrian Orthodox Christians (also sometimes called Suryanis). Their total population in Turkey is between 20 and 40 thousand members. By repute they are the best jewelers of the country. Their everyday language is Syriac.

TUR ABDİN

Tur Abdin means "the plateau of the servants of God." The plateau is an extensive highland region stretching from Mardin to Cizre; the main town in between is Midyat. This has been the center of the Syrian Orthodox Church since the 6th century when Bishop Jacob Baradi converted the people here to Christianity.[12] In medieval times there were as many as 150 ordained bishops and 80 monasteries. Bishops from the Jacobite and Armenian persuasions who had rejected the decisions against the Monophysites of the Fourth Ecumenical Council, met together in Manzikert (Malazgirt) in 728 hoping, but without success, to effect a union. Today there

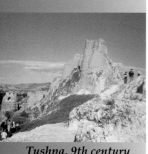

Tushpa, 9th century BC citadel on shores of Lake Van

are three Christian monasteries here struggling to exist, **Mor Gabriel**, **Mor Yakub** and **Deyrulzafaran**. Their membership has dwindled and their financial resources are low, but their libraries hold priceless volumes of early Christian literature. Mor Gabriel is a 4th century establishment where St. Simeon and St. Gabriel are said to be buried; the church at Deyrulzafaran dates from the late 6th century. Deyrulzafaran was the seat of the Syrian Orthodox Patriarchate from 1293 until 1932. Mor Yakup is located in Nusaybin, the Roman Nisibin. Mor Gabriel, east of Midyat, was founded in 396/7. The present complex has been built up through the vision and efforts of its community within the last 20 years.

Several other old churches dot the area, including, on the road between Midyat and Hasankeyf, the 14th century **Mor Yakup** (at Salah), the 6th century **Mor Kyriako**s (at Bağlarbaşı), and the **Mor Sovo** and the 7th century **El Hadra** (at Khakh). The whole area has been affected by the political instability of the recent fighting and influx of Kurdish refugees.

Tenth and 9th century BC Urartian gold and silver work was so prized that it was exported to Greece and Italy. There, historians believe, it was copied in Greek and Etruscan art objects.

CUDİ DAĞI

The Koranic account of Noah differs from the biblical on several points. Only one of Noah's sons appears in the Koran. This man refused to join his father in the Ark, choosing instead to seek refuge on a mountain where he, along with the unbelievers, was drowned. When the waters abated — the Koran suggests they were boiling hot waters — Noah pled for his son with God, to which God responded, "My ways are not to be questioned." (Sura xi: 38-49). The Koran gives Cudi Dağı (at 2,114 m a much lower and much less pronounced peak than Ararat) as the resting place of Noah's Ark. Cudi Dağı is about 25 km east of Cizre and the Tigris River.

Mosque of Hüsrev Paşa, Van

VAN - TUSHPA

Van, (or Tushpa, its ancient name) was a major city of the land of Urartu, a state that was known as Ararat in biblical history between the 9th to the 6th centuries BC. One of its early rulers, King Sardur I (840-830 BC) built the foundations of the citadel on the large butte near Lake Van. His successor, King Menua, rendered a public service to the community with a canal that brought fresh water from the mountains. Some scholars think that the writers of Genesis used Ararat as their image of the Garden of Eden because it was so fertile during these years. It also was a growing power, and as such was a threat to the Assyrian Empire.

The Van markets today are famous for the local flatweave kilims. Van cats with one blue eye and one green and long white fur have been a second commercial item, but their sale is now greatly restricted.

Lake Van is the world's largest soda lake. The water is good for neither drinking nor irrigation, but it is fun to swim in because it leaves a silky feeling on one's skin.

Assyrian kings figure in both Van's history and that recorded in the Old Testament. The Assyrian Sargon II invaded and laid waste the land in the 8th century BC. Sargon had also defeated a Hittite-Mushki army led by King Midas at Carchemish in 717 BC. Sargon's son was Sennacherib, the king against whose attack Hezekiah built the tunnel for water from the Gihon spring to the Pool of Siloam in Jerusalem. The night before Sennacherib was to enter that city his army died in some catastrophic event. Not long after, he was murdered by his sons who then fled to the land of Ararat (2 Kings 19:37). The deeds of the Urartian kings are recorded on stone in Van.

Xerxes I, the Persian king who was later defeated at the Battle of Salamis (26 September 480 BC), left a trilingual inscription (Babylonian, old Persian and Median) on the face of the citadel about half-way up, detailing his exploits. The **inscription** is visible from below, but it is too far away and too small to be read at a distance. Such an inaccessible cliff is an odd place for Xerxes to have left his curriculum vitae since he apparently wanted so much to be remembered by later generations.

Not long after, in 401 BC, the Greek soldier/historian Xenophon fought several battles in the area as he and his Ten Thousand plodded northwards. Alexander the Great was here in 331 BC and later in the 1st century BC the Roman general Pompey came through; he accepted the surrender of the Urartian kingdom from Tigranes I. Tigranes had been allied with Mithradates, the king of Pontus who was responsible for the revolt against Rome in 88 BC known as the "Asian Vespers." Under Persian domination the

Ahtamar

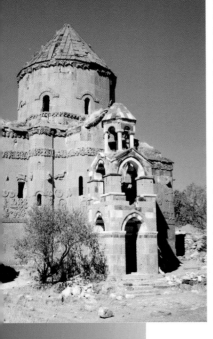

resident Armenians became buffers between Byzantine, Persian, and Arab control. Turkish nomads who came upon the lake in the 11th century must have wondered at the verdant fields. In the early 15th century AD Tamelane worked his destructive power against the citadel. Van became part of the Ottoman Empire in 1548. It was completely destroyed in the fighting during the War of Independence in 1917/18. Following that, the old city on the lake was abandoned and the present new one grew up about four kilometers inland.

The buildings of religious and historic interest are the ruins of the citadel, and the mosques and tombs grouped at its foot. Perhaps the oldest building is the **wall** of the old city, of which only small sections remain. The ruined **Ulu Cami** was built in the 13th century by leaders of the Turkish Ilkhan tribe. The three Ottoman mosques are the **Hüsrev Paşa** (a Sinan building), the **Kurşunlu** and the **Kaya Çelebi**. Two small **kümbets** (tombs) stick up above the rubble a bit farther south.

The path up the citadel begins at the western edge of the cliff. It is a bit of a scramble to reach the top. Among the

places to explore (but some caution is recommended because of many pitfalls) are a number of tombs on the south side, the Urartian fortress wall, the castle and another Ottoman mosque. The crest of the hill is about two kilometers long; the terrain is broken enough that it is not always easy to find one's way. The view from the top of the lake and the surrounding mountains has few equals for dramatic quality, particularly as an electrical storm approaches over the lake.

Mt. Ararat (Ağrı Dağı) and Kurdish villagers

AHTAMAR

On the south side of Lake Van, about 38 km west of Van and in the lake itself, is the island of Ahtamar famous for its church. Lake Van is said by geologists to have been formed by the lava from the now inactive volcano Nemrut Dağı[13] located on the west shore of the lake; the lava blocked several rivers from joining the Murat. This took place about 10,000 years ago. Nemrut Dağı last erupted in AD 1444.

Ahtamar is approached by boat from west of the town of Gevaş. Not much more than a dot in the lake, Ahtamar is the site of the **Armenian Church of the Holy Cross**, built by King Gagil Artsruni in 921. Originally there was a monastery on the island; from the 10th to the 19th century it was a religious and cultural center. For a while in the 10th century it was the seat of the Armenian Orthodox Patriarchate. Thereafter until 1900 it was a bishop's seat; it was abandoned as a residence in 1917.

The outside walls of the cruciform church are lavishly covered with reliefs illustrating biblical scenes, Armenian saints and stylized animals and flowers. Inside there are 10th century frescoes but they have been damaged by smoke and defacement. In addition to its setting, the church is charming for the lively spirit and detail of these reliefs. A cow appears to be sleeping undisturbed between David and Goliath; the whale that is about to attack Jonah is a curiously scaly animal, hardly big enough to swallow even his arm.

A number of hills obscure the distant view of Mt. Ararat, so it is not until one is quite close that its immensity strikes one with awe. Insignificant only in comparison, Little Ararat (Küçük Ağrı Dağı) rises to the east 3,925 m and is joined across an 11 km saddle to Ararat.

The first fragments of the Gilgamesh Epic, *and the earliest known version, were found at Nineveh (Mosul) in the mid-19th century AD. The story must have been a popular one because fragments of Hittite and Hurrian versions have turned up in Boğazkale. A later version from Sultantepe, 8th century BC in date, suggests that by then the* Epic *may have been rewritten as a satire.*

MALAZGİRT - MANZIKERT

Little of interest for the casual tourist exists in Malazgirt at the foot of the volcanic Suphan Dağı. At 4,058 m Suphan Dağı is the third tallest mountain in Turkey. It is also at the edge of the Murat Nehri, one of the two large rivers that come together in the Keban Dam to form the Euphrates. The city was an important army post for the Byzantines. When the Eastern Roman Emperor Romanus IV Diogenes was defeated and captured here by the Selçuk leader Alp Arslan on 19 August 1071, the whole of Anatolia was opened to Turkish inroads. A **fortress** of black basalt remains from that time, but there are no other physical scars from the battle. Probably neither army could comprehend the long-term significance of what had happened that day.

AĞRI DAĞI - ARARAT

Ararat is the mountainous region of eastern Turkey stretching from south of Lake Van north to the Araxes River (Aras Nehri). While there are several high mountains in Ararat (Mor Dağı at 3,807 m, Suphan Dağı at 4,058 m, Uludoruk at 4,135 m), by far the highest is the volcanic cone of Mt. Ararat (Ağrı Dağı) at 5,165 m. It is higher than any of the European Alps. Rising with an unobstructed view 4,000 m above the surrounding plain, it has acquired renown as the place where the Ark came to rest.

Mt. Ararat, a dormant volcano, looms majestically over the far eastern tip of Turkey Even through the summer the summit is capped in snow. The last time it erupted was on June 2, 1840. At that time a rock fall destroyed the village of Arghuri where legend held that Noah planted the first vineyard. The snow on the upper hundred meters of the mountain is ice, and below the snow line the slopes are littered with huge blocks of black basalt. Many mountaineers have been challenged by Mt. Ararat, at best a deceptive, dangerous climb. At present no permission is given for any climbing here: Ararat borders Armenia, and is therefore a sensitive military area. Those who hope to see the mountain need to be cautioned that it is chary of revealing itself: Early morning before it has gathered its cloud wraps about it is reported to be the most likely time to see its full extent, but it can also be misty in the early light.

The story of the Flood in which Noah builds the Ark to save himself, his family, and a selection of animals from God's cleansing waters is a common element found in much of the religious literature of the Middle East. Of these, two stand out, the *Gilgamesh Epic* which perhaps originated in southern Mesopotamia and the story of Noah

Artist's rendering of Gilgamesh

which is told both in the Bible (Gen. 6: 9 - 9: 29) and in the Koran (Sura xi: 27-51). Both are much more, however, than the story of the Flood, and older even than the biblical telling of it.

The *Gilgamesh Epic* contains about 3,000 lines of dramatic, lyrical poetry. The earliest known written copies are from about 2,000 BC; partial copies have been found with the excavations at Boğazkale, Urfa, Sultantepe, Zincirli and Carchemish in Turkey. A masterpiece, the *Epic* is a powerful narrative involving love and lust, heroism, optimism and despair in Gilgamesh's quest for immortality. Gilgamesh's will to live, in the face of inexorable death, makes him one of literature's great epic heroes who transcends the boundaries of culture and time.

The story of the *Epic* centers on **Gilgamesh**. He may have been a real Sumerian king thought to have lived during the first half of the third millennium BC. Gilgamesh, the urbane leader, is contrasted in the beginning with Enkidu, a man who lived among the animals. (Is this a parallel with Cain?) One of their joint exploits was to overcome the giant Huwawa, the guardian of a forest thought to be located in the Amanus Mountains (Nur Dağı) near İskenderun in the Hatay.

İshak Paşa Camii, Doğubeyazıt

When he lost his friend Enkidu through sickness, Gilgamesh wished for eternal life. In his search he met Utnapishtim who had attained immortality, and he asked him how he did it. Utnapishtim's answer involved his description of how he built a ship in which he, his craftsmen and the seed of all living things rode out the Deluge. When the storm subsided, Utnapishtim sent forth a dove and then a swallow, but both returned. Last he set a raven free. The raven ate and circled and cawed but did not come back. Thereupon Utnapishtim let his other animals out of the ship and offered a sacrifice which was accepted by Ishtar, whose many-colored necklace is reminiscent of the rainbow. Together, she, the storm god Enlil and the god of wisdom Ea gave immortality to Utnapishtim and his wife, but with the restriction that they were always to live where the two rivers empty into the sea. (This story of the Deluge is incidental to the main thread of the Epic, but, including it, the *Epic* embodies myths common to the Hebrews, the Syrians, the Greeks and the Romans.)

Road signs in Doğubeyazıt point east a few kilometers to "Noah's Ark." This is a tourist site where mud and basalt form a large, roughly shaped lozenge in which the credulous can imagine a large ship.

Willing to help Gilgamesh attain immortality, Utnapishtim challenged Gilgamesh to stay awake for seven days. Although Gilgamesh failed that test, Utnapishtim told him that he could find a plant at the bottom of the sea which would make him youthful again. Gilgamesh weighted himself down, dived into the water and got the plant, only to be robbed of it by a snake when he came up again. (The snake had the power of rejuvenation because it

The American composer Alan Hovhannes wrote his Ani *Symphony No. 23 in 1972 to recall the famous city.*

Kilims, such as those produced in Kars and many other places in eastern Turkey, have a special place in the culture of the people. In contrast to pile rugs which are woven for a commercial market, flatweaves are intended for the family. Their creators are women. A girl's dreams might be expressed in the care with which she weaves this part of her dowry. Or the colors and designs may identify her tribe, or be a combination of the symbols of her new husband's tribe and hers. Thus some regions can be identified, and some movements of people. Few really old kilims have survived because, as household items, their value has been their great usefulness.

slipped off its old skin to escape from him.) Gilgamesh at last was advised by Utnapishtim, in words similar to those in Ecclesiastes, to eat, drink and be happy. The well-known Turkish composer Nevit Kodallı has composed an opera based on the *Gilgamesh Epic*. The opera is performed frequently on the İstanbul and Ankara stages.

The *Gilgamesh Epic* undoubtedly echoes in the biblical story of Noah, with the Ark which rides out the Deluge carrying with it the seed of every living thing. According to the biblical telling, Noah's Ark came to rest "upon the mountains of Ararat." (Gen. 8:4) "Ararat" is one of the puzzles of scholarship. In the oldest use of the word, it appears only as three consonants: "RRT". According to the rules of the Semitic languages, this could be translated in a variety of forms including both "Urartu" (the name of people who lived in this region between the 9th and the 6th centuries BC) and "Ararat" (the name now given to a specific mountain). Moreover, "RRT" at first was a general word meaning "a land somewhere up north" and "a place that is a long ways off."

In his book, *The Antiquities of the Jews*, Josephus reported in about AD 70 that he had heard about the existence of the Ark on Mt. Ararat, and Marco Polo in AD 1300 said the same thing. Josephus said that what remained of it was in a museum for everyone to look at without the bother of hunting for it on the peak. Whatever the truth of the story, the Ark remains an intriguing puzzle.

The intent of the account of **Noah** is both about how God punished the whole earth because of human sin and about how all the peoples known to the writer (or writers) were related through Noah's three sons, Shem, Ham and Japheth. The thesis is that God works through history. Shem, Ham and Japheth are used in Genesis (Gen. 10:1-32) to group and identify the peoples and their geographic locations. Several of the groups have possible connections with Anatolia, although the farther afield they were located from the writer in Palestine the more tenuous is their identity. These connections help locate Ararat in eastern Anatolia; they both help and confuse the relations among the family members.

Shem's family included Asshur (the Assyrians), Arphaxad (progenitor of Terah and Abraham) and Aram (the Arameans). In Ham's family Mizraim appears to be the father of the Lydians, and Canaan is related to the Hittites and the Hurrians. It is Japheth's family names that occur most commonly in Anatolia: Japheth's sons were the people living generally north of Israel: Gomer (the Cimmerians on the Black Sea), Magog (the Scythians), Madai (the Medes), Javan (the Ionians), Tubal and Meshech (both living in Asia Minor), Togarmah (in south central Anatolia), Ashkenaz (northeastern Anatolia) and Riphath (perhaps on the southwest edge of the Black Sea). (See pp. 57 - 59.)

KARS

Kars is a city known for its long, very cold winters, and for its short, cool summers. Religious interest in Kars focuses mainly on its Ottoman mosques. A frontier city, many of its residents are soldiers posted here on duty, and the city seems like it is always in transition. Visitors often characterize it with the dark, gloomy colors of the black basalt rock underlying it. The city is located on the Kars River, a tributary of the Araxes. It is thought that the city's name comes from the Karsaks, a Bulgarian-Turkish tribe who migrated through the region in the 2nd century AD.

Most foreigners visit Kars in order to obtain permission to continue on to Ani. The Ministry of Tourism and the Turkish *Emniyet Müdürlüğü* are the offices giving that official paper.

The history of Kars is similar to the rest of Eastern Asia Minor. Little is known in detail about it before the 10th century AD when the Armenian Bagratids made it their capital for a brief period. That seat was later transferred to Ani. Alp Arslan, the Selçuk leader, took the city in 1064 a few years before he defeated the Byzantine emperor at Malazgirt. From the 13th century into the 20th it has gone back and forth between Georgian-Russian control and Ottoman-Turkish.

The Russian influence is most visible in some buildings uncharacteristic of Armenian or Ottoman architecture. They date from the most recent Russian occupation between 1878 and 1920. One built as a neo-classical style **Russian Orthodox church** is now a mosque. It might have been the work of Aladdin's djinns who levitated it from St. Petersburg. Also, the main streets are laid out in a grid plan, unlike the usual haphazard wandering of Anatolian streets that follow old trails.

Several buildings, however, do date from an earlier history. The crenelated **citadel** on the rocky north hill overlooking the river has probably always been the focus of the city's defenses. Urartians, Byzantines, Armenians (perhaps they were responsible for the present foundations), Selçuks, Mongolians, Turcomans, Arabs, Russians and Turks have all held it, sometimes more than once, for varying lengths of time, storming or defending it in sequence. An inscription on the central tower gives the date of 1152 for work done on it by the governor, Firuz Akay. Tamerlane took the citadel and razed the town in 1386; Süleyman the Magnificent repaired it in the 16th century. In contrast to its turbulent history, the citadel is now a park; its ramparts and its more than 200 towers are a place for a gentle stroll with the family on Sundays.

Located at the foot of the citadel, **Kümbet Camii** originally was the 10th century Church of the Apostles. (It is not open to the public.) The carved figures of the twelve apostles in the blind arches on the outside are from the time of its first builders. It is built of the same dark basalt as the castle. There are two Ottoman

From 961 to 1046 Ani was the capital of the Bagratid Armenian kingdom. The Byzantines held it from 1046 only until 1064 when the Selçuks took it. Between 1125 and 1209 it went back and forth five times from the Selçuks to the Georgians to the Armenians. In 1239 the Mongols sent by Genghis Khan's son Ogodei ravaged it along with Kars and Diyarbakır. An earthquake in 1319 did major damage, and the complete ruin of the once flourishing city was accomplished by Tamerlane in 1401.

Bagratid kings claimed that they were descendants of Herod the Great. They had a long history as rulers. Their power in Georgia began when the Byzantine emperor Justin II made one of their princes, Guaram, viceroy of Georgia in 571. The Bagratid kingdom of Georgia continued to exist after the Selçuks defeated the Byzantines in 1071. The dynasty lasted until 1803 in today's Georgia.

mosques, a bridge and several hamams. Of the Ottoman mosques, **Evliya Camii**, a 16th century building, is the largest mosque in Kars. The minaret of **Ulu Cami** is all that is left of a 17th century mosque. A 17th or 18th century stone **bridge** arches across the Kars River at the foot of the citadel near where the river enters a gorge. Kars has three 18th century Ottoman hamams: the **İlbeyioğlu** (still in use), the **Mazlum Ağa** and the **Cuma**. The **Ahşap Paşa** or **Abdullatif Paşa Konak** was once the home of the famous 19th century Turkish poet Namık Kemal.

Besides its buildings, Kars is also known for its cheeses and for its folklore traditions. The dancers are accompanied by a men playing drums and a local, 3-stringed lute (_kemençe_).

A modern **museum** in Kars contains some finds from Ani and a good kilim collection.

ANI

The ruins of once prosperous Ani are found on the border between Turkey and Armenia. While Europe was lost in the Dark Ages, Ani's rulers knew that its fortune depended on their control of the shortest, safest trade route to the East; its rulers understood the equation of political stability and economic prosperity.

Ani sits on a triangular bluff about 2 km long by 1 km wide defined on two sides by deep gorges. The Arpa Çayı which flows through one of the gorges makes the border between Turkey and Armenia; the other river is the Alaca. The double walls of the city on the level side of the bluff complete its fortification. The height of power for Ani came in the late 10th and early 11th centuries when the Armenian Bagratids had it as their capital and established their dominance over most of the Armenian principalities. A city of 100,000 inhabitants, at that time its only other rivals in culture and elegance were Constantinople, Cairo and Baghdad. Today a visit to Ani requires permission from the authorities in Kars. The extensive area deserves at least a half a day to explore the churches and the castle and to return to Kars.

Ani was fabled as the city of 1001 churches, a fable that lingers in spite of earthquakes, fires and the mass exodus of its residents in the 14th century. Now hardly ten churches remain — and they are in ruins. However, the irregularly interspersed black and rosy brown blocks of stone and the classically balanced dimensions of the buildings help bring Ani's ancient values to life. These buildings are the **Church of St. Gregory of Tigranes Honentz** (1215), the **Cathedral** (1000), the **Church of St. Gregory Abugamrents** (10th century), the **Church of St. Gregory** (Gagik I) (10th century), the **Church of the Redeemer** (1036), and the **Church of the Holy Apostles** (1013). An 11th century **mosque of Ebu Menucher** (1072) and a 13th century **Convent of the Three Virgins** (Kusanats, on a ledge below the bluff) add to the buildings of note. The mosque is reputed to be the one built by the earliest Selçuks in Anatolia. Visible below the convent, a broken stone bridge over the Arpa River must have born the weight of hundreds and hundreds of camel caravans plodding along the Silk Route. Probably at least once the members of those caravans included the Venetian family of Marco Polo.

St. Gregory, Ani

The Church of St. Gregory of Tigranes Honentz (also called the Resimli Kilise — the church with pictures) is decorated on the outside with stone-carved peacocks and dragons encircled in foliage. Inside, against a deep blue background, the frescoes show scenes from the New Testament and from the life of St. Gregory the Illuminator. St. Gregory was instrumental in convincing King Tiridates to accept Christianity as the state religion of Armenia about 290, some years before Constantine the Great did the same for the Roman Empire.

Tridat, the man who restored the dome of St. Sophia in Constantinople after the earthquake of 989, was the architect of the cathedral in Ani. It is the largest standing Armenian church in Turkey. Although it is a ruin, its pleasing proportions, classic style, and details of decoration (blind arches outside, massive stone columns inside) mark it as a masterpiece of Armenian architecture.

Next to the ruins of the Church of the Holy Apostles is a small domed room decorated with Iranian-style figures over its door. One can imagine that the walls of this 13th century addition to the church, used mainly as the customs office, heard their share of pleading voices.

ERZURUM - THEODOSIOPOLIS

Two Selçuk medreses in Erzurum carry elaborate stone carvings of floral and geometric designs. The grace and quality of these carvings place the city's religious institutions among the most attractive of the country. In 1919 revolutionaries supporting Mustafa Kemal met here and helped set the course for the emergence of the Turkish Republic.

Bitter cold in winter, dusty and dry in summer, Erzurum is on the saddle between the head of the Araxes River which empties into the Caspian Sea and the Karasu, a main tributary of the Euphrates. Thus, located at a crucial crossroads on the trade routes, it has had a long history as a military post. In Byzantine times it was called Theodosiopolis after Emperor Theodosius I who fortified it in

Georgian churches were built of local burnt orange sandstone. A barrel dome that rises high above the nave is topped by a conical tiled roof. Blind arches mark the main walls of the buildings. Carved animals, geometric figures, and saints articulate many of the surfaces. The walls inside once had frescoes, but these are difficult to distinguish now.

Yakutiye Medresesi, Erzurum

Mustafa Kemal took the decisive step of resigning from the sultan's army just before the congress convened in Erzurum. He already was a hunted man, with only his courage and charisma to command leadership. But a growing revolutionary movement had begun to form behind him which took political shape through the Erzurum and Sivas Congresses.

the 4th century. Its present name dates from its occupation by Arabs who called it Ard ar-Rum (the land of the Romans — or Byzantines).

The foundations of the **citadel** walls near the center of the city may be the work of Theodosius's 4th century stonemasons; those which are visible are from medieval times, as are the most interesting buildings of the city. The citadel encloses a ruined Selçuk mosque and its minaret which is now the city's **clock tower**.

Not far from the citadel are four rather small round towers (*kümbet*) built as mausoleums in the 12th century. The face of one of them is decorated with reliefs of animals such as bats, snakes, eagles and rabbits — probably some reference to the ancient central Asian calendar which identifies a cycle of years characterized by animals.

All of the main attractions are on or close to the main street, Cumhuriyet Caddesi, and in the center of town. The **Çifte Minareli Medresesi**, Erzurum's best known and most photographed building, was built in 1253 either by the Selçuk Sultan Alaettin Keykubat II, grandson of the man who built the fortress in Alanya, or by his daughter, Mahperi Huand Hatun. The carved stone entrance is similar to the Gök Medrese in Sivas, which also has two minarets. The türbe inside the courtyard may be the burial place of the sultan or his daughter.

Ulu Cami (Great Mosque) dates from 1179. The columns supporting the main hall of the mosque are staggered diagonally, an unusual arrangement called "quincuncial" which was also used in the Selçuk Ulu Cami in Afyonkarahisar. **Lala Paşa Camii**, a large, active mosque, was built by one of Süleyman the Magnificent's viziers in 1562/63. Its architect was the great Sinan.[14]

An older and more interesting building is the **Yakutiye Medresesi** which dates from 1310. The medrese was founded by the city's Mongol administrator, Yakut, in honor of his emperor, Timur Khan (also known as Oldjeitu), the son of Kublai Khan and great-grandson of Gengiz Khan. Its portal is richly decorated with roses, stars and birds and is guarded by lions and an eagle.

Erzurum is also known for its jet black stone (*Erzurum taşı* or *oltutaşı*) mined in Oltu between Erzurum and Artvin. The stone is used in jewelry and for prayer beads (*tesbih*).

The Palendöken winter ski resort 4 km south of Erzurum is being developed with hotels and ski lifts.

YUSUFELİ

Yusufeli is located on the Barhal Çayı, a tributary of the Çoruh Nehri, in its season reputedly the river that rushes most wildly of any in Turkey. Sports enthusiasts gather here in the spring to enjoy the thrills of white water rafting. A little later in the year Yusufeli is a staging place for hikers who will climb the Kaçkar Mountains, some of the most rewarding and scenic of the high mountains of Turkey.

Yusufeli is also a center from which to explore the Georgian churches. The conversion of this region to Christianity was spurred by the work of the Cappadocian missionary nun Nino in the 4th century. This was the same time that Gregory was converting the Armenian King Tiridates farther east. However, the churches here date mostly from the time of its Bagratid rulers between the 9th and 13th centuries. The area was called Tao by the Byzantine emperors who were its overlords. Its church orientation was to the Eastern Orthodox, not to the Monophysite Armenian faith. Of the rulers, Queen Tamara (Thamar) (1184-1212) stands out. Under her, Georgia experienced its greatest period. By political and military means she extended the area of Georgia as far east as the Caspian Sea. She was also wise in her internal politics, being known for her tolerance and her philanthropy. Georgia's decline was hastened by Tamerlane's attack in 1401. The Georgians had become Muslims by the 17th century.

Yusufeli is about 10 km off the main road from Erzurum to Artvin. It is a pleasant place from which to explore the area. Starting from Erzurum and moving north, the places most often visited include the following:

About 90 km south of Yusufeli there are two crumbling castles on either side of the road, the indication of the southern entrance to the area of the Georgian churches. From there the road follows the valley of the Tortum Çayı. **Bağbaşı** (Haho) is about 35 km north-west of the village of Tortum. The church here, originally part of a monastery complex, was built between 961 and 1001 by David the Great, great-grandfather of Tamara. Now a mosque, it has a number of stone reliefs illustrating religious scenes including angels, apostles and Jonah and the whale. (Is this whale related to the strange animal in Ahtamar?)

Some 15 km beyond the turn off the main road to Bağbaşı is the

Stately even as ruins, the Georgian churches of the Yusufeli - Artvin area remind Western visitors that, while Europe marked time until the Renaissance, the residents of eastern Anatolia enjoyed a period of religious and artistic splendor and political importance.

Kümbets (tombs), Erzurum

*Dörtkilise,
Yusufeli*

Honey gathered by
the bees from wild
rhododendrons in
the Kaçkar
mountains around
Artvin has been
known since the
time of Xenephon
for causing
temporary
insanity. Still
called deli bal
(crazy honey), it
makes people act
like they are drunk
when they eat it
even in moderate
amounts. Strabo
reported that the
local people in the
1st century BC
tempted Pompey's
soldiers to drink
the mead they
made from it.
When the soldiers
became sick the
locals easily routed
them.

sign to the village of Çamlıyamaç which is 7 km off on the side road. This is the place of the impressive **Öşk Vank**, a stately monastery church dedicated to the Deisis. It, too, was built by David the Great in the late 10th century. The frescoes in the southern transept wall are the best preserved of any in the Georgian churches.

Farther on are Lake Tortum and the Tortum Falls (little water goes over the falls except in the spring). Then, off from the road to Olur and up a gravel road with many hairpin turns reached after a precipitous climb is the village of **İşhan**. İşhan is a green oasis on top of a very dry mountain. The **Church of the Virgin Mary** is the reason for a visit to İşhan. One of the most impressive Georgian churches for its size and its proportions, it was built between the 7th and the 11th centuries. Reliefs and frescoes include a lion and a snake in mortal combat, and vision of Zechariah (Luke 1:5-79).

The road to **Dörtkilise** goes from Yusufeli through the village of Tekkale. An unmarked, narrow, bumpy road leads right from the center of Tekkale 7 km over three bridges to where a path (again unmarked) takes off from the left side of the road. About 100 m ahead, but not clearly visible from the road, is the grassy clearing and the ruins of the 10th century church. Although identified as "four" (*dört*) churches, only one major building remains, but it stands as a tribute to the skill of its builders and its founder, David the Great.

David the Great also built the monastery complex of **Parhalı** between 961 and 973. Now a mosque, the church which is in good condition is located in the village of Barhal (about 40 km north of Yusufeli.) It is similar in design and construction to Dörtkilise. Exterior decorations include stylized geometric and floral motifs. One of the interior pilasters has a truncated figure of a praying angel.

Several other Georgian churches are scattered in the mountains, often where some spring or stream has made a small, pleasant

*Church of Öşk
Vank*

pastureland. One such is at Hamamlı, east of Artvin and 7 km up a steep gravel road that barely hugs the side of the hill. Now cared for as a mosque, this church of **Doluşhane** is a 10th century building.

Many of these churches are difficult to reach if one is not prepared for a hike. The local people are generous and eager to be helpful to strangers and often know more than the guidebooks contain.

TRABZON - TREBİZOND, TRAPEZUS

Trabzon has perhaps appeared more often in recorded history than all the rest of the places on the Black Sea put together. The 10th to 13th century churches (now museums) hold masterpieces of Byzantine art. The city's name meant "tableland," reflecting the flat land on which the old city was located. It was between two streams, the Tabakhane Deresi and the Kuzgun Deresi. Trabzon is shielded from the extreme temperatures of Eastern Turkey by the high mountains to the south. This southeastern coast of the Black Sea with its warm, humid climate is ideal for growing tea, hazelnuts, kiwis and avocados. The grasslands of the surrounding mountains even in September are a lush green, in part from the tea plantations that are terraced up the sides of the valleys.

It was from the mountains above Trabzon in February of 400 BC that Xenophon's Ten Thousand weary soldiers who had slogged across Anatolia all winter, looked and shouted half unbelievingly, "Thalassa! The Sea!! We've made it!!!" Strabo was here about the turn of the Christian millennium and wrote about the town, as did the 17th century Ottoman traveler Evliya Çelebi. Napoleon claimed as part of his fame that he was a member of the Comneni family who ruled from Trabzon, and Don Quixote dreamed that he was its emperor. More recently in her book, *The Towers of Trebizond*, the satirist Rose Macaulay used its towers as the symbol of that which haunts men's minds.

Hadrian and Justinian supported it as one of the ports on the Silk Route. When the Mongols cut the routes to the other Black Sea

*The **Monastery of Panaghia Theoskepastos** was founded in about 1340, possibly by Eirene, mother of Alexius II of Trabzon. Named for the God-protected Virgin, it enjoyed the security of a large endowment and continued to function until the exchange of populations between Turkey and Greece in 1923.*

Church of St. Sophia, Trabzon

ports in the 13th century Trabzon's importance grew, encouraged by the influx of Genoese and Venetian merchants, among whom were Marco Polo, his father, and his uncle. They were in Trabzon about 1295, returning to Venice after their 20-year stay in China. (Twenty years? No wonder that the Venetians doubted the identities of these men who were wearing such strange clothes!) Trabzon broke its ties with the Byzantine Empire centered in Constantinople when the Latin Fourth Crusaders captured that capital in 1204. Beginning as a refuge for the scion of the Byzantine Comneni emperor, it posed as a cultural and political center more influential than its size justified. Although the Byzantines returned to their capital in 1261, Trabzon by then had become a proud, independent state. It was captured by Sultan Mehmet II in 1461 in the last of the Ottoman battles against the Eastern Roman Empire.

The center of Trabzon is a shady square, the Atatürk Alanı or the Taksim Meydanı. From there you can get a *dolmuş* (shared taxi) to take you to the Cathedral of St. Sophia (3 km west) or a bus to the Kaymaklı Monastery southeast of town. Somewhat less than half a kilometer west of the main square is the market area with its 14th century Genoese **bedesten** (originally a market, now a lumber mill) and the large Ottoman **Çarşı Camii** (Market Mosque).

The small Church of **St. Anne (Küçük Ayvasil Kilisesi)** was built probably in the 8th century and restored by Basil I in the 9th, making it the oldest church in Trabzon. It is south of the market between Maraş Caddesi and Uzun Yol.

The **Church of St. Eugenius** — now the **Yeni Cuma Camii** — is an 11th century building (possibly much older); its restoration took place in the 14th century. Mehmet II is supposed to have celebrated his capture of the city in 1461 first in this building.

The walls of the fortified Ortahisar (Middle Fortress) enclose the **citadel** of the old town. The **Fatih** or **Ortahisar Camii** inside the citadel was the 10th century **Church of the Golden Headed Virgin** (Panaghia Chrysocephalos), so named because during the Comneni reign the dome was gilded. It was here that the coronations of the Trapezuntine emperors took place. Ruins of the Byzantine palace are farther up the hill to the south. Not far from them is the **Gülbahar Hatun Camii**, a 1514 building commemorating the mother of the Ottoman Sultan Selim I. She

Sumelas monastary perched on the hill

is reputed to have been a Comneni princess, which is the presumed reason for her burial here. Her grandson Süleyman the Magnificent was born in Trabzon while his father was the governor.

West and just outside the walls of the citadel is the **Zaganos Bridge** that was built by Mehmet the Conqueror's Grand Vizier Zaganos Paşa; he had previously built the south tower of Rumeli Hisar on the Bosphorus in İstanbul. Some of the early 20th century homes up the hill in Soğuksu are palatial. Of them, the Karayannidhis house has become the **Atatürk Köşkü,** a museum to Mustafa Kemal Atatürk who wrote part of his will here, leaving all his possessions to the Turkish nation.

The **Cathedral of St. Sophia** (1238, 1263) overlooks the sea; it is the most famous site in the town. The building is now a museum. It was built on the place of a Temple to Apollo by the Comneni Manuel I during the time that Constantinople was in Latin hands. Manuel's wealth came from silver mines; he lav-

13th century frescoes of St. Sophia, Trabzon

ished his money on the church, using both Christian and Muslim architectural elements. The floor was a mosaic pattern of marble and porphyry, now mostly destroyed. Four large columns of Proconnesian marble held up the central dome. There are stalactite niches reminiscent of Selçuk work, painted angels in the dome, a marble eagle capital from 6th century Constantinople, and many, many frescoes which have been painstakingly restored. These latter include scenes of the Last Supper, the Last Judgment, SS. Sergius and Bacchus, Doubting Thomas, the Miracle at Cana, Feeding the Five Thousand (John 2: 1-11, Mark 5: 30-44), and Christ's Ascension. Alone they justify a visit to Trabzon. A tall bell tower stands a short distance from the church.

A short distance above Trabzon near the village of Çukurçayır is the **Monastery of Kaymaklı,** a 15th century Armenian institution. Frescoes in the main church (currently serving as a hay barn) are from the 18th century. They depict scenes from Revelation similar to those in the Cathedral of St. Sophia in Trabzon.

SUMELAS - MERYEMANA

The distance from Trabzon to Sumelas is 54 km; if you don't have your own transportation you can get a taxi or a public minibus from Trabzon, or you can go with an organized tour, several of which start from Trabzon. Sumelas is identified as "Meryemana" on the road signs. Sumelas is in the Altındere National Park in the Zigana Mountains. A poor road goes close to the **monastery,** but many people prefer to park some distance below and hike up the steep path to it.

Tradition credits two monks from Athens, Sophronius and his uncle Barnabas, with founding the monastery of Sumelas in AD 368. They followed the guidance of an icon to a cave in this mountain setting. They believed it had been painted by the

The Empire of Trabzon was founded in 1204 by Alexius Comnenus. He was a member of the Comneni dynasty that had been started in 1056 by the Byzantine emperor, another Alexius I Comnenus. This state maintained its independence of Constantinople until it was overcome by Sultan Mehmet II in 1461. The library which the Comneni collected in their palace was a lodestone for scholars.

Apostle Luke. In the 6th century the emperor Justinian ordered a silver reliquary made for the monastery in order to preserve the remains of Barnabas who by then had been raised to sainthood.

Some old manuscripts and icons from Sumelas are still preserved in museums and private collections in Europe and the United States.

The Sumelas monastery was the goal of many pilgrims, both Orthodox Christians and Muslims, until it closed in 1923. In the late 19th century a number of buildings had been built to house pilgrims, but they are now gone. Now a museum protected by the Turkish government and being repaired, the site still draws people for its sanctity.

The monastery buildings probably date from the 12th century. Nothing is left inside except some art work. The best frescoes are from the 14th century, but most of them are much later — 18th or 19th century. Much of the art has been defaced, some recently by European and American tourists. More than the art and architecture, it is the setting of the buildings of Sumelas against the sheer cliff that inspires the usual descriptions of "breath-taking, powerful, grand and mystic" for this retreat.

South of Sumelas, at the Zigana Pass, is a ski resort for winter sports enthusiasts.

Church of Abughamrents, Ani

DİVRİĞİ - TEPHRICE

Located well off the usual route of tourists and about 100 km southeast of Sivas, Divriği is hidden in the valley of the Çaltı Çayı, a tributary of the Euphrates River. During the time of the Byzantine Empire, Divriği was called Tephrice.

From the beginning of the 5th century AD, Tephrice was the center of a heretical Christian sect, the Paulicians who believed, among other things, that Christ was two persons. Their name referred both to Paul the Apostle and to a 3rd century heretic, Paul of Samosata. They professed to have modeled their interpretation of Christianity on early Church traditions. Such things as infant baptism, repetition of the Nicene Creed, the use of a cross that was not made of wood, and the building of churches they rejected on the grounds that Jesus had not done so. Their missionaries were active throughout the

Byzantine Empire, provoking persecutions against them particularly under Leo V the Armenian (813-820) and Theodora (842-857).

In 873 Basil I the Macedonian captured Tephrice, thus enlarging his empire to where it would soon be attractive to the Selçuk Turks. More immediately, Basil sent the surviving Paulicians into the Balkans and Russia where they influenced the sect of the Bogomils, likewise a heretical sect that was important in the 12th century and continued into the 17th.

North and on the hill is the **citadel** whose foundations probably go back to the late 9th century when the Byzantine Emperor Basil I captured it. The Mengücheks restored it and left inscriptions of 1236, 1242 and 1252 on its walls. An early **Mosque of Shahanshah** (1180) inside the citadel is simple and plain in contrast to the lavishly decorated Ulu Cami. From this hilltop there is a view of the town and the valley that makes the climb well worth the effort.

The attraction in Divriği now is the Selçuk **Ulu Cami**, the Great Mosque, built between 1228 and 1229 by the Mengüchek ruler Ahmad Shah. (The Mengücheks were one of a number of tribes related to and vassals of the controlling Selçuks.) Part of the mosque complex is a medical center of the same date; it is ascribed to Malika Turan Malik, the wife of Ahmad Shah. Both are remarkable because of their stone-carved doorways. The designs are intricate and rich. The deeply incised geometric patterns, calligraphy, floral and faunal detail (a pair of double-headed eagles, for instance, on the northwestern doorway), even a few human faces conjure descriptions from "exceptional" and "ostentatious" to "exuberant," "extravagant" and "outrageous." Other details are worth special mention: Inside the hospital is a central fountain whose splashing water was reputed to help soothe the patients. The minber of the mosque, made of ebony and dated 1241 is a masterpiece of carved wood.

The Mengücheks were one of several Turkish tribes who controlled small principalities in eastern Turkey under the Selçuk sultans. While they were the local administrators, the people who were there before them - largely Jews and Greeks, perhaps also descendents of the Hittites - carried on the commerce.

[1] Nemrut, or Nimrod in biblical references, is both "a mighty hunter before the Lord" (Gen. 10:9) and the first-named powerful ruler. His territory included a large part of Mesopotamia. The 1st century AD Jewish historian Josephus credited him with building the Tower of Babel. There is some doubt about whether he was a single historical figure who lived in the 13th century BC, a general name for a number of kings whose armies threatened Israel for many years, or a Babylonian god. Several places in Anatolia carry references to him including the "Throne of Nimrod" in Şanlıurfa, Nemrut Dağı northwest of Lake Van, and this Commagene Nemrut Dağı near Adıyaman.

[2] See p. 246.

[3] Aramaic is a Semitic language. Others include Arabic and classical Hebrew. Syriac is an eastern dialect of Aramaic. The Semitic languages are generally based on main words made of three consonants; related meanings are controlled by various additions to the consonants. Thus for instance with those changes KTB can mean "writer," "letter," "correspondent," "school" and so on.

[4] Paraphrase, Sura ii: 130.

[5] The Fertile Crescent is a recently conceived metaphor suggesting the arch of land spanning on its eastern arm the basin of the Tigris and Euphrates from their delta, stretching on the north to include Nineveh, Van, Urfa and Aleppo (all of this is Mesopotamia), and continuing west and then south from İskenderun through Syria, Lebanon, Palestine and part of Egypt. This is the stage on which many of the first true settlements evolved, the bridge over which people still surge back and forth.

[6] Sabians were pagans who hid their practice of magic and star worship behind a name that was acceptable to their Muslim overlords. Several Sabians from Harran and Baghdad were celebrated physicians and astronomers between the 9th and the 11th centuries AD.

[7] The relationships among these groups are tangled. As examples, Chaldean and Assyrian are Semitic languages but Hittite and Hurrian are not. Then there is the unanswered question of whether Hurrians, Hivites and Horites are the same people.

[8] According to the Bible, this King Nimrod also built Nineveh. One of the early ideograms identifies Nineveh with a fish inside a sacred container or pool.

[9] This was in part the library from Pergamum which Mark Anthony had given to Cleopatra.

[10] The Roman historian Marcellinus Ammianus was in the Byzantine army when the Persian King Shapur II captured Diyarbakır in AD 359. He left a graphic account of how he barely escaped with his life in that battle. He also has given a clear and unprejudiced account of the social conditions and history of the Roman Empire from AD 353 to 378.

[11] See p. 66 for a discussion of the differences between these two groups.

[12] Jacob Baradi was a Monophysite bishop. The Monophysites believed that Christ had a single divine nature and therefore they were disowned by the Eastern Orthodox Church. (See p.67 for a discussion of the Fourth Ecumenical Council.) Baradi's influence was so great that his followers were at one time called "Jacobite Christians". Among his contemporary supporters was the Empress Theodora who protected him against her husband Justinian's policies of supporting the established Church.

[13] This mountain is not the same as that near Adıyaman where Antiochus built his self-glorifying monument.

[14] See p.104.

Çifte Minareli Medrese, Erzurum

FINAL COMMENTS

Turkey is a land of great physical beauty and great natural resources, making it also a land greatly valued and desired by many people. From the beginning it has served as a bridge and a crossroads, a theater, a battleground, a council chamber and a place of pilgrimage, challenging people to envision new and more complex concepts in political, economic, artistic, and religious terms.

A surprising number of themes and symbols have persisted: The symbol of the earth's fertility in the figures of the Mother Goddess continues in the recognition of human dependence on God's bounty for food and water. The nagging questions about the reality (and proximity) of an apocalyptic end to life, and the problems of moral standards of conduct are still with us, modified but unresolved. Emblems of the crescent moon, the stars and the cross appear from the time of the Hittites, now overlaid with Muslim, Jewish and Christian meanings. The history might in a way be compared to a fugue and variations on the search for divine meaning in the patterns of our lives.

Questions with which I began work on this book are still with me: What events, what geography — over all, what grace has been responsible for such a concentration of places and history in Turkey? Is it mere chance that the three great monotheistic religions were centered in the Middle East? Did the geographic fertility of northern Mesopotamia influence the intellectual and religious ferment? Does it still? Why have some symbols persisted while others have become meaningless? What have we lost from past civilizations?

By an ironic twist in the emphasis in our educational system, a guide book writer has become a high priestess responsible for transmitting the culture and traditions of the past. I acknowledge this with some trepidation, conscious of the misinterpretations, particularly in religious outlook, possible in a work of this sort. But instead of encouraging heresy, skepticism or boredom, I hope that the book may challenge its readers to appreciate the richness of the entire mosaic of culture, imagination, myth, conflict, invention and religious understanding that continues to inform the history of Turkey.

SUGGESTED READINGS

For copies of works by the Greek and Latin classical authors, see among others the Loeb Classical Library or the Penguin Classics.

Achtemeir, Paul J., ed., *Harper's Bible Dictionary*, Harper & Row, Publishers, San Francisco, 1985

Akurgal, Ekrem, *Ancient Civilizations and Ruins of Turkey*, Haşet Kitabevi, İstanbul, 1985

Arseven, Celâl Esad, *L'art Turc depuis son Origine jusqu'à nos Jours*, İstanbul Devlet Basımevi, İstanbul, 1939

Barks, Coleman, tr, with John Moyne, A. J. Arberry and Reynold Nicholson, *The Essential Rumi*, Harper San Fransisco, 1994

Bean, George E., *Aegean Turkey, An Archeological Guide*, Ernest Benn Limited, London, 1966

—, *Lycian Turkey, An Archeological Guide*, Ernest Benn Limited, London, 1978

—, *Turkey Beyond the Meander, An Archeological Guide*, Ernest Benn Limited, London, 1971

—, *Turkey's Southern Shore, An Archeological Guide*, Ernest Benn Limited, London, 1968

Blair, Sheila S. and Bloom, Jonathan M., *The Art and Architecture of Islam 1250-1800*, Yale University Press, 1994

Blake, Everett C., and Edmonds, Anna G., *Biblical Sites In Turkey*, Redhouse Press, İstanbul, 1986

Cahen, Claude, (tr. J. Jones-Williams) *Pre-Ottoman Turkey, A General Survey of the Material and Spiritual History c. 1071-1330*, Taplinger Publishing Company, New York, 1968

Çelebi, Evliya, *Narrative of Travels in Europe, Asia and Africa in the Seventeenth Century*, tr. von Hammer, Johnson Reprint Corporation, 1968

Davison, Roderic, *Turkey*, Eothem Press, England, 1985

Darke, Diana, *Guide to Aegean and Mediterranean Turkey*, Michael Haag, London, 1989

—, *Guide to Eastern Turkey and the Black Sea Coast*, Michael Haag, London, 1987

deLange, Nicholas, *Atlas of the Jewish World*, Facts on File, Inc., 1984

Dimand, M.S., *A Handbook of Muhammadan Art*, Hartsdale House, NewYork, 1947

Emre Yunus, *Yunus Emre and His Mystical Poetry*, tr. Talat Sait Halman, Indiana University Press, 1981

Encyclopedia Britannica, 11th edition, Encyclopedia Britannica, Inc., New York, 1911

Encyclopedia of World Art, McGraw-Hill Book Company, London, 1960,1963, 1967

Eusebius Pamphili, *Ecclesiastical History*, Books 1-5, 6-10, in *The Fathers of the Church*, The Catholic University of America Press, Inc., Washington, D.C. 1953

Gerber, Jane S., *The Jews of Spain*, The Free Press, New York, 1994

Gibb, H. A. R., and Kramers, J. E., eds., *Shorter Encyclopedia of Islam*, E. J. Brill, Leiden, 1953

Goodwin, Godfrey, *A History of Ottoman Architecture*, The Johns Hopkins Press, Baltimore, 1971

Graves, Robert, *The Greek Myths*, vols. 1 & 2., Penguin Books, Middlesex, 1955

Gurney, O. R., *The Hittites*, Penguin Books, Middlesex, England, 1969

Halman, Talat Sait, *The Humanist Poetry of Yunus Emre*, R.C.D. Cultural Institute, İstanbul, n.d.

Halman, Talat Sait, and Metin And, *Mevlana Celalettin Rumi and the Whirling Dervishes*, Dost Yayınları, İstanbul, 1983

Harrell, Betsy, *Mini Tours Near İstanbul*, Book II, Redhouse Press, 1978

Harrell, Betsy and Kalças, Evelyn Lyle, *Mini Tours Near İstanbul*, Book I, Redhouse Press, 1975

Herodotus, *The Persian Wars*, George Rawlinson, trans., The Modern Library, New York, 1942

Homer, *The Iliad, The Odyssey*

Josephus, Flavius, *Complete Works*, Kregel Publications, 1960

Kedouri, Elie, ed., *The Jewish World, History and Culture of the Jewish People*, Harry N. Abrams, Inc., New York, 1979

Kuran, Aptullah, *Sinan, The Grand Old Master of Ottoman Architecture*, Ada Press Publishers, İstanbul, 1987

Lewis, Bernard, *The Jews of Islam*, Princeton, 1985

Martinovitch, Nicholas, N., *The Turkish Theater*, B. Blom, New York, 1968

McCarthy, Justin, *The Ottoman Turks*, Longman, New York, 1997

McDonagh, Bernard, *Blue Guide, Turkey*, A. & C. Black, London, 1995

New English Bible, 2nd edition, Oxford and Cambridge University Presses, Oxford, 1970

Polo, Marco, *The Travels of Marco Polo*, the Complete Yule Cordier Edition, 1903

Ramazanoğlu, Gülseren, ed., *İstanbul At Your Fingertips*, DAMKO, İstanbul, 1994

Restle, Marcell (tr. Irene R. Gibbons), *Byzantine Wall Painting in Asia Minor*, New York Graphic Society Ltd., Greenwich, Conn. 1967

Runciman, Steven, *Byzantine Civilization*, Meridian Books, New York, 1960

Rodwell, J. M., tr. *The Koran*, J. M. Dent & Sons Ltd., London, 1948

Seyfert, Oscar, *A Dictionary of Classical Antiquities*, The Meridian Library, Meridian Books, New York, 1956

Shaw, Stanford, *The Jews of the Ottoman Empire and the Turkish Republic*, New York University Press, 1991

Sumner-Boyd, Hilary, and Freely, John, *Strolling Through İstanbul*, Redhouse Press, İstanbul, 4th ed., 1989

Tucker, Alan, ed., *Berlitz Travellers Turkey 1993*, Berlitz Publishing Company, Inc., New York, 1993

Uzunçarşılı, İsmail Hakkı, *Osmanlı Tarihi*, Türk Tarih Kurumu Basımevi, Ankara, 1982

Vasiliev, A. A., *History of the Byzantine Empire*, Vols. 1 & 2, The University of Wisconsin Press, Madison, 1961

INDEX

Religious Heritage of Turkey

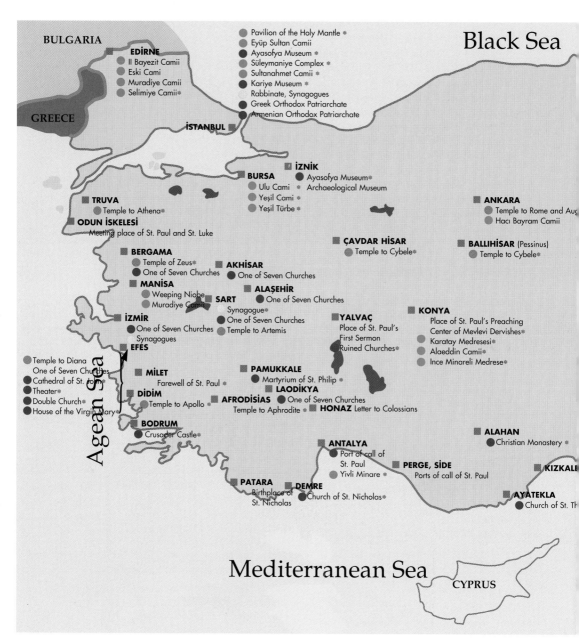

BULGARIA

Black Sea

- Pavilion of the Holy Mantle ✳
- Eyüp Sultan Camii
- Ayasofya Museum ✳
- Süleymaniye Complex ✳
- Sultanahmet Camii ✳
- Kariye Museum ✳
- Rabbinate, Synagogues
- Greek Orthodox Patriarchate
- Armenian Orthodox Patriarchate

EDİRNE
- Il Bayezit Camii
- Eski Cami
- Muradiye Camii
- Selimiye Camii ✳

GREECE

İSTANBUL

TRUVA
- Temple to Athena ✳

ODUN İSKELESİ
- Meeting place of St. Paul and St. Luke

İZNİK
- Ayasofya Museum ✳

BURSA
- Ulu Cami
- Yeşil Cami ✳
- Yeşil Türbe ✳
- Archaeological Museum

ANKARA
- Temple to Rome and Aug
- Hacı Bayram Camii

ÇAVDAR HİSAR
- Temple to Cybele ✳

BALLIHİSAR (Pessinus)
- Temple to Cybele ✳

BERGAMA
- Temple of Zeus ✳
- One of Seven Churches

AKHİSAR
- One of Seven Churches

MANİSA
- Weeping Niobe
- Muradiye Camii

ALAŞEHİR
- One of Seven Churches

SART
- Synagogue
- One of Seven Churches
- Temple to Artemis

YALVAÇ
- Place of St. Paul's
- First Sermon
- Ruined Churches ✳

KONYA
- Place of St. Paul's Preaching
- Center of Mevlevi Dervishes ✳
- Karatay Medresesi ✳
- Alaeddin Camii ✳
- Ince Minareli Medrese ✳

İZMİR
- One of Seven Churches
- Synagogues

EFES

Agean Sea

- Temple to Diana
- One of Seven Churches ✳
- Cathedral of St. John
- Theater ✳
- Double Church
- House of the Virgin Mary

MİLET
- Farewell of St. Paul ✳

DİDİM
- Temple to Apollo ✳

PAMUKKALE
- Martyrium of St. Philip ✳

LAODİKYA
- One of Seven Churches

AFRODİSİAS
- Temple to Aphrodite ✳

HONAZ Letter to Colossians

BODRUM
- Crusader Castle ✳

ALAHAN
- Christian Monastery ✳

ANTALYA
- Port of call of
- St. Paul
- Yivli Minare ✳

PERGE, SİDE
- Ports of call of St. Paul

KIZKALE

PATARA
- Birthplace of
- St. Nicholas

DEMRE
- Church of St. Nicholas ✳

AYATEKLA
- Church of St. Th

Mediterranean Sea

CYPRUS

✳ The sites that are **musts**.

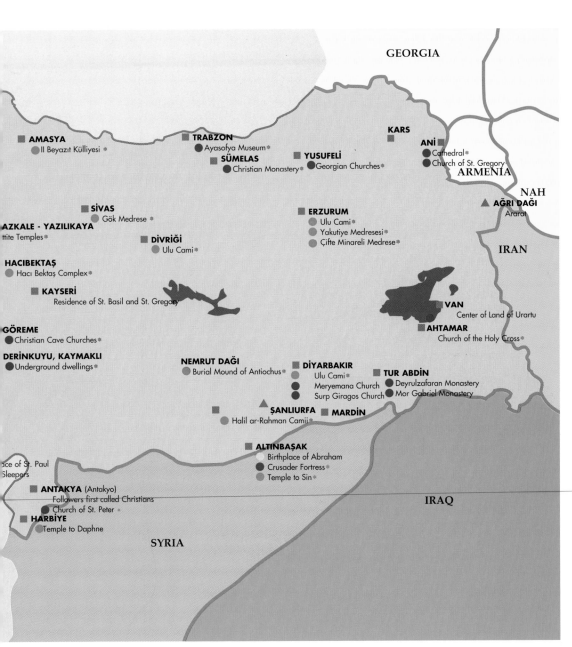

GEORGIA

AMASYA
● Il Beyazıt Külliyesi ✳

TRABZON
● Ayasofya Museum ✳
SÜMELAS
● Christian Monastery ✳

YUSUFELİ
● Georgian Churches ✳

KARS

ANİ
● Cathedral ✳
● Church of St. Gregory ✳
ARMENIA

NAH

SİVAS
● Gök Medrese ✳

AZKALE - YAZILIKAYA
ttite Temples ✳

DİVRİĞİ
● Ulu Cami ✳

ERZURUM
● Ulu Cami ✳
● Yakutiye Medresesi ✳
● Çifte Minareli Medrese ✳

▲ **AĞRI DAĞI**
Ararat

IRAN

HACIBEKTAŞ
● Hacı Bektaş Complex ✳

KAYSERİ
Residence of St. Basil and St. Gregory ✳

VAN
Center of Land of Urartu

AHTAMAR
Church of the Holy Cross ✳

GÖREME
● Christian Cave Churches ✳

DERİNKUYU, KAYMAKLI
● Underground dwellings ✳

NEMRUT DAĞI
● Burial Mound of Antiochus ✳

DİYARBAKIR
● Ulu Cami ✳
● Meryemana Church
● Surp Giragos Church

TUR ABDİN
● Deyrulzafaran Monastery
● Mor Gabriel Monastery

▲ **ŞANLIURFA**
● Halil ar-Rahman Camii ✳

MARDİN

ALTINBAŞAK
○ Birthplace of Abraham
● Crusader Fortress ✳
● Temple to Sin ✳

ce of St. Paul
Sleepers

ANTAKYA (Antakyo)
Followers first called Christians
● Church of St. Peter ✳

IRAQ

HARBİYE
● Temple to Daphne

SYRIA

(Names of locations are in Turkish for the convenience of the readers).

RELIGIOUS HERITAGE OF TURKEY
(Summary)

Ağrı Dağı. Mt. Ararat towers over the land where Noah's ark came to rest. The same story appears in the Babylonian myth of *Gilgamesh.*

Akhisar. An agricultural center, Thyatira was one of the Seven Churches admonished by St. John.

Alaşehir. One of the Seven Churches, Philadelphia was a border post in the 1st century AD.

Altınbaşak. Birthplace of Abraham, it was here that he heard the call to found a great nation that believed in One God. A 9th century BC Temple to Sin was part of a university complex. Crusaders held the fortress in the 12th century AD.

Ani. Ani's continuing fame is as a city of a thousand churches.

Ankara. The 15th century Hacı Bayram Mosque and the Roman Temple to Rome and Augustus with its inscription about Caesar's census are located back-to-back.

Antakya. City where Christians were first named, the 11th century Crusaders believed that they found St. Peter's sword in the Church of St. Peter. St. Paul began his missionary journeys from Antioch.

Bergama. One of the Seven Churches, St. John denounced the Throne of Satan in his reference to church members.

Bursa. Beautiful mosque complexes from the 13th and 14th centuries enrich the early Ottoman capital.

Divriği. Exquisite designs on Ulu Cami are a record of the skill of Selçuk stone carvers.

Diyarbakır. It comes second to İstanbul in the number of handsome mosques in the city.

Edirne. The complex of the Selimiye Camii is the masterpiece of the 16th century architect Sinan.

Efes. Once renowned for its gleaming Temple to Diana, the archaeological site of Ephesus is famous for the missionary work of St. Paul, and as one of the churches addressed by St. John. The Home of the Virgin Mary has been a quiet mountain retreat.

Erzurum. The Yakutiye and Çifte Minareli Medreses are evidence of the Selçuk religious activities in Erzurum in the 12th and 13th centuries.

Hacıbektaş. The Bektaşi dervish community dates its inspiration from the life and work of Hacı Bektaş Veli who lived here in the 13th century.

İstanbul. The museums of St. Sophia, St. Irene, and Kariye hold masterpieces of Christian art. Unrivaled Muslim relics are found in the Pavilion of the Holy Mantle in the Topkapı Museum. Among the famous mosques are the Süleymaniye Complex and the Sultanahmet. A number of Jewish synagogues are active in the city.

İzmir. One of the Seven Churches, İzmir's Church of St. Polycarp memorializes the 2nd century martyred bishop. Many synagogues serve the Jewish community of İzmir.

İznik. Both the first and the last of the Christian Ecumenical Councils took place in İznik.

Kapadokya (Cappadocia). Center of monastic cave churches, Christians also tunnelled many stories underground for refuge.

Kayseri. Residence of the 4th century church leaders, St. Basil and St. Gregory, Kayseri is also known in the Mahperi Huand Hatun Complex for its Selçuk Muslim art.

Konya. For Christians, Konya was one of St. Paul's centers of preaching; for Muslims the tomb of the Whirling Dervish saint, Mevlana Celaleddin Rumi, is a place of pilgrimage.

Laodikya. The last of the Seven Churches, which was neither hot nor cold, Laodicea is close to the hot springs and travertine deposits of Pamukkale.

Mardin/Tur Abdin. Since earliest times the Tur Abdin region has been the location of Christian monasteries such as Deyrulzarafan and Mor Gabriel.

Şanlıurfa. Legendary place of the contest between Abraham and Nimrod, the Halil ar-Rahman Camii is a place of pilgrimage for Muslims.

Sart. The Temple to Artemis, the synagogue and the position of Sardis as one of the Seven Churches identify its varied religious significance.

Tarsus. Birthplace of St. Paul, Tarsus lies in the fertile Çukurova plain.

Trabzon. The ceiling of the 13th century Museum of St. Sophia is covered with Christian frescoes. Nearby in the mountains is the famous Sumelas Monastery.

Van/Ahtamar. Historically the region around Van was the center of Urartu-Ararat. The 10th century Church of the Holy Cross on the island of Ahtamar is a classic example of Armenian art.

Yalvaç. St. Paul preached his first recorded sermon in Pisidian Antioch and was expelled from the city.

Yazılıkaya. Second millennium BC priest-gods march in procession to the altar of the Hittite temple in Yazılıkaya.